KU-758-602

Matrimonial Offences

WITH PARTICULAR REFERENCE TO THE MAGISTRATES' COURTS

By LIONEL ROSEN, O.B.E., LL.M., Ph.D. (Lond.)

John Mackrell Prizeman

Solicitor of the Supreme Court of Judicature

THIRD EDITION

LONDON
Oyez Publishing

OYEZ PUBLISHING LIMITED
OYEZ HOUSE, 237 LONG LANE
LONDON SE1 4PU
1975

SBN: 85120222 5

First Published .   .   .   .   . *May*, 1962
Second Edition .   .   .   . *February*, 1965
Third Edition .   .   .   . *January*, 1975

An Leabharlann

B

346.42.016

Leitir Ceanainn

Ceárd Choláiste Réigiún

PRINTED IN GREAT BRITAIN BY
THE EASTERN PRESS LIMITED
OF LONDON AND READING

PREFACE TO THE THIRD EDITION

OF the many Acts passed by Parliament in the last ten years relating to matrimonial law, only one refers exclusively to proceedings in the magistrates' courts, namely, the Maintenance Orders Act, 1968, which removed the limitation on the amount the magistrates could award in domestic proceedings. Apart from this the Matrimonial Proceedings (Magistrates' Courts) Act, 1960, retains its integrity. Section 1 of the Matrimonial Causes Act, 1963, now replaced by s. 42 of the Matrimonial Causes Act, 1965 (a section unrepealed by the consolidating Matrimonial Causes Act, 1973) which deals with the presumption of condonation and certain other matters, and ss. 34 and 35 of the Matrimonial Causes Act, 1973, which deal with separation agreements, appear to be the only other statutory provisions which apply to matrimonial law in the magistrates' courts.

In 1969 Parliament altered the whole basis of the law of divorce (and judicial separation) by substituting breakdown of the marriage, instead of matrimonial offences, as the only ground for obtaining a divorce or a judicial separation, the only difference between the two being that, for divorce, the breakdown had to be shown to be irretrievable, while for judicial separation breakdown itself was sufficient. The Divorce Reform Act, 1969, has been repealed but re-enacted in the consolidating Act, the Matrimonial Causes Act, 1973.

There are now two codes of law relating to relief in matrimonial cases. One relates to the law in operation in the High Court Family Division and the divorce county courts, and the other—a very different code—applies in the magistrates' courts. One would have thought that immediately after the 1969 legislation Parliament would have attempted to bring the two codes into harmony so that the law in the magistrates' courts would so far as circumstances permitted be the same as in the other courts. No Bill has been brought before Parliament for this purpose, but preparations for the introduction of such a Bill have been made rather tentatively.

The Law Commission has set up a Working Party whose

Working Paper No. 53, " Family Law: Matrimonial Proceedings in Magistrates' Courts," has been published. The Working Party recommends that the basis of jurisdiction in these courts should be three matrimonial offences, namely: —Wilful Neglect to Maintain; Desertion and Intolerable Conduct. These recommendations are only provisional, and definitive proposals will be made after criticisms have been considered. One may comment that it is illogical to have Intolerable Conduct, and in addition Wilful Neglect and Desertion, when the two latter are obviously examples of Intolerable Conduct; but quite apart from this, since the basis for relief in the divorce court, both for divorce and judicial separation, is the breakdown of the marriage, why should not this be the basis in the magistrates' courts? It is suggested that if a married couple are in trouble, there should be ready access to a court of summary jurisdiction, whose first duty should be to try and mend the marriage, but failing this to adjust their affairs, in face of the fact that the marriage has broken down, as would be just in the circumstances.

However, if the recommendations of the Working Party are accepted in their present form, matrimonial offences will be dealt with in the magistrates' courts for a long time to come.

It is worth pointing out that matrimonial offences are still with us in the divorce court, since in proving that a marriage has irretrievably broken down (or merely broken down in case of judicial separation) evidence can be given of the respondent's adultery; or conduct which formerly would have been called cruel, but is now said to be behaviour which the petitioner cannot reasonably be expected to tolerate; or desertion. So that, although the matrimonial offence has been thrown out of the front door, it has crept in through the back door.

In bringing this book up to date all the relevant reported cases in the last ten years have been considered and noted. I have also added a section on the principles relating to the award of maintenance, since conduct of the parties is one of the considerations to be taken into account.

LIONEL ROSEN

Hull,
January, 1975

PREFACE TO THE SECOND EDITION

ALTHOUGH this book was first published as recently as May 1962, already a new edition has been called for. In the short intervening period there have been considerable developments in the law on this subject. There has been the enactment of the Matrimonial Causes Act, 1963. The promoters of this Bill endeavoured to introduce seven years' separation as a ground for divorce, but their efforts failed, and at the last moment an entirely new clause was introduced, that adultery which has been condoned shall not be capable of being revived, and this was passed virtually without debate in either House. The purpose of the Bill, according to the preamble, was to facilitate reconciliation, but such a clause is more likely to impede than facilitate reconciliation. Clause 1, which puts husband and wife on the same footing as to presumptions of condonation, and cl. 2, which provides for a three months' trial period, are welcome but will give rise to some questions of interpretation.

The House of Lords has given three notable decisions—*Gollins* v. *Gollins* [1964] A.C. 644, which decided that intention is not a necessary element in cruelty; *Williams* v. *Williams* [1964] A.C. 698, which decided that insanity is not necessarily a defence to cruelty; and *Godfrey* v. *Godfrey* [1964] 3 W.L.R. 524, which decided that the doctrine " once connivance, always connivance " is not now valid.

The Court of Appeal decision in *Hall* v. *Hall* [1962] 1 W.L.R. 1246 on drunkenness and constructive desertion is also of considerable interest. An interesting feature of these cases is the doubt that they have thrown on the decision in *Buchler* v. *Buchler* [1947] P. 47, but though it is probable that that case was wrongly decided, the reasoning of Asquith L.J., it is submitted, still stands. On the other hand, the reasoning in another celebrated case, *Lang* v. *Lang* [1955] A.C. 402, can now be seen to be somewhat confused although the decision was unquestionably correct.

In the first edition and in the supplement I was at pains to show that *Kaslefsky* v. *Kaslefsky* [1951] P. 38 and *Eastland* v.

Eastland [1954] P. 403 were wrongly decided, and that the so-called doctrine of " aimed at " was unnecessary and unfortunate. As long ago as 1954 I wrote in the *Modern Law Review*, vol. 17 at p. 442, that " aimed at " was malignity raising its ugly head in another form. I am naturally gratified that the House of Lords in *Gollins* has now overruled these cases unanimously and has decided that " aimed at " is not a test of cruelty. In the recent case of *Le Brocq* v. *Le Brocq* [1964] 1 W.L.R. 1085 the Court of Appeal have said that " cruel " must be understood in its ordinary and natural meaning, whatever that may be. As five judges in *Gollins* held that the conduct there was not cruelty in its natural meaning, one can see that the new ruling has the seeds of future confusion. Is it not better to stick to the words that the conduct must be grave and weighty?

I have taken the opportunity of rewriting (and I hope thereby improving) large sections of the chapter on Desertion. I have also eliminated the appendices, partly because some of the unsolved problems have now been resolved, and partly because what remains is more conveniently dealt with in the text.

LIONEL ROSEN

Hull,
January, 1965

PREFACE TO THE FIRST EDITION

THERE appears to be no work devoted exclusively to a detailed and comprehensive study of the substantive law of matrimonial offences. I have felt for a long time that the subject was of such importance that it was worth while to devote an entire book to it, and the coming into force of the Matrimonial Proceedings (Magistrates' Courts) Act, 1960, which codifies the law on the subject so far as it applies to courts of summary jurisdiction, seemed an opportune moment to attempt the work. The law in the High Court and in the magistrates' court is pretty much the same. Such differences as there are are inconsiderable and easily identified, and therefore, although the emphasis in this book is on the magistrates' courts, I believe that it will be equally useful to practitioners in the High Court.

A good law should be clear, unambiguous, precise and certain. The laws as to matrimonial offences seem far too often to be deficient in one or more of these elements. Although the main matrimonial offences are the creation of statute, such important offences as Desertion, Cruelty and Wilful Neglect to Maintain are not defined and judges have deprecated the attempt at definition. The remark of Lord Greene, M.R., " The decided cases upon the matter of desertion do not present a very illuminating body of jurisprudence " (*Williams* v. *Williams* [1939] P. 365, at p. 368), is one of many similar remarks by judges in respect of the law of matrimonial offences.

Differences between judges seem to be more rife, and expressed more vigorously than in other branches of the law. As recently as last year, Lord Merriman, P., said, " I have never quite understood how Lord Evershed, M.R., dealt with the question of the condonation of desertion . . ." (*W.* v. *W.* (*No.* 2) [1961] 3 W.L.R. 473, at p. 476).

If the late and very experienced President of the Divorce Court could not understand, what is to be expected from lesser mortals?

I have had the feeling in reading some of the reported cases that, while the decision was probably right, the reasons given by the tribunal do not satisfactorily match up to the decision. It is

ix

as though the court, having heard the spouses and their witnesses and the tangled tale of matrimonial woe they have to tell, has got the feeling that A is right and B is wrong, or that A is more in the right than B and should have the verdict, but to say why in rational terms has not been easy, with the result that the reasoning is faulty in that it goes beyond the facts of the case, or while paying lip service to a supposed doctrine, has missed the spirit of it, or that instead of giving real reasons, there has been an incantation of shibboleths. These faults are well known to the courts, but are difficult to guard against. For instance, Lord Merriman, P., in *Churchman* v. *Churchman* [1945] P. 44, at p. 52, said: —

"... Much of the difficulty in dealing with the question of connivance arises from the fact that in the past judges have gone beyond the facts of the particular case in an attempt to lay down general principles of wider application."

This is very true, but as an example of how difficult it is not to do this, in this very case the President committed himself to the general principle: "The same strict proof is required in the case of a matrimonial offence as is required in connection with criminal offences properly so called " (p. 51), which certainly went beyond the facts of the case. This principle has not been generally accepted and is probably incorrect.

In *Simpson* v. *Simpson* [1951] P. 320, Lord Merriman complained that it had been increasingly difficult to obtain consistent guidance from the decisions of the Court of Appeal in two matters, one of which related particularly to matrimonial offences, and he quoted the Master of the Rolls (this time with approval) in an unreported case of *Allen* v. *Allen* as follows (p. 328): —

"It has so often been said that it is obvious, yet it is worth repeating, that all cases that come before this court must be determined upon their own facts, and I should imagine that in no class of case is that trite observation truer than in matrimonial cases. The circumstances vary infinitely from case to case. The fact is, I think, another reason for a sense of danger in trying to formulate principles of law out of particular circumstances in particular cases, and then treating those principles of law as being, so to speak, explanations or riders to the actual statutory language."

What then is a judge to do? In arriving at his decision, he has to be guided by some principle and in order to show that he is adopting the right principle, he must formulate it, and it is most difficult to state a principle which is confined to the facts of a particular case. After all, inductive reasoning is the only useful form of reasoning, both in science and in law. It must be recognised that in law, as in science, principles have to be modified in the light of further information, and therefore any statement of principle is tentative.

Magistrates, too, must arrive at their decision on the basis of reasoning. They must first find the facts, and then apply the law. They must not allow themselves to be guided by a feeling that one party is right and the other party wrong. They are not obliged to state their reasons there and then, but if there is an appeal, then they must give their reasons in writing (Matrimonial Causes Rules, 1957, r. 73 (3)). Indeed, they should supply their reasons on request when an appeal is under consideration (*Padley* v. *Padley* [1954] P. 302). In *Sullivan* v. *Sullivan* [1947] P. 51, Lord Merriman, P., said: —

> " Justices are not, like judges of the High Court, obliged to give their reasons at the time of the decision. They are entitled to make the order, or decline to make the order, without giving reasons, but they are bound to give this court, in the event of an appeal, a proper and sufficient statement of the reasons upon which their decision was based. There should never be any difficulty whatever in doing so, for whether the court is or is not bound openly to express the reasons for its decision in court; whether it be the highest court in the land or the humblest, and whatever its jurisdiction may be, no court can give a proper decision in any case without formulating to itself at the time of the decision the reasons upon which such decision is based."

While the justices are guided, on matters of law, by the advice of their clerk, they have to understand the law applicable to the particular case. All the more necessary, therefore, that the principles concerned should be clear and intelligible.

The cases divide themselves into three groups. The first are the decisions of the ecclesiastical courts up to 1857. Here, the judges first formulated the principles relating to matrimonial offences, and some of their decisions are still effective and binding today. From 1857 to 1937 there was a steady trickle of cases which then after 1937 burst into a flood, as a result of the widening of the grounds for divorce. It so happens that Lord Merriman was

President of the Divorce Court for almost the whole of the last period. With characteristic trenchancy and clarity of language he tried, with some measure of success, to impose consistency in the law of matrimonial offences. It is safe to say that, as long as there is a law of matrimonial offences in this country, it will bear the indelible mark of his firm hand.

The difficulty in laying down accurate principles in the law of matrimonial offences seems to be greater than in other branches of the law. Why is this? I hazard the following reasons:

(1) Many problems can only be resolved by the House of Lords, but there are singularly few cases on this subject in the House of Lords. Of the few we have, we are indebted to Scotland (*Jamieson* v. *Jamieson* [1952] A.C. 525) for much illumination on the law of cruelty, and Australia (*Lang* v. *Lang* [1955] A.C. 402, a Privy Council case) for clearing up the question of intention in constructive desertion.

(2) A consideration of the reported cases for the last 200 years shows that the patterns of matrimonial behaviour have not varied over the years, but the climate of opinion has. The decisions of the courts have reflected the change in public opinion. This, of course, introduces an element of uncertainty.

(3) The subject matter is one which is not as susceptible to regulation as, say, the transfer of property. Here we are dealing with deepseated human emotions, and questions of religion, morality and public policy are also involved, on each or all of which opinions may differ widely. Judges, being human, cannot wholly abandon their own personal predilections. The psychological make-up of the judge may play its part in the decision as much as those of the parties. This is shown where judges seem to entrench themselves in certain positions from which they will not move, with the result that respect for precedent is perhaps more shaky in this branch of the law than in any other.

(4) The law is in constant process of development, and because of the infinite variety of circumstances, principles are difficult to state or apply.

Whatever the duty of a judge, that of the writer on this subject is clear. If his book is to be of any use at all, his job is to set out the principles concerned as lucidly as possible, to point out contradictions where they occur, to harmonise conflicting decisions where this can be done and, where it cannot, to set out the arguments on both sides. Accordingly, I have set out what I understand to be the law, and I have includes two appendices to analyse a number of difficult points.

I would like to acknowledge my indebtedness to my friend, Mr. H. K. Bevan, LL.B., Senior Lecturer in Law, Hull University, for his extraordinary kindness and patience in reading the whole of my manuscript and for making many suggestions, correcting errors, and his general encouragement. I find it difficult adequately to express my appreciation for all he has done. The section on the *Glenister* rule owes much to his article, " Belief in the other spouse's adultery " (1957), 73 L.Q.R. 225, and the section on Condonation, to the following articles by him: —

" Which matrimonial wrongs may be condoned? " (1960), 27 *Solicitor* 351.

" Knowledge and belief in relation to condonation " (1961), 28 *Solicitor* 40.

" The elements of forgiveness and reinstatement in condonation " (1961), 28 *Solicitor* 71.

" The rule in *Henderson* v. *Henderson* " (1961), 111 *Law Journal* 116.

I have to thank the General Editor, editorial committee and proprietors of the *Modern Law Review* for permission to use material in various articles I have written for that journal.

My brother Calman Rosen, LL.B., and my son John H. Rosen, LL.B., have also made useful suggestions, for which I am grateful. Finally, I would like to thank my secretary, Mrs. Molly Giles, who typed out the whole of the manuscript (in addition to her normal duties) with care, patience and tireless skill.

LIONEL ROSEN

Hull,
March, 1962.

CONTENTS

Chapter One

MATRIMONIAL OFFENCES

Chapter Two

DESERTION

Chapter Three

CRUELTY

Chapter Four

MISCELLANEOUS OFFENCES

Chapter Five

ADULTERY

Chapter Six

WILFUL NEGLECT TO MAINTAIN

Chapter Seven

CONDONATION; CONNIVANCE AND CONDUCT CONDUCING

TABLE OF CASES

TABLE OF STATUTES

CHAPTER 1

MATRIMONIAL OFFENCES

I. NATURE AND CLASSIFICATION

UNTIL 1969, in order to get relief in the divorce court, or the magistrates' court, a spouse had to satisfy the court that the other spouse had committed a matrimonial offence (except that in the divorce court insanity in certain circumstances was a ground for a divorce). The Royal Commission on Divorce, 1912, Cd. 6478, p. 10, para. 13, said: —

> ". . . in all ages and countries and under all religious systems, serious breach of the obligations involved in matrimony has always been regarded as constituting a legal as well as a moral wrong and as entitling the innocent spouse to a legal remedy."

So far as the termination of a marriage is concerned, one could accept one or more of three general principles as the basis for the dissolution of a marriage, namely: —

(1) that the marriage has irretrievably broken down;

(2) that of mutual agreement of the parties;

(3) that one party has been guilty of one or more grave matrimonial offences.

Until 1969 the third principle only had been accepted, not only for divorce (with the exception mentioned above) but also for relief in the magistrates' court.

> " Certain acts (which are termed ' matrimonial offences ') are regarded as being fundamentally incompatible with the undertakings entered into at marriage; the commission of these acts by one party to the marriage gives to the other an option to have the marriage terminated by divorce. With one exception (that of insanity, to which special considerations apply) all the present grounds of divorce, being conduct of a grave nature which cuts at the root of the marriage, conform to this principle " (Royal Commission on Marriage and Divorce, 1956, Cmd. 9678, para. 56).

Until recently, therefore, the concept of the matrimonial offence

1

as the basis for relief in the courts was deeply embedded in our law. From the earliest times it was the basis of the jurisdiction exercised by the ecclesiastical courts in matrimonial disputes, and when the Matrimonial Causes Act, 1857, created the new divorce court, the court was expressly directed to continue the practice of the ecclesiastical courts. Magistrates were first given jurisdiction by the Matrimonial Causes Act, 1878, and then only in the cases of aggravated assault by a husband upon his wife (with no limit on the amount to be awarded). This jurisdiction was extended to deal with other matrimonial offences by the husband, particularly by the Summary Jurisdiction (Married Women) Act, 1895, which continued in force, as amended from time to time, until it was repealed and replaced by the Matrimonial Proceedings (Magistrates' Courts) Act, 1960, which is still in force, and which affords relief to husbands as well as wives. This statute (hereinafter referred to as the Act of 1960) codified the law and procedure with regard to matrimonial offences for which there is a remedy before the magistrates.

Nine years after the passing of the Act of 1960 Parliament enacted the Divorce Reform Act, 1969, which radically altered the law of divorce and judicial separation in the divorce court. Matrimonial offences were no longer to be the bases for a divorce or judicial separation, and in their place was one ground only, namely, that the marriage had irretrievably broken down (in the case of divorce) or merely broken down (in the case of judicial separation). These provisions were subsequently repealed and re-enacted by the Matrimonial Causes Act, 1973, a consolidating Act which is now the current Act on this subject, and which will hereinafter be referred to as the " Act of 1973." The relevant provisions are set out in Appendix II.

None of these provisions at present applies to the magistrates' court.

It will be noticed that while a matrimonial offence is not a ground for divorce or a judicial separation, nevertheless it still has some significance, since it is provided that, to prove to the court that the marriage has irretrievably broken down, it may in some circumstances be necessary to prove adultery, or desertion, or conduct which has affinities to cruelty or misconduct of some kind or other, and in s. 17 similarly to prove the marriage has broken down, though not necessarily irretrievably.

Matrimonial offences are offences committed by one spouse against the other and consist of acts or omissions which are incompatible with the obligations entered into at marriage. They may be divided into five categories: —

(1) Those which a spouse may prove in order to show that the marriage has broken down irretrievably if a divorce is sought or merely broken down if a judicial separation only is desired, e.g.—

    (a) adultery, and the petitioner finds it intolerable to live with the respondent;

    (b) behaviour such that the petitioner cannot reasonably be expected to live with the respondent;

    (c) desertion for two years.

(2) Those not referred to in (1) above for which a remedy is available in the magistrates' court, e.g., wilful neglect to maintain; desertion for less than two years; persistent cruelty; and others more particularly referred to hereafter.

(3) Those for which there is no direct remedy but which nevertheless have legal consequences. These are sometimes referred to as acts of conjugal unkindness; refusal of sexual intercourse is one example; drunkenness not amounting to habitual drunkenness and short of cruelty is another. It may form part of a course of conduct which taken as a whole amounts to cruelty or just cause for the other spouse leaving the matrimonial home. In *Beard* v. *Beard* [1946] P. 8, at p. 22, Scott, L.J., said: —

"A 'matrimonial' or 'marital offence within the cognizance of the Divorce Court' in my opinion simply means conduct which in the eye of that court is wrong, whether it does or does not reach the duration or gravity or completeness which is necessary to permit of a decree, provided always that it be sufficiently serious for the court to regard it as a substantial breach of duty."

(4) Those which bar relief such as connivance or conduct conducing.

(5) Conduct which may be taken into account in assessing maintenance or periodical payments (see *Wachtel* v. *Wachtel* [1973] 1 All E.R. 829, at p. 835).

All matrimonial offences for which a direct remedy is available are now laid down by statute, but some were well-known to the ecclesiastical courts before they became offences by statute. The statutes with which we are now concerned are the Matrimonial Causes Act, 1973, which deals with the High Court and divorce county courts, and the Act of 1960 which deals with magistrates' courts. The innocent spouse (and sometimes the guilty spouse) has a right to apply for relief to the court, which may be in the form of divorce, judicial separation or an order for maintenance, or certain other relief in the High Court. The main relief in the magistrates' courts is maintenance for the wife and children. In addition, a wife or husband may obtain relief on the ground of wilful neglect to maintain (s. 27 of the Act of 1973).

The matrimonial offences in respect of which the magistrates' courts have jurisdiction are set out in s. 1 of the Act of 1960 (see Appendix I). All the offences are dealt with in detail hereafter, but briefly they are: —

(1) Desertion.
(2) Persistent cruelty to the complainant, his or her child or a child of the family.
(3) Various assaults.
(4) Adultery.
(5) Knowingly inflicting a venereal disease, or permitting intercourse while aware of it.
(6) Being an habitual drunkard or drug addict.
(7) Compelling the wife to submit to prostitution.
(8) Wilful neglect to maintain.

The desertion for which a remedy may be had before the magistrates may be for any period, however short.

It is obvious that the offences for which a remedy is given before the magistrates differ widely in gravity. A remedy is given in a number of cases for a single assault, which in most cases may well be much less serious than persistent cruelty. Nevertheless, serious or not, when once the offence is proved, the court may make an order. The word " may " really means " must " for, although the court has a discretion to refuse making an order, the discretion must be exercised judicially, and it is not a judicial exercise of the discretion to say it is a hard case, or that the parties may get together (*Dawson* v. *Dawson* (1929), 93 J.P. 187). What order the court may make is set out in s. 2 of the 1960 Act, and it may include provisions as to maintenance, non-cohabitation and custody of children.

II. FORGIVENESS

The innocent party can forgive the guilty party as to cruelty and adultery, and probably other matrimonial offences as well. If in addition to forgiveness the guilty party is reinstated the offence is condoned (see p. 295 et seq.).

Can the guilty party, by appropriate action, such as repentance and an offer of reconciliation and a promise of reformation expunge the offence? This is certainly so in the case of desertion, in the absence of any aggravating feature. No action by the guilty party, of itself, can cure the offence of an adulterer. There is a hint by Evershed, M.R., in *W.* v. *W.* (*No.* 2) [1954] P. 486, at p. 503, that cruelty may be extinguished in this way. See also *Wilkins* v. *Wilkins* (1962), 106 Sol. J. 433 (D.C.), to the same effect. There appears to be no case which gives guidance on this matter with regard to single assaults, but it is submitted that where the assault is isolated, and not very serious, the guilty spouse may rehabilitate himself or herself.

III. CHANGES IN THE LAW

(a) By the Act of 1960

1. Before the Act of 1960, a complaint could only be made by a husband in three cases: —

   (i) Where the wife was alleged to have committed adultery (Matrimonial Causes Act, 1937, s. 11 (3)).

   (ii) Where the wife was alleged to be a habitual drunkard (Licensing Act, 1902, s. 5 (2)).

   (iii) Where the wife was alleged to be guilty of persistent cruelty to the children of the marriage (Summary Jurisdiction (Separation and Maintenance) Act, 1925, s. 1 (3)).

Now, a married man as well as a married woman may apply by way of complaint and the two are placed almost, if not quite, on an equality. The only exceptions are that a wife can, in addition, make a complaint in respect of being compelled by her husband to submit to prostitution, and a wife is liable in respect of wilful neglect to maintain only in certain restricted circumstances. Nevertheless, the occasions when a husband can usefully make a complaint must be very rare. Statistics are not available to show the number of occasions, if any, when a husband has applied for an order on the three grounds stated above. There are no reported cases of such complaints, and in a wide experience the present writer has not heard of a case. It seems, therefore, that the provision that a husband may apply for an order is more of a gesture than of any likely utility. Nor are statistics available of the number of complaints by a husband since the 1960 Act came into force, but as far as one can gather, the number is very small. The remedies in the magistrates' courts were designed for the protection and maintenance of the wife, and as far as one can see, those objects will remain the main purpose of the Act of 1960.

It is true that a husband could apply for an order of non-cohabitation, but this is only granted for the protection of the spouse, and if the wife has been so cruel that he is in need of protection, divorce would appear to be a more appropriate remedy.

2. The time limit for making a complaint in respect of adultery used to be six months from the date of the adultery. This is now changed by s. 12 to six months from the date when that act of adultery first became known to the complainant.

3. Formerly, the defendant could seek the revocation of the order against him on the ground of the wife's adultery at any time, whether the marriage had been dissolved or not. Now the adultery must take place during the subsistence of the marriage (s. 8 (2)).

4. In place of a conviction for aggravated assault, there are new provisions covering a great variety of offences against the person (s. 1 (1) (c)).

5. Formerly, the only children in respect of which an order could be made were children of the marriage. This has now been extended to a " child of the family," which is defined by s. 16 as—

   (a) any child of both parties; and
   (b) any other child of either party who has been accepted as one of the family by the other party (see p. 292 et seq.).

6. Maintenance was increased to £7 10s. maximum for the wife, and £2 10s. maximum for each child, but by the Maintenance Orders Act, 1968, all limitations have been removed.

7. Formerly, there was no liability under an order, and it could not be enforced, while the married woman in respect of whom the order was made resided with her husband, and if she continued so to reside for three months after the order was made, it ceased to have effect. This provision led to a controversy between the divorce court and the Queen's Bench as to the meaning of

" reside." The latter considered that mere residence without cohabitation was sufficient for the purposes of s. 1 (4) of the Summary Jurisdiction (Separation and Maintenance) Act, 1925, whereas the divorce court said that to have effect, the residence must amount to cohabitation. The whole subject is discussed at length in *Naylor* v. *Naylor* [1962] P. 253.

The Act of 1960 has settled this controversy by adopting the view of the divorce court, and provides by s. 7 (1) that the order shall not be enforceable and no liability shall accrue thereunder until the spouses have ceased to cohabit, and if they continue to cohabit for three months after the date of the order, the order shall cease to have effect.

8. The definitions of " Habitual Drunkard " and " Drug Addict " have been widened.

(b) By the Matrimonial Causes Act, 1965, s. 42

This section re-enacts the Matrimonial Causes Act, 1963.

1. The rule in *Henderson* v. *Henderson and Crellin* [1944] A.C. 49, that one act of sexual intercourse is conclusive evidence that a husband has condoned his wife's offence is now abolished, and both husband and wife may rebut any presumption of condonation by evidence sufficient to negative the necessary intent (s. 42 (1)) (see p. 301 et seq.).

2. Adultery or cruelty shall not be deemed to have been condoned by reason only of a continuation or resumption of cohabitation for one period not exceeding three months, if this is done with a view to a reconciliation (s. 42 (2)) (see p. 305 et seq.).

3. Adultery which has been condoned shall not be capable of being revived (s. 42 (3)) (see p. 309).

IV. THE STANDARD OF PROOF

What is the standard of proof with regard to matrimonial offences is a question of great difficulty, and one upon which the courts have given confused guidance. It is not even known whether the same standard is required for all matrimonial offences, or whether they differ. Lord Merriman, P., in *Churchman* v. *Churchman* [1945] P. 44, at p. 51, said: —

> " The same strict proof is required in the case of a matrimonial offence as is required in connection with criminal offences so-called."

This clear statement has not been generally accepted. The standard in criminal cases is that the court shall be satisfied beyond reasonable doubt. In civil cases, the standard is the balance of probabilities. The reason for the difference is this. While it is in the interest of the State that guilty persons should be convicted and punished, it is of greater importance that an innocent person should not be convicted. It is better, therefore, to have a standard of proof so strict that while some guilty persons may escape, the conviction of the innocent shall be rendered as unlikely as possible. An injustice to the State, that is the public at large, is not so serious a matter as an injustice to a particular individual. In civil actions, however, there is not the fate of one individual to consider but at least two, and it is essential to do justice to both. If the standard of proof is too high, in seeking to give justice to one party, one may be doing injustice to the other by depriving an injured party of a remedy which he ought to have. On this basis, the standard of proof in matrimonial cases should be the civil standard. This is reinforced by the fact that there is the highest authority for saying that proceedings with regard to adultery were civil proceedings, and not criminal, and this is true of all matrimonial proceedings (*Mordaunt* v. *Moncrieffe* (1874), L.R. 2 Sc. & Div. 374).

However, there is a factor which differentiates matrimonial proceedings from civil proceedings, namely, that stated by Lord MacDermott in *Preston-Jones* v. *Preston-Jones* [1951] A.C. 391, at p. 417: —

> " The jurisdiction in divorce involves the status of the parties and the public interest requires that the marriage bond shall not be set aside lightly or without strict inquiry."

This reasoning does not apply at first hand to proceedings in the magistrates' courts, since there is no jurisdiction in divorce. It would, however, be extraordinary if there were a different standard in the divorce court from that in the magistrates' courts, for the same matrimonial offence. No one has suggested there is a different standard, and furthermore, the decision of a magistrates' court may have repercussions in the divorce court (see Matrimonial Causes Act, 1973, s. 4 (2)).

But on this point see *Ellis* v. *Ellis and Wilby* [1962] 1 W.L.R. 450. The magistrates had adjudged the husband to be a deserter in proceedings which the husband did not contest. A commissioner dismissed the husband's petition alleging desertion by the wife, in proceedings undefended by the wife. The Court of Appeal reversed the decision of the commissioner, holding that the uncontradicted evidence of the petitioner, accepted as a reliable witness, was of greater weight than a magistrates' order made in the petitioner's absence, and also the husband's offers to return, and the wife's refusals, had terminated his desertion and made her the deserter. Willmer, L.J., said that, although the court paid great attention to magistrates' orders, they were no more than some evidence, and in this case could not outweigh the uncontradicted evidence of the husband.

By s. 2 (1) (a) of the Act of 1960, a non-cohabitation clause has in all respects the effect of a judicial separation. Such a clause does not estop the divorce court, but it has evidential value (*Harriman* v. *Harriman* [1909] P. 123 and 142).

Lord Greene, M.R., in *Kara* v. *Kara and Holman* [1948] P. 287, at p. 288, said on the weight to be attached to a magistrates' order—" There may, however, be something less than an estoppel, i.e., the findings may be treated as of strong probative value."

In *Turner* v. *Turner* [1962] P. 283, a wife obtained a maintenance order on the ground of persistent cruelty, and the magistrate also inserted a non-cohabitation clause in the order, but the divorce commissioner dismissed her petition for divorce on the ground of cruelty. The Court of Appeal ordered a new trial, and Holroyd Pearce, L.J. ([1961] 3 W.L.R. 1269, at p. 1275) said that the divorce judge may come to a different conclusion from the magistrates, but he must do so with a realisation that the order is prima facie of definite probative value. The more leisurely and scientific investigation in the divorce court must be weighed against the advantage of a more contemporary and direct confrontation of the parties in the magistrates' court before time and the reiteration of their stories to their advisers has had its effect. A wife who has obtained an order in her favour cannot properly be described as having no corroboration at all.

One may assume, therefore, that the same standard of proof should be applied before the magistrates as in the divorce court.

The real difficulty is that while the courts have tried to indicate that the standard of proof is not as great as that in a criminal case, and yet is higher than that in a civil case, the judges have

used the expression " that the court must be satisfied beyond
reasonable doubt," which is the same expression as that used in
criminal cases. To use the same expression for two different things
naturally causes confusion.

Adultery has been usually treated as a special case (see pp. 237,
243) and the Court of Appeal in *Ginesi* v. *Ginesi* [1948] P. 179 decided that adultery must be proved with the same degree of strictness as a criminal case. In *Preston-Jones* v. *Preston-Jones, supra,*
the House of Lords seemed to come to the same conclusion, not
because of any analogy with the criminal law, but because of the
gravity and public importance of the issues (per Lord Mac-
Dermott).

In *Bater* v. *Bater* [1951] P. 35, a case of cruelty, the Court of
Appeal said the proof must be beyond reasonable doubt, but
Denning, L.J., said that a doubt may be regarded as reasonable
in the criminal courts which would not be so in the civil courts.

It cannot be said that the courts have found a suitable expression
which accurately describes what the standard of proof is, and
whether it is the same in all matrimonial cases (see *Davis* v. *Davis*
[1950] P. 125; *Gower* v. *Gower* [1950] 1 All E.R. 804, and *Galler*
v. *Galler* [1954] P. 252). Something may depend on the actual
subject matter of the case. Charges, such as adultery, which are
easy to make and hard to rebut, must be treated with special
caution.

CHAPTER 2

DESERTION

I. INTRODUCTION

BY s. 1 (1) (*a*) of the Act of 1960 either spouse may apply by way of complaint to a magistrates' court for an order under this Act on the ground that during the subsistence of the marriage the defendant has deserted the complainant (see Appendix I).

A. History

In Scotland desertion has been a ground for divorce *a vinculo* since 1573. In England, even before this date, there seemed a likelihood that provision might be made for divorce on various grounds including desertion. A commission was appointed under 3 & 4 Edw. 6, c. 2, presided over by Archbishop Cranmer, which resulted in a draft code entitled " *Reformatio Legum Ecclesiast-arum.*" This recommended (*inter alia*) desertion for two years as a ground for divorce. The recommendations were not adopted.

A Royal Commission on Divorce appointed in 1850 made no recommendations for divorce on the ground of desertion, but when the Bill, which resulted in the Matrimonial Causes Act, 1857, was debated in the Commons, an amendment to make divorce available on the ground of five years' desertion was defeated. Although the Commissioners did not recommend desertion as a ground for divorce *a vinculo*, they said that this offence " so entirely frustrates all the objects of the marriage union, that it may reasonably be doubted whether it should not be put on the same footing as cases of cruelty " and recommended that it should be a ground for judicial separation.

The position as to desertion as a matrimonial offence up to 1857, when the jurisdiction in matrimonial matters was vested in the newly created divorce court, is described by Lord St. Helier, formerly Sir Francis Jeune, P., as follows: —

> " It is remarkable that desertion by either party to a marriage, except as giving rise to a suit for restitution (of conjugal rights) was not treated as an offence by canon law in England.

11

It founded no ground for a suit for divorce, and constituted no answer to such a suit by way of recrimination. It might indeed deprive a husband of his remedy if it amounted to connivance, or perhaps even if it amounted to culpable neglect " (Article Divorce in 1911 ed. of *Encyclopædia Britannica*).

Desertion by the wife was not recognised as a matrimonial offence, except to enable a husband to obtain an order for restitution of conjugal rights.

The next Royal Commission on Divorce reported in 1912. A majority of the Commissioners was in favour of desertion for three years and upwards as a ground for divorce.

The last Royal Commission on Divorce, which reported in 1956, made certain recommendations with regard to constructive desertion.

Desertion was a matrimonial offence well-known to the ecclesiastical courts, but for which they provided no direct remedy. The deserted spouse could apply for a decree for restitution of conjugal rights, disobedience to which resulted in the disobeyer being pronounced contumacious and excommunicated. By the Ecclesiastical Courts Act, 1813, imprisonment for not more than six months was substituted for excommunication. The Matrimonial Causes Act, 1857, made desertion by the husband for two years a ground for a judicial separation, and, if coupled with adultery, a ground whereby a wife might get a divorce. The Matrimonial Causes Act, 1937, made desertion for three years a ground for divorce, and this provision was re-enacted in the Matrimonial Causes Act, 1965, s. 1 (1) (*a*) (ii).

By s. 5 of the Matrimonial Causes Act, 1884, desertion was made an express ground in the High Court for a decree of restitution of conjugal rights, and it was provided that disobedience to a decree carried a statutory presumption of desertion without reasonable cause.

The first Act to provide a remedy in the magistrates' courts was the Married Women (Maintenance in the Case of Desertion) Act, 1886, which provided a remedy for a wife who had been deserted, but the court had to be satisfied that the husband, being able wholly or in part to maintain his wife, or his wife's family, had wilfully refused or neglected so to do, and had deserted his wife. In other words, the wife had to prove both desertion and wilful neglect to maintain.

The Summary Jurisdiction (Married Women) Act, 1895, s. 4, made desertion itself a ground whereby a wife could get an order before the magistrates, and that provision has been re-enacted by the Act of 1960.

B. Definitions

Lord Jowitt in *Weatherley* v. *Weatherley* [1947] A.C. 628, at p. 631, said: —

" . . . in all of them (the decided cases) the judges have declined and, in my view, wisely declined to attempt any definition of ' desertion.' In this respect I propose to follow their example."

This is one of the many cautious statements on this subject which appear in the decided cases from the House of Lords downwards. Another example is that of Sir Henry Duke, P., in *Jackson* v. *Jackson* [1924] P. 19, at p. 23, where he says: —

" If there is abandonment by one of the spouses of the other, that is desertion. If one of the spouses causes the other to live separate and apart, that is desertion. I am not going to attempt an exhaustive definition of desertion. No judge, so far as I am aware, has sought to do so, and certainly there is no prospect of its being successfully done."

Lord Romer in *Cohen* v. *Cohen* [1940] A.C. 631, at p. 645, said: —

" The question whether a deserting spouse has reasonable cause for not trying to bring the desertion to an end and the corresponding question whether desertion without cause has existed for the necessary period must always be questions of fact, and the determination must depend upon the circumstances of the particular case. I deprecate attempts to lay down any general principle applicable to them all."

The following are examples of judicial attempts at definition or description of desertion: —

1. " Without attempting to lay down a precise definition of ' desertion ' I think it undoubtedly must mean a wilful absenting himself by the husband; and that such absence or cessation of cohabitation must be in spite of the wish of the wife; she must not be a consenting party " (Sir Creswell Creswell, J.O., in *Thompson* v. *Thompson* (1858), 1 Sw. & Tr. 231, at p. 233).

2. " To desert is to forsake or abandon . . . To neglect opportunities of consorting with a wife is not necessarily to desert her.

Indifference, want of solicitude, illiberality, denial of reasonable means, and even faithlessness, are not desertion. Desertion seems pointed at a breaking off, more or less completely, of the intercourse which previously existed " (Lord Penzance, J.O., in *Williams* v. *Williams* (1864), 3 Sw. & Tr. 547, at p. 548).

3. "A husband deserts his wife if he wilfully absents himself from the society of his wife in spite of her wish. There must be a deliberate purpose of abandoning the conjugal society " (Lopes, L.J., in *R.* v. *Leresche* [1891] 2 Q.B. 418, at p. 420).

4. " The party who intends to bring the cohabitation to an end, and whose conduct in reality causes its termination, commits the act of desertion " (Gorell Barnes, J., in *Sickert* v. *Sickert* [1899] P. 278, approved in *Thomas* v. *Thomas* [1924] P. 194, at p. 199).

5. " Desertion means the cessation of cohabitation brought about by the fault or act of one of the parties " (Jeune, P., in *Frowd* v. *Frowd* [1904] P. 177, at p. 179).

6. " It has been almost a commonplace in this court to hold that in order to ascertain whether there has been desertion, you must look at the conduct of the parties. There may be no matrimonial home, and yet no forfeiture of the rights of the spouses. Desertion is not the withdrawal from a place, but from a state of things. The husband may live in a place, and make it impossible for his wife to live there, though it is she and not he that actually withdraws; and that state of things may be desertion of the wife. The law does not deal with the mere matter of place. What it seeks to enforce is the recognition and discharge of the common obligations of the married state. If one party does not acknowledge them, the party who has offended cannot be heard to say that he or she is not guilty of desertion on the ground that there has been no desertion by departure from a place " (Duke, P., in *Pulford* v. *Pulford* [1923] P. 18, at p. 21).

7. " If there is abandonment by one of the spouses of the other, that is desertion. If one of the spouses causes the other to live separate and apart, that is desertion " (Duke, P., in *Jackson* v. *Jackson* [1924] P. 19, at p. 23).

8. ". . . the spouse who leaves the matrimonial roof is not necessarily the deserter. Constructively, the deserter may be the party who remains behind, if that party is guilty of conduct which justifies the other party in leaving. Secondly, to afford such justification the conduct of the party staying on need not have amounted

to a matrimonial offence, such as cruelty or adultery. But thirdly, it must exceed in gravity such behaviour, vexatious and trying though it may be, as every spouse bargains to endure when accepting the other ' for better, for worse ' " (Asquith, L.J., in *Buchler* v. *Buchler* [1947] P. 25, at p. 45).

9. " [Desertion] is nothing less than a total repudiation of the obligations of marriage " (du Parcq, L.J., in *Williams* v. *Williams* [1943] 2 All E.R. 746, at p. 752).

10. " One of the essential elements of desertion is the fact of separation. . . . If that separation is brought about by his fault, why is not that desertion? " (Denning, L.J., in *Hopes* v. *Hopes* [1949] P. 227, at p. 235).

11. " It is as necessary in cases of constructive desertion as it is in cases of actual desertion to prove the *factum* and the *animus* on the part of the spouse charged with the offence of desertion " (Lord Greene, M.R., in *Buchler* v. *Buchler* [1947] P. 25, at p. 29).

In the Report of the Royal Commission on Marriage and Divorce 1951–55 (Cmd. 9678), para. 155 (iii), the majority recommended a statutory definition of desertion as follows: —

> " One spouse shall be held to have deserted the other spouse when without reasonable cause and against the will of that other spouse he or she shall have brought cohabitation to an end or shall have prevented its resumption either—
> (*a*) by departing or remaining away from that other spouse or the matrimonial home, or
> (*b*) by causing that other spouse to depart or remain away from him or her or the matrimonial home—
> > (1) by actual expulsion, or
> > (2) by conduct of a grave and weighty nature which is such that the other spouse could not on the face of it reasonably be expected to continue with the conjugal life."

Other attempts at definition are: Rayden on Divorce, 12th ed. (1974), p. 232: —

> " The court has discouraged attempts at defining desertion, there being no general principle applicable to all cases. In its essence desertion is the separation of one spouse from the other, with an intention on the part of the deserting spouse of bringing cohabitation permanently to an end without reasonable cause and without the consent of the other spouse; but the physical act of departure by one spouse does not necessarily make that spouse the deserting party. Desertion is not a

withdrawal from a place, but from a state of things, for what the law seeks to enforce is the recognition and discharge of the common obligations of the married state."

Latey on Divorce, 14th ed., p. 104: —

" There is no judicial definition of desertion that can be applied to meet the facts of every case, but it is in essence the abandonment of one spouse by the other with the intention of forsaking him or her without just cause. To constitute desertion, the acts relied on must have been done against the will of the person setting up desertion.

Desertion has also been defined as ' the cessation of cohabitation brought about by the fault or act of one of the parties.'

Desertion is not the withdrawal from a place, but from a state of things. The husband may live in a place, and make it impossible for his wife to live there, though it is she and not he that actually withdraws; and that state of things may be desertion by the husband of the wife."

Stone's Justices' Manual (1974), p. 1396: —

" To prove desertion it is necessary to establish a termination of cohabitation brought about by the intention of the defendant and the absence of consent thereto of the complainant."

C. The Elements of Desertion

In analysing the subject of desertion one usually finds four separate elements, namely: —

1. The fact of separation (*factum*).
2. A mental element (*animus deserendi*).
3. The absence of consent by the party alleging desertion.
4. The idea of just cause.

These elements will be considered separately for the sake of convenience, but here one must add a caution. These elements are so bound up one with the other, that they are often only fully effective in combination.

There is a further complication. Desertion is of two kinds, actual and constructive, each radically different from the other, and this is the main reason why desertion is so difficult to define.

"Actual desertion rarely gives rise to legal problems of any difficulty. The spouse charged with desertion must be shown to have abandoned in fact the matrimonial consortium and to have done so with the intention of bringing it permanently to an end. Both of these are questions of fact which are so infrequently disputed that there are few reported cases on the subject. On the other hand, constructive desertion, which also requires *factum* and *animus* on the part of the spouse charged with desertion, due to his wrongful actions which have driven the wife from the matrimonial home, has been the subject of exhaustive legal arguments, and is still so unsettled that it is impossible to state the law with any certainty " (Prof. A. L. Goodhart, 79 L.Q.R., p. 110).

II. ACTUAL DESERTION

This is sometimes called " Simple Desertion." It occurs when the deserter leaves the home. Constructive desertion occurs when the deserted party leaves the home.

In actual desertion, not only must the deserter withdraw from the matrimonial home, but he must do so with the intention, at the time, of not returning. In other words, he must intend permanently to abandon his wife. There was another matrimonial offence known as " wilful separation without cause " where the intention to remain absent permanently was not necessary. This offence was analogous to " absence without leave." It was referred to only in the Matrimonial Causes Act, 1965, s. 5 (4), proviso (iii), which provided for discretionary bars to divorce.

In practice, when one spouse leaves the other without just cause, there is a presumption that the leaving was intended to be permanent. Certainly the onus is on the one leaving to show that it was not. Even if he left with the intention of staying away permanently, he might have a good defence for so doing, such as that he left because of an agreement with his wife, or that he had good cause or excuse, such as the fact that she had committed adultery. It is not necessary for him to leave the matrimonial home to be proved an actual deserter. The man who abandons his wife at the church door deserts her effectively (*De Laubenque* v. *De Laubenque* [1899] P. 42).

It may also happen that the original parting was by agreement, but for some reason or other the agreement comes to an end, or becomes ineffective. The spouse who refuses to return to cohabitation, in the absence of reasonable excuse, will be an actual deserter.

In divorce, since a continuous period of two years has to be proved (see s. 1 (2) (c) of the 1973 Act), the date of the commencement of desertion may be vital. Since desertion does not necessarily begin when the husband withdraws from the matrimonial home, it has to be established when the parting changed its nature from an innocent one to a culpable one. A wife was left by her husband on the pretence that his business compelled him to be absent. He supplied her with necessaries, corresponded with her and visited her occasionally, and she had a child by him. She then discovered that he had been living in adultery for years. Hannen, J., expressed the view that desertion began when the wife discovered the adultery (*Farmer* v. *Farmer* (1884), 9 P.D. 245).

III. CONSTRUCTIVE DESERTION

When a matrimonial home is broken up the person who stays behind may be the deserter. The deserter is the one who is to blame, or whose fault it was which caused the other party to leave. The principle is clear and has been recognised for over 100 years. The description of the offence has found various modes of expression. It has been said that: —

(*a*) One spouse has driven the other away, or

(*b*) has pursued a course of conduct with the intention of driving the other away, or

(*c*) has expelled the other by—

    (i) force, or

    (ii) words, or

    (iii) conduct, or

(*d*) the conduct was such that the leaving of the other spouse was a natural consequence, or

(*e*) the deserted spouse had good cause for leaving.

The circumstances whereby one spouse can constructively desert another are infinite, but in general they come within three recognisable categories: —

(1) Actual physical expulsion from the home, or locking the other spouse out.

(2) Telling the other spouse to go.

(3) A course of conduct by one spouse which causes the other to leave.

The first two present little difficulty. When a man seizes his wife and throws her out of the house, and throws her clothes after her, in the absence of any legal excuse, e.g., catching her in the act of adultery, there can be little doubt that he is deserting her.

18760181

Similarly, if he says to her, to quote the expression most commonly used, " Clear out," and she goes, he is equally in desertion.

But when the expulsion consists of " a course of conduct," difficulties arise. The subject will be dealt with in detail under the heading " Just Cause," but certain general considerations can be considered here. The circumstances which determine whether desertion is actual or constructive may be very narrow. Assuming there is no question of agreement or consent between the parties, if one spouse abandons the other without just cause, that is actual desertion; but if a spouse leaves the other with just cause, then the party remaining is the deserter. This is considered in detail later. It is submitted that the cases of *Gollins* v. *Gollins* [1964] A.C. 644 and *Williams* v. *Williams* [1964] A.C. 698, in the House of Lords, reinforce this view. Therefore, which party is in desertion depends upon the determination by the court of the nature of the conduct concerned.

One of the best discussions on the subject appears in one of the older cases, *Sickert* v. *Sickert* [1899] P. 278.* The husband lived an adulterous life and in consequence his wife left him. She said she was willing to return if he gave up that mode of life, but he said he was unable to alter it. It was held that he was guilty of desertion. Gorell Barnes, J., at p. 282, said: —

> " In order to constitute desertion there must be a cessation of cohabitation and an intention on the part of the accused party to desert the other. In most cases of desertion the guilty party actually leaves the other, but it is not always or necessarily the guilty party who leaves the matrimonial home. In my opinion, the party who intends bringing the cohabitation to an end, and whose conduct in reality causes its termination, commits the act of desertion. There is no substantial difference between the case of a husband who intends to put an end to a state of cohabitation, and does so by leaving his wife, and that of a husband who with the like intent obliges his wife to separate from him."

and at p. 283:—

> "A wife whose husband is carrying on an adulterous intercourse with another woman or other women is not bound to remain in cohabitation with him: she can at once obtain a judicial separation. She may however be willing to remain

---

* N.B. Sickert was the famous artist. The report [1899] P. 278 makes amusing reading.

B/346.42'016

with her husband provided he will give up the connection complained of, and, if he refuses to do so, a wife with any self-respect has only one course to take—that is, to withdraw from cohabitation. The husband in such a case must be taken to intend the consequences of his action—that is to say, that his wife shall not live with him. The situation then produced is just the same as if the guilty husband left his wife. Desertion is not to be tested by merely ascertaining which party left the matrimonial home first."

A. Grave and Weighty

It has been said that the conduct must be " grave and weighty " or " grave and convincing." This has been contrasted with " the wear and tear " of married life. Certain conduct a spouse has to put up with. Other conduct may be unbearable. There is no sure guide as to where the line has to be drawn. In *Buchler* v. *Buchler* [1947] P. 25 the Court of Appeal gave the matter very careful consideration.

The wife objected to her husband's association with a pigman in his service. There was no suggestion of the husband having committed any matrimonial offence, but it was said that the husband's liking for the company of the pigman showed a lack of consideration for his wife's feelings and caused her unhappiness and a feeling of humiliation. It was not suggested that the relationship was homosexual, though it was said that the husband's conduct was such as to lead people to think it might be. The wife thought the association unnecessary. He thought she was a snob. She asked him to give up the association and he refused, saying if she did not like it she knew what she could do. The wife left. Lord Greene, M.R., said at p. 29: —

" The practical difference between the two cases lies in the difference in the circumstances which will constitute such proof [i.e., the *factum* and *animus* of desertion]. In actual desertion the spouse charged must be shown to have abandoned the matrimonial consortium in fact, and to have done so with the intention of deserting. In constructive desertion the spouse charged must be shown to have been guilty of conduct equivalent to ' driving the other spouse away ' (per Bucknill, L.J. in *Boyd* v. *Boyd* [1938] 4 All E.R. 181, 183) from the matrimonial home and to have done so with the intention of bringing the matrimonial consortium to an end. In each case the intention may, of course, be inferred if the circumstances are such as to justify the inference. In the case of

actual desertion the mere act of one spouse in leaving the
matrimonial home will in general make the inference an easy
one. In the case of constructive desertion where there is no
such significant act as a departure by the spouse who is alleged
to be in desertion, the acts alleged to be equivalent to an
expulsion of the complaining spouse must be of such gravity
and so clearly established that they can fairly be so described.
If they do not satisfy this test, not only is expulsion in fact not
proved, but it is not legitimate to infer an intention to desert.
A man may wish that his wife will leave him; but such a wish,
unless accompanied by conduct which the court can properly
regard as equivalent to expulsion in fact, can have no effect
whatever. Conversely, where the conduct of the required
nature is established, the necessary intention is readily
inferred since no one can be heard to say that he did not
intend the natural and probable consequences of his acts:
Sickert v. *Sickert* [1899] P. 278. The crucial matter for consideration, therefore, is the nature of the conduct relied on as
equivalent to an expulsion of the complaining spouse."

Asquith, L.J., said at p. 45: —

"In the first place it is common ground—and a commonplace—that the spouse who leaves the matrimonial roof is not
necessarily the deserter. Constructively, the deserter may
be the party who remains behind, if that party has been
guilty of conduct which justifies the other party in leaving.
Secondly, to afford such justification the conduct of the party
staying on need not have amounted to a matrimonial offence,
such as cruelty or adultery. But thirdly, it must exceed in
gravity such behaviour, vexatious and trying though it may
be, as every spouse bargains to endure when accepting the
other ' for better, for worse.' The ordinary wear and tear
of conjugal life does not in itself suffice. Where the learned
judge seems to have erred is in supposing that on the evidence
before him conduct complying with this last test had been
established.

It is difficult to deduce from the decided cases any principle
of law by reference to which it can be determined in every
case on which side of this line the case falls. To say that the
petitioner must establish conduct by the respondent which
has made it ' practically impossible for the parties to live
properly together ' or which ' drove the petitioner out ' is to
propound a criterion too vague to be very helpful. It is, I
think, possible to say of certain courses of conduct that they
could not amount to constructive desertion, and of certain
other courses that they could not fail to do so. This would
appear to be a question of law, involving, as it does, the issue
whether there was any evidence or no evidence to support

the judge's conclusion. But between the extremes indicated there is obviously a no-man's land where the issue is one of fact . . ."

The decision in this case cannot be regarded as satisfactory. Danckwerts, L.J., in *Hall* v. *Hall* [1962] 1 W.L.R. 1246, at p. 1254, said, " I must confess that I find his [Lord Greene's] conclusion that the facts relied upon were not of sufficient gravity difficult to swallow." Lord Pearce, too, in *Gollins,* at p. 694, said, " I find it hard to understand how the court on the reported facts came to overrule the decision of the judge of first instance." Nor are the instances cited by Asquith, L.J., as being conduct which a wife must put up with valid today. He cited habitual drunkenness, persistent nagging and insult, even incest forgiven but followed by indecent assault. It has now been decided that drunkenness of itself can amount to just cause (*Hall* v. *Hall* [1962] 1 W.L.R. 1246 (C.A.)), and that the other instances amount to cruelty (*Usmar* v. *Usmar* [1949] P. 1; *Boyd* v. *Boyd* [1938] 4 All E.R. 181; *Ivens* v. *Ivens* [1955] P. 129).

Nevertheless, it is submitted that the first two paragraphs of the judgment of Asquith, L.J., are an accurate statement of the principles of constructive desertion. Formerly the expression " intention to drive away " was favoured, but in recent years this has been dropped in favour of " just cause for leaving." This is illustrated by *Hall* v. *Hall, supra.* This case emphasises that whether the conduct of a husband is sufficient to justify a wife leaving him is a question of fact, and that there is no yardstick or formula other than the time-honoured expression " grave and weighty."

The facts were that the husband drank constantly and stayed out late at night, waking the family and causing a disturbance in the street, before the wife left him. There was no evidence that the husband was violent in drink. The magistrates made an order on the ground of constructive desertion. The Divisional Court [1962] 1 W.L.R. 478 (Sir Jocelyn Simon, P., and Cairns, J.), allowed the appeal, but this was reversed by the Court of Appeal who reinstated the magistrates' order.

The Divisional Court took the view that drunkenness only entitled the other spouse to matrimonial relief when it amounted to cruelty (and then, of course, it had to be shown that the health of the wife had been affected, or that there was a reasonable apprehension of this), or where it was of so extreme a nature that it made matrimonial life virtually impossible, or where it was accompanied by physical violence, or involved possible danger to members of the household. The Court of Appeal refused to accept these limitations.

The Divisional Court even went so far as to suggest, without actually deciding this, that a spouse's drunkenness, falling short of being an habitual drunkard within the meaning of s. 1 (1) (f) of the Matrimonial Proceedings (Magistrates' Courts) Act, 1960, could not constitute just cause for the other spouse leaving.

Cairns, J., expressed the rather surprising view that drunkenness, with its ordinary accompaniments of rowdiness and inconvenience to those who have to deal with the drunkard, cannot be said to be such conduct that any reasonable man would know that his wife would not stay and put up with it.

Sir Jocelyn Simon, P., said at [1962] 1 W.L.R. 483: —

> " I certainly must not be taken to hold that in no circumstances could drunkenness constitute the *factum* of constructive desertion. But in the present case, it seems to me impossible to hold that the husband must have known that his behaviour would cause his wife to leave, so that one could reasonably infer from it an intention to expel her."

The view of the Court of Appeal ([1962] 1 W.L.R. 1246) in this case (and also in *Parmenter* v. *Parmenter* (1962), *The Times*, 13th October, where it was held that drunkenness of this sort amounted to cruelty) was that a drunken husband must expect a wife to reach a point when she could put up with it no longer, and this will commend itself to most people. The sort of drunkenness described by Cairns, J., is much harder to bear than an occasional blow.

It is important to notice, too, that in this case there was no evidence that the wife had warned the husband that she would leave him if he did not mend his ways, or that the husband knew or suspected that his habits were causing his wife such distress that she was likely to leave him.

Ormerod, L.J., said at p. 1251: —

> " The question is not whether drunkenness of itself is sufficient to amount to expulsive conduct. The question is whether the conduct of this husband (caused no doubt, initially, by the drunkenness) was sufficient to justify his wife in leaving him and saying that she found it impossible to live with him. The

circumstances are such that any decent wife must have been caused considerable trouble and unhappiness by the husband's conduct. He came home drunk regularly; and it is clear that when he did come home drunk, he came home noisily late at night, created a considerable disturbance, and so deprived his wife and other members of the household of their sleep and peace of mind. It does not seem to me to be surprising that in such circumstances the wife found that she could not put up with it for an indefinite period, and finally left him. It may be that this conduct was not committed by the husband with the intention that it should drive the wife from their home. But, in my judgment, it was the sort of conduct which might well do this, and the husband, if he did not know, should have known what the result of his conduct might be."

He thought the justices were in a better position to decide the issue of fact.

Danckwerts, L.J., said that the Divisional Court referred to a large number of cases, but he thought there was danger in this course since every case of this kind must depend on its own particular facts. He went on to say, at p. 1253: —

" I would respectfully suggest that there is too much talk in matrimonial cases about a party accepting the other ' for better or for worse,' or about the behaviour which a party ' bargains to endure.' It must be exceptional for parties who marry to bargain, even in a figurative sense, to endure drunkenness or disgusting conduct. The phrase ' for better or for worse ' in jurisdictions in which divorce is not recognised might have some sense, but in this country, where the law provides for divorce, it seems to me to be something of a cynical jest."

Diplock, L.J., described the *animus* at p. 1256: " That this husband must have known that this wife would in all probability not continue to endure his conduct if he persisted in it . . . it does not need a specific warning to make a husband realise that he is driving his wife beyond the bounds of her endurance."

There is a useful analysis of the ingredients of constructive desertion by Lord Merriman, P., in *Lane* v. *Lane* [1951] P. 284. He begins by recalling Lord Merrivale's statement in *Pulford* v. *Pulford* [1923] P. 18, at p. 21, that desertion is not a withdrawal from a place but from a state of things, which for short Lord Merriman called " the home." Desertion occurs when the husband either leaves the home or drives the wife away from the home with the intent to bring the home to an end and without her consent or fault. When the fact of separation is proved, the intent can be inferred. As to this inference he gives three examples: (a) from the nature of the parting, as where the husband bolts in a false name to the ends of the earth, (b) from conduct so brutal that although nothing is said, the wife must leave the home for fear of her life, (c) from words so plain that the husband may be taken to mean what he says.

There are, of course, infinite variations.

The learned President pointed out that when the wife leaves as a result of brutal conduct the fact that she voluntarily opens the door and goes does not mean that she consents to go. No more is it consent if, when told to go, she goes. There is a confusion of thought by those who say that the voluntary act of departure amounts to consent to ending a state of things. If the husband's words are proved to be intended to be final, conclusive and effective, there is no better evidence of the cause of the separation and the intention of the husband. The point of *Charter* v. *Charter* (1901), 84 L.T. 272, was that the wife must prove that the husband meant what he said. In *Charter* v. *Charter* the husband spoke in temper and immediately afterwards repented. He obviously had not meant his wife to go. Whether the husband means it depends on all the circumstances.

The case of *Lane* v. *Lane* [1951] P. 284, and on appeal [1952] P. 34, was itself near the borderline because Willmer, J., in the Divisional Court had doubts and Jenkins, L.J., in the Court of Appeal dissented. The facts were that in April, 1950, the wife had got an order on the ground of constructive desertion, and her evidence was that the husband had frequently told her to leave. On her own initiative in October, 1950, the parties resumed cohabitation and after a few days she left again and took out another summons for desertion. The justices found that the conduct of the husband was such as to show her return was not welcome and she was often taunted with the phrase, " I never asked you to come back." It was held by the magistrates, and on appeal by both the Divisional Court and the Court of Appeal, that these words taken in the context of all the circumstances showed an intention by the husband to drive his wife from the home.

A useful illustration is *Saunders* v. *Saunders* [1965] 1 All E.R.

838. The facts briefly were that the wife worked in a shop belonging to both parties as well as doing the household work and was overburdened, and the husband neglected to help her and was inconsiderate. The justices found he was callous and lacked consideration. There was trouble about a male assistant and the wife left. She returned after the husband had signed an admission that he was to blame for his wife leaving. Later she left again and issued a summons alleging constructive desertion and wilful neglect to maintain. The justices found that the husband had deserted his wife. The Divisional Court (Sir Jocelyn Simon, P., and Scarman, J.) had doubts about the justices' findings of fact, and the head note, curiously using a double negative, states " the conduct described in the evidence was not such that it would not under any circumstances have been misconduct of the grave and weighty character that would justify a finding of constructive desertion, and so the justices were not shown to have erred in law." On the facts this was a borderline case, but once again the court emphasised that the test was that the conduct of the erring spouse must be grave and weighty.

The following is an extract from the judgment of the President (at p. 841): —

> " The generally accepted test of what conduct amounts to constructive desertion is this: has the defendant been guilty of such grave and weighty misconduct that the only sensible inference is that he knew that the complainant would in all probability withdraw permanently from cohabitation with him, if she acted like any reasonable person in her position. So stated, *factum* and *animus* and, indeed, absence of consensuality are intimately bound up. Unless the conduct is so grave and weighty as to make matrimonial cohabitation virtually impossible, the defendant cannot know that his wife will *reasonably* withdraw from cohabitation. Unless the conduct is of such a nature as to overbear the complainant's willingness to remain in cohabitation, her withdrawal will have an element of consensuality. On the test of constructive desertion as I have ventured to state it, see *Oldroyd* v. *Oldroyd* [1896] P. 175, at pp. 183, 184 (itself firmly founded on earlier authorities); *Buchler* v. *Buchler* [1947] P. 25; *Lang* v. *Lang* [1955] A.C. 402; and *Gollins* v. *Gollins* [1964] A.C. 644, at p. 666, per Lord Reid.
>
> It is true that the actual decision in *Buchler* v. *Buchler* has been criticised by Danckwerts, L.J., in *Hall* v. *Hall* [1962] 3 All E.R. 518, and by Lord Pearce in *Gollins* v. *Gollins*; but

the propositions of law contained in the judgments have been
cited with approval and applied over and over again in cases
of the highest authority—one example is the decision of the
Court of Appeal in *Lane* v. *Lane* [1952] P. 34, which was
cited to us in this case."

Examples of conduct, where constructive desertion found: —

(1) Where the husband brought his mistress into the house—
Dickinson v. *Dickinson* (1889), 62 L.T. 330.

(2) Where the husband adhered to his mistress—*Pizzala* v.
Pizzala (1896), 12 T.L.R. 451.

(3) Where the husband induced belief in his adultery—*Baker*
v. *Baker* [1954] P. 33.

(4) Where the husband refused to dismiss the maid with whom
he was too friendly—*Morse* v. *Morse* (1959), *The Times*,
2nd June.

(5) Where the wife committed treason—*Ingram* v. *Ingram*
[1956] P. 390.

(6) Where the justices were not acting, or purporting to act,
judicially in telling the husband that he would have to
leave, but that in all the circumstances the inference was
that the direction to leave was given at the direct instigation of the wife—*Jones* v. *Jones* [1952] 2 T.L.R. 225.

(7) Where the wife kept an inordinate number of cats—
Winnan v. *Winnan* [1949] P. 174.

(8) Refusal of sexual intercourse—*Lawrance* v. *Lawrance*
[1950] P. 84.

(9) Adulterous association in the past with intention to persist
—*Teall* v. *Teall* [1938] P. 250.

(10) Cruelty to child—*Wright* v. *Wright* [1960] P. 85.

(11) Conviction for several acts of indecent exposure—*Crawford* v. *Crawford* [1956] P. 195.

(12) Boorishness, taciturnity and uncleanliness—*Waters* v.
Waters [1956] P. 344.

(13) In *Howell* v. *Howell* (1964), *The Times*, 10th June, the wife
was obsessed with cleanliness and went to bed at dawn
and rose at dusk and cleaned at night making sleep
impossible. The husband's health was affected and he left
her. The court held this was cruel conduct, and the wife
was guilty of constructive desertion.

(14) Drunkenness—*Hall* v. *Hall* [1962] 1 W.L.R. 1246.

Examples where constructive desertion not found: —
1. (1) Frivolous conduct such as kissing which aroused sexual desire—*Cox* v. *Cox* [1958] 1 W.L.R. 340.
2. (2) Isolated incident of indecent assault of not too serious a nature—*Lewis* v. *Lewis* [1956] P. 205*n*.
3. (3) Innocent association by the husband with a male employee against wife's wishes—*Buchler* v. *Buchler* [1947] P. 25.
4. (4) Husband came home drunk once, and when she left asked forgiveness—*Pratt* v. *Pratt* (1962), *The Times*, 18th October (C.A.).

Notice

Where a wife alleges, in summary proceedings, conduct by the husband in relation to other women, albeit not giving rise to a reasonable belief in adultery, but nevertheless so inconsistent with the married relationship as to amount to expulsive conduct, general notice of the charge must be given to the husband in the same way as where there is a charge of adultery or reasonable belief in adultery. Sir J. Simon, P., said that a case of adultery should no more be dressed up as a case of constructive desertion than a case of persistent cruelty should be (*Hind* v. *Hind* [1969] 1 All E.R. 1083, 1085; see also *Burton* v. *Burton* (1969), 113 Sol. J. 852, D.C.).

B. The factum of Separation

In the majority of cases, the question whether spouses are living separate and apart presents no difficulty; but as it can happen that parties not living in the same house may still in the eyes of the law be living together, and on the other hand, parties living in the same house may yet be living apart, it will be recognised that the subject is not without its complexities.

There have been unsuccessful attempts to persuade the courts that there can be desertion without separation when there has been a gross breach of matrimonial duty (*Weatherley* v. *Weatherley* [1947] A.C. 628 approving *Jackson* v. *Jackson* [1924] P. 19, where it was held that refusal of sexual intercourse in itself did not amount to desertion).

Husband and wife are entitled to each other's society. This is known as consortium. There was a time when this could be enforced by a decree of restitution of conjugal rights, but the power to imprison for refusal to obey such a decree has long been abolished. Nor can the parties use self-help in such matters (*R.* v. *Jackson* [1891] Q.B. 671, where the Court of Appeal held that a husband had no right to seize his wife and imprison her person until she consented to restore conjugal rights).

When spouses live separate and apart they cease to cohabit. The question therefore is—what is cohabitation?

The *factum* of separation is an essential element in desertion.

(i) *Cohabitation*

Cohabitation is important in the law of desertion, in that, if cohabitation exists between the parties, there can be no desertion by either: and if there is a state of desertion, then the resumption of cohabitation brings it to an end. Lord Merriman said in *Mummery* v. *Mummery* [1942] P. 107 at p. 109: —

> " I doubt whether any judge could give a completely exhaustive definition of cohabitation . . ."

Certain it is that it has been used in different senses by different judges and writers. In its normal sense, it means living together in the same house as man and wife, which usually includes sleeping and eating together, and the usual close association of man and wife. For some purposes it means living in the same house provided that the parties are not living in two separate households. Parties not living in the same house, because of the exigencies of their employment, may still be cohabiting. Work may keep them apart but they try to be together when they can. In all these cases it is a question of fact whether the parties are cohabiting or not; but attempts have been made to have notional cohabitation. Thus Stone's Justices' Manual (1974), p. 1397: " The legal relationship known as ' cohabitation ' exists immediately upon marriage." This proposition is arrived at by these stages: —

First, by defining desertion as follows (p. 1396): To prove desertion, it is necessary to establish a termination of cohabitation brought about by the intention of the defendant and the absence of consent thereto of the complainant.

Second, the cases of *De Laubenque* v. *De Laubenque* [1899] P. 42 and others show that there can be desertion where a husband leaves his wife at the church door and refuses to cohabit. Ergo: cohabitation " in the legal sense " must commence at marriage.

Actually the headnote of *De Laubenque* refutes this argument. It reads as follows: —

> " There may be desertion without previous cohabitation. Where a husband and wife separated immediately after their marriage and never cohabited although it appeared that it was the husband who refused to cohabit, the wife having always been willing to do so, the court found the husband had been guilty of desertion."

It was Lord Penzance in *Fitzgerald* v. *Fitzgerald* (1869), L.R. 1 P. & D. 694, at p. 697, who enunciated the doctrine that " Desertion means abandonment, and implies an active withdrawal from a cohabitation that exists." In the cases of *Pulford* v. *Pulford* [1923] P. 18, *Jordan* v. *Jordan* [1939] P. 239, *Beeken* v. *Beeken* [1948] P. 312 (C.A.), and *Everitt* v. *Everitt* [1949] P. 374, this doctrine has now been decisively rejected.

The argument is as follows: —

The judgment of Lord Penzance is confused because he is using cohabitation in different senses and he contradicts himself thus: —

> " But if the state of cohabitation has already ceased to exist, whether by adverse act of husband or wife, or even by the mutual consent of both, ' desertion ' in my judgment, becomes from that moment impossible to either, at least until their common life and home has been resumed."

On the other hand, Lord Penzance says that there are cases in which actual cohabitation does not exist and in respect of which desertion can take place, and he gives as an example *Williams* v. *Williams* (1864), 3 Sw. & Tr. 547, where cohabitation did not exist at all because the circumstances did not permit it.

Then there are cases where the parties are living apart, separated by the calls of everyday life, or the exigencies of public duty. Here he says cohabitation is suspended, though only a few lines back he says it does not exist at all.

Cohabitation means that parties are living together as man and wife and that includes living together as best they can, even though physically separated due to the exigencies of earning a living, public duty and the like. It may be suspended while one party is in prison or in a mental hospital. The inception of desertion is not confined to the case where cohabitation is brought to an end, but includes cases where the two factors of actual separation, and intention to desert, coincide. The importance of cohabitation in the inception of desertion is negative, that is, it must be shown not to exist. In the termination of desertion, cohabitation is important in a positive sense, that is, the fact that the parties have resumed cohabitation brings the desertion to an end.

(ii) *Withdrawal from a state of things*

In *Pulford* v. *Pulford* [1923] P. 18 (Divisional Court, Duke, P., and Hill, J.), the parties were married in 1882 and lived together until 1883, and then the wife was in an asylum until 1902. When she came out there was no resumption of cohabitation. In 1922 the wife took out a summons for desertion and the magistrates made an order from which the husband appealed, relying on the dictum of Lord Penzance in *Fitzgerald* v. *Fitzgerald* (1869), L.R. 1 P. & D. 694, at p. 697: "Desertion means abandonment and implies an active withdrawal from cohabitation that exists." Duke, P., pointed out that Lord Penzance had qualified the above statement, and that there may be desertion when the parties are separated by the exigencies of public duty, and that there may be cases where the cohabitation is merely supended and not wholly relinquished. He continued at p. 21: —

> "It has been almost a commonplace in this court to hold that in order to ascertain whether there has been desertion, you must look at the conduct of the parties. There may be no matrimonial home, and yet no forfeiture of the rights of the parties. Desertion is not the withdrawal from a place, but from a state of things. The husband may live in a place and make it impossible for his wife to live there, though it is she and not he that actually withdraws; and that state of things may be desertion of the wife. The law does not deal with the mere matter of place. What it seeks to enforce is the recognition and discharge of the common obligations of the married state. If one party does not acknowledge them, the party who has so offended cannot be heard to say that he or she is not guilty of desertion on the ground that there has been no desertion by departure from a place."

He went on to say that the misapprehension was that Lord Penzance's dictum had been treated as a comprehensive definition of desertion.

Lord Merrivale's (formerly Duke, P.) own celebrated dictum that desertion is not the withdrawal from a place but from a state of things has itself been elevated into a definition, which of course it was not intended to be. The President was concerned to show that the abandonment of the obligations of marriage is a vital element of desertion. Desertion might occur through the withdrawal from a place. It might also occur when the parties are in fact parted, and the deserter " withdraws " from the obligations of marriage by signifying his intention to abandon the obligations of marriage, but " withdrawal " here is used in a notional sense and not a physical one, so that in fact there may be desertion without any withdrawal in fact by the deserter, and that is what happened in *Pulford* v. *Pulford*. When the wife came out of the asylum, the husband did not withdraw from anything in a physical sense. He simply declined or neglected to resume the obligations of his marriage. While his wife was in the asylum, the husband began an adulterous association. The President accurately described his conduct as " a complete renunciation by him of every conjugal duty."

The following year, 1924, the President in *Jackson* v. *Jackson* [1924] P. 19, quoted with approval the words of Lopes, L.J., in *R.* v. *Leresche* [1891] 2 Q.B. 418 and 420: —

" A husband deserts his wife if he wilfully absents himself from the society of his wife in spite of her wish."

In spite of *Pulford*, Lord Penzance's dictum was not completely defunct and was dealt with comprehensively by Lord Merriman in *Jordan* v. *Jordan* [1939] P. 239. From p. 249 he shows that the words of Lord Penzance's judgment are capable of more than one meaning, that in various subsequent cases, such as *Mahoney* v. *M'Carthy* [1892] P. 21, 25; *Bradshaw* v. *Bradshaw* [1897] P. 24, 27; *Pulford* v. *Pulford* [1923] P. 18, 20, and *Papadopoulos* v. *Papadopoulos* [1936] P. 108, 114, it has been explained that the judgment was not intended to be an exhaustive exposition of the law relating to desertion, and that the subsequent history of the case itself showed that a resumption of cohabitation was unnecessary before there could be desertion.

Lord Merriman probably thought he had at last given the quietus to *Fitzgerald*, but its ghost continued to walk, and he tells us in *Everitt* v. *Everitt* [1949] P. 374 that it was pressed upon the Divisional Court in an unreported case, *Volp* v. *Volp* in 1940, and he hoped that was for the last time.

The upshot of these cases is that it is now established that there need not be a state of cohabitation immediately preceding, or preceding at all, the state of desertion, but that the absence of cohabitation is an essential element in desertion.

(iii) *Living under the same roof*

It is possible for parties to cohabit although they are living in separate places. On the other hand, it is possible for parties to be living separate and apart although living under the same roof. The first case to be decided on the subject was *Powell* v. *Powell* [1922] P. 278, where the husband and wife lived in the same dwelling-house but the husband forsook his wife's bed, avoided her society and secluded himself from her in a separate part of the house with a separate entrance from the street. He refused to associate with her, but made her an allowance and occasionally wished her good morning. Lord Buckmaster, at p. 279, said: —

> " [Desertion] is an offence difficult to define. Neglect or contempt, however hard to bear, do not constitute desertion. . . . Except that these two persons were sheltered by one and the same roof there was desertion of this wife by the husband in every meaning of the word."

This case was followed in *Smith* v. *Smith* [1940] P. 49. The facts were that the house belonged to the husband, but the basement was occupied by his mother. After a quarrel with his wife, he left her bedroom and went to live with his mother in the basement. He slept with his son on the first floor. In fact, he lived with his mother and received no services from his wife, but he made her an allowance.

This case has been described as a high-water mark in this type of case. Thus, in *Littlewood* v. *Littlewood* [1943] P. 11, where the parties slept in separate bedrooms and hardly conversed but the wife cooked the food and occasionally performed her domestic duties, there was held to be no desertion. In *Wilkes* v. *Wilkes* [1943] P. 41 and *Angel* v. *Angel* [1946] 2 All E.R. 635, where in effect there were two separate households, both in the same house, *Smith* v. *Smith* [1940] P. 49 was followed. The leading case is *Hopes* v. *Hopes* [1949] P. 227, in the Court of Appeal. This was a case where the parties had separate bedrooms. There was no sexual intercourse. The wife did no mending or washing, but they ate together. It was held that the parties were not living apart. Bucknill, L.J., at p. 234, said: —

> "The cases to which I have referred establish that there may be desertion, although husband and wife are living in the same dwelling, if there is such a forsaking and abandonment by one spouse of the other that the court can say that the spouses were living lives separate and apart from one another. On the other hand, when husband and wife are living together, as they were in the present case, it seems that to grant a decree of divorce on the ground of conduct by the wife, which *ex hypothesi* did not amount to cruelty, and which did not amount to a life separate and apart from her husband, would be to introduce a new ground for divorce."

and Denning, L.J., at p. 235, said: —

> "One of the essential elements of desertion is the fact of separation. Can that exist whilst the parties are living under the same roof? My answer is: 'Yes.' The husband who shuts himself up in one or two rooms of his house, and ceases to have anything to do with his wife, is living separately and apart from her as effectively as if they were separated by the outer door of a flat. They may meet on the stairs or in the passageway, but so they might if they each had separate flats in one building. If that separation is brought about by his fault, why is that not desertion? He has forsaken and abandoned his wife as effectively as if he had gone into lodgings."

It would appear, therefore, that the criterion is: are there two households or one? This is not always easy to decide.

A husband and wife can have two households under the same roof even though they share certain parts of the house in common. For instance, they may use the same bathroom and lavatory, and cook in the same kitchen. This is illustrated by the case of *Walker* v. *Walker* [1952] 2 All E.R. 138, in the Court of Appeal. There the parties lived in the same house. The wife withdrew to a separate bedroom which she kept locked. She performed no household duties for her husband, who had to do his own washing, mending and ironing. The husband had his meals out except on Sunday mornings, when he cooked for himself when his wife was not in the kitchen. They communicated by notes and the wife refused attempts at reconciliation. Birkett, L.J., at p. 141, said: —

> "The only element of living together was that the husband

and wife were actually residing in one house and there was no physical separation between the parts of the house in which they were living. They were compelled to cook their meals in the same kitchen, and the only thing the husband did in that way was to cook his meal on Sunday morning at some time different from the time at which his wife used the kitchen. To say that these people were in any sense living together—that in any sense there was one household—is impossible on the facts of this case. There was an imperative need to use the same kitchen, as indeed for all I know there was an imperative need to use the same w.c. or anything else which was essential, but in no other sense could it be said that there was one household."

The above case deals with the inception of desertion. Is the principle the same during the continuance of desertion? In other words, if a wife, say, deserts her husband and after a time returns to his house, under what conditions does the desertion end? If cohabitation is resumed, then of course desertion ends (see p. 116 et seq.). If the parties continue to live as separate households, as if they were living in two flats, then clearly it does not. The facts may be such, however, as to make it difficult to determine whether there is cohabitation on the one hand, or two separate households on the other, and then the court has to determine on which side of the line the case falls. The court does not wish to discourage attempts at reconciliation, and yet in a proper case it does not wish the period of desertion to be interrupted. Isolated acts of intercourse, for instance, have been held not to put an end to desertion. Cases on either side of the line are *Bartram* v. *Bartram* [1950] P. 1, desertion not interrupted, and *Everitt* v. *Everitt* [1949] P. 374 and *Bull* v. *Bull* [1953] P. 224, where it was.

In *Bartram* v. *Bartram* the wife deserted her husband but eighteen months later she went to live at his house and, according to Bucknill, L.J., she went there purely as a lodger because there was no other accommodation and she wanted to be near her employment. She did not sleep with her husband and paid no attention to him. She did not mend his clothes or cook for him, or go out with him or treat him in any way differently from the way she would have treated another lodger in the house whom she cordially disliked. There were times when she had meals at the same table. Bucknill, L.J., said at p. 6: —

" If the facts do not establish any intention on the part of the

wife to set up a matrimonial home, the mere fact that, as a
lodger, she went to live under the same roof as her husband,
because she had nowhere else to go, does not remove the
desertion which she had already started and which continued
to run."

and Denning, L.J., said at p. 6: —

" Once the period of desertion has begun to run, it does not
cease to run simply because the parties attempt a reconciliation and for that purpose come together again for a
time. That was laid down by Lord Merriman, P., in
Mummery v. *Mummery* [1942] P. 107, and has never been
doubted since. Indeed, I would say in such a case the period
of desertion does not cease to run unless, and until, a true
reconciliation has been effected [as to which see *Mackrell*
v. *Mackrell* [1948] 2 All E.R. 858]. Any other view would
greatly hamper attempts at reconciliation, because it would
mean that the deserted party would be disinclined to take the
other back for fear of losing his legal rights in case the
reconciliation was unsuccessful."

(The words in square brackets do not appear in the Law Reports
but only in [1949] 2 All E.R., at p. 273.)

In *Everitt* v. *Everitt* [1949] P. 374, the facts were that the
parties were married in April, 1943, and during the first few months
of the marriage the husband pursued his association with a
woman with whom he had had sexual relations before his marriage
—a fact well-known to his wife. The husband left within six
months and lived with the other woman and the wife got an
order before a magistrate on the ground of desertion. Later the
husband informed his wife that the other woman had married and
left the country and he wished to resume cohabitation with his
wife. She refused to have him back but he installed himself in
her flat and lived there for four months before she left. The
husband swore they had lived as man and wife. The wife denied
this. The commissioner who tried the wife's petition for divorce
on the ground of desertion did not decide the question of cohabitation, but the Court of Appeal received in evidence a letter from
the wife from which it was clear that the parties resumed
cohabitation while the husband was in the flat. Lord Merriman,
P., at p. 387, said: —

" The fundamental point about this part of the case [i.e., that
the husband had returned and installed himself in the flat
of his wife and lived there for four months] is that it was

decided by this court in *Hopes* v. *Hopes* [1949] P. 227 that the necessary element of separation cannot subsist when a husband and wife are living under the same roof unless they have ceased to share one household and have set up two households there. In my opinion it is impossible to limit that decision merely to the inception of the alleged desertion. The same principle must apply to the interruption of a period of desertion. . . ."

and at p. 388: —

" Taking the wife's evidence at its highest, and assuming that it has been accepted by the commissioner not only as regards the allegation that there was no sexual intercourse, but that she was living in this three-roomed flat with the husband for four months virtually under duress; still I doubt whether it would be possible even if the husband had forced his way in in the first instance, to hold that for the whole period of four months a state of separation still subsisted. I doubt very much whether it would be possible to hold, applying the test laid down in *Hopes* v. *Hopes*, that there was not only the creation but also the subsistence of two households in those three rooms. It is not, however, necessary to express a concluded opinion. . . ."

In *Bull* v. *Bull* [1953] P. 224, in the Court of Appeal, the wife had deserted her husband for a number of months. She returned to the matrimonial home at his request and lived there for over three years. She refused his requests for sexual intercourse, and would not converse with him, or sit in the same room, or go out with him, or have his friends in the house. She cooked his meals and sometimes mended his clothes. It was held that the wife's desertion terminated.

Somervell, L.J., said that he considered the cases of *Mummery* v. *Mummery* [1942] P. 107 and *Perry* v. *Perry* [1952] P. 203 were only concerned with occasional acts of intercourse. The distinction between *Bartram* and *Bull* was that in the former the wife returned, not at the husband's request, but because she had nowhere to go. Asquith, L.J., had held she was acting under the spur of necessity; whereas in the latter the wife did not come back because of necessity and she did not come back at the husband's request. At p. 228 he said: —

" I therefore, speaking for myself, do not think that *Bartram* supports the wide proposition for which Mr. Loudon contends, nor do I think in principle that any such proposition could be accepted or laid down. We are dealing simply with the present case and in the present case during the relevant three years the parties were living under the same roof as one household."

and Jenkins, L.J., said, at p. 228 (referring to *Bartram*): —

"Her residence in that house, which belonged to the husband, was put an end to by the husband selling it with a view to forcing her to come and live with him. There was no house other than the one occupied by the husband in which she could live consistently with her continuance in the employment in which she was engaged. She therefore came against her will and lived in the same house as the husband. The terms upon which she lived in the house were put thus: ' The wife refused to sleep with her husband and slept with the adopted daughter of her husband's mother. She never went into his rooms. She paid no attention at all to him as a husband, never mended his clothes, cooked for him, or went out with him. She never treated him in any way differently from the way she would treat a lodger whom she disliked. At times, however, she sat at the same table with her husband and ate the common food provided for them. . . .'

The circumstances relied on in support of that view are weaker than those in *Bartram* v. *Bartram* and the element of compulsion on the wife to live under the same roof as the husband, which was a decisive factor in that case, is wholly absent here."

It is clear, therefore, that the principles which apply to the inception of desertion apply equally to its interruption, and if there are not two separate households, desertion cannot either begin or continue.

Suppose the parties occupy the same room under compulsion, as in a prisoner of war camp, and one party wishes to desert the other and ceases cohabitation as far as the conditions allow, can there be desertion? There is no authority on this, but Bucknill, L.J., in *Beeken* v. *Beeken* [1948] P. 302 thought there could be desertion (see p. 41).

The Matrimonial Causes Act, 1973 (re-enacting a similar provision in the Divorce Reform Act, 1969) provides that proof of the irretrievable breakdown of the marriage can be shown on proof that the parties have lived apart for two years in certain cases and five years in other cases. The court therefore has had to consider what amounts to " living apart," and as living apart is essential for desertion these cases are helpful in desertion cases. The Court of Appeal considered the subject in *Fuller (otherwise Penfold)* v. *Fuller* [1973] 2 All E.R. 650. The facts were that the husband left his wife in 1964 and she went to live with P. In 1968 the husband became ill and was medically advised not to live alone and so he went to live at P's as a lodger. The wife slept with P but the husband joined them for meals. The wife petitioned for divorce on the ground of separation for five years. The divorce judge refused a decree on the ground that she had not been living apart, but this decision was reversed by the Court of Appeal.

Lord Denning, M.R., at p. 652, pointed out that s. 2 (5) of the Act of 1969 (now s. 2 (6) of the Act of 1973) says that the parties are to be treated as living apart " unless they are living with each other in the same household." With each other meant as husband and wife. He contrasted this with *Mouncer* v. *Mouncer* [1972] 1 All E.R. 289, where husband and wife were living with their children in the same household but were not having sexual intercourse together. That was not living apart. He also referred to *Santos* v. *Santos* [1972] Fam. 247, C.A., where it was pointed out that " living apart " meant not mere physical separation. In addition there had to be the intention not to return, but this intention need not be communicated to the other spouse (see *Nutley* v. *Nutley* [1970] 1 W.L.R. 217).

Although Lord Denning based his decision on the words of the 1969 Act it is submitted that the criteria are exactly the same as in *Bartram* v. *Bartram* [1950] P. 1 and *Hopes* v. *Hopes* [1949] P. 227, which he referred to.

(iv) *Cohabitation may exist although the parties do not live under the same roof*

The parties to a marriage, though willing to live together, may for various reasons not be able to live in the same home, as where the husband has to go abroad on business, as in *Stickland* v. *Stickland* (1876), 35 L.T. 767 (where the husband went to Australia gold-digging), or *Chudley* v. *Chudley* (1893), 69 L.T. 617 (where the wife went to her mother's for a confinement), or *Henty* v. *Henty* (1875), 33 L.T. 263 (where the husband, who was a soldier, was sent to India) and *Davis* v. *Davis* (1920), 124 L.T. 795 (where the husband was a soldier abroad).

Where the parties are in domestic service in different establishments but meet when they can, they are cohabiting (*Williams* v. *Williams* (1864), 3 Sw. & Tr. 547).

Sir Francis Jeune, P., in *Huxtable* v. *Huxtable* (1899), 68 L.J.P. 83, at p. 85, said: —

> "What is or is not cohabitation is not a simple question. Cohabitation may be of two sorts, one continuous, the other intermittent. The parties may reside together constantly, or there may be occasional intercourse between them, which nevertheless may amount to cohabitation in the legal sense of the term. . . .
>
> The circumstances of life, such as business duties, domestic service, and other things may separate husband and wife and yet notwithstanding there may be cohabitation."

He referred to *Bradshaw* v. *Bradshaw* [1897] P. 24, a decision of a Divisional Court, of which he was a member, where the wife was a domestic servant who had never lived with her husband under the same roof, though he had visited her, and it was held that she had been in cohabitation with him. It was said they cohabited together in the wider sense of that term.

(v) *It is not necessary for cohabitation to precede desertion*

As has been stated (p. 30), it was at one time thought that cohabitation was a necessary prelude to desertion. In other words, cohabitation had immediately to precede the act of desertion. This is clearly not the law now and probably never was, though certain expressions in *Fitzgerald* v. *Fitzgerald* (1869), L.R. 1 P. & D. 694, were to that effect.

In *De Laubenque* v. *De Laubenque* [1899] P. 42 the parties had married because a child was expected, and never lived together. The husband left the wife at the church door. It was held that the husband had deserted the wife.

In *Fassbender* v. *Fassbender* [1938] 3 All E.R. 389 the wife petitioned for restitution of conjugal rights. It was conceded the parties had never cohabited and it was argued that therefore no order could be made. Henn Collins, J., in making the order said: —

> "I think that it really means a suit to oblige one of the spouses to afford those matrimonial amenities which the marriage tie renders obligatory. I do not think that it is a test of that, that they should already have been enjoyed."

A man can continue to be in desertion even though he is in prison. In *Drew* v. *Drew* (1888), 13 **P.D.** 97, the husband left his wife saying he was going to Ireland, but he went to Australia to evade arrest. Up to then he had been carrying on with a woman, and he was found living in Australia with another woman. He was brought back to England in custody and sentenced to ten years' imprisonment. It was held, on the wife's petition for divorce, that he was nevertheless in desertion.

Desertion can commence whilst the spouses are living apart, the separation being by compulsion, e.g., by reason of imprisonment. This was decided in *Beeken* v. *Beeken* [1948] **P.** 302. The parties were captured by the Japanese and interned in a camp in Amoy, China, in December, 1941, where they occupied twin beds in the same bedroom. From June, 1942, the wife formed a friendship with a Norwegian and thereafter refused intercourse with her husband, and all wifely duties, and spent all her time with the Norwegian. There was no evidence that either spouse made any attempt to get leave to live separately. In June, 1943, they were removed to Shanghai and each interned in a different camp. The wife was permitted to visit her husband once a year for twenty minutes. On the second visit in March, 1944, she asked him if he had seen any lawyers in the camp about a divorce, and she said she intended to marry the Norwegian. On release in August, 1945, they travelled to England separately, where she said she would not live with him.

The husband petitioned for divorce on the ground of desertion putting forward December, 1942, and alternatively March, 1944, as the inception of the desertion. Mr. Commissioner Eddy refused a divorce, but on appeal the Court of Appeal (Lord Merriman, P., Bucknill, L.J., and Hodson, J.) reversed his decision, holding that there was desertion certainly from March, 1944.

There was a difference of opinion whether it was possible for one party to desert the other while living in the same room, since they had to live there under compulsion. Lord Merriman, who thought this proposition was unarguable, said at p. 307: —

> " There was no evidence before the court that either spouse made any attempt to get leave to live in different conditions and it is impossible to contend that the mere failure to render wifely duties could constitute the fact of separation."

Bucknill, L.J., preferred another view at p. 311:—

> " Apart from the fact that the husband and wife were com-
> pelled to sleep in the same bedroom, I should have thought
> that the wife had committed the matrimonial offence of
> desertion which in its essence is the forsaking and abandon-
> ment by one spouse of the other, whilst the parties were still
> living at Amoy, at all events as from December, 1942, when
> the wife said to her husband that she refused to alter her
> attitude unless he undertook to commence divorce proceed-
> ings. . . . But, if spouses are compelled by their gaolers to live
> in the same bedroom, the reasoning which prevents a spouse
> from establishing desertion where they voluntarily share
> the same bedroom seems to me to disappear."

It would be interesting to know if Lord Merriman would have
agreed with this if there had been evidence that the wife had tried
to get leave to live in another place and failed.

Beeken v. *Beeken* illustrates the point that the *factum* and the
animus cannot be put into separate compartments, but must be
considered together. For instance, when the parties were com-
pulsorily separated in different camps and only allowed to meet
for a few minutes each year, they were in fact separated, but
whether they were cohabiting depended entirely on the intention
of one of the parties. Once the wife had formed the intention to
desert, and told her husband so, cohabitation ceased. If she had had
no such intention, then it would have continued.

(vi) *The parting must be permanent*

A temporary withdrawal by one spouse does not amount to
desertion. When it is said that the parting must be permanent,
that is, that one party has abandoned the other, all that is meant
is that the spouse in default has the intention at the time of
making the parting permanent. He may of course change his
mind at a later stage. The presumption is that he intends to leave
permanently and the onus would be on him to prove otherwise. If
his intention was merely to leave temporarily without the consent
of the other party, and without just cause, this would formerly
have constituted the offence of wilful separation without cause
(Matrimonial Causes Act, 1965, s. 5 (4), proviso (iii), which made it
a discretionary bar to divorce). There is no other statutory
reference to this offence.

Lilley v. *Lilley* [1960] P. 158 (C.A.), is an important case on wilful neglect to maintain, but it also illustrates the importance of "permanence" in desertion. The wife in that case refused to live with her husband owing to a neurosis from which she suffered. Medical evidence given on her behalf was that the presence of her husband would make this neurosis worse. The wife, who was a rational person, had stated in writing that she would never return to her husband. If she had said she would not go back for the time being, this would not have been desertion, but because of her categorical "never," the Court of Appeal held that she was in desertion.

C. Intention

It is frequently asserted that an *animus deserendi* is an essential element in desertion (*Pardy* v. *Pardy* [1939] P. 288, and *Buchler* v. *Buchler* [1947] P. 25). This is true of actual desertion, and in most cases of constructive desertion, but it will be argued here that there may be cases of constructive desertion where it is not necessary.

In actual desertion the words "*animus deserendi*" mean that the deserter intends to leave for good, without consent, and without just cause. In constructive desertion it has been said that these words mean an intention to drive away or expel the other spouse (*Boyd* v. *Boyd* [1938] 4 All E.R. 181, and Denning, L.J., in *Hosegood* v. *Hosegood* (1950), 66 T.L.R. (Pt. I) 235). It is true that a husband who drives his wife away and intends to do so is guilty of constructive desertion; but the question remains whether conduct of a husband such that his wife is justified in leaving him, although he has no intention of driving her away —indeed may sincerely wish her to stay—can still be a ground of constructive desertion. It will be demonstrated that there are such cases.

There is a series of cases known as " the mistress cases " which, although decided many years ago, are still good law: —

Dickinson v. *Dickinson* (1889), 62 L.T. 330, where the wife left because her husband wished to have his mistress in the house.

Koch v. *Koch* [1899] P. 221, where the wife left because the husband refused to discharge a maid with whom he was committing adultery.

Pizzala v. *Pizzala* (1896), 12 T.L.R. 451, and *Sickert* v. *Sickert* [1899] P. 278, where, in each case, the husband refused to give up his mistress and the wife left.

In all these cases the husband did not intend to drive his wife away, but it was said that he was presumed so to intend. One may well ask why it is necessary to import a legal fiction here, namely, to presume an intention which was the opposite of his real intention.

As the courts have felt their way to a solution of the problem, there developed two schools of thought. The first school represented by *Boyd* and *Hosegood* (per Denning, L.J.) (*supra*), asserted that the spouse's intention to drive away the other spouse had to be shown as a matter of fact, though the intention may be inferred from conduct. The other view to be found in *Sickert* (*supra*), and *Edwards* v. *Edwards* [1948] P. 268, was that if the conduct is so bad or so unreasonable, he must be presumed to intend her to leave, however much he may in fact have desired her to remain.

Lord Denning's view was that the difference between the two schools amounted to this: that the first school held the presumption of intention to be rebuttable, while the second school asserted it was irrebuttable. It is submitted that if there were two such schools, then neither was correct. As will be shown, in this type of case, the question of intention is beside the point. The solution is the answer to the question—Had the complainant just cause for leaving? This is the test laid down by Asquith, L.J., in *Buchler* v. *Buchler* [1947] P. 25.

The subject was considered at length by the Privy Council in *Lang* v. *Lang* [1955] A.C. 402. This was an appeal from the High Court of Australia, and concerned a petition by a wife for divorce on the ground of desertion. By the law of Victoria, desertion for three years was a ground for divorce, but cruelty was not. The husband had unquestionably been cruel to his wife and on that account she had left him. It was argued on behalf of the husband that as he had no intention to drive his wife out, he could not be said to have had a constructive intention to do so, if his real intention was to the contrary. Lord Porter, who gave the judgment of the court, discussed the alleged two schools of thought. He said (at p. 424) that in *Boyd*, *supra*, and *Bartholomew* v.

Bartholomew [1952] 2 All E.R. 1035 (where the wife was dirty in her person and kept the matrimonial home dirty), language had been used suggesting that if the respondent desired the petitioner to remain there cannot ever be constructive desertion: in other words, in those cases the courts applied a subjective test, viz., the husband's intention. Logically, therefore, if a husband wished to have his wife at home so that he could ill-treat her, he cannot be guilty of constructive desertion.

Lord Porter expresses it thus in *Lang* v. *Lang, supra*, at p. 428: —

> " Prima facie, a man who treats his wife with gross brutality may be presumed to intend the consequences of his acts. Such an inference may indeed be rebutted, but if the only evidence is of continuous cruelty and no rebutting evidence is given, the natural and almost inevitable inference is that the husband intended to drive out the wife. The court is at least entitled and, indeed, driven to such an inference unless convincing evidence to the contrary is adduced. In their lordships' opinion that is the proper approach to the problem. . . ."

Lord Porter then went on to point out that there may be a conflict between intention and desire, e.g., where a man hopes his actions will not produce their natural consequences: —

> " If the husband knows the probable result of his acts and persists in them, in spite of warning that the wife will be compelled to leave the home, and indeed, as in the present case, has expressed an intention of continuing his conduct and never indicated any intention of amendment, that is enough however passionately he may desire or request that she should remain. His intention is to act as he did, whatever the consequences, though he may hope and desire that they will not produce their probable effect " (p. 429).

Finally, Lord Porter said that they were fortified in their view by the mistress cases; for such actions by the husband have always been regarded as justifying the wife's withdrawal and a holding that she had been constructively deserted if she left the house.

Although Lord Porter asks more than once what is meant by " intention," he nowhere analyses or defines that term, though it is true he says it has to be voluntary, that is an act of the will, whereas a wish or desire is not. Nor does he pursue the distinction between a real intention, an inferred intention, and an imputed or constructive intention. While he stresses that conduct raises an inference of an intention, which inference may be rebutted, he gives no instances of the sort of evidence that will rebut it. It is clear from the whole tenor of his speech that if a man pursues a cruel course of conduct, it is not sufficient for him to say that his intention was not to drive his wife away, for it will be said that this is merely his wish, or his desire, or his hope. What of the man who beats his wife because he enjoys seeing her suffer, and locks her in the house so that he can continue to enjoy his sadism? Surely his intention is not to drive her away, but in fact keep her in.

From his reference to the mistress cases, it would seem he approved of the submission that if a man behaves in such a manner that his wife is justified in leaving him, that is constructive desertion. Why bother with intention at all, in the sense that he intended certain consequences? If we must retain " intention," why is it not sufficient to say that he intended the acts without reference to consequences?

Again, is not the reference to rebuttable presumptions supererogatory? Is it not easier to say that a man is responsible for the natural and probable consequences of his acts? See 79 L.Q.R., p. 9, where the editor, referring to the case of *Moorgate Mercantile Co., Ltd.* v. *Finch and Read* [1962] 1 Q.B. 701, says: —

> " This case is an interesting illustration of the confusion that has been introduced into the law by the statement that a man must be ' presumed to intend the natural and probable consequences of his act.' Why is it not sufficient to say that a man will be held liable for the natural and probable consequences of his act, without introducing the unnecessary and often untrue statement concerning his intention."

See also Dr. Goodhart's article in the same issue. Lord Reid in *Gollins* v. *Gollins* [1964] A.C. 644, at p. 662, said: —

> " Why should we drag in intention at all? It seems to me to be a very poor defence to say ' I know the disastrous effect on my wife of what I have been doing. Probably I could have resisted temptation if I had really tried. But my conduct is innocent because I had not the slightest desire or intention to harm my wife. I have acted throughout from pure selfishness.' And the evidence may make it quite clear that he had no intention at all of causing pain to his wife. If he knew, or the evidence shows that he must have known, the effect of his conduct, if there was no justification or excuse for it, if the effect was really serious, if the wife was not unusually

sensitive and he had not reached the stage of mental disorder, why does intention matter? "

It is true that *Gollins* was a case of cruelty, but the reasoning is equally apt for constructive desertion. Moreover, Lord Reid was fortified in his conclusions on cruelty by *Lang* v. *Lang*, which of course was a case of constructive desertion, and about which he said at p. 666: —

" He (the husband) did not act with the intention of driving her out, but he acted with the knowledge that that was what would probably happen. There are references to what a reasonable man would have known; but it is said that this man must have known, which I take to mean that it was proper to hold on the evidence that he did know. So in the result his desire to keep his wife or lack of intention to drive her out was irrelevant. The Act said nothing about intention: it used the word ' wilful.' So the decision was that if without just cause or excuse you persist in doing things which you know your wife will probably not tolerate, and which no ordinary woman would tolerate, and then she leaves, you have wilfully deserted her, whatever your desire or intention may have been. That seems to me to be in line with what I am now submitting to your lordships is the law in cases of cruelty."

Nor does the matter stop there. Since *Williams* v. *Williams* [1964] A.C. 698, the test whether one spouse has treated the other with cruelty is wholly objective and, therefore, proof of insanity is not necessarily an answer. There is no reason to suppose that the position is not exactly the same in the conduct which justifies one spouse in leaving the other.

Lang v. *Lang* was a Privy Council case and therefore not technically binding on the English courts, but since its approval by the House of Lords in *Gollins* (as explained by that case) it is now authoritative, and before that it was referred to by Lord Merriman, P., sitting with Collingwood, J., in *Marjoram* v. *Marjoram* [1955] 1 W.L.R. 520 as " that . . . most authoritative case."

A good illustration of the misunderstanding which can arise on the subject of intention is *Waters* v. *Waters* [1956] P. 344 (D.C.—Lord Merriman, P., and Wallington, J.). The husband behaved with extreme boorishness, unbearable taciturnity, and personal uncleanliness. The justices refused an order because they said he had no intention of being cruel, and had not deliberately conducted himself so as to drive the wife away. The wife's appeal was allowed. Lord Merriman said at p. 352: —

" Now one of the things which is said in this case is that the husband's conduct was due to his natural disposition, which, I suppose, was a reflection of a remark made in *Horton* v. *Horton* ([1940] P. 187, at p. 193), about conduct being a manifestation of character acting in its own sphere. It was an excuse which was put forward, but did not succeed, in *Lauder* v. *Lauder* ([1949] P. 277) and a long way further back than that, in the leading case of *Kelly* v. *Kelly* ((1870), L.R. 2 P. & M. 59 (C.A.)), which was the first reported case depending solely upon mental cruelty, where the excuse was put even higher, namely, that the conduct was due to the clerical husband's response to the call of a Higher Authority, and actuated, so it was said, by the best possible motives. Nevertheless it was an excuse that did not prevail."

Sachs, J., in *Ingram* v. *Ingram* [1956] P. 390, held that a conviction for treason as a result of which a husband left his wife, amounted to constructive desertion.

In *W*. v. *W*. (*No.* 2) [1962] P. 49 (D.C.—Lord Merriman, P., and Baker, J.), it was held that a husband who had committed incest as a result of which his wife left him, was guilty of constructive desertion.

Conclusions

1. Intention cannot be a satisfactory test for course of conduct cases in constructive desertion. In cases where obviously the wife should have a remedy as in *Lang* v. *Lang*, the husband has no such intention. It is better to abandon intention altogether rather than impute to the wrongdoer an intention he has not got.

2. Matrimonial cases are as a rule more complicated than criminal cases. In the latter there is a particular act which is forbidden. In constructive desertion, there is no particular act, but a course of conduct. What has to be considered is not only whether this conduct has been grave and weighty, but what is the effect on the particular spouse concerned.

3. Examination of intention shows that " intention to drive away " is not a sufficiently apt test for constructive desertion. A man who strikes his wife must foresee that she will be hurt, but not necessarily that she will go away.

4. Until *Gollins* and *Williams* it could be said that while an intention to drive away was unnecessary, yet there had to be an *animus deserendi* and for this purpose an intent to do the acts which caused her to go away was sufficient. *Gollins* and *Williams* show that even this may not be necessary. Since insanity is not necessarily a defence, the acts need not be voluntary. There will be cases where an intent to hurt will make all the difference between just cause and not just cause. For instance, an accidental blow would be excusable, but a blow given with intent to hurt, even though it actually did not, might be inexcusable.

5. An intention is required in actual desertion, that is, an intention to abandon the other spouse.

6. Constructive desertion can take two forms: —

   (*a*) Where the spouse is ejected by words or physical means, an intention to drive away permanently is essential.

   (*b*) Where a spouse leaves because the conduct of the other is unendurable, there is just cause and a specific intent is not essential though there may be cases where it is required.

D. Consent—Separation Agreements

The absence of consent is an essential element in desertion. A spouse who has consented to the other spouse leaving cannot complain of desertion. What amounts to consent is a question of fact, and may be a difficult matter, but if the parties agree to separate, while the agreement lasts, there can be no desertion. The consent may be expressed by way of a separation agreement, or implied from the spouses' conduct.

The effect of such an agreement is to exclude desertion or to bring to an end an existing state of desertion.

If one spouse deserts the other, and subsequently they enter into a separation agreement, neither can successfully claim that the other is in desertion, unless coercion or fraud can be shown, or that the agreement is void (*Piper* v. *Piper* [1902] P. 198). If a husband fails to pay under the agreement, the wife has a remedy on the ground of wilful neglect to maintain (as well as a civil remedy for breach of contract).

1. *Form of the agreement*

The agreement may be by deed, or in writing or oral. Naturally, an oral agreement is more difficult to prove. The following are illustrations of the effect of agreements.

In *Buckmaster* v. *Buckmaster* (1869), L.R. 1 P. & D. 713, a husband, having refused to cohabit with his wife or provide a home for her, offered her £100 on condition that she did not molest him in the future by insisting on her conjugal rights. She agreed and accepted the money, and did not live with him thereafter. Lord Penzance said that the wife chose to bargain that they should not live together, and unless they cohabited after that bargain, there could be no desertion.

In *Townsend* v. *Townsend* (1873), L.R. 3 P. & D. 129, a husband had committed several thefts and separated from his wife with her consent to avoid arrest. Later she was unable to resume cohabitation because he was in prison. It was held there that as the original separation had been by consent there could be no desertion. In this case, too, the wife had refused to rejoin her husband because of his criminal life, and the judge held this was not just cause, but that is a more doubtful proposition.

Even if the parties were under a misapprehension about the effect of the agreement, nevertheless if it provides for the parties living separate and apart, then it will bar desertion. *Long* v. *Long* [1940] 4 All E.R. 230 was a case where the wife had deserted the husband, but some months later they entered into a separation deed which, after reciting the wife's desertion and that they had agreed to live separate and apart, stated that both undertook not to take proceedings for restitution of conjugal rights. Later the husband sought a decree for divorce on the ground of his wife's desertion saying that he had executed the deed on the understanding that it would not be a bar to divorce. It was held that the agreement prevented desertion continuing. The Court of Appeal distinguished this case from *Pardy* v. *Pardy* [1939] P. 288, where the agreement had been repudiated by the deserting spouse and treated as a dead letter by the other spouse (see p. 55). It was obvious that the absence of consent by the spouse alleging desertion was necessary before it could be said that desertion without cause existed. In the present case, consent had been given in the most formal and solemn manner and could not be withdrawn as long as the deed remained in effective operation.

A strong case is *Tickler* v. *Tickler* [1943] 1 All E.R. 57, where the Court of Appeal upheld a decision of Henn Collins, J., who granted a divorce to a husband on the ground of his wife's desertion. There had been a settlement of an action concerning rights of property, and the husband had agreed he would not assert any right or claim for any purpose to come upon or reside with his wife, the plaintiff, at her residence or elsewhere. He also agreed not to molest her. There was no corresponding promise by the wife, who remained free to request him to return. The court held that an undertaking not to molest would not exclude attempts at reconciliation. Scott, L.J., who gave the judgment of the court (Mackinnon, L.J., and du Parcq, L.J., with him), after mentioning that the husband had written letters which the wife said had justified her in staying away, continued at p. 59: —

> " Ultimately, the question for the court is whether, in the light of all the circumstances, the language or the conduct of the deserted spouse has been such as to excuse the deserting spouse from making an attempt to put an end to the desertion. Has he ' made it plain to his deserting wife that he will not receive her back? '."

and he referred to *Cohen* v. *Cohen* [1940] A.C. 631, where Lord Romer said that this was a question of fact, and he deprecated the laying down of general principles applicable to all cases. Scott, L.J., at p. 60, further said: —

> " Intemperate complaints of a spouse's desertion and the circumstances leading up to, or accompanying, it do not of necessity afford an excuse for its continuance, nor do we think that every angry expression used by a husband, from which a reluctance to resume cohabitation might be inferred, can necessarily be treated as making (in the words of Lord MacMillan [in *Pratt* v. *Pratt* [1939] A.C. 417 at p. 420]) ' it plain to his deserting wife that he will not receive her back '."

The court held that the agreement endorsed on counsels' briefs did not amount to an agreement to live separate and apart.

2. *Void agreements*

An agreement which is void for any reason will not bar desertion.

(a) *Public Policy*

Thus an agreement before marriage to live separate is void as against public policy, and even a second agreement after marriage confirming the first would be void also (*Brodie* v. *Brodie* [1917] P. 271).

In *Papadopoulos* v. *Papadopoulos* [1936] P. 108, the parties were married in England, and later proceedings in Cyprus were compromised by an agreement which stated the marriage was null and void. Subsequently, the English courts held the agreement was a nullity and cohabitation was never resumed. On a petition for judicial separation by the wife, it was held that the husband was in desertion.

It was held in *Hindley* v. *Westmeath* (1827), 6 B. & C. 200, that a deed stated to be in contemplation of immediate separation, when in fact no separation took place, nor was it intended at the time, was void. Similarly, in *Bindley* v. *Mulloney* (1869), L.R. 7 Eq. 343, there was a deed of separation but no separation in fact took place; it was held that the deed was wholly void.

(b) Coercion

A deed of separation executed under coercion is void. In *Adamson* v. *Adamson* (1907), 23 T.L.R. 434, a husband, before leaving his wife, told her that if she would sign a deed of separation, he would make her an allowance of £1 per week, otherwise she would get nothing. He took her to a solicitor's office and the solicitor told her that the only way to get any money from her husband was to sign the deed which was already prepared. She consented. She had a child three months old, for whose maintenance she was very concerned. She had no independent advice. She received the allowance for some years. The husband then committed adultery, and the wife applied for a divorce on the grounds of adultery and desertion. Bucknill, J., after saying there was no duress and there was no complaint about the solicitor concerned, said: " But I am satisfied that she was not in fact a consenting party to the first deed so as to bind herself contractually, and that she was forced into doing so by the circumstances of her then position."

This decision was followed in *Holroyd* v. *Holroyd* (1920), 36 T.L.R. 479. The husband, for four years before he left her, pressed his wife to sign a paper accepting a small weekly sum. Then he left her and some weeks later she found him and he declined to return or provide her with money unless she signed an agreement. He said he would leave the country if she did not sign. She signed and received an inadequate allowance. McCardie, J., in following *Adamson* v. *Adamson*, said the wife had really no alternative but to sign or starve.

3. *Agreement for maintenance only*

There are a number of cases which decide that a maintenance agreement, as distinguished from a separation agreement, will not preclude the inception or the continuance of desertion. This is always a matter of construction. In *Long* v. *Long* [1940] 4 All E.R. 230 it was said that if the deed had been confined to financial matters, there would have been no difficulty about desertion. A recital that parties are living separate and apart does not amount to an agreement to separate and so preclude desertion.

In *Crabtree* v. *Crabtree* [1953] 1 W.L.R. 708 the husband deserted his wife and then entered into an agreement to pay maintenance during joint lives. The commissioner who tried the wife's petition for divorce dismissed it on the ground that desertion ceased on the signing of the agreement, but the Court of Appeal reversed this decision, Denning, L.J., saying that if the agreement had bound the parties to live separate and apart it would stop desertion running, but if it was an agreement to pay maintenance it would not; and Hodson, L.J., said that an agreement which contains no express or implied stipulation that the petitioner agrees to the respondent living apart will not prevent desertion from running. See also *Nott* v. *Nott* (1866), L.R. 1 P. & D. 251, *Macdonald* v. *Macdonald* (1859), 4 Sw. & Tr. 242, and *Yeatman* v. *Yeatman* (1868), L.R. 1 P. & D. 489.

That there should be a real consent is indicated by *Smith* v. *Smith* [1954] 2 All E.R. 452. The husband left the wife and the husband made her an allowance. He attempted through his solicitors to get her to sign a separation agreement in the usual form, stating that they had agreed to live separate and apart. She was unwilling to sign this and it was amended by stating that it was the desire of the husband to live separate and apart from his wife. There was a non-molestation clause, and a clause not to bring proceedings for restitution of conjugal rights. On a petition by the wife for divorce it was held the husband had deserted her.

Pilcher, J., held that neither the non-molestation clause nor the clause against proceedings for restitution amounted to an agreement by her to live separate.

4. *Desertion where there has been a valid agreement*

The fact that parties have been separated under a valid agreement does not preclude desertion for all time. The courts have shown considerable ingenuity in avoiding the effect of a separation agreement. The circumstances under which this can be done are as follows: —

1. Where the agreement is for a limited period, the party who refused to resume cohabitation at the end of that period is a deserter.

2. Where the agreement is repudiated.

    (*a*) Where the agreement is for a definite period, e.g., joint lives, then both must contribute to the termination of the agreement, such as the repudiation by the husband acquiesced in by the wife.

    (*b*) Where the agreement is for an indefinite period, a genuine offer by one party to resume cohabitation, refused by the other, makes that other a deserter.

3. A resumption of cohabitation puts an end to an agreement.

(*a*) *Agreement for a limited period*

Where the agreement to separate is for a limited period, at the end of that period it loses its effect. The spouse who then refuses to resume cohabitation is the deserter. In *Shaw* v. *Shaw* [1939] P. 269, after a clandestine marriage, each of the parties agreed to live for a short time with their own parents until the husband could afford to set up a home. When he obtained employment, he refused the wife's repeated requests to make a home. There never was cohabitation nor was the marriage consummated. The President, Sir Boyd Merriman, held that the husband was guilty of desertion. He said at p. 272: —

> "It is clear from this case [*Mahoney* v. *M'Carthy* [1892] P. 21, 25] and from the cases of *Smith* v. *Smith* (1888), 58 L.T. 639, and *Sifton* v. *Sifton* [1939] P. 221, that if cohabitation has ceased by agreement, only for a limited time or for a particular reason, that spouse is guilty of desertion who, without cause, refuses to resume cohabitation at the expira-

tion of the time or the cessation of the reason for the separation. It is also settled by *De Laubenque* v. *De Laubenque* [1899] P. 42 that a spouse may be guilty of desertion in spite of the fact that the marriage has not been consummated, and that cohabitation has never begun, if that state of things is brought about by his or her fault. In *Buckmaster* v. *Buckmaster* (1869), L.R. 1 P. & D. 713, the wife only failed, in similar circumstances, because she had bargained away her rights for a money consideration. It seems to me to follow that a spouse who without excuse refuses to start cohabitation after the expiration of an agreement merely to postpone its inception can also be guilty of desertion."

(b) Where the agreement is repudiated

The *locus classicus* is *Pardy* v. *Pardy* [1939] P. 288. In that case, after four years of unhappy married life, the parties executed a separation deed in May, 1932, whereby the husband agreed to pay the wife 25s. a week so long as she led a chaste life. Payments were made under the deed until September, 1932, and no more was paid until 1934 when he made two payments, one of 10s. and one of £1. In 1935 the wife committed adultery and thereby the husband's liability under the deed ceased. The wife brought a petition for divorce on the ground of the husband's desertion, and Langton, J., held that as the separation was under the deed, her case was not proved. Lord Greene, M.R., posed the question whether or not it is possible in law for a separation which began by being consensual to acquire the character of desertion without a previous resumption of cohabitation, and he answered the question in this way (at p. 302): —

"Looking at this question on principle and apart from authority, I can see no reason why the answer to it should not be in the affirmative. The word ' desertion ' may describe an act, or it may describe a state. For the act of desertion both the *factum* of separation and the *animus deserendi* are required. A *de facto* separation may take place without there being an *animus deserendi*, but, if that *animus* supervenes, desertion will begin from that moment, unless, of course, there is consent by the other spouse. Thus a husband who leaves his wife for a business voyage may nevertheless become guilty of desertion without the necessity of a previous return. All that is required to establish desertion in such a case is the presence of a supervening *animus deserendi* (a matter to be inferred from the words and conduct of the deserting spouse), a continuance of the *de facto* separation, and the absence of consent by the other spouse. I do not see why, in a case where the original separation was due to the agreement of both spouses to live apart, it should be impossible in law for a similar change in the quality of the separation to take place without there being any previous resumption of the common life. In such a case the burden of proving that the change has taken place may not be easy to discharge; but this is no reason for saying that the court must refuse to admit the possibility. It appears to me that the first question which the court ought to put to itself is: ' Was the separation which *de facto* existed during the relevant period attributable to the agreement under which the parties separated, or was it due to a supervening *animus deserendi* on the part of the respondent? '."

He went on to say that if one spouse has repudiated the deed and the other can show that during the relevant period he or she has not had any intention of relying on the separation deed, and was always ready and willing in spite of it to resume cohabitation, it would be unreal to say he or she consents to the separation. There must be repudiation of the whole deed.

He summarised his findings as follows (at p. 306): —

" (i) that where the original separation was by mutual consent, desertion may supervene without the necessity of a resumption of cohabitation; (ii) that this can happen where (*a*) on the part of the spouse alleged to be in desertion there is repudiation of the agreement under which separation took place, no step taken towards the resumption of cohabitation in fact, and, in addition to repudiation, the *animus deserendi*, and (*b*) on the part of the spouse alleging desertion there is not only no insistence on the terms of the separation agreement, but a bona fide willingness to resume cohabitation without regard to its terms—in short, if it can be said that both parties are, during the relevant period, regarding the agreement as a dead letter which no longer regulates their matrimonial relations; (iii) that whether or not these conditions exist during the relevant period is a question of fact in each case, the answer to which depends upon the true inference to be drawn from the words and conduct of the parties; (iv) that, once these conditions are fulfilled, all the elements necessary to constitute a state of desertion are present, namely *de facto* separation, *animus deserendi*, and absence of consent on the part of the spouse alleging desertion."

Lord Greene made the reservation that a separation agreement which has been approbated by the wife remains effective even if repudiated by the husband. Approbation is best shown by the wife suing on the agreement. See *Clark* v. *Clark* (*No.* 2) [1939] P. 257, where Henn Collins, J., described the wife's action as a conclusive election, and *Roe* v. *Roe* [1916] P. 163 to the same effect.

What is a repudiation of the agreement is not always easy to decide. The following are examples: —

In *Pape* v. *Pape* (1887), 20 Q.B.D. 76, where the parties separated under a separation agreement, the mere non-payment by the husband was held not to amount to a repudiation of the agreement.

In *Balcombe* v. *Balcombe* [1908] P. 176, a deed of separation was entered into after the husband's cruelty and adultery. The wife covenanted not to sue on any ground of complaint which existed, and that she condoned them. Subsequently the husband went abroad and lived in adultery. It was held the husband had wholly repudiated the deed, having failed to pay under it or comply with any part of it, and that he was in desertion.

Ratcliffe v. *Ratcliffe* [1938] 3 All E.R. 41. The husband paid for a month only under a separation deed. He was a heavy drinker and made promises to return which he never kept. Langton, J., held that while failure to pay of itself was not a repudiation of the agreement, nevertheless the further facts proved that there had been a repudiation.

Watson v. *Watson* [1938] P. 258. A husband deserted his wife and later entered into a separation deed in which the desertion was recited. The husband did not carry out the terms of the deed. Hodson, L.J., held, on the wife's petition for divorce, that the husband had been in desertion prior to the deed, that the husband had not observed its terms and the wife had not sought to enforce it, and therefore the execution of the deed was merely an incident in the desertion. He went on at p. 261: —

" There have been, however, cases where notwithstanding the existence of agreements of separation, the court has been able to find desertion, and two cases to which I have been referred are *Hussey* v. *Hussey* (1913), 29 T.L.R. 673, and *Smith* v. *Smith* [1915] P. 288. In both these cases, desertion having taken place, the deserting spouse entered into an agreement with the deserted spouse and repudiated the agreement after making a few payments. Horridge, J., said in the latter case: ' I am prepared to hold that there was desertion,

but I do so on the particular facts of this case,' and he goes
on: 'It must not be taken, where parties separate under a
deed, that I should hold there has been desertion merely
because the husband has failed to pay the allowance provided
by the deed.'

In this case the parties did not separate under a deed at
all but because the husband deserted the wife, and the
execution of the separation agreement was a mere incident
in that desertion. It was not followed by the respondent
observing the terms of the agreement, nor was it in any way
sought to be enforced by the petitioner."

Tate v. *Tate* [1938] 4 All E.R. 264. A husband was cruel to his
wife and she left. When she returned he told her to go. They
entered into a separation agreement, and after paying £6 he
disappeared. Bucknill, J., at p. 266, said: —

"In my view, the husband cannot rely upon the deed as
protecting him from his original wrongful acts of desertion
if it is clear on the evidence that he had treated the deed as
not binding on him in any way, and it seems to me quite
clear on the facts that this is what he has done. If it is not quite
a legal way of putting it, he has repudiated the deed by completely failing to make the all-important payments to his wife
for herself and her child, and by disappearing and failing to
keep in touch with the wife, and failing in any way to give
her the help and support to which one spouse is entitled from
the other."

Stockley v. *Stockley* [1939] 2 All E.R. 707. A wife deserted her
husband. Thereafter the husband, primarily on account of the
child, entered into a separation agreement to pay weekly sums
to the wife for herself and the child, and providing for him to have
access to the child once a week at places he should reasonably
select. The wife did not keep to the agreement as respects access
and also refused an offer to resume cohabitation. The husband
stopped payments and petitioned for divorce. Henn Collins, J.,
held that the provision in the agreement as to access was a condition which went to the root of the agreement, that the wife was
in breach thereof, and that the husband had accepted the
repudiation of the agreement and the wife was therefore in
desertion.

In *Nutley* v. *Nutley* [1970] 1 All E.R. 410 the parties agreed
that the wife should leave the matrimonial home to look after
her ailing parents. A year later she decided not to return to

her husband but did not communicate her intention to him. Her parents died a few years later, and a few months afterwards her husband brought a petition for divorce on the ground of his wife's desertion, which was dismissed. The Court of Appeal agreed with this decision since desertion did not run until she had informed her husband of her intention, or on the death of her parents, and sufficient time had not elapsed since that had happened.

(c) Where the agreement to part is for an indefinite period

In such a case the agreement may be terminated unilaterally by one of the parties offering to return.

In *Bosley* v. *Bosley* [1958] 1 W.L.R. 645 the parties parted by consent. Both signed copies of an agreement for the wife's maintenance but there was no provision that they should live apart. Before the agreements were exchanged, the wife asked the husband to take her back. He refused and the agreements were then exchanged. It was held by the Court of Appeal that the husband was in desertion after his refusal to take his wife back. Pearce, L.J., at p. 653, said: —

" The question here is: was the oral or implied agreement such that it precluded any future unilateral change of heart on the part of either party? Often in the rather haphazard parting of husband and wife the fact of a mutual agreement to separate has to be deduced from things done and things said in emotion and temper. The court should, I think, be slow to decide that there is imported a term that the separation shall be for ever and that there shall be no opportunity for any unilateral change of mind, no right ever to ask the other party to return to cohabitation."

Hodson, L.J., distinguished *Pardy* v. *Pardy* [1939] P. 288 where there was presumably a claim to maintain for joint lives. He said that that case and the other authorities cited were not in point because here at most was an agreement to live apart for an indefinite period.

This case was followed in *Hall* v. *Hall* [1960] 1 W.L.R. 52. The parties agreed to separate but for an indefinite period. The wife rejected the husband's request to return and he continued to pay under the agreement. It was held by Wrangham, J., that an agreement to live apart for an indefinite period was terminable by the will of either party. After quoting *Bosley* v. *Bosley*, he said at p. 54: —

> " This I think implies that an agreement to live separately for an indefinite period is terminable upon the will of either party either immediately (as in the case of tenancy at will) or, perhaps, upon reasonable notice if the other terms of a particular agreement are such as to lead to the inference that such a term should be implied."

Where there is a consensual separation before desertion can run, the petitioner must prove the withdrawal of consent, communicated to the other party, and to make that party guilty of desertion there must be an offer to resume cohabitation which must: —

(1) be genuine, i.e., having the intention and the means to implement it;

(2) not be subject to unreasonable or unnegotiable conditions; and

(3) if prior to the separation the petitioner was guilty of grave and weighty conduct, contain an expression of regret and a promise to be of good behaviour in the future (*Fraser* v. *Fraser* [1969] 3 All E.R. 664, following *Gallagher* v. *Gallagher* [1965] 2 All E.R. 967, *Barrett* v. *Barrett* [1948] P. 277 and *Gaskell* v. *Gaskell* (1963), 108 Sol.J. 37).

5. *Resumption of cohabitation*

This puts an end to the agreement whether it is so provided in the agreement or not. The question here usually is whether as a fact there has been such a resumption. In *Rowell* v. *Rowell* [1900] 1 Q.B. 9, the fact that there had been several acts of intercourse while the parties were separated was held not sufficient to make the deed of no effect.

On the other hand, in *Eaves* v. *Eaves* [1939] P. 361 the acts of intercourse were held sufficient to put an end to the agreement. Hodson, J., at p. 363, said: —

> " The fact that intercourse has taken place is not in itself conclusive evidence that a separation has come to an end so as to make the deed of no effect (see *Rowell* v. *Rowell* [1900] 1 Q.B. 9) and the court has to determine in a case such as the present whether there was any intention by the parties to come together again. In the words of Lord Russell of Killowen

in *Rowell* v. *Rowell*: ' If the court comes to the conclusion that there was an intention by both parties to come together again there would be an end of the deed '."

E. Consent—Inferred from Conduct

(a) *What is consent ?*

The authorities are agreed that there can be no desertion if the parties separate by consent, or having parted for other reasons, the parting becomes consensual. While the principle is clear, it is not easy to establish precisely what is meant by " consent." Clearly, if the parties enter into an agreement, formal or informal, not to live with one another, while the agreement subsists the parting is by consent. But is there more to it than that?

In the early cases it was said that the parting must be against the will of the other spouse. Not to part against the will of the other was equated with parting by consent. Thus Cockburn, C.J., in *Ward* v. *Ward* (1858), 1 Sw. & Tr. 185: —

" Though the husband may have left her, yet if there were a corresponding *animus* on the part of the wife, if she were a party to his leaving and consented to it, that would not constitute desertion. The act of desertion must be done against the will of the wife."

Sir Cresswell Cresswell, J.O., said that the fact of the husband living with another woman did not necessarily prove that a husband has deserted his wife, meaning presumably that the wife may have consented to it.

In *Thompson* v. *Thompson* (1858), 1 Sw. & Tr. 231, at p. 233, Sir Cresswell Cresswell, J.O., said: —

" Such absence (by the husband) or cessation of cohabitation must be in spite of the wish of the wife; she must not be a consenting party."

But *Smith* v. *Smith* (1859), 1 Sw. & Tr. 359, a decision of the full court, Lord Chelmsford, Wightman, J., and the Judge Ordinary, is most remarkable. This was a wife's petition for divorce on the ground of her husband's adultery and desertion. He treated her with great harshness. On one occasion he turned her out on a cold night in January. He sold the furniture to buy drink, threatened to leave her and said she could walk the streets for a living. Then saying he was going away and she would never see him again, he left and took his clothes. She waited a fortnight and then left the matrimonial home and went to live with her sister. She never inquired after him. Some years later a witness saw him and urged him to do something to support his wife. He said he would do nothing voluntarily, and if an attempt was made to force him, he would leave the town as he was determined to do nothing for her. He admitted living in adultery. During argument, the Judge Ordinary asked Dr. Spinks, the wife's counsel, " Have you any evidence to show that the separation was against the wish of the wife? " Counsel pointed out that she had waited a fortnight for him to return, and there was no evidence that she had assented to his departure. Lord Chelmsford, L.C., said: —

". . . the proof of desertion entirely fails. There is nothing to satisfy the court that, when the parties separated, the husband went against the will of the wife. On the contrary, there are circumstances in the case which induce the court to believe that it is extremely probable that they parted by mutual consent. It is shown that the respondent was a man of vile habits and bad temper, and treated the petitioner with great cruelty, and he told her ' he should leave her and that she might walk the streets for a living ' . . . There is nothing to show that the wife was desirous of retaining the husband at that time; on the contrary, there appears to have been a desire on her part to separate, for she goes to live with her sister and makes no enquiries after her husband for a considerable period of time, and there is no proof that he knew where she was living. If the court were to permit this evidence to be taken as satisfactory proof of desertion, it would lead to great laxity."

One might add that if the court had continued to hold the view that this sort of evidence was not satisfactory, it would have been virtually impossible to have proved desertion in any case. It is puzzling why the wife in this case did not base her petition on adultery and cruelty.

An extreme case like this is illuminating. The Full Court here required the wife to prove a negative, that she had not consented to his departure. A wife may try to keep the home together with a cruel husband, but once he has gone saying he will not return, she would not be human if she did not feel relief.

The Lord Chancellor's final remark about leading to great laxity has become a parrot cry by all judges who dislike the extension of divorce. As Professor Goodhart has pointed out, the greater danger is injustice to innocent spouses, for surely Mrs. Smith was treated unjustly in this case.

The arguments of the Lord Chancellor are more akin to the former law of Scotland, where there was the doctrine of adherence and the pursuer had to swear that he or she had all along been willing to fulfil the duties of marriage, that the desertion was against his or her will, and that if the defender had returned during the triennium, the pursuer would have been willing to resume the normal relationship of marriage.

This is not the law of England. Consent means a full and free consent amounting to an agreement. The law of England has no place for the doctrine of adherence. What, then, is meant by saying that the parting must be against the will of the other spouse? If it is not against his or her will, does this amount to a parting by consent? Once the parting has taken place, has the innocent spouse to " leave the door open "?

It is contended that consent means a full and free consent amounting to an agreement. If it were not so, it would mean that the worse the conduct of the husband, the more difficult it would be to show that the parting was not by consent, since the worse he was the more glad would she be to see him go. To be content that the erring spouse has left is not to consent.

An analogy can be found in the maxim *Volenti non fit injuria* as applied to cases of master and servant. Owing to his contract of service, a servant is not in a position to choose freely between the acceptance and rejection of risk. In *Bowater* v. *Rowley Regis Corporation* [1944] K.B. 476 (applied in *London Graving Dock* v. *Horton* [1951] A.C. 731), Goddard, L.J., said at p. 481: " It must be shown that he agreed that what risk there was should lie upon him." Lord Reid (in *London Graving Dock* v. *Horton*), at p. 783, quoted with approval Scott, L.J., at p. 479): —

> ". . . a man cannot be said to be truly ' willing ' unless he is in a position to choose freely, and freedom of choice predicates, not only full knowledge of the circumstances on which the exercise of choice is conditioned, so that he may be able to choose wisely, but the absence from his mind of any feeling of constraint so that nothing shall interfere with the freedom of his will."

This, it is submitted, is exactly the position in the law of desertion. There has to be a true consent, not one that is forced on the innocent party by circumstances. In a sense in many cases of undoubted constructive desertion, the parties are *ad idem*. The husband says, " Clear out." The wife feels in the circumstances it is the only thing to do. In a sense therefore they are both agreed that she should go. The husband has a free choice, but the wife has not, like the man who said, " It is my poverty and not my will that consents."

What amounts to a " real consent " was explored in *T*. v. *T*. [1964] P. 85 (C.A.). The wife had petitioned for a divorce on the ground (*inter alia*) of sodomy. She said she had submitted to it on three occasions because her husband had told her that his friends' wives allowed it, that it was normal between married couples and that it was part of her matrimonial duty. The majority of the Court of Appeal held that the consent was not real, Donovan, L.J., quoting from Story, Commentaries on Equity Jurisprudence, 3rd English ed., para. 222: " Consent is an act of reason accompanied with deliberation, the mind weighing, as in a balance, the good and evil on each side."

(b) Consent is a question of fact

It was held in *Haviland* v. *Haviland* (1863), 32 L.J.P. M. & A. 65, that a wife who had said to her husband, " Go if you like, and when you are sick of her, come back to me," and made him swear on the Bible that he would return, had not consented to his leaving her; also a wife who had signed a separation agreement virtually by force, without legal advice and under great mental stress because she thought it was the only way to get maintenance from him, had not consented to living apart (*Holroyd* v. *Holroyd* (1920), 36 T.L.R. 479).

There is now ample authority for saying that, because one spouse is glad to see the other go, that does not mean that he or she consents to a separation. There is the well known passage in the judgment of Buckley, L.J., in *Harriman* v. *Harriman* [1909] P. 123, at p. 148: ——

> " Desertion does not necessarily involve that the wife desires her husband to remain with her. She may be thankful that he has gone, but he may nevertheless have deserted her."

Lord Merriman, P., after quoting this passage, says in *Kinnane* v. *Kinnane* [1954] P. 41, at p. 47: ——

" To deal with the thing as a matter of commonsense, supposing, at the moment when he announced his intention of walking out of the house, she said, ' Well, I don't mind your going. I shall be thankful to see the last of you. But let us understand what this means. What are you suggesting about the future?' and the husband said, ' Please understand that the moment I am outside the front door I wash my hands of you altogether. I have no further liability to support you or the child.' It is unnecessary to ask the rhetorical question ' What would her answer to that have been? ' I decline to hold that she is to be taken to have consented to a parting on those terms; of course she did not: and to say, having brought her charge of desertion, that because she said she did not want her husband back then because of the way he treated her in the past and was likely to treat her in the future, that prevents her from asserting that he has deserted her, is, in my opinion, to fly in the face of authority."

The Court of Appeal (Denning, Birkett and Parker, L.JJ.), in *Gibson* v. *Gibson* (1956), *The Times*, 18th July, gave judgment to the same effect. In that case, there was a maintenance agreement with no separation clause. Nevertheless, Mr. Commissioner Bush-James, Q.C., held that the parties were heartily glad to get rid of each other, and both were content to remain separate and apart, and that it was a mutual agreement to separate.

Denning, L.J., said that there was no evidence of a parting by consent. It may be true they were both heartily glad to be rid of one another, but that did not prevent the wife being in desertion. It did not make it a separation by consent. There was nothing in our laws like Scottish law on " willingness to adhere." If a wife left a husband and deserted him, the fact that the husband was heartily glad to see her go, and did not want her back, did not amount to separation by consent such as to bar the grant of a decree.

Two other modern cases are good examples. In *Wevill* v. *Wevill* (1962), *The Times*, 15th February, husband and wife were on bad terms and wished to leave each other but neither wished to be in the wrong. In 1957 the husband decided to move to another place, believing that his wife would refuse to join him. He found a place and then asked her to join him, in a manner which was neither kindly nor conciliatory. She refused, did not discuss the matter with him as a reasonable wife would, and was delighted that he was going. Both sought decrees on the ground of desertion.

Wrangham, J., said that it was not necessary for a spouse to regard his or her abandonment of the other as unwelcome, but the matrimonial cohabitation must have ended on the initiative of one spouse without the co-operation by the other in the taking of that initiative. The fact that one spouse helped the other to carry out a determination already formed did not amount to consent. A spouse who was determined so to arrange matters that cohabitation was likely to be brought to an end was the true cause of its termination, even though the other spouse behaved in a manner which, in other circumstances, would make him or her a deserter. The motive behind what the husband did was vital, and matrimonial cohabitation came to an end as a result of his scheme, and accordingly the wife was granted a decree.

In *Phair* v. *Phair* (1963), *The Times*, 5th July (C.A.) (Willmer, Danckwerts and Diplock, L.JJ.), the wife told the husband to get out. He left but admitted he had wanted to leave since he thought that they were unsuited to one another. The Commissioner dismissed the husband's petition for divorce on the ground of desertion, but this was reversed by the Court of Appeal. Willmer, L.J., said that it was abundantly clear that it was the wife's act which was the immediate cause of the separation. She had intended to bring the cohabitation to a permanent end and had not defended the petition. While absence of consent was essential, the mere fact that the deserted spouse was glad to see the other go did not amount to consent. There was no agreement here. An agreement necessarily involved an exercise of choice. The husband was never consulted by the wife; he was asked to go and given no option.

(c) Changing the locks

There has been an attempt to show that a parting which was non-consensual can be turned into a consensual one by an overt act of one of the parties. For instance, a husband deserts his wife, and she remains in the matrimonial home. After he has gone the wife then changes the locks, and it is said that by this simple action she has consented to his parting. The two cases which so held are reported one after the other in the Law Reports [1955] P., *Barnett* v. *Barnett* at p. 21, and *Fishburn* v. *Fishburn* at p. 29.

Barnett v. *Barnett*.—In this case the husband deserted his wife by leaving the matrimonial home. Shortly afterwards the wife changed the locks and, by letters from her solicitors, evinced a firm and settled intention not to have him back. The husband at no time made an approach to his wife to return. At the time he left and thereafter he was glad to be gone. The wife was and remained glad he had left. Sachs, J., held that the husband's desertion had been terminated. He took the view that it was contrary to sound sense for a wife to be able to claim she was being wronged by the continuing absence of a husband whom she has decisively declared she will not have back. He found support in the view of Lord Macmillan in *Pratt* v. *Pratt* [1939] A.C. 417, at p. 420 (which was a case where a deserted spouse refused to consider an offer to return) who said: —

> " In fulfilling its duty in determining whether on the evidence a case of desertion without cause has been proved the court ought not, in my opinion, to leave out of account the attitude of mind of the petitioner."

He also cited *Cohen* v. *Cohen* [1940] A.C. 631, and *Harriman* v. *Harriman* [1909] P. 123, especially Fletcher Moulton, L.J., at p. 137, " It is impossible to hold that the husband is committing a marital offence by non-cohabitation when he has not the right to cohabit " (which referred to a separation order and therefore is irrelevant here) and *Ward* v. *Ward* (1858), 1 Sw. & Tr. 185, where Cockburn, C.J., said, " the act of desertion must be done against the will of the wife." He thought that Willmer, J.'s view in *Church* v. *Church* [1952] P. 313, that Lord Macmillan's statement in *Pratt* v. *Pratt* was obiter, unsupported by authority and in some degree contrary to authority, was incorrect. He summarised the effect of *Pratt, Cohen* and *Harriman* by saying they were authorities " at least for the proposition that if the possibility of the husband returning has been decisively negatived by the wife then she so rejects her husband as to make her unable to call herself deserted by him " (p. 28).

He went on to say that the parties were living apart by consent. They were living apart by agreement; or, each party having made it plain to the other that he or she would on no account live together in future, such a state of affairs constituted in itself a separation by consent.

Fishburn v. *Fishburn.*—Willmer, J., was so impressed by the

judgment of Sachs, J., in *Barnett* v. *Barnett* that he preferred to
follow it rather than his own judgment in *Church* v. *Church*. In this
case the wife had withdrawn from the marital bed because of
reasonable suspicions of the husband's association with another
woman. The husband allowed relations to deteriorate, never
asked her to return to his bed, or sought to convince her of his
innocence, ceased to support her, threw her clothes from his bedroom and kept the door locked against her. Shortly afterwards
she locked her door against him and told him if he would not have
her, she would not have him. Willmer, J., held that the husband
had in the first place deserted his wife, but that this desertion had
been terminated by the wife's conduct.

These cases have not been favourably received. They are rather
like mules "without pride of parentage, or hope of posterity."
They are not based on firm authority, or principle or realities.

Lord Macmillan's words in *Pratt* were, it is submitted, obiter,
and clearly carry overtones from the Scottish doctrine of
adherence. The principle is that the wrongdoer, the deserter,
remains in desertion until it is brought to an end (*a*) by resumption
of cohabitation or (*b*) a bona fide offer which ought to be
accepted but is not, or (*c*) an agreement to live separate and apart,
or (*d*) adultery by the deserted party which has so affected the
mind of the deserter as to preclude a resumption of cohabitation.

As has been emphasised, the agreement must be a true agreement. What is more natural than for a wronged wife to say, "Well
if he won't live with me, I won't live with him "?

The reasoning of Sachs, J., may be attacked as follows: —

   (*a*) There was never a true consent. The wife's reactions were
       a natural effect of the husband's wrongdoing.

   (*b*) There is no analogy between the wife's actions and a non-
       cohabitation clause.

   (*c*) It is for the wrongdoer to approach the innocent party to
       make up.

   (*d*) There is no real distinction between changing locks and
       saying, "I am glad to see him go." Both are merely
       demonstrations. Everyone knows that locks cannot keep
       love out. Who knows what the wife's response would have
       been if the husband made a proper approach. Byron was
       describing every woman when he wrote, "Who vowing

she would ne'er consent, consented." Scott, L.J., said in *Tickler* v. *Tickler* [1943] 1 All E.R. 57, at p. 60, "Intemperate complaints of a spouse's desertion and the circumstances leading up to it do not of necessity afford an excuse for its continuance."

A Divisional Court (Lord Merriman, P., and Collingwood, J.), in *Bevan* v. *Bevan* [1955] 1 W.L.R. 1142, where a wife said she did not want to see her husband again after he had deserted her, decided that *Fishburn* and *Barnett* could be distinguished on the rather flimsy ground that the wife had merely spoken and not acted, as though speech is not a form of action. Contrast this with Lord Merriman's own words in *Lane* v. *Lane* [1951] P. 284, at p. 288: "words, after all, are conduct." The court said that by bolting the door the wife had effectively stopped the husband's approach. This is unreal as was pointed out by the Court of Appeal in *Beigan* v. *Beigan* [1956] P. 313.

In *Beigan* v. *Beigan* condoned adultery was revived by the husband's desertion. When he left his wife she said that if he went she would not have him back, and she changed the locks. The Court of Appeal (Denning, Birkett and Parker, L.JJ.) held that the husband's desertion had not been terminated. Denning, L.J., at p. 319, said of *Fishburn* and *Barnett*: —

"I must say that I have considerable doubt whether those cases were rightly decided. There has since been a decision of the Divisional Court in *Bevan* v. *Bevan, No.* 2 [1955] 1 W.L.R. 1142, in which it was held that, even though a wife says in terms that she does not want to see her husband again, she does not thereby automatically terminate his desertion. The Divisional Court applied the reasoning of Henn Collins, J., in *Sifton* v. *Sifton* [1939] P. 221, and of Willmer, J., in *Church* v. *Church* [1952] P. 313. I, too, agree with that reasoning, and I must say that I see no distinctions in principle between a wife's words and her actions. I should have thought that, if a wife locks the door against her husband, it does not automatically terminate his desertion any more than her own adultery would do. It depends on whether it has any effect on the husband by preventing him from seeking a reconciliation. If he would never have returned in any case, then he remains in desertion, nothwithstanding the locking of the door. I know that in Scotland it is necessary for the petitioner to prove that she was throughout the three-year period ' willing to adhere ' to her husband, but this has never been part of English law, and I do not think it should now be introduced."

Birkett, L.J., did not express an opinion on *Barnett* v. *Barnett* and *Fishburn* v. *Fishburn*, though he quoted them, but Parker, L.J., had grave doubts as to their correctness.

The Court of Appeal in *Brewer* v. *Brewer* [1962] P. 69, considered all the above cases and others. The facts briefly were that a wife in July, 1955, wrote to her husband (who was serving in the R.A.F.) that she would never join him. This was held to establish her desertion. Early in 1956 the husband committed adultery, and in February, 1956, the husband wrote to his wife that he intended to petition for divorce, and that whatever she said or did would make no difference as his mind was made up. Mr. Commissioner Latey, Q.C., on the husband's petition, granted a divorce on the ground of the wife's desertion, holding that neither the husband's adultery nor his expressed view communicated to the wife had prevented the desertion running. The Court of Appeal dismissed the wife's appeal, since the husband had satisfied the court that neither his adultery, nor his letter that he would not live with her again, had had any effect on his wife's intention to desert him, and had not deterred her from seeking a reconciliation.

Willmer, L.J., who gave the leading judgment, quoted at p. 80 with approval the following from the commissioner's judgment: —

" None of these cases, however, appear to dissent from the root principle that once desertion has been established there is no obligation on the deserted spouse to appeal to the deserting spouse to change his or her mind; and, as was stated by Scrutton, L.J., in *Bowron* v. *Bowron* [1925] P. 187, at p. 195, an intention to desert is presumed to continue, unless the deserting party proves genuine repentance and makes reasonable attempts to get the deserted spouse back."

Willmer, L.J., said that the passage quoted above, from the speech of Lord Macmillan in *Pratt* v. *Pratt*, approved by the House of Lords in *Cohen* v. *Cohen* [1940] A.C. 631, must be accepted as authoritative, but he interpreted it as follows, at p. 82: —

" It seems to me that what Lord Macmillan must have meant was that a deserted husband cannot complain if what he has said or done has in fact caused his wife to desist from making any attempt at reconciliation which she otherwise would have made."

Willmer, L.J., quotes, apparently with approval, the passage from the judgment of Denning, L.J., in *Beigan* v. *Beigan, supra,* quoted above, doubting the correctness of *Barnett* v. *Barnett* and *Fishburn* v. *Fishburn.*

Then the learned lord justice refers to *Tickler* v. *Tickler* [1943] 1 All E.R. 57 (C.A.), and in particular to the judgment of Scott, L.J., who emphasised that the inclination and disposition of the person to whom a written communication is addressed is as important as the intention of the writer, and from the authorities, Willmer, L.J., draws these two conclusions, at p. 85: —

> "First, the question whether a deserted spouse has so acted as to bring to an end the desertion of which he seeks to complain cannot be decided as a question of abstract law, but must depend on the actual facts of each particular case. Secondly, the issue of fact which arises is peculiarly one for the determination of the judge who has the advantage of seeing and hearing the parties, and his finding on that issue is one with which this court must necessarily be reluctant to interfere."

Holroyd Pearce, L.J., in his judgment, agreed with Willmer, L.J., but said at p. 90 that he did not doubt the correctness of the decisions in *Barnett* v. *Barnett* and *Fishburn* v. *Fishburn,* since the pre-emptive refusal of the deserted spouse occurred at so early a stage in the desertion. This view, it is submitted, is unfortunate, for these reasons. It is against the current of opinion in the Court of Appeal, and therefore reintroduces an element of uncertainty, and seems to be inconsistent with the views later stated in the final paragraph of his judgment. In both *Barnett* v. *Barnett* and *Fishburn* v. *Fishburn,* it was evident that the mind of the deserting spouse was not affected as to desertion or reconciliation by the conduct of the deserted spouse. The introduction of the criterion of the time factor is not helpful. How is one to tell whether the desertion has become a settled and an accomplished fact, when it is one week, one month, six months or a year old? The learned lord justice says at p. 90: —

> "Where, however, the desertion has become a settled and accomplished fact, it is a not unusual feature for the deserted spouse to develop an aversion to the deserter who has scorned him or her, and to form perhaps another attachment. And in my view such aversion or other attachment does not bar relief unless they have the effect of preventing a reconciliation

and driving away a spouse who is or might otherwise become willing to return."

One may observe as to this, that an aversion—love turned to hate—in such circumstances can arise very quickly. Often the aversion occurs immediately after desertion, while the insult is still smarting.

The learned lord justice continues at pp. 90–91: —

"It is conceded that an uncommunicated intention by the deserted to have nothing more to do with the deserter need not prevent desertion running. If, however, it is communicated to the deserter, it may do so. The reason why it may do so is that it may deter him or her from reconciliation. If then it is clear that, though communicated to the deserter, it will have no effect at all on his or her conduct, there is no reason why it should automatically prevent desertion running (see the reasoning in *Herod* v. *Herod* [1939] P. 11). *Church* v. *Church* is an example of such a situation; and there Willmer, L.J., correctly, as I respectfully think, held that desertion had been made out. Where, therefore, the deserted spouse satisfies the court that his or her declared refusal of reconciliation has had no effect at all on the deserter, there is no rule of law that desertion is necessarily terminated by it."

It is submitted, it is hoped without presumption, that this last paragraph is an accurate exposition of the law, but it is not consistent with the decisions in *Barnett* v. *Barnett* and *Fishburn* v. *Fishburn.*

(d) Content not consent

Content is not consent, that is to say, if one spouse leaves the other without good reason, and the remaining spouse is content, or says to himself or herself "I am glad," that is not consent in law. In *Warburton* v. *Warburton* (1965), 109 Sol.J. 290 (C.A.) (Lord Pearce, Willmer and Russell, L.JJ.), the wife left her husband and they did not meet for six years. The husband then asked her if she had any feelings left and she said she wanted a divorce. On a divorce petition the judge held the parting was by consent. Lord Pearce said that because each was content to be apart did not mean there was a consensual parting. He referred to *Church* v. *Church* [1952] P. 313, 317, and *Sifton* v. *Sifton* [1939] P. 221. Once desertion had started it was no longer necessary to show that the other spouse actually wanted the deserter back. He approved of *Brewer* v. *Brewer* [1962] P. 69. Willmer, L.J., said that the deserted spouse may be thankful the other spouse had gone. The parting was not therefore consensual. Nothing less than true consent or agreement was required.

(e) *Effect of a Jewish divorce*

The courts have considered this subject in connection with Jewish divorces where the Rabbinical courts have dissolved a Jewish marriage by ordering the husband to give the wife a bill of divorcement. Does this amount to a separation by consent?

This depends on the circumstances. In *Joseph* v. *Joseph* [1953] 1 W.L.R. 1182 a wife whose husband had deserted her obtained a *get* from the Beth Din and the Court of Appeal (Somervell, Jenkins and Hodson, L.JJ.) held that this amounted to an agreement by the wife to the husband living separate and apart from her, thus terminating his desertion. In Jewish law only the husband can apply for the *get*, and if the wife wishes to have one she has to persuade the husband to apply for it, which was done in this case. This case was distinguished in *Corbett* v. *Corbett* [1957] 1 W.L.R. 486. There it was the husband who took the initiative in obtaining the *get* and as Jenkins, L.J., had said in *Joseph* v. *Joseph* that the *get* did not operate in this country as a decree of divorce or as an agreement to separate, Barnard, J., felt able to say that the wife never really consented to her husband leaving her or remaining separate from her.

(f) *Tacit consent*

Langton, J., in *Spence* v. *Spence* [1939] 1 All E.R. 52 held that the parties had tacitly agreed to separate. He found both parties were equally at fault, and that it was not possible for separation to be attributed to either party alone. The wife had often threatened to go. The husband, while sorry to see his children go, was not displeased to get rid of her. He went on to say at p. 57: —

> "To my thinking, it is quite impossible to describe a parting of this kind between the spouses as desertion by either side. As Gorell Barnes, J., said in *Sickert* v. *Sickert* [1899] P. 278, at p. 282: 'In order to constitute desertion, there must be a cessation of cohabitation and an intention on the part of the accused party to desert the other. In most cases of desertion,

the guilty party actually leaves the other, but it is not always or necessarily the guilty party who leaves the matrimonial home. In my opinion, the party who intends bringing the cohabitation to an end, and whose conduct in reality causes its termination, commits the act of desertion. There is no substantial difference between the case of a husband who intends to put an end to a state of cohabitation, and does so by leaving his wife, and that of a husband who with the like intent obliges his wife to separate from him.' It has always seemed to me that this paragraph constitutes a most comprehensive compendium of the law of desertion."

After referring to the dictum of Buckley, L.J., in *Harriman* v. *Harriman* [1909] P. 123 about a wife being glad to see her husband go, he continued: —

" In other words, the parting must be unfairly or unreasonably imposed by the offending spouse in order to constitute desertion. In the present case, it is unnecessary to go further than to recognise the position created by the tacit consent of Mr. Spence to the departure of his wife.

Mr. Middleton, in an able and instructive argument, contended that, where the faults of conduct are equal on each side, the act of a spouse leaving the matrimonial home with the intention not to return constitutes desertion. Without deciding the point, I am inclined to think that this contention is correct if the leaving be unaccompanied by any agreement or concurrence upon the other side."

The last sentence is probably the clue to this decision. In *Spence's* case before the wife went, the spouses did discuss the division of the household goods, which was probably some, if not strong, evidence of an agreement to part.

F. Just Cause

The Act of 1960 gives the complainant a remedy when the defendant " has deserted the complainant." Section 1 (1) (*a*) (ii) of the Matrimonial Causes Act, 1965, gave the petitioner a ground for divorce when the defendant " has deserted the petitioner without cause " for three years. In the first divorce Act, the Matrimonial Causes Act, 1857, the expression was desertion " without reasonable excuse." In *Frowd* v. *Frowd* [1904] P. 177, at p. 179, Jeune, P., said: —

" The expression ' desertion without reasonable excuse ' in the Matrimonial Causes Act, 1857, ss. 27, 31, and the equivalents of that expression ' without just cause ' or ' without good cause' have always struck me as somewhat loose and inaccurate language. Desertion means the cessation of cohabitation brought about by the fault or act of one of the parties. Therefore the conduct of the parties must be considered. If there is good cause or reasonable excuse, it seems to me there is no desertion in law."

It is now settled that "desertion" with or without the above expressions is the same thing (*Oldroyd* v. *Oldroyd* [1896] P. 175, at p. 182). If *A* leaves *B* without just cause, *A* is the deserter; but if *A* leaves *B* with just cause, then *B* is the deserter. The first proposition is established beyond doubt. The second is by and large true, though it cannot be said that the controversy about it is completely settled. What then is " Just Cause " ?

(a) Grave and weighty

It has been said time and time again that " just cause " must be conduct that is " grave and weighty " or " grave and convincing." See, for example, *Buchler* v. *Buchler* [1947] P. 25; *Edwards* v. *Edwards* [1950] P. 8; *Hall* v. *Hall* [1962] 1 W.L.R. 1246; *Gollins* v. *Gollins* [1964] A.C. 644. The same expression is used to describe conduct amounting to cruelty. Conduct of this kind is such that a spouse is not bound to endure it; while conduct described as the " wear and tear of conjugal life " is conduct which a spouse is expected to endure. There is no precise dividing line between one and the other. It is a matter of degree, and there is no formula or yardstick by which a court can say, in any particular case, on which side of the dividing line the case falls to be decided. There is a no man's land between the two poles where the court has a discretion. The decided cases have to some extent narrowed down this no man's land by indicating categories of conduct which might be one thing or the other.

(b) Conduct less than a matrimonial offence

As we have seen, matrimonial offences can be divided into at least five categories. For our present purpose, they may be divided into two classes (a) matrimonial offences properly so called where a direct remedy is given, e.g., a maintenance or a separation order in the magistrates' court, or which are evidence proving breakdown of the marriage in the divorce court, and (b) other matrimonial offences known as conjugal unkindness. When the cases refer to conduct less than a matrimonial offence, they mean less than (*a*), that is, conduct of the kind mentioned in (*b*).

As Vaisey, J., pointed out in *Buchler* v. *Buchler, supra,* if constructive desertion was based on misconduct for which there was a separate remedy, there would be no reason for the doctrine at all. If conduct less than a matrimonial offence amounts to just cause, *a fortiori,* matrimonial offences themselves (properly so called) must be just cause too. This seems too obvious for discussion, and yet it has been seriously argued that in certain cases cruelty did not amount to just cause (see *Boyd* v. *Boyd* [1938] 4 All E.R. 181, and *Hosegood* v. *Hosegood* (1950), 66 T.L.R. (Pt. 1) 833). This proposition cannot now be sustained.

The expression "conduct falling short of a matrimonial offence" is found in early cases. In *Yeatman* v. *Yeatman* (1868), L.R. 1 P.D. 489, it was said that reasonable cause was not necessarily a distinct matrimonial offence on which a decree of judicial separation or dissolution could be founded; but it must be grave and weighty. Mere frailty of temper (unless shown in some marked and intolerable excesses) and distasteful habits were not sufficient. The Judge Ordinary, Lord Penzance, relied on *Haswell* v. *Haswell* (1859), 1 Sw. & Tr. 502, where the wife had been discovered in indecent behaviour.

In *Ousey* v. *Ousey* (1874), L.R. 3 P. & D. 223, the husband left his wife because of persistent refusal to consummate the marriage, and the court held he was not in desertion since the husband bona fide believed his wife had wronged him. The state of affairs between husband and wife on these facts was intolerable.

du Parcq, L.J., in *Williams* v. *Williams* [1943] 2 All E.R. 746, at p. 752, said: —

> "Counsel for the husband suggested, however, that as a general rule there could not be reasonable cause or excuse for desertion unless some matrimonial offence on the part of the deserted spouse were proved. This suggestion is wholly erroneous. Conduct which falls short of adultery may excuse desertion, and so in some circumstances may the honest, though mistaken, belief of one spouse that he or she has been wronged by the other. This seems to me to be plain as a matter of construction and good sense, and the courts have always so held: see *Haswell* v. *Haswell and Sanderson* (1859), 1 Sw. & Tr. 502, *Ousey* v. *Ousey* (1874), L.R. 3 P. & D. 223, and *Wickins* v. *Wickins* [1918] P. 265."

The *locus classicus* that something less than a matrimonial offence is just cause provided that it is " grave and weighty " is to be found in *Buchler* v. *Buchler* [1947] P. 25, where Asquith, L.J., said: —

> " To afford such justification [that is, for a party leaving the matrimonial home] the conduct of the party staying on need not have amounted to a matrimonial offence such as cruelty or adultery but . . . it must exceed in gravity such behaviour, vexatious and trying though it may be, as every spouse bargains to endure when accepting the other ' for better or worse.' The ordinary wear and tear of conjugal life does not in itself suffice. . . . It is difficult to deduce from the decided cases any principle of law by reference to which it can be determined in every case on which side of this line the case falls. . . ."

The headnote in *Edwards* v. *Edwards* [1950] P. 8 reads: —

> " Conduct of ' a grave and convincing character ' but short of cruelty or other matrimonial offence may afford cause for desertion."

This was a decision of the Court of Appeal (Bucknill, Cohen and Asquith, L.JJ.). The commissioner found that the wife had failed to prove cruelty by the husband, but that she had proved a course of conduct which justified her in leaving him. It was argued for the husband that in view of the decision of Hodson, J., in *Barker* v. *Barker* [1949] P. 219, once the commissioner had negatived cruelty, it was not open to him to find the wife justified in leaving her husband. *Barker* v. *Barker* was a case in the Divisional Court, and Hodson, J., giving the second judgment, said at p. 225: —

> " It will not do to say that because a grave and weighty matter will justify one spouse in leaving the other, therefore something less than cruelty will do. The grave and weighty matter which justifies one spouse in leaving the other is very often something different from cruelty, and something which might even be regarded as more calculated to disrupt family life, such as the persistence in a false allegation of a criminal charge, which was the subject of the decision in *Russell* v. *Russell* [1895] P. 315 itself. Many people might regard this as something worse than cruelty involving the mere infliction of a physical injury causing injury to health. The existence of cruelty depends not on the magnitude but rather on the consequence, actual or apprehended, of the offence; and dealing with conduct which is either cruelty or not cruelty, it is, in my view, not open to any court to say ' This is not cruelty,

but is so near it that it amounts to a grave and weighty matter justifying separation '."

Bucknill, L.J., examined this statement carefully in *Edwards* v. *Edwards*. After citing *Russell, Oldroyd* and *Buchler*, he then quoted the above passage from the judgment of Hodson, J., in *Barker* v. *Barker*, and continued, at p. 14: —

" If Hodson, J., meant to say that, once a charge of cruelty has failed to be established, it is impossible for a wife to establish grounds justifying her refusing to live with her husband, with great respect to him I think that inconsistent with the decisions to which I have referred, and that this court ought to follow *Russell* v. *Russell* and *Buchler* v. *Buchler*. I think, however, that that is not what Hodson, J., meant to say. What I think he meant to say was that either the blows inflicted by the husband on the wife amounted to cruelty in that they injured her health or were likely to injure her health, or they were not of such a nature. If they were not of such a nature then, there being no other evidence in the case at all, the court ought not to say that although they were trivial blows in effect, they justified the wife in leaving her husband."

He also said in terms at p. 11 " there can be sufficient cause for desertion which falls short of legal cruelty."

Cohen, L.J., interpreted the findings of the commissioner as being that although the facts sworn to by the wife were proved they did not have the effect on the health of the wife requisite to justify her getting relief on the ground of cruelty, but that the conduct of the husband was of such a serious nature as to justify her in leaving him.

(c) Conduct less than cruelty

If the conduct (or rather misconduct) of the offending spouse is cruel, even though it does not cause injury to health, it amounts to good cause for the complainant to leave. In *Slon* v. *Slon* [1969] P. 122 the Court of Appeal gave a petitioning husband leave to amend his petition alleging cruelty to desertion where he had alleged his wife's unreasonable refusal of sexual intercourse.

Although the conduct in constructive desertion need not amount to a matrimonial offence (as defined above), difficulties have been experienced in distinguishing this conduct from cruelty, and there has been considerable discussion whether conduct less than or different from cruelty can be sufficient " just cause."

Cruelty may be divided into (i) actual physical cruelty and (ii) acts or a course of conduct which do not have an actual physical impact on the other spouse but which cause or tend to cause injury to health.

Cruelty as in (ii) may not be so obvious as direct physical cruelty but it can be very real and often more distressing. It is plain now that the test is objective, and intention is not an essential element (*Gollins* v. *Gollins* [1964] A.C. 644, and *Williams* v. *Williams* [1964] A.C. 698).

The individual reaction is important in cruelty. A sensitive person will become ill where a more phlegmatic person will not. Nevertheless the latter may feel that, illness apart, he or she has endured enough and must go.

Conduct which causes a spouse to leave must be of an intolerable nature, and such conduct must either be cruel or potentially cruel. The ways in which one person can be cruel to another are infinitely various and therefore, if one says on the one hand that conduct causing constructive desertion must be grave and weighty (or intolerable which is the same thing) and yet can be less than or different from cruelty, then the only meaning that can be attached to those words is that the conduct must be conduct of a cruel kind without necessarily resulting in injury to health or a reasonable apprehension of such injury.

It is sometimes said that such conduct can fall short of cruelty in that there is no intention to be cruel (*Young* v. *Young* [1964] P. 152). In other words, the conduct which in fact hurts the other spouse is not cruel unless it is intended to be cruel; whereas for just cause there has to be an intention to drive away, without an intention to be cruel. This reasoning was never very convincing and, after *Gollins* v. *Gollins,* is impossible.

Nor must it be assumed that the expression " grave and weighty " necessarily means the same thing in the context of cruelty and in the context of just cause, though doubtless it frequently does. The inquiry in each case is different. In cruelty, the question is " Has the conduct caused injury to health or is it likely to do so? " In other words, whether the conduct is grave and weighty depends on the likelihood or otherwise of injuring the health of the other party.

The question in constructive desertion is, " Has the conduct been so grave and weighty that the other spouse has found it intolerable and therefore was justified in leaving? " The question used to be put in other words, for instance, " Was the conduct so grave and weighty that the party committing it knew or ought to have known that it would lead to the other spouse leaving? " or again, " Was the conduct such that it amounted to expulsive conduct? " For the sake of this argument, it does not matter in which of these ways the question is put. The point is that the gravity or weightiness of the conduct is not directed to the end of injury to health; but to the end that it would justifiably lead to the other party leaving.

The cases amply support this view. There are many acts which are unlikely to lead to injury to the health of the other party which however justify that party in leaving. Instances are: False charges of homosexuality (*Russell* v. *Russell* [1895] P. 315); indecent behaviour by the wife (*Haswell* v. *Haswell* (1859), 1 Sw. & Tr. 502); belief in wife's wilful refusal to consummate the marriage (*Ousey* v. *Ousey* (1874), L.R. 3 P. & D. 223); belief in wife's adultery (*Glenister* v. *Glenister* [1945] P. 30; and *Baker* v. *Baker* [1954] P. 33); excessive sexual demands (*Holborn* v. *Holborn* [1947] 1 All E.R. 32); persistent extravagance (*G* v. *G* [1930] P. 72); unreasonable refusal to provide a proper home (*Jackson* v. *Jackson* (1932), 146 L.T. 406).

There are four cases which have caused difficulties: *Barker* v. *Barker* [1949] P. 219; *Pike* v. *Pike* [1954] P. 81; *Timmins* v. *Timmins* [1953] 1 W.L.R. 757; and *Young* v. *Young* [1964] P. 152.

Barker v. *Barker* was a case in the Divisional Court. The wife complained of five assaults and the justices had made an order on the grounds of wilful neglect and persistent cruelty. The real question was whether the husband's conduct amounted to persistent cruelty or not. The Divisional Court (Lord Merriman, P., and Hodson, J.) held that the husband's conduct was not serious enough for cruelty and had at least in part been provoked. The court also held that " cruelty " meant the same whether the case was in the High Court or in a court of summary jurisdiction. So far the case was unexceptional and would call for little, if any, comment. Hodson, J., however, took the opportunity to make some observations, which have been quoted on p. 77. Counsel for the wife had argued that something less than cruelty would justify a wife remaining apart from her husband. The President said that the case stood or fell on the finding of persistent cruelty " without drawing any fine distinction between cruelty and conduct of such a grave and weighty character as to justify the wife in living separate and apart, for on the facts of this case no such distinction falls to be drawn." In other words in this case the conduct was either cruelty or nothing. Hodson, J.'s observations went further than this.

If Hodson, J., meant by cruelty, direct physical cruelty, then his views are acceptable, but if he meant something different from this then they do not seem based on authority.

Then comes the case of *Timmins* v. *Timmins* [1953] 1 W.L.R. 757. On any view, this is an unsatisfactory case.

The husband petitioned for restitution of conjugal rights. The wife petitioned for divorce on the ground of cruelty. Wallington, J., found the husband was domineering and overbearing, but did not attribute the wife's mental breakdown to his conduct. He did express anxiety that if she went back she would have another breakdown as a result of her husband's conduct.

These findings are contradictory. He refused to grant a decree of divorce and felt he was bound to order restitution.

In the Court of Appeal, Hodson, L.J., would have dismissed the appeal under both heads, but Denning, L.J., and Lloyd-Jacob, J., agreed in allowing the wife's appeal against the order for restitution, but not against the dismissal of her divorce petition. Denning, L.J., said that the husband's conduct had affected his wife's health and expressed surprise that the judge had not found cruelty, but he thought the judge's finding was justifiable because there was no intent by the husband to injure or inflict misery on his wife, though the husband lacked this intent in the leading case of *Kelly* v. *Kelly* (1870), L.R. 2 P. & D. 59 (and now see *Gollins* v. *Gollins* and *Williams* v. *Williams*, *supra*) but was found guilty of cruelty. Nevertheless, Denning, L.J., thought the husband's conduct so grave and weighty that the wife was entitled to refuse to return. Hodson, L.J., thought the conduct was not grave and weighty.

Lloyd-Jacob, J., said, at p. 764: —

" The preservation of her sanity is, in my judgment, a grave and weighty matter, and for the husband to behave in an overbearing, dominating and dictatorial manner when he has once appreciated the consequences of such behaviour to her state of mind would no longer be an exercise of his frailty, but a wickedly cruel matrimonial offence. The husband's conduct in relation to the removal of his second child from the other's custody, and his rejection of his wife's offer to return to the matrimonial home for a few days, illustrate such a lack of consideration as to satisfy me that a return under an order of the court might be fraught with the gravest peril."

Although Lloyd-Jacob, J., agreed with the facts as stated by Denning, L.J., and also with his conclusions, his reasons were different. For instance, he thought that the reason why the wife's petition should be refused was because the only act of violence proved against the husband had been condoned. This leaves out of account the main ground of cruelty, namely, the husband's domineering manner and the other conduct which this judge described as a wicked matrimonial offence, and that in any event such conduct would have eliminated the condonation. Denning, L.J., was the only judge who said that the conduct was not cruel because it was not intended to be cruel.

Denning, L.J., felt it necessary to explain (or explain away) what he had said in *Pike* v. *Pike* ([1954] P. 81) and said, at pp. 761–762: —

"We were referred to *Pike* v. *Pike*, and in view of some comments made on it by Davies, J., in *Dixon* v. *Dixon* [1953] P. 103, I think that I ought to explain some of the things which I there said. In considering whether one party has good cause for leaving the other, much depends on whether the conduct complained of is of a ' grave and weighty ' character or not. Conduct which is of a grave and weighty character may sometimes fall short of cruelty because it lacks the element of injury to health (as in *Russell* v. *Russell* [1895] P. 315, and *Edwards* v. *Edwards* [1950] P. 8), or because it lacks the element of intent to injure (as in the case of drunkenness or association with other women); but nevertheless it may give good cause for leaving as the cases which I have cited earlier amply show. On the other hand, conduct which is not ' of a grave and weighty character,' and is for that reason not cruelty, does not give good cause for leaving; see *Yeatman* v. *Yeatman* (1868), L.R. 1 P. & D. 489. It is conduct of that kind to which I referred in *Pike* v. *Pike* when I said that conduct ' less than cruelty ' does not justify a spouse in leaving. In the present case the conduct of the husband was, I think, of a grave and weighty character, and the only reason why it was not cruelty was because there was no intent to injure. It comes, therefore, within the earlier cases to which I referred."

It will be seen that all the judges differed and only Denning, L.J., made the point about intention.

Buchler and *Edwards* were clear decisions that conduct less than a matrimonial offence (properly so called) was sufficient for " just cause." The law there set out was reasonably clear. The dicta in *Barker*, *Pike* and *Timmins* have caused confusion. Expressions like " less than cruelty " or " different from cruelty " are misleading and obscure unless the cruelty referred to is direct physical cruelty, since all intolerable conduct is or can be cruel. In *Pike* the decision was right but the dicta were unnecessary and went much too far. In *Timmins* the findings of fact were absurd and contradictory. To say that conduct of a domineering kind (which obviously must be deliberate even if a man had that sort of nature) and which was described by one judge as a wicked matrimonial offence, and which caused a breakdown in the wife's health, and was conduct which two judges said was grave and weighty, did not amount to cruelty, because the husband did not intend to be cruel was ridiculous (as *Gollins* and *Williams* made clear). *Hadden* v. *Hadden* (1919), *The Times*, 5th December, has been many times approved and establishes that although the husband did not intend to be cruel, his conduct amounted to cruelty if the acts complained of were intended. In the words of Macbeth the acts " trammel up the consequences."

Sir Jocelyn Simon, P., in the case of *Young* v. *Young* [1964] P. 152, however, said that *Pike* and *Timmins* were perfectly reconcilable. In *Timmins* the husband had no desire [*sic*] to injure his wife and for that reason alone, it was not cruelty. The learned judge in this passage does not distinguish between desire and intention (see *Lang* v. *Lang*, *supra*). Desire, and motive (he also used this word) are not necessary ingredients in cruelty or desertion. He pointed out that in *Russell* v. *Russell*, *supra*, the conduct was not cruel only because it did not injure the husband's health. True, but in that case the judges did not enter into any metaphysical arguments about " just cause " being less than " or different from " cruelty. All they said was that injury to health was a necessary element in cruelty, but although the wife's conduct could not in that sense be said to be cruel, nevertheless the fact that she wilfully disseminated lies that he was a sodomite, was just cause for his refusal to live with her.

In *Ogden* v. *Ogden* [1969] 3 All E.R. 1055, C.A., the wife issued summonses for desertion, wilful neglect and persistent cruelty. The justices dismissed the summons for persistent cruelty although the wife's health had been affected, but found conduct sufficiently grave and weighty to justify her leaving and made an order in her favour on both desertion and wilful neglect. This decision was upheld by a Divisional Court but reversed by the Court of Appeal (Davies, Winn and Phillimore, L.JJ.). They held that in this case having dismissed cruelty they could not find constructive desertion on the same facts. They followed *Pike* v. *Pike*, *supra*, and referred to *Slon* v. *Slon* [1969] 1 All E.R. 759. In *Ogden's* case the Court of Appeal found that there was a genuine offer of reconciliation by the husband not accepted by the wife, and on this ground alone the appeal succeeded. If the wife was right then she had proved cruelty. The court held that the justices were right in negativing cruelty and there were no special circumstances to find constructive desertion. *Slon's* case, *supra*, showed that grave and weighty conduct on account of which a wife left her husband, though her health was not affected, could not amount to cruelty but was good cause for constructive desertion.

(d) *The effect of* Gollins v. Gollins *and* Williams v. Williams

These cases now establish that an intention to injure is not an essential element in cruelty. Indeed *Williams* decided that when the conduct was cruel, insanity is not necessarily an answer to the charge. Cases of constructive desertion, where a spouse has left the matrimonial home because he or she has found the conduct of the other intolerable, have close similarities to cruelty and indeed the courts have on many occasions recognised this affinity, e.g., *Howard* v. *Howard* [1962] 3 W.L.R. 413, at p. 418, and *W.* v. *W.* (*No.* 2) [1962] P. 49. The question is bound to arise whether in view of these decisions of the House of Lords, intention is a necessary element in this type of constructive desertion. It is submitted that these cases strongly reinforce the view, expressed in this book, that intention is not a necessary element. Conduct which is cruel and which causes injury to health, or a reasonable apprehension thereof, would be just cause for the injured spouse leaving. We know now that in respect of such conduct intention to hurt, even intention to do the acts which hurt, is not necessary. Therefore it is clear that in that type of constructive desertion, intention is not a necessary element. Supposing, however, the conduct is intolerable but the health of the other party is not affected. Why should the presence or absence of injury to health affect the question of intention? In either case the law should (and does) take an objective view of the conduct and its consequences. See p. 206 for Lord Reid's views.

(e) As a defence

Once the cause of the separation has been found "not to be just," then a spouse cannot rely on it as a defence to desertion. As Lord Merriman said in *Rice* v. *Raynold-Spring-Rice* [1948] 1 All E.R. 188, where it had been held that the husband had reasonable cause for leaving his wife because of her refusal to allow normal complete intercourse (at p. 190): —

> "There is nothing irrevocable about . . . these matters. The wife can mend her ways. She can determine, and show she is determined, to resume cohabitation in the full sense of the word, and to render her husband wifely duties, not merely in connection with sexual matters, but in the daily conduct of married life. If so, the husband is not entitled to take up the view that it is finally decided that this marriage is at an end. Far from it. It will be his duty, in turn, to be ready and willing to resume cohabitation. If not, always assuming that the wife, in the true sense of the word, is ready and willing to resume cohabitation, it will be he who will assume the character of deserter."

This was clearly shown by the Divisional Court in *Marjoram* v. *Marjoram* [1955] 1 W.L.R. 520, where the husband had left his wife because of her dirty habits. He alleged that she slept in her clothes, never washed and wore her underclothes until they fell off. The wife relied on the case of *Bartholomew* v. *Bartholomew* [1952] 2 All E.R. 1035 (Court of Appeal), where the court had held that dirty habits were not sufficient to show an intention to expel the other spouse. Lord Merriman said it was necessary to consider this case with caution because it was based on the *Boyd*

v. *Boyd* school of thought, which had been discredited by the later case of *Lang* v. *Lang* [1955] A.C. 402, which the President described as a most authoritative case, and he suggested that at the re-hearing of the case before the justices, the questions they should ask themselves were: was the wife's alleged sluttishness the real and effective cause of the husband leaving the matrimonial home? or was the cause in whole or part to continue what the wife said was an improper association with the woman mentioned? It will be noticed that the word " expel " is noticeably absent.

(f) Examples

Examples of cases where the court has held " just cause " has been proved are the following:

(1) Bringing and persisting in a false charge against the husband of sodomy with a third person. Husband had just cause for leaving his wife. *Russell* v. *Russell* [1895] P. 315.

(2) Habitual drunkenness by a wife justifies a husband in leaving her. *Beer* v. *Beer* (1906), 94 L.T. 704.

(3) Persistent refusal to consummate the marriage. *Ousey* v. *Ousey and Atkinson* (1874), L.R. 3 P. & D. 223. (But if the refusal was due to illness, whether physical or psychological, it would not afford just cause: *Beevor* v. *Beevor* [1945] 2 All E.R. 200.)

(4) Refusal of normal sexual intercourse. *Rice* v. *Raynold-Spring-Rice* [1948] 1 All E.R. 188.

(5) Excessive sexual demands, and sexual activities which to the wife were revolting and to which she had objected. *Holborn* v. *Holborn* [1947] 1 All E.R. 32.

(6) Persistent extravagance. *G.* v. *G.* [1930] P. 72.

(7) Where a husband finds his wife submitting to indecent liberties. *Haswell* v. *Haswell and Sanderson* (1859), 1 Sw. & Tr. 502.

(8) Drunkenness and violence short of cruelty. *Butland* v. *Butland* (1913), 29 T.L.R. 729.

(9) Wife's persistent friendship with another man. *Russell* (*Marchioness of Tavistock*) v. *Russell* (*Marquis of Tavistock*) (1935), 80 Sol.J. 16.

(10) The husband due to mental instability frightened the

children. Wife left. *G.* v. *G.* [1964] 1 All E.R. 129, D.C. " Common sense indicates that separation may be caused without blame to either party ": per Sir J. Simon, P.

(11) A wife kept the child of an adulterous union knowing that if she did so her husband would leave her. He did. Held by Divisional Court he was entitled to do so. *Rothery* v. *Rothery* (1966), *The Times*, 30th March.

Justices should not disregard the conduct of other members of the husband's family when considering whether the wife was justified in leaving the husband. The husband was not entitled to say that his family had driven the wife out of the house and he was not involved. *Devi* v. *Gaddu* (1974), 118 Sol.J. 579; Divisional Court appeal from justices.

Examples where the court has held that the conduct complained of was not " just cause " for one spouse leaving the other: —

(1) The innocent contraction of venereal disease by a wife transmitted to the husband who knew of her condition did not justify the husband leaving her. *Butler* v. *Butler* [1917] P. 244.

(2) Frailty of temper and distasteful habits. *Yeatman* v. *Yeatman* (1868), L.R. 1 P. & D. 489.

(3) A conviction for larceny. *Williamson* v. *Williamson* (1882), 7 P.D. 76.

(4) Pregnancy of wife at marriage, and false representation of seduction by husband. *Holt* v. *Holt* (1908), 53 Sol.J. 84.

(5) Adultery which has been conduced to cannot be claimed as just cause by the other party. *Callister* v. *Callister* [1947] W.N. 221.

(6) Husband's persistent friendship with an employee, the wife taking strong objection to the association. *Buchler* v. *Buchler* [1947] P. 25.

(g) *Refusal of sexual intercourse*

Sexual intercourse is regarded by the courts as one of the essential obligations of married life, and a wilful refusal of intercourse, without reasonable excuse, such as ill health, is a breach of that obligation.

Denning, L.J., in *Kaslefsky* v. *Kaslefsky* [1951] P. 38, at p. 47, has described the seriousness of the obligation: —

"The wilful and unjustifiable refusal of sexual intercourse is destructive of marriage, more destructive, perhaps than anything else. Just as normal sexual intercourse is the natural bond of marriage, so the wilful refusal of it causes a marriage to disintegrate. It gives rise to irritability and discord, to nervousness and manifestations of temper, and hence to the breakdown of the marriage."

(i) *Where no separation*

It has been argued that a mere refusal without actual separation was sufficient to constitute desertion. The argument failed in *Jackson* v. *Jackson* [1924] P. 19, as it did also in the House of Lords in *Weatherley* v. *Weatherley* [1947] A.C. 628, which approved the decision in *Jackson* v. *Jackson.*

The facts in *Jackson* v. *Jackson* were that the husband refused to sleep with his wife because she insisted on having her little girl in bed with her, but the case was argued on the basis that there had been an unqualified refusal of sexual intercourse. The Divisional Court (Duke, P., and Hill, J.), held there could not be desertion without the *factum* of separation. Duke, P., said of the refusal of sexual intercourse, at p. 24:

"It is not abandonment; it is not living apart. If it is a refusal of a duty it does not purport to conclude the matrimonial relationship."

This was approved by the Lord Chancellor in *Weatherley* v. *Weatherley.*

(ii) *Where wronged party leaves*

In neither *Jackson* v. *Jackson* nor *Weatherley* v. *Weatherley* were the parties living apart. When there is the *factum* of separation, as well as the refusal of sexual intercourse, different considerations arise.

When one spouse refuses sexual intercourse to the other persistently and without good reason, this constitutes good cause for the other leaving. This was decided in an early case, *Ousey* v. *Ousey and Atkinson* (1874), L.R. 3 P. & D. 223, where a husband had left his wife because of her persistent refusal to allow him to consummate the marriage. The question was whether the husband had deserted his wife.

The Judge Ordinary at p. 225 said: —

" In such a state of things, I think that a husband taking the view that the fault was not with himself but with the wife, and in that state of mind coming to the conclusion that the connection between them was intolerable, leading to misery and not to happiness, because the wife was either unable or resolutely unwilling to consummate, and therefore leaving her, cannot be said to have been guilty of such desertion as is contemplated by the statute."

This was followed in *Synge* v. *Synge* [1901] P. 317, where the Court of Appeal held that a wife who without cause refuses to permit marital intercourse to her husband cannot allege desertion without reasonable excuse.

In *Rice* v. *Raynold-Spring-Rice* [1948] 1 All E.R. 188 a wife summoned her husband before the magistrates alleging desertion and wilful neglect to maintain. The husband's defence was that the wife had consistently refused him normal complete intercourse and refused to bear him a child, and this led to quarrels until finally, deciding it was impossible to go on living with her, he left her. The magistrates dismissed the summons and a Divisional Court (Lord Merriman, P., and Barnard, J.) dismissed the wife's appeal. The President took a hint from *Baxter* v. *Baxter* [1947] A.C. 274, where the Lord Chancellor indicated that, although refusal to consummate a marriage, that is by the use of contraceptives and the like, was not a ground for nullity, nevertheless there may well be another remedy.

In addition to being a defence to a summons for desertion, unreasonable refusal of sexual intercourse can be the basis of constructive desertion, that is, the one who refuses becomes the deserter if the other party leaves. This is subject to some qualifications. Something will depend on the age and health of the parties, and the period of time over which the refusal has extended. It has also been said that it should be supported by other complaints as well, but it is conceived that, in a proper case, prolonged refusal is in itself sufficient.

In *Davis* v. *Davis* [1918] P. 85, a refusal of intercourse without sufficient reason was held to give just cause for withdrawal. This was a wife's petition for restitution. The husband alleged the wife's refusal of sexual intercourse. Coleridge, J., at p. 87,

referring to the judgment of Jeune, P., *Synge* v. *Synge* [1900]
P. 180, at p. 195, said: —

> "Later on he makes use of this language, which ought to
> be written in letters of gold over the doors of all houses where
> husband and wife have to make allowances for each other:
> 'The objects of married life, as expressed in the Marriage
> Service, are not the less true because they are utterances of a
> more plain-spoken age than the present; and while human
> nature remains what it is, I think a husband has a right to
> decline to submit to a groundless demand of his wife that
> he should live with her as a husband only in name. Neither
> party to a marriage can, I think, insist on cohabitation unless
> she or he is willing to perform a marital duty inseparable
> from it '."

In *Scotcher* v. *Scotcher* [1947] P. 1 the wife refused sexual
intercourse and the husband said that if she continued in this
course he would leave her. She did not change and he left her
and subsequently petitioned for divorce on the ground of desertion. Willmer, J., held the wife was in desertion and granted a
decree. He relied upon *Synge* v. *Synge* and also on the dictum
of Hill, J., in *Jackson* v. *Jackson* [1924] P. 19, at p. 27: —

> "Refusal to occupy the same bed and refusal to have sexual
> intercourse may be a fact which, taken with other facts, has
> weight in considering whether the husband has really caused
> the wife to live apart. I say may be because even so, in my
> view, the refusal of sexual intercourse would have to be con-
> sidered in connection with the age of the parties, the state of
> their health, the number of children they already had, and a
> number of other circumstances. It may be a circumstance
> which ought to be taken into account, but at the best it is only
> a circumstance which ought to be taken into account along
> with others, and in my view it would be entirely wrong to
> suppose that, taken by itself and independent of anything
> else, it would ever be possible to base upon it a finding of
> desertion."

It will be remembered that in *Jackson* v. *Jackson* there was
absent the *factum* of separation, and it was to this Hill, J., was
referring in the last sentence of this quotation.

Willmer, J., concluded at p. 10: —

> ". . . it appears to me that in the long run the question
> which I have to decide in this case is one of fact, namely
> whether the conduct of the respondent, taken as a whole,
> including her refusal of sexual intercourse, constituted such

a total disregard of the fundamental obligations of matrimony as to afford evidence of an intention to desert. As was pointed out by counsel for the petitioner, the respondent must be taken to intend the natural and probable consequences of her acts, and if she behaves with a reckless indifference to the natural and probable (and, I may add, expressly threatened) consequences of her conduct, this would be sufficient evidence of an intention to desert."

Lord Merriman, P., in *Lawrance v. Lawrance* [1950] P. 84, in giving the decision of a Divisional Court which upheld a finding by the magistrates that the husband had deserted his wife by causing her to leave by the refusal of ordinary conjugal rights, when the wife ardently wanted a child, said there was really no doubt about the law on the subject. He referred to the decision in *Rice v. Raynold-Spring-Rice* [1948] 1 All E.R. 188, and added at p. 90: —

" I am satisfied that this wife has proved that she was justified in withdrawing from cohabitation because of the wrongs done to her by the husband in and arising from this vital aspect of married life."

If the refusal is based on a physical incapacity or what is equivalent thereto, beyond the spouse's control, that would not afford an excuse to the other spouse to leave.

In *Beevor v. Beevor* [1945] 2 All E.R. 200 the wife consistently refused sexual intercourse in spite of the husband's warning that if this continued he would leave her. This continued for fifteen years, and then he left her. Evidence was that the wife had developed an invincible repugnance to the sexual act. The husband petitioned for divorce and the wife cross-petitioned. Henn Collins, J., held that the position was the same as though the wife had been rendered structurally incapable by accident or disease, and therefore the husband's petition failed. The wife's refusal has to be wilful and without excuse.

See also *Cann v. Cann* (1967), 111 Sol.J. 819, where the wife found sexual intercourse disgusting and distasteful and refused. But where a wife's sexual instincts diminished with the years the husband was not entitled to leave (*Chapper v. Chapper* (1966), *The Times*, 25th May).

(iii) *Where party refusing sexual intercourse leaves*

In *Lilley v. Lilley* [1960] P. 158 it was the wife who left the husband on the ground of her repugnance to sexual intercourse, and also because on medical advice to live with him would injure her health. The Court of Appeal, differing from the Divisional Court, held that she was in desertion. The wife was neurotic but quite capable of rational thought, and she elected to treat the separation as permanent.

It was held in *Casey* v. *Casey* [1952] 1 All E.R. 453 that where there was refusal of sexual intercourse by the deserting husband, the wife was justified in refusing to have him back.

In the recent case of *Slon* v. *Slon* [1969] P. 122 the Court of Appeal (Harman, Davies and Sachs, L.JJ.) held that refusal of sexual intercourse was a just cause for the wronged party leaving the other. In this case the home was sold up and each left the other.

(h) Illness

When a man and woman marry they undertake to live with one another in sickness and in health. Generally speaking, therefore, it is not just cause to abandon the other spouse, if that other is ill, whether physically or mentally. As Goddard, L.J., said in *Sotherden* v. *Sotherden* [1940] P. 73, at p. 79: —

" A man does not get rid of his obligations as a husband because his wife is in the hospital."

Nor is it just cause for the sick spouse to leave the other merely on account of this sickness.

A husband is not entitled to turn his lunatic wife out, though it may be his duty to place her in proper custody, under proper care (*Hayward* v. *Hayward* (1858), 1 Sw. & Tr. 81), but where a husband's mania endangered the safety of a wife, it was held in *Hanbury* v. *Hanbury* [1892] P. 222, affirmed 8 T.L.R. 559, that she was entitled to a judicial separation.

In *Keeley* v. *Keeley* [1952] 2 T.L.R. 756, the wife, who was a voluntary patient in a mental home, refused to return to her husband because she was happy where she was. As the wife was perfectly able to make this decision, the Court of Appeal held she was in desertion. Singleton, L.J., at p. 761, said: —

" If the respondent is stricken by illness which compels him or her to be in hospital for the relevant period, it is difficult to see that the petitioner can prove desertion without cause; and it seems to me that this reasoning would apply equally in

the case of mental illness as it would in the case of (say) prolonged heart disease . . . if the case is that the patient remains
there on advice given to her in the interests of her health, that
is a case which ought to be pleaded. In such a case it would
be for the judge to consider whether she remained there for
that reason or whether her real reason for not returning to
her husband was merely that she did not wish to do so. This
is of course on the assumption that the patient is competent
to make a decision for herself."

The neurotic condition of a husband, and nothing more, is not
sufficient ground for a wife's refusal to live with him (*Leng* v. *Leng*
[1946] 2 All E.R. 590), nor was the neurotic condition of a wife
good cause for refusing to live with her husband, at any rate, if
she says the refusal is for all time (*Lilley* v. *Lilley* [1960] P. 158).

The latter is a particularly strong case, the medical evidence
being that her neurosis was such that she would be taking a grave
risk to her mental health if she returned at that time, but the wife,
who had the mental capacity to make a decision, said that not
only would she not return at that time, but said "never will."
Hodson, L.J., who gave the judgment of the Court of Appeal,
said at p. 184: —

"In this case we do not think that the neurotic wife can in
law justify a refusal ever to return to cohabitation, now that
the state of desertion for which her husband was responsible
has been terminated. From this it follows that she is herself
in desertion."

A similar case to *Lilley* v. *Lilley* is the more recent case of
Tickle v. *Tickle* [1968] 2 All E.R. 154 (Divisional Court, Sir
Jocelyn Simon, P., and Willmer, L.J.), where the husband
developed mental trouble and went into a mental hospital. When
he left hospital he told his wife he would not return to her. His
wife issued a summons for desertion and the husband told the
court he would never return to his wife. A doctor told the
court that if he did return he would have to go back to hospital.
The magistrates dismissed the summons because they took the
view that the separation was temporary and in view of the medical
evidence they thought the husband had no intention to bring
cohabitation permanently to an end. The court allowed the appeal
following *Lilley* v. *Lilley* and also *G.* v. *G.* [1964] P. 133. The
President said the husband would have been justified, on the medical advice, in a temporary separation from his wife, but he said he

would never return, and therefore he was in desertion. Willmer, L.J., concurred but with considerable doubt.

(i) Crime

The fact that one spouse has been convicted of a criminal offence does not in itself justify the other spouse leaving. Persistence in a criminal life may amount to just cause and so may the commission of certain serious crimes (*Stanwick* v. *Stanwick* [1971] P. 124, where persistent dishonesty in financial matters was held to be cruel).

(i) Sexual offences

Unnatural practices with a third party by the husband have been held to justify the wife in leaving (*Mogg* v. *Mogg* (1824), 2 Add. 292, where the husband was convicted of an indecent assault on his apprentice) (following *Bromley* v. *Bromley* (1793), 2 Add. 158n, where the husband was convicted of attempts at unnatural practices). It is plain from the tenor of the judgments in *Buchler* v. *Buchler* [1947] P. 25 that if the husband's association with the pigman had been of a homosexual nature, the court would have held this to be just cause. False charges of unnatural offences were held to be just cause in *Russell* v. *Russell* [1895] P. 315.

Sexual offences might amount to cruelty (see p. 189).

(ii) Other offences

In *Townsend* v. *Townsend* (1873), L.R. 3 P. & D. 129, the husband, having committed several thefts, separated from his wife with her knowledge and consent to avoid arrest. He was arrested and imprisoned, and after his release, committed other thefts and was again imprisoned. He made repeated attempts to persuade his wife to resume cohabitation, but she refused and cohabitation was never resumed. Later the wife brought a petition for divorce on the ground of his adultery and desertion, but the Judge Ordinary refused on the ground that there was no desertion. His reason was that the husband never intended to desert her, and (in contrast with *Lawrence* v. *Lawrence* (1862), 2 Sw. & Tr. 575) always wanted to live with her. This reasoning would not be accepted today. The question whether the wife was justified in refusing to live with him because of his criminal activities was neither asked nor answered by the Judge Ordinary, and so this case can hardly be said to be an authority on the subject.

It was held in *Williamson* v. *Williamson and Bates* (1882), 7 P.D. 76, that a wife's conviction and sentence of six months for theft was not just cause for her husband refusing to live with her. This decision is doubtless correct, but the judgment of Hannen, P., stated the law too widely when he said, at p. 76: —

> "The conviction and imprisonment of a husband or wife for an offence against the criminal law is no justification to the other party for refusing to live with him or her. However painful it may be for a respectable man to have a wife who has been convicted of felony, such conviction does not in this court justify him in deserting her. It sometimes happens that wives have husbands who have been convicted of infamous crimes, and yet those husbands are legally entitled to cohabitation with them."

Contrast this with *Ingram* v. *Ingram* [1956] P. 390, where Sachs, J., held that a conviction for treasonable conduct by a spouse may amount to just cause for the husband leaving. It also could amount to cruelty. The words of the judge at p. 408, referring to conduct amounting to cruelty, are equally applicable to conduct amounting to just cause: —

> ". . . in principle, it does not matter if the conviction relates to a sexual, violent, fraudulent or treasonable matter. The first questions in each case must be: does the single conviction, viewed against the background of the particular marriage, tend to strike at the roots of the matrimonial relationship, and has it inflicted injury on the health of the other party? If the single conviction is of the requisite degree of gravity, and has the above effect, then the court can look at the circumstances as a whole and see whether or not there is to be inferred that intention to injure which leads to a finding of cruelty."

The references to injury to the health of the spouse are unnecessary where constructive desertion is concerned.

Criminal conduct which may amount to cruelty, and therefore, *a fortiori,* to just cause, is dealt with at p. 189.

(j) Belief in adultery

This is another example of the doctrine that something less than a matrimonial offence constitutes " just cause." It was first formulated in *Glenister* v. *Glenister* [1945] P. 30, where Lord Merriman defined it in precise terms as follows (at p. 38): —

> "I think that where the wife has so conducted herself as to lead any reasonable person to believe, until she gives some explanation, that she has committed adultery, the husband becoming aware of the facts and honestly drawing that inference, and leaving his wife on that ground, ought not to be held to have left her without reasonable cause."

So stated it is a defence by a spouse to proceedings for desertion by the other spouse, and it will be seen to consist of three elements: —

(1) There must be "conduct" by the complainant,

(2) inducing thereby a belief in the complainant's adultery by a reasonable person, and

(3) the defendant must have a belief in the complainant's adultery.

(i) *Conduct*

If a wife behaves in such a way that her husband believes he has good grounds for proving that she has committed adultery, then if he continues to cohabit with her it may be said he has condoned the offence, or connived at it (*Hartley* v. *Hartley* [1955] 1 W.L.R. 384, at p. 386, subject to s. 42 (2) of the 1965 Act). If, on the other hand, he leaves her, it would be said he has deserted her, unless genuine belief in such circumstances is a defence. This was the reasoning whereby Lord Merriman arrived at the *Glenister* rule.

The conduct of the wife in *Glenister* v. *Glenister* was this. The husband, who was in the Army, came home early one morning and found three men in the house, one of whom the wife admitted had been in her bedroom. She gave no explanation in detail. When he found her to be three months pregnant, many months after he had had intercourse with her, he turned her out of the house. He also suspected she had infected him with gonorrhea. When she summoned him for desertion, he pleaded she had committed adultery. The magistrate was not satisfied of the adultery, and made an order. Lord Merriman, P., held that the magistrate had ample material on which to make a finding of adultery, although he was not disposed to disturb the finding, but he held the husband was justified in turning his wife out on the ground that her conduct was such that a reasonable man would have believed she had committed adultery, and that the husband had such a belief. In coming to this conclusion, he relied on *Haswell* v. *Haswell* (1859), 1 Sw. & Tr. 502, where a wife had allowed indecent overtures, and *Ousey* v. *Ousey* (1874), L.R. 3 P. & D. 223, where the wife had refused sexual intercourse, and in both cases the court held that the husband had a belief that his wife was wronging him and that constituted just cause negativing desertion. The President did not refer to one of his own decisions (*Roast* v. *Roast* [1938] P. 8) where a wife had said that her husband would have to keep her child whether he was the father or not, and it was held that the husband was justified in leaving, since he had reasonable grounds for believing that she had committed adultery.

In *Glenister* v. *Glenister*, Lord Merriman had said that there were previous authorities, but he could not call them to mind. Seven years later in *Chilton* v. *Chilton* [1952] P. 196, he stated that the authorities he had had in mind in *Glenister* v. *Glenister* were *Morris* v. *Edmonds* (1897), 77 L.T. 56, and *Biggs* v. *Burridge* (1924), 89 J.P. 75. These were cases under the Vagrancy Act, 1824, where the husband was charged with wilful neglect to maintain his wife, and it was held that his bona fide belief in her adultery was a good defence to that charge. The case of *Chilton* v. *Chilton* also decided that the *Glenister* rule was a good defence to a summons not only for desertion, but also for wilful neglect to maintain, Pearce, J., saying, at p. 202: —

> "Unless there is some agreement, made expressly or by implication between the parties, the duty to cohabit and the duty to maintain are co-extensive and in my opinion, where circumstances have excused the husband from his duty to cohabit, he cannot be held guilty of wilful neglect to maintain."

On the other hand, *Glenister* was distinguished in *Wood* v. *Wood* [1947] P. 103, where there had been a pregnancy of 346 days, and Lord Merriman held that that circumstance alone, without any evidence of misconduct by the wife, was not sufficient to invoke the *Glenister* rule.

A distinction has been made between conduct of which the defendant actually knows and information about conduct obtained from third parties. In the latter case, the *Glenister* rule does not apply (*Beer* v. *Beer* [1948] P. 10, and this decision of Willmer, J., was followed by the Court of Appeal in *Elliott* v. *Elliott* [1956] P. 160). In the *Elliott* case, the husband pleaded, in answer to his wife's petition for divorce on the ground of desertion, that he believed that she had committed adultery because of information about a miscarriage told him by his mother. He did not allege that this was true, or that he had made enquiries about it. This plea was rejected as it would put the wife at the mercy of idle gossip. Morris, L.J., said at p. 166: —

> " It seems to me that if the husband says: ' I was told by somebody . . . that my wife has gone to a hospital because of a miscarriage,' and does not allege the truth of that statement, or does not allege any conduct on the part of the wife inducing a belief in its truth, he is not entitled to say: ' I believed the statement which was made to me, and so I was justified in staying away from my wife '."

See also *Hunter* v. *Hunter* (1961), *The Times*, 14th November.

(ii) *Reasonable belief*

Not only must the defendant believe in the complainant's adultery but that belief must be reasonable, that is to say, based on reasonable grounds. As was stated above, a belief induced by mere idle gossip would not be sufficient. It is difficult to see how a man can allege a reasonable belief in his wife's adultery unless he is prepared to go so far as to say that he has evidence which proves she has committed adultery.

Lord Merriman, in one case, gave an example of a wife who, for her own purposes, gave a false confession of adultery. The court, at a later date, might find that it was false, but the husband's belief would be genuine and based on reasonable grounds. Sir Raymond Evershed, M.R., in *Allen* v. *Allen* [1951] 1 All E.R. 724, at p. 731, said: —

> " . . . it seems to me that if a man says: ' I bona fide and reasonably believe that my wife is an adulteress ' as a defence in proceedings of this character, the result is neither irrational nor unjust if he be regarded as saying this: ' I say and allege that the evidence and materials in my possession are such that on them a court should and would find that adultery has been committed '."

In *Edwards* v. *Edwards* (1965), 109 Sol.J. 175, the husband argued that he had a bona fide belief in his wife's adultery and therefore had just cause for leaving her. To find adultery a court had to be satisfied beyond reasonable doubt but for him as a layman to justify his belief it was sufficient to show he was justified on a balance of probabilities. Sir Jocelyn Simon, P., rejected this argument and said that the test was the same for the court and the layman, following *Allen* v. *Allen, supra*, otherwise if a court had dismissed a charge of adultery, on the husband's argument he could still be justified in holding a reasonable belief in her adultery as he was relying on a lesser test.

(iii) *Notice*

In the magistrates' court, whenever there is a charge of adultery, the party making the charge must give notice to the other party. In *Duffield* v. *Duffield* [1949] 1 All E.R. 1105, Lord Merriman at p. 1106 said: —

> " I wish to emphasise, as has been emphasised repeatedly by this court, that it is of the utmost importance that, whenever a charge of adultery is made, in whatever context, under the summary jurisdiction procedure, full and proper particulars should be given."

In *Sullivan* v. *Sullivan* [1956] 1 W.L.R. 277, Lord Merriman stated that notice was similarly required where the allegation was a reasonable belief in the other spouse's adultery. But he went on to say that it was not essential to allege adultery if the only allegation relied on was a reasonable belief in adultery. He said, at p. 279: —

> "But there is an essential difference between making a charge of adultery and alleging that the conduct of one spouse or the other has induced a reasonable belief that adultery has been committed. In my opinion, a specific allegation of adultery should not be made merely as a matter of course unless it is intended to make the actual charge of adultery. In this case it would have been appropriate and sufficient to give notice that the wife intended to rely in support of the charge of desertion on a reasonable belief that adultery had been committed at the time and in the circumstances specified: in other words, to state the substance of her case. I think that this is the true effect of the decisions of this court in *Frampton* v. *Frampton* [1951] W.N. 250 and *Jones* v. *Jones* [1954] 1 W.L.R. 1474; but I am saying what I am in deference to [the statement of counsel for the wife] that there is a practice which is supposed to necessitate

the making of a charge of adultery merely because the charge of reasonable belief in adultery is being put forward, whether by way of defence or as the case may be. Therefore it is desirable, I think, that the matter should be brought back to where it is left in *Jones* v. *Jones* . . . namely, that what is required is a correct statement of what is the substance of the wife's case, but that adultery should not be charged merely as a matter of course."

Although, as a matter of practice, it is right not to make allegations of adultery where none can be proved, nevertheless it is very difficult to see how a party can prove a bona fide belief on reasonable grounds of the other party's adultery unless adultery is also alleged. As Davies, L.J., said in *Forbes* v. *Forbes* [1954] 1 W.L.R. 1526, at p. 1534: —

" The fact that a petitioner has not chosen to bring and does not now make a charge of adultery may well be a most relevant matter for consideration when the court is asked to find that the petitioner on reasonable grounds believes, and has believed for three years preceding the presentation of the petition, that the respondent had committed adultery."

In *Sullivan's* case, the allegation in fact was of adultery, and the justices found that the adultery was not proved but that the husband had reasonable grounds for believing his wife had committed adultery, and therefore the President's remarks were strictly obiter. It seems that a spouse who says in the witness box: " I cannot prove my wife has committed adultery " faces a hopeless task if he proceeds to say: " I have reasonable grounds for believing she has committed adultery." Therefore, in practice, it is inevitable that if the allegation of reasonable belief is to be made seriously, it can only succeed if it is put in the alternative to an allegation of adultery.

(iv) *Not easy to establish this defence*

The *Glenister* defence is not easily established, and Karminski, J., in *Jones* v. *Jones* [1953] 1 W.L.R. 867, at p. 871, in emphasising this, said that it fell into the category of charges easy to make and less easy to prove.

The rule was applied in *Everitt* v. *Everitt* [1949] P. 374. A husband continued to associate with a woman with whom he had had sexual relations before marriage, and this the wife knew. Within six months of his marriage he had gone to live in the house of the other woman, and the court held that this was conduct "calculated to make the wife believe that he had resumed and intended to continue an association with his old love which, by reason of his intervening marriage, had now become an adulterous association." On the other hand, when a woman confessed to her husband that she was in love with another man and genuinely sought her husband's help to overcome her feelings, the court held the husband had not reasonable grounds for believing in his wife's adultery (*Forbes* v. *Forbes* [1954] 1 W.L.R. 1526).

In *Kemp* v. *Kemp* [1953] 2 All E.R. 553 (Divisional Court) the husband had committed adultery, which the wife had condoned, and some years later began to stay out regularly until the early hours of the morning. He admitted he had been out with a woman, but said there was nothing wrong in their association. The wife went, with the husband's consent, to spend Christmas with relatives, but did not return and took out a summons alleging desertion. The justices, by a majority, dismissed the summons stating that the husband's conduct was not such as to compel her to leave the house, nor was it his intention to break off matrimonial relations. Lord Merriman said such an inference was unjustifiable, and that as the husband was carrying on a clandestine association, she had every right to object, having regard to the circumstances under which she had taken him back. He referred to the case of *Winscom* v. *Winscom and Plowden* (1864), 3 Sw. & Tr. 380, which decided that condoned adultery may be revived by subsequent misconduct and improprieties short of, but tending to, adultery, which was approved in *Tilley* v. *Tilley* [1949] P. 240. Lord Merriman commented that if such conduct was sufficient to revive condoned adultery, surely it was sufficient to justify a wife leaving her husband, and to sustain a charge of desertion.

(v) *The spouse under suspicion should be asked for an explanation*

If this is not done, the court may come to the conclusion that the spouse who is invoking the *Glenister* defence is merely doing so as a pretext for bringing cohabitation to an end (*Beer* v. *Beer* [1948] P. 10), and in *Allen* v. *Allen* [1951] 1 All E.R. 724, at p. 726, Hodson, L.J., commented on the husband's failure to seek an explanation, and said: —

"I should be slow to say that a man or woman who finds

incriminating documents in the possession of his or her
spouse is entitled by that circumstance alone to draw an
inference entitling him or her to refuse to live with the other
spouse without giving the spouse an opportunity of making
an explanation."

If no explanation is given, or the one given is unreasonable,
the defendant's case will be strengthened. If the explanation
is reasonable, then the defence fails.

In *Marsden* v. *Marsden* [1968] P. 544 (Divisional Court, Sir J.
Simon, P., and Cairns, J.) the husband suspected his wife had
committed adultery but never asked her for an explanation or
told her of his suspicions or the grounds of his belief. The
husband's attitude because of his suspicions made the wife
miserable. Magistrates dismissed summonses for persistent cruelty,
desertion and wilful neglect to maintain but the Divisional Court
allowed her appeal, holding that the wife was justified in leaving
since the husband could not rely on reasonable grounds for his
suspicions since he had not given her a chance to explain.

Where the wife has been associating with men for company's
sake, Bucknill, L.J., in *Kafton* v. *Kafton* [1948] 1 All E.R. 435,
thought that the husband could not possibly establish that he had
good grounds for leaving her, but if there is something more,
such as incriminating documents, the defence could be established.

Where the conduct upon which the belief is based is brought
about or actively promoted by the other spouse, the *Glenister* rule
has no application (*Hartley* v. *Hartley* [1955] 1 W.L.R. 384) for
the defendant would be the author of his own wrong, and his
conduct is clearly analogous to connivance or conduct conducing.
In *Hartley's* case, the husband was suspicious of his wife's association with one *P*. One night he saw them kissing and embracing,
but said nothing until a week later when his wife denied it. This
was in February, 1954. In September, *P* said in front of the
husband that he preferred the husband's wife to his own, and
would stay with her. In November the husband left. It was held
that although he might have taken a firmer line, there was
nothing in his conduct to suggest he had promoted or brought
about the conduct on which he was relying to base his belief in
her adultery.

(vi) *The temporary nature of the rule*

The defence is only valid so long as the belief is reasonably held. It may be dispelled by an explanation or further evidence, or the decision of a court on whether adultery has been committed (*Allen* v. *Allen* [1951] 1 All E.R. 724; *Everitt* v. *Everitt* [1949] P. 374).

Allen v. *Allen* is a direct authority for saying that the *Glenister* defence cannot justify a separation from the other spouse which has taken place, or which has continued, after a court has acquitted that other of adultery, but this finding does not prevent a spouse from saying that until the date of that finding, his or her belief in the alleged adultery was good cause for living apart from the other spouse (*James* v. *James* [1948] 1 All E.R. 214, and *Everitt* v. *Everitt* [1949] P. 374).

In *West* v. *West* [1954] P. 444 the wife applied for maintenance in the High Court under s. 23 of the Matrimonial Causes Act, 1950, and two days later the husband petitioned for divorce on the ground of the wife's adultery. This petition was dismissed. The Court of Appeal held that as the husband had a bona fide and reasonable belief in her adultery until the date of her summons, he had an effective answer to it.

If a charge of adultery is not proved, the spouse in question is cleared of the charge, and the other spouse cannot say that, because the judge had said the charge was not proved, and not positively that adultery did not take place, he still had reasonable grounds for a belief in her adultery (*Allen* v. *Allen, supra*). See *Edwards* v. *Edwards* (1965), 109 Sol.J. 175.

(vii) *Can be used offensively*

The rule in *Glenister*, which originated as a defence, can be used offensively as well. In *Baker* v. *Baker* [1954] P. 33 a wife left her husband after repeated protests against her husband's association with another woman. She issued a summons for desertion, and gave notice alleging her husband had committed adultery. The magistrate rejected this allegation, but held the wife had reasonable grounds for believing he had committed adultery, and made an order.

This is an illustration of the rule that if a spouse has just cause for leaving, then the other spouse is guilty of constructive desertion. Lord Merriman, at p. 35, said: —

" In my opinion, the magistrate was justified in saying as a matter of law, that if a man (I am putting it hypothetically now) deliberately induces the belief that he is carrying on an adulterous association, and his wife leaves the matrimonial home in consequence, he can be held to have expelled her, and therefore to have deserted her, even though she fails to bring a charge, or to prove the fact of adultery."

Lord Merriman did indicate that there was a simpler approach in this case, namely, that the husband had by his conduct expelled the wife.

The word " expelled " was probably used to conform to the current jargon, but since *Lang* v. *Lang* (decided two years later— [1955] A.C. 402) " just cause " would be more in conformity with the facts.

The divorce court in *Hunter* v. *Hunter* (1961), *The Times,* 14th November, laid down three questions that magistrates should ask themselves in this type of case. A wife had told her husband to go, and he went. She then alleged desertion on the ground that he had by his conduct induced in her the belief that he was misconducting himself with another woman. The questions set out by Lord Merriman, P., were: —

(1) Did the wife reasonably believe that the husband was misconducting himself with another woman or other women?
(2) Did the husband, by his conduct and the explanations he gave to his wife, induce that belief?
(3) Was the wife actuated by that belief in directing the husband to go?

Lord Merriman went on to say that if a husband induced by his conduct—it must not be induced by gossip or hearsay—a belief in his wife that he was conducting an improper affair with another woman, and the wife, acting on that belief, left the husband, or turned the husband out, she could not be held to be in desertion. Indeed, he would be the deserter.

The discovery of past adultery may be just cause for one spouse leaving the other, and then bringing a summons for desertion (*Kemp* v. *Kemp* [1961] 1 W.L.R. 1030, which corrected a previous ruling in *Teall* v. *Teall* [1938] P. 250 that the mere discovery of a past adulterous association was not sufficient).

(viii) *Reasonable belief in* ADULTERY *and nothing else*

In *Cox* v. *Cox* [1958] 1 W.L.R. 340 the husband heard a conversation between his wife and her sister in which the wife stated that a man at work had shown affection for her, and she had embraced him in daytime which had caused him sexual excitement, and this had led to jests by fellow employees. The husband left his wife and, on a complaint by the wife that she had been deserted, the husband alleged he had an honest and reasonable belief in her adultery. This was accepted by the justices, but on appeal the Divisional Court (Lord Merriman, P., and Collingwood, J.) held the husband guilty of desertion since there was no evidence that there had been an opportunity to commit adultery.

Collingwood, J., at p. 344, said the husband had put the worst construction on anything the wife had done, but the test was an objective one. He referred to *Haswell* v. *Haswell and Sanderson* (1859), 1 Sw. & Tr. 502, where the husband had seen his wife behaving indecently in a room upstairs. The court there had found that the husband was justified in leaving his wife because she had submitted to indecent liberties.

> " With regard to that decision it is to be noted that the Judge Ordinary expressly refrained from deciding whether the wife's conduct was such as to justify the husband in turning her out, or would have afforded an answer to a suit for restitution. Further, the circumstances differ considerably from those in the present case. In *Haswell* v. *Haswell* the wife was found in the home indulging in an act of sexual familiarity."

He went on to say with reference to *Glenister*: —

> " But we think that, because of the nature of the offence of adultery, the principle of that case should not be extended beyond its proper scope. For example, it would be going further than is warranted by the reasoning upon which the decision in *Glenister* v. *Glenister* is based to hold that a husband would be justified in leaving his wife upon the belief that she had been cruel to him; or that she had given him some other ground for complaint which he reasonably believed would afford him the right to leave her."

The last remarks were obiter, and seem to be in conflict with the case of *Ousey* v. *Ousey* (1874), L.R. 3 P. & D. 223, where the husband had left the wife because of her refusal to consummate the marriage and the Judge Ordinary held the husband was justified in leaving his wife in consequence of his belief that she was wronging him. *Ousey* was not cited in argument in *Cox* v. *Cox*.

(k) Harm to child

In *G.* v. *G.* [1964] 2 W.L.R. 250 (D.C.—Sir Jocelyn Simon, P., Cairns, J.) the husband summoned the wife alleging desertion. The wife had refused to allow the husband to reside in the matrimonial home on the ground that he had endangered the health of the children, because his behaviour had terrified them. He suffered from a mental illness. The justices dismissed the summons, holding the wife had just cause for living apart. The husband's appeal was dismissed.

It was argued on behalf of the husband that only misconduct on the part of the husband constitutes in law a justification for the wife to live apart, and this misconduct must be either a matrimonial offence or some grave and weighty matter approximating to a matrimonial offence. On the facts the simple answer to that was that the husband's conduct amounted to misconduct since his behaviour to his children amounted to cruelty since he frightened them and caused one of them to have serious nervous disorders.

The learned President, however, said there could be good cause without any fault, so that neither party was a deserter, if for instance a spouse was deported, or sent to prison for life, or where there is danger to health of the other spouse or a child. He went on to say that if the wife manifested an intention to live apart permanently she would be in desertion.

It should be noticed that this case was decided before *Williams* v. *Williams* [1964] A.C. 698. Two of the cases on which the learned President relied, *Hayward* v. *Hayward* (1858), 1 Sw. & Tr. 81 and *Hanbury* v. *Hanbury* [1892] P. 222, have to be considered in the light of this decision in the House of Lords. It is submitted that on the facts of *G.* v. *G.*, the husband's conduct amounted to cruelty to his children, that his mental illness afforded no excuse for this conduct and that therefore in law it amounted to matrimonial misconduct, and that, the wife having refused to let him live in the matrimonial home, he was constructively in desertion.

(l) Drunkenness

In the important case of *Hall* v. *Hall* [1962] 1 W.L.R. 1246, a wife left her husband because of his continual drinking and the

magistrates made an order on the ground of constructive desertion. This was reversed by the Divisional Court [1962] 1 W.L.R.
478, but restored by the Court of Appeal. The dictum of
Asquith, L.J., in *Buchler* was quoted with approval. Ormerod,
L.J., said at p. 1251: —

> "The question is not whether drunkenness of itself is
> sufficient to amount to expulsive conduct. The question is
> whether the conduct of this husband (caused, no doubt
> initially, by the drunkenness) was sufficient to justify his
> wife in leaving him and saying that she found it impossible
> to live with him."

(m) Choice of a home

Which spouse has the right to say where the matrimonial home
shall be? There is no answer to this question. Normally, the
home is chosen near to the husband's place of employment.
Henn Collins, J., in *Mansey* v. *Mansey* [1940] P. 139, at p. 140,
said: —

> "The rights of a husband, as they used to be, have been
> considerably circumscribed in favour of the wife without very
> much, if any, curtailment of his obligations, but we have not
> yet got to the point where the wife can decide where the
> matrimonial home is to be, and if the husband says he
> wants to live in such and such a place, assuming always that
> he is not doing it to spite his wife and the accommodation
> is of a kind that you would expect a man in his position to
> occupy, the wife is under the necessity of sharing that home
> with him. If she will not, she is committing a matrimonial
> offence: she is deserting him."

(i) May be settled by agreement

That the home should be chosen by mutual consent is common
sense and the usual case; but there are exceptions. Much depends
on the special circumstances of the case. For instance, in *King* v.
King [1942] P. 1, at the time of the marriage the husband was
73 and the wife 37. The wife was in business which she conducted
from her place of residence, and the husband agreed at the time
of the marriage that the matrimonial home should be at her
residence. Seven months later, without any material change of
circumstances, the husband moved to his former home and asked
his wife to join him. She refused and cohabitation was never
resumed. It was held that the agreement was not against public

policy, that the wife had a reasonable excuse for refusing to comply with her husband's demand that they should live in his house, and that she was not a deserter but he was.

Lord Merriman said that, speaking generally, he did not in the least dissent from *Mansey* v. *Mansey* that a husband has the right to say where the matrimonial home shall be. The present case had this special feature, that there was an agreement between the parties which amounted to this, that for good reasons common to both sides, the parties had agreed that the wife's residence should be, *rebus sic stantibus*, the proper matrimonial home. That did not mean that the wife was entitled to dictate where the matrimonial home should be if the good reasons on which the agreement was based ceased to exist, or if for some good reason through a change of circumstances called for a change. In the present case the husband had no right to go back on the understanding.

(ii) *Each entitled to an equal voice in deciding*

The case of *Dunn* v. *Dunn* [1949] P. 98 was more difficult. The husband was a sailor. The wife, who was very deaf, had lived in the neighbourhood of Morpeth all her life and her husband, at her suggestion, bought a house there which became the matrimonial home. The husband signed on for a long term in the Navy, and after quarrels, found himself stationed in Immingham, where he got rooms, and asked his wife with their child to join him. She refused. They never resumed cohabitation, and the husband committed adultery. Then he brought a petition alleging desertion by his wife, and asked for discretion. Jones, J., dismissed the petition, and the Court of Appeal dismissed the appeal. As the three judges differed among themselves, it is not easy to arrive at the *ratio decidendi*. Nor is the decision easier to understand, when it is said by Denning, L.J., that neither party had been unreasonable. According to Denning, L.J., the decision turned on the onus of proof, and the husband had not discharged the burden of proving that his wife had deserted him without cause. He said that the proposition that the husband has a right to say where the home should be was not a proposition of law, and at p. 103: —

> " It is simply a proposition of ordinary good sense arising from the fact that the husband is usually the wage earner

and has to live near his work. It is not a proposition which
applies in all cases. The decision where the home should be
is a decision which affects both the parties and their children.
It is their duty to decide it by agreement, by give and take,
and not by the imposition of the will of one over that of the
other. Each is entitled to an equal voice in the ordering of
the affairs which are their common concern. Neither has a
casting vote, though, to be sure, they should try so to arrange
their family affairs that they spend their time together as a
family and not apart. If such an arrangement is frustrated
by the unreasonableness of one or the other, and this leads
to a separation between them, then the party who has
produced the separation by reason of his or her unreasonable
behaviour is guilty of desertion. The situations which may
arise are so various that I think it unwise to attempt any
more precise test than that of unreasonableness."

(iii) *The test is reasonableness*

Two cases, in which Lord Merrivale gave judgments in the same
year, illustrate the difficulties of this class of case, and the way
they should be approached.

In *Millichamp* v. *Millichamp* (1931), 146 L.T. 96, the parties
had agreed, while engaged, to live with the husband's mother.
Differences arose between the wife and her mother-in-law, and
she left. The wife summoned the husband for wilful neglect to
maintain, and the husband, in defence, said that he was prepared
to have her back in his mother's home for that was all he could
afford. Lord Merrivale, at p. 97, said: —

"The husband submits that he has not neglected his duty.
His first duty was to his wife. It could be limited by an
arrangement, but his first duty was to provide her with a
home according to his circumstances. The justices came to
the conclusion that by reason of the difficulty about his
marriage he failed in that duty because he put his mother
first, instead of putting his wife first, subject to such limitation as I have mentioned."

The court confirmed the decision of the justices.

Contrasted with this is *Jackson* v. *Jackson* (1932), 146 L.T.
406, where the husband required his wife to live next door to his
mother. The magistrates held that this, plus control of the purse
and housekeeping with the assistance of his mother, constituted
unbearable conditions, and made an order on the ground of wilful
neglect, though they negatived desertion. In passing, it may be

mentioned that the cases often reveal this compromise by magistrates. In the section on Wilful Neglect to Maintain, it will be shown that it is not permissible to make an order under such circumstances, unless the parting was by mutual consent (see p. 267 et seq.). In allowing the appeal, Lord Merrivale said: —

> " Is it right to say that the conditions imposed on the wife were unbearable for her or any other wife, conditions which it was not competent for a reasonable husband to set up? Were they such conditions that a reasonable wife, being so treated by an unreasonable husband, could not be expected to proceed with the conjugal life? The husband took a house next to his mother's. The wife resolved not to be in contact with his mother if she could avoid it. It could not be said that taking the house next to the mother's was an abuse of the husband's marital duties, despite the irritation it was likely to cause. I am not able to say that the taking of the house next to the mother's, if he did not put his wife under his mother's domination, was necessarily wrong."

The result is that if one party is reasonable and the other is unreasonable then the reasonable party wins. But what if both are unreasonable? There's the rub, for matrimonial disputes are the bitterest of all disputes, and temper, unreason and hatred displace love in many cases. Two cases of unreasonable spouses had different results.

In *McGowan* v. *McGowan* [1948] 2 All E.R. 1032 the parties were married in 1945 while the husband was in the services, but on his demobilisation they went to live with his parents. After three days the wife left, refusing to live any longer with his parents. In 1947 she secured a flat and asked her husband to join her, but he refused. She took out summonses for desertion and wilful neglect, and once more the magistrates compromised by dismissing the desertion summons and making an order on the wilful neglect summons. They held the wife had no good reason for leaving the matrimonial home, but that the husband was unreasonable in not joining her in the flat. The Divisional Court (Hodson and Pilcher, JJ.) allowed the appeal.

Hodson, J., accepted the test of reasonableness. *Millichamp* v. *Millichamp* was distinguished because there the husband put his mother first. After referring to Denning, L.J.'s judgment in *Dunn* v. *Dunn* [1949] P. 98, he said, at p. 1035: —

> " So long as the husband's obligation to maintain his wife

remains, he can fulfil this obligation by providing his wife with a reasonable home. She does not succeed in establishing that he has not provided her with a reasonable home by showing that, having left him unreasonably she has, by her independent action, found accommodation somewhere else which he is unwilling to accept. To put the matter in another way, having deserted him in the first place, she does not bring her desertion to an end by offering to live with her husband elsewhere than in the place of his choice, unless she can show that the place of his choice is not a reasonable home for him to offer her, having regard to all the circumstances."

Pilcher, J., said: —

" The authorities referred to by my lord make it clear that neither husband nor wife has any legal right to dictate the whereabouts of the matrimonial home. In the event of any unfortunate difference of view, the rights of the parties must be governed by reason."

In *Munro* v. *Munro* [1950] 1 All E.R. 832 (C.A.) (Bucknill and Denning, L.JJ., and Roxburgh, J.) the parties, on marriage, went to live with the husband's mother in the south of France. The mother had a dominating personality, and the husband was addicted to drink and was unemployed. The wife left. The husband visited his wife in London, but refused to make a home there. He suggested they should return to his mother's home in France. She refused. The wife applied for restitution of conjugal rights, and it was held the wife was entitled to refuse.

Willmer, J., was faced in *Walter* v. *Walter* (1949), 65 T.L.R. 680, with the following facts. The husband had taken employment at *G* which was too far from the matrimonial home at *E* to journey there each day, and he wished his wife to join him at *G*. The wife worked at *E* and would not move to *G*. Willmer, J., referred to both *Dunn* v. *Dunn* and *McGowan* v. *McGowan,* and said the husband had no absolute right to say where the matrimonial home should be. Neither could dictate to the other. Where the home should be should be settled by agreement and mutual give and take. Neither party had proved that the separation had been brought about by the fault of the other.

(iv) *Guiding principles*

It is difficult to discern in the judgments in the above cases a guiding principle whereby the magistrates can decide every case of this kind.

The judges have been at pains to emphasise that both parties to the marriage are entitled to an equal say in deciding where the matrimonial home shall be, and that there is no rule of law that the husband has the casting vote. On the other hand, as a matter of practical convenience the home should be reasonably near the husband's place of employment. This would apply to the great majority of cases, but there may be exceptions, as where the parties have agreed otherwise. It may also be that the home is unsuitable for various reasons, and the wife can rightly object to living there, as where she is asked to live with a mother-in-law who is particularly unfriendly to her.

The best test is reasonableness. The parties should, if possible, agree where the home should be, and if they cannot, the one who is unreasonable is in the wrong. What is to happen if both are unreasonable? In the magistrates' court it is the wife who almost invariably issues the summons, and if she proves her husband has been unreasonable, she will establish desertion, but if the break up of the home is due to her own unreasonableness, even though her husband has been unreasonable too, then she should fail.

G. Can both parties be in desertion at the same time?

Even if it were theoretically possible for both husband and wife to desert one another at the same time, it is only in exceptional cases that this could happen. Desertion is not a static conception but a developing one. Lord Merrivale said that desertion was not a withdrawal from a place but from a state of things. Of course, it can be withdrawal from a place as well. It also includes withdrawal from the society of the other spouse. There is no reason why both parties cannot simultaneously withdraw from a place, or a state of things or from each other. If it should be said that the withdrawal must be against the will of the other, then that too can happen simultaneously for both may be willing to live together subject to a condition that neither will accept. One feels that the decision in *Walter* v. *Walter* (1949), 65 T.L.R. 680, was an unfortunate and undesirable one. Both parties were willing to live together but only at a home of their own choosing. Because both were unreasonable, each had injured the other. Each was responsible for the break up of the marriage, and therefore each was guilty of desertion.

Lord Denning is the chief protagonist of this point of view.

In *Hosegood* v. *Hosegood* (1950), 66 T.L.R. (Pt. 1) 735, he considered, at p. 739, that state of affairs in *Walter* v. *Walter* and said that each must know full well that if he or she does not give way, the married life will be brought to an end, and continued: —

" I see no reason why the court should be forced to choose between them and say that one only is a deserter . . . I say this because I am afraid that the last seven lines of my judgment in *Dunn* v. *Dunn* [1948] P. 98 misled Willmer, J., in *Walter* v. *Walter* into thinking that where each is obstinate, neither is guilty of desertion; whereas the truth is that both may be."

No arguments have been advanced by any judge against this view, although it has been frowned upon by Lord Merriman (*Simpson* v. *Simpson* [1951] P. 320) and Jenkins, L.J. (*Lang* v. *Lang* (1955), *The Times,* 7th July) said he found the concept of mutual desertion difficult to understand while Hodson, L.J., in the same case thought on facts of this kind the parting amounted to separation by consent.

Denning, L.J., repeated his views in *Beigan* v. *Beigan* [1956] P. 313, at p. 320, and thought the only solution, where both were to blame, was to give each a decree.

While the usual case in desertion is that one party is in the wrong and the other in the right, it is submitted that this is not an essential requirement. It is common enough for both parties to be in the wrong, each having committed a matrimonial offence against the other and each being given relief. For instance, each may have committed adultery. Each can obtain a decree of divorce. In *Walter* v. *Walter* it was not correct to say that neither had proved the other in fault. The truth was that each had proved the other in fault.

In *Wevill* v. *Wevill* (1962), *The Times*, 15th February, Wrangham, J., thought it was not impossible for both parties to be in desertion at the same time, but he limited this to cases where the act of each spouse was outside the knowledge of the other, so that no inference of consent should arise. This limitation seems to be unnecessary. It is for the court to draw the correct inference.

The same judge in *Price* v. *Price* [1968] 1 W.L.R. 1735 saw no logical reason why both spouses could not be in desertion at the same time, and granted decrees to each spouse. Due to a quarrel each spouse determined to get rid of the other. Each made up his or her mind to desert the other. Wrangham, J., referred to *Beigan* v. *Beigan* [1956] P. 313 and *Hosegood* v. *Hosegood* (1950), 66 T.L.R. (Pt. 1) 735, C.A.

H. Is there a half-way house?

Just cause is a good defence to actual desertion. It has been held in many cases to be a good ground for complaint in constructive desertion. Can there be a case where the just cause is good enough for a defence, but not sufficient as a ground of complaint? Since just cause in either case has to be grave and weighty, it is difficult to visualise a half-way house. This view is supported to some extent by the following quotation from the judgment of Sargant, L.J., in *Thomas* v. *Thomas* [1924] P. 194, at p. 202: —

> "It was strongly urged by counsel for the appellant that though the facts might be such as to justify the wife in resisting an application for restitution for conjugal rights, it does not follow that they are sufficient to establish a continuing desertion by the husband; and it was suggested that there might be a half-way house, an intermediate position in which the one spouse may be released from the obligation of cohabitation, while the other is nevertheless not guilty of a continuance of desertion. The reasoning of the learned President rather tends to negative this suggestion . . . it is unnecessary to decide this question for the purposes of this case."

Consent would appear to be the only exception to the above proposition. Certainly, the absence of intention to expel is not (*Gollins* v. *Gollins* [1964] A.C. 644 and *Hall* v. *Hall* [1963] P. 378).

Furthermore, if there were a half-way house, it would make nonsense of the doctrine of turning the tables where a bona fide offer to return by a deserter is rejected (see p. 142).

I. Misconduct short of just cause

There is the curious case of *Postlethwaite* v. *Postlethwaite* [1957] 1 All E.R. 909, where the wife refused to join her husband and was found to be in desertion. Reliance was placed by the wife on Matrimonial Causes Act, 1950, s. 4 (2), proviso, which read: —

" Provided that the court shall not be bound to pronounce a decree of divorce and may dismiss the petition . . . if, in the opinion of the court, the petitioner has been guilty . . . (iv) where the ground of the petition is . . . desertion, of such wilful neglect or misconduct as has conduced to the . . . desertion."

The difficulty facing Willmer, J., was that if there was misconduct by the husband which in fact conduced to her leaving, then it caused her to leave and that would be just cause, and therefore there would be no offence of desertion. Willmer, J., accepted the position that there was a no man's land between just cause and wear and tear of married life and that since some meaning must be attributed to the statute it must refer to conduct which is not sufficiently bad to amount to just cause, but which is something worse than ordinary wear and tear. Counsel suggested there might be conduct which would not justify the separation but which would excuse it. This, said the judge, was a question of fact. As the judge found there was nothing beyond ordinary wear and tear, his views on the law were obiter. One may comment that to distinguish between conduct which justifies a separation and conduct that excuses it is a refinement which ought not to be introduced into the law on this subject. There appears to be no decided case which has in fact made the distinction.

Cannot reasonably be expected to live with the respondent

The case of *Pheasant* v. *Pheasant* [1972] 1 All E.R. 587 was decided by Ormrod, J., on the wording of the Divorce Reform Act, 1969, s. 2 (1) (*b*) (now s. 1 (2) (*b*) of the Matrimonial Causes Act, 1973) which provided that proof that the marriage has irretrievably broken down can be provided by satisfying the court that the respondent has behaved in such a way that the petitioner cannot reasonably be expected to live with the respondent.

This section is not applicable in the magistrates' court, but the learned judge's judgment is useful in connection with constructive desertion.

The husband's case was that the wife did not give him that spontaneous affection for which his nature craved and that in consequence it was impossible for him to live with her. He did not criticise his wife's conduct, and the wife said she would welcome her husband back and did not believe the marriage had irretrievably broken down.

Ormrod, J., in dismissing the petition, said the test to be applied was similar to that used in constructive desertion. There had to be shown a breach in the wife's obligations to her husband. He said that the subject had to be approached more from the point of view of breach of obligation rather than in terms of the idea of a matrimonial offence. This is, with respect, a distinction without a difference, or much difference, since a breach of marital obligation is a matrimonial offence, though it may be of more or less gravity.

The case of *Pheasant* v. *Pheasant* was not followed in *Livingstone-Stallard* v. *Livingstone-Stallard* [1974] 2 All E.R. 766, where Dunn, J., said that the notion of constructive desertion is unhelpful in construing s. 1 (2) (*b*) of the 1973 Act, the proper test being to ask whether any right thinking person would conclude in all the circumstances that one spouse has behaved in such a way that the other cannot reasonably be expected to live with him.

In this case the wife petitioned for divorce relying upon the said section. She had had to live in a constant atmosphere of criticism, disapproval and boorish behaviour by the husband and she was granted a decree nisi.

IV. TERMINATION OF DESERTION

A. Resumption of cohabitation

Desertion can be put an end to by cohabitation. What amounts to a resumption of cohabitation is not always an easy question to decide. It is the policy of the law to facilitate reconciliation and encourage efforts in that direction (*Cohen* v. *Cohen* [1940] A.C. 631). Therefore, casual acts of sexual intercourse have been held not to amount to a resumption of cohabitation. On the other hand, a resumption of cohabitation need not amount to a full reinstatement of married life. The difficulty in each case is to find out where the line is to be drawn.

In *Williams* v. *Williams* [1904] P. 145, where the wife had summoned the husband for desertion, and before the hearing the parties had first resumed cohabitation and then separated again, Jeune, P., said at p. 147: —

> " The effect of the condonation was to put an end to the cause of complaint—not by virtue of the Act, but by force of law. The principle acted on by the judges of this court, and, in the ecclesiastical courts, by our predecessors, that the moment you find a resumption of cohabitation there is an end to any previous desertion, is founded on or has been recognised by the courts of common law."

In *Cook* v. *Cook* [1949] 1 All E.R. 384, a wife left her husband because he was living with another woman, but later she returned as his housekeeper and the husband paid for her services. The Divisional Court (Lord Merriman, P., and Pearce, J.) reversed the magistrates and held that cohabitation had not been resumed. Pearce, J., at p. 388, said: —

> " The words ' resumption of cohabitation ' must mean resuming a state of things, that is to say, a setting up of a matrimonial home together, and that involves a bilateral intention on the part of both spouses to do so."

Mummery v. *Mummery* [1942] P. 107 was a case where the husband deserted his wife in 1937 and on a single occasion in June he spent a night with her and marital intercourse took place. She hoped that married life would be resumed, but he had no such intention, left her the next morning and never returned. The question was whether this act of intercourse interrupted the continuous desertion of the husband. Lord Merriman, P., held that it did not. He pointed out that a resumption of cohabitation puts an end to desertion not only because it condones it, but because such a resumption is the exact negation of desertion. He doubted whether any judge could give a completely exhaustive definition of cohabitation, but it involved setting up a matrimonial home together, and that involved a bilateral intention on the part of both spouses to do so. He also relied on *Rowell* v. *Rowell* [1900] 1 Q.B. 9, where three or four acts of intercourse were held not to have put an end to a separation deed.

Mummery v. *Mummery* was followed in the case of *Bartram* v. *Bartram* [1950] P. 1 which, however, was a much more difficult case. There a wife had deserted her husband but returned to his roof only because there was no other accommodation near to her work, but did not sleep with him, cook for him, or associate with him except that she sometimes had meals at the same table. It was held by the Court of Appeal that the mere fact that she lived there as a lodger did not amount to a resumption of cohabitation.

The difficulties of this subject are illustrated by the following three cases: *Whitney* v. *Whitney* [1951] P. 250, *Viney* v. *Viney* [1951] P. 457 and *Perry* v. *Perry* [1952] P. 203, where there was considerable conflict of judicial opinion.

In *Whitney* v. *Whitney* [1951] P. 250 the wife deserted her husband in 1945, and between then and 1947 her husband visited her on about half a dozen weekends, stayed with her and had sexual intercourse. It was held by Willmer, J., following *Mummery* v. *Mummery* [1942] P. 107 and *Bartram* v. *Bartram* [1950] P. 1, that there had not been a resumption of cohabitation.

In the same year, the case of *Viney* v. *Viney* [1951] P. 457 was heard by a Divisional Court, and the judges, Lord Merriman, P., and Havers, J., purported (according to the headnote in the Law Reports) to overrule *Whitney* v. *Whitney*. They certainly disapproved of some of the observations of Willmer, J., in that case. The facts, however, differed in this important respect, that the wife in *Viney* v. *Viney* had committed adultery. She had obtained an order from the magistrates on the ground of wilful neglect to maintain, but that order had subsequently been discharged on the ground of her adultery. This was in 1947. In 1950 she returned to her husband's home and tried to effect a reconciliation, and on at least three occasions intercourse took place, and she subsequently gave birth to a child. From March to October she lived with the husband in the same house and then he turned her out. She took out a summons for desertion, and this was dismissed by the magistrates, and the wife appealed. The magistrates said that cohabitation had not been resumed.

On general principles one would have thought that there had been a resumption of cohabitation, and that by his intercourse the husband had condoned his wife's adultery, and that by turning her out he was in desertion.

One of the difficulties of this case is that both judges treated the doctrine of condonation as being the same for adultery and desertion. As will be seen, condonation only applies to adultery and cruelty, and special considerations apply to desertion. A husband, therefore, can by intercourse be held to have forgiven his wife for adultery, but not to have resumed cohabitation with her so as to stop desertion by her.

Lord Merriman's criticism of the judgment of Willmer, J., in *Whitney* v. *Whitney* is as follows (*Viney* v. *Viney* [1951] P. 457, at p. 462): —

> " I venture to say that the judge misdirected himself, because he ignored the vital fact that in *Bartram* v. *Bartram* [1950] P. 1, there was lacking the essential element, which is present in the case we are now deciding, that the husband had voluntarily had sexual intercourse with his wife, and that *Henderson* v. *Henderson* [1944] A.C. 49 decides that that is absolutely conclusive of the fact that he has thereby re-installed her as his wife."

Henderson v. *Henderson* [1944] A.C. 49 was a case of adultery and not desertion and was overruled by s. 1 of the 1963 Act (now s. 42 of the Matrimonial Causes Act, 1965). The President distinguished his own decision in *Mummery* v. *Mummery* on the ground that there the wife was the petitioner and submission to intercourse by a wife is not conclusive of condonation.

The Court of Appeal in *Perry* v. *Perry* [1952] P. 203 approved *Whitney* v. *Whitney* and the strictures on it, in *Viney* v. *Viney*, were disapproved.

(i) *Condonation and desertion*

Does the law with regard to condonation properly apply to desertion? By condonation is meant reinstatement of the guilty spouse by the innocent spouse with the result that the offence is completely blotted out, subject to the condition that it may be revived if the guilty spouse offends again. This doctrine applies to cruelty and possibly to other matrimonial offences as well, and until recently applied to adultery, but now by s. 42 (3) of the Matrimonial Causes Act, 1965, adultery which has been condoned shall not be capable of being revived.

Condonation has been held not to apply to desertion, though it is probable that this applies to actual desertion only, and not constructive desertion. It was thought that because of the rule in *Henderson* v. *Henderson, supra,* reconciliation would be impeded if condonation applied to desertion, but as we have seen that rule does not now apply. Casual acts of intercourse do not put an end to desertion (*Mummery* v. *Mummery* [1942] P. 107). It is in the power of the deserter to bring desertion to an end by making a bona fide offer to return. In other words, the onus is on the deserter and not the deserted spouse to bring the desertion to an end in this respect, whereas in adultery and cruelty the initiative is with the innocent party.

Evershed, M.R., in *Perry* v. *Perry* [1952] P. 203 said that condonation cannot properly be applicable to the offence of desertion.

In *Harvey* v. *Harvey* [1956] P. 102, at p. 107, Hodson, L.J., referred to his own judgment in *Perry* v. *Perry* [1952] P. 203, at p. 232, where he said: —

> "Accordingly, in my opinion, as I ventured to suggest in *Lane* v. *Lane* [1952] P. 34, when considering a current period of desertion, the primary question is: Aye or No, 'is it terminated?'—not 'is it condoned?' It can be terminated by a resumption of cohabitation involving a mutual or, as it has been called, a bilateral act, or it can be terminated by the deserter returning, or even offering to return, provided the offer is not one which for some reason the offeree is entitled to refuse, but it is not necessarily terminated as a matter of law by the sexual act."

Both *Whitney* v. *Whitney* [1950] P. 250 and *Viney* v. *Viney* [1951] P. 457, and the whole subject of condonation and desertion were considered by the Court of Appeal in *Perry* v. *Perry, supra.* In this case the wife deserted her husband in 1944 and went to live with her mother. The husband visited her from time to time and two or three isolated acts of intercourse took place between December, 1949, and March, 1950, as a result of which a child was born. The *animus deserendi* of the wife throughout never changed. The husband petitioned for divorce, and the commissioner, holding that he was bound by *Viney* v. *Viney,* dismissed it. The Court of Appeal allowed the appeal, and they held that the conception of condonation either in strictness or by analogy has no application to desertion, and to end or interrupt desertion there has to be a resumption of cohabitation, in the sense of setting up a home together accompanied by a common intention to do so. Therefore, sexual intercourse by itself does not bring desertion to an end even if it leads to the birth of a child. *Whitney* v. *Whitney* was approved, and the strictures of the Divisional Court in *Viney* v. *Viney* on the question were disapproved.

Evershed, M.R., at [1952] P. 215, said that, looking at the matter apart from authority, whether cohabitation had been resumed was a question of fact and degree, to be determined according to common sense principles. Just as the refusal of sexual intercourse by itself was not desertion, it was not unreasonable that participation in one or two acts of intercourse by the parties, who in all other respects repudiated the marriage relationship, should not be regarded as necessarily constituting a resumption of that relationship.

Jenkins, L.J., at p. 221, took a contrary view. He thought that, apart from authority, sexual intercourse between the parties was in itself essentially inconsistent with the continuance of desertion between them. It seemed to him inconsistent that sexual intercourse should be so decisive in condonation of adultery and cruelty, and not desertion. He pointed out the difficulty when the wife has committed adultery and is also in desertion (at p. 222): —

"The husband, by his conduct, has taken his wife back as his wife, adultress though she has been. How can it consistently be said that, although he has taken her back and reinstated her as his wife, she has not come back to him, but has been continuously, even during the decisive act of intercourse, in a state of desertion from him?"

Both judges, however, held that the authorities bound them to decide that in fact sexual intercourse of itself was not cohabitation, and that the law as to condonation was not applicable even by analogy to desertion.

Jenkins, L.J., said at p. 225: —

"The judgment in *Mummery* v. *Mummery* [1942] P. 107 received the unqualified approval of this court in *Bartram* v. *Bartram* [1950] P. 1, and must therefore be regarded as an authority binding on us, and it seems to me to establish the proposition that, in order to terminate or interrupt the state of desertion between a deserted and a deserting spouse, there must be a resumption of cohabitation, that is to say, the setting up of a matrimonial home together pursuant to a 'bilateral,' which I take to mean a 'common' or 'mutual' intention to do so."

and he referred to the words of Denning, L.J., in *Bartram* v. *Bartram* that any other view hampered attempts at reconciliation.

The lords justices in *Perry* v. *Perry* based their conclusion that condonation did not apply to desertion on two intrinsic factors, namely: —

1. Condonation involves the right of the injured spouse to elect whether to affirm the marriage notwithstanding the condoned offence, but desertion is a continuing offence requiring the deserted spouse, at all times up to the presentation of the petition or hearing of the summons, to affirm the marriage, otherwise the desertion becomes in effect by consent.

2. The doctrine of revival of a condoned offence by subsequent misconduct cannot apply to desertion, at any rate for divorce purposes, since the continuity of the desertion required by s. 1 (1) (b) of the Matrimonial Causes Act, 1950, would be irretrievably broken. (See Evershed, M.R., and Jenkins, L.J. [1952] P. 203, at p. 213 and p. 228 respectively.)

Perry v. *Perry* is an established authority, but two more recent cases show that there remained a certain judicial uneasiness about the doctrine it laid down. Lord Merriman in *W.* v. *W.* (*No.* 2) [1962] P. 49 said he could not understand how one can condone cruelty, and yet not condone desertion based on that cruelty. This was a case where the wife had left her husband on account of his convictions for incest against a daughter and an offence against another daughter. After his release from prison, the husband attempted to be reconciled and the parties had intercourse on a number of occasions. The magistrates made an order on the ground of constructive desertion, on the ground that his criminal behaviour was just cause for the wife excluding him from the home, and that the intercourse was not condonation of his desertion. Lord Merriman said that resumption of cohabitation was a more apt description than condonation, when applied to simple desertion, but constructive desertion raised other considerations. The conduct in constructive desertion often amounted to cruelty. At p. 53 he said: —

"There is no doubt . . . that one can condone cruelty. Nobody has doubted that, and supposing one is dealing with a cruelty case which is also a case of constructive desertion, identical in every respect on the facts with the charge of cruelty, it does seem to me, although I only say this as one of the things I have not succeeded in understanding, that it

cannot be right to say that one can condone the cruelty but
not at the same time condone the desertion."

Nevertheless he recognised the binding authority of *Perry* v.
Perry.

The case of *Pizey* v. *Pizey* [1961] P. 101, in the Court of
Appeal, has to some extent weakened the authority of *Perry* v.
Perry, or at any rate reduced its scope. A wife, in the course
of an argument, spontaneously admitted she had committed
adultery nine years before, and left her husband. In the course
of the next two years the husband frequently visited the wife, had
intercourse on a number of occasions, and once stayed five days
with her. Later the husband petitioned for divorce on the grounds
of adultery and desertion. The petition was dismissed by Steven-
son, J., and his decision was upheld by the Court of Appeal
(Ormerod, Willmer and Danckwerts, L.JJ.) who held that the
wife's leaving was an act of desertion even though the husband
was willing to see her go, because she left in consequence of her
own adultery (*Baker* v. *Baker* [1954] P. 33, a decision based on
Glenister v. *Glenister* [1945] P. 30, followed), but the wife's
desertion terminated for two reasons. One was really a question of
fact, namely that the husband's visits had amounted to a resumption of cohabitation, and the course of conduct amounted to a
consensual separation. It is the other ground which distinguishes
it from *Perry* v. *Perry* and lends added force to Lord Merriman's
strictures in *W.* v. *W.* (*No.* 2) [1962] P. 49, namely that since the
desertion arose from the wife's adultery, and since intercourse had
condoned that adultery, the state of desertion ceased to exist
since the cause was removed. Willmer, L.J., who gave the leading
judgment, said this at p.108 : —

" *Perry* v. *Perry* [1952] P. 203, of course, is a decision which
is binding upon us, and I do not wish to say anything which
can possibly be thought to be in conflict with that decision.
But I do not think it covers the facts of the present case.
I say that for two reasons. The first reason is this: the wife's
desertion in the present case arose out of rather peculiar
circumstances. It depended on the circumstances that the
wife's confession of adultery, whether it were true or false,
was such as to make further married life between these
spouses virtually impossible. That is to say, the desertion
depended—and, as I see it, depended entirely—on the wife's
confession of adultery. It seems to me that it would be a very

odd result if desertion which depended entirely upon the confession of adultery should be held to continue after the adultery which was the cause of it had already been condoned. I confess that I do not see any answer to that difficulty. It seems to me, in the special circumstances of the present case, that the acts of sexual intercourse whereby the adultery was condoned must be regarded as having at one and the same time removed the cause on which the desertion depended.

My second reason for saying that this case is not within the principle of *Perry* v. *Perry* is this: On the evidence which was accepted by the judge, we have here something much more than mere casual acts of sexual intercourse. There was a regular course of conduct, extending over a period of about two years, during which the husband was constantly going down for weekends and for even longer periods, as and when he could, to stay with the wife. Obviously a question of degree must be involved in deciding whether parties who come together and have sexual intercourse are thereby resuming cohabitation. But on the facts of the present case, bearing in mind the course of conduct which was pursued over such a lengthy period, I find it impossible to say that, on the principle of *Perry* v. *Perry*, the desertion none the less continued to run."

Although Willmer, L.J., says that he does not purport to differ from *Perry* v. *Perry*, nevertheless he does differ, because Jenkins, L.J., had pointed to the very same difference with regard to adultery. If Willmer, L.J., is right, then the same arguments would apply where cruelty is the cause of the desertion. If the cruelty is condoned the cause is removed.

The trouble is that there are two principles in conflict and, in the state of the authorities, it is hopeless to find a logical solution that applies to all cases. On the one hand, there is the principle that sexual intercourse may condone adultery and cruelty. (The details are dealt with later at p. 301 et seq.). In desertion, another principle has been followed that casual acts of intercourse do not constitute condonation because this would discourage reconciliation. Where cruelty and adultery are mixed up with desertion, illogicalities are bound to occur.

What amounts to a resumption of cohabitation is, as has been said, a question of fact. See *Bull* v. *Bull* [1953] P. 224. Another example is *Abercrombie* v. *Abercrombie* [1943] 2 All E.R. 465, where a wife obtained a separation order in 1940 on the ground of cruelty. Later the husband wrote wanting a reconciliation, and the wife wrote affectionate letters in reply. The husband was a doctor and held a post as a locum. They met at two different places and had sexual intercourse. Then they stayed two nights at a friend's home and a weekend in London. When the husband applied to have the order discharged, the question was whether cohabitation had been resumed. The magistrates refused the discharge but were reversed on appeal, the Divisional Court holding that it was not essential to establish a resumption of cohabitation to show that the parties had lived together in a new house. Where the special circumstances make the establishment of a new home impossible, there may be a resumption of cohabitation by a resumption of intercourse, and in this case there had been a resumption of cohabitation.

In *Glasson* v. *Glasson* (1962), 106 Sol. J. 901, the wife obtained an order on the grounds of persistent cruelty, desertion and wilful neglect to maintain, which included a non-cohabitation clause. The husband wrote asking for forgiveness, and the parties met and had sexual intercourse, but the wife said she was not willing to return. Two days later the wife told the husband she was expecting a baby, and both agreed to make a fresh start. There were two further acts of intercourse but the wife, finding that she was not pregnant, said she did not wish to resume married life. The husband applied for revocation of the order, and the wife did not give evidence. The magistrates accepted the husband's evidence, held that cohabitation had been resumed and varied the order, but the report does not say in what respect the order was varied. The wife appealed.

The Divisional Court (Sir J. Simon, P., and Scarman, J.) dismissed the appeal, but revoked the order except for the provisions regarding the child, holding that resumption of cohabitation was a question of fact, that sexual intercourse having taken place was not in itself sufficient, that there must be a bilateral intention, and that it was not essential that the parties should establish a matrimonial home together.

Howard v. *Howard* [1962] 3 W.L.R. 413 is yet another case where the justices reached a compromise decision by dismissing a summons for desertion and finding wilful neglect to maintain, but the importance of the case is that the Divisional Court (Sir Jocelyn Simon, P., and Cairns, J.), held that condonation applied to constructive desertion.

The spouses after a quarrel both left the matrimonial home. Thereafter the husband intermittently visited the wife and had sexual relations with her but, though she repeatedly asked him to make her a home, he did not do so. The husband's case was that his wife had left him without just cause, and her violent conduct thereafter had compelled him to live apart from her, or amounted to just cause for his doing so.

After this case was decided, the 1963 Act was passed overruling *Henderson* v. *Henderson* [1944] A.C. 49, which was relied on by the court, that a husband condones his wife's offences by intercourse. As the law now stands, by s. 42 (1) of the 1965 Act (replacing s. 1 of the 1963 Act), the husband could have rebutted this presumption. This, however, does not affect the court's decision that constructive desertion is capable of condonation, while actual desertion is not (*Perry* v. *Perry* [1952] P. 203).

The result in *Howard's* case was that the husband had condoned his wife's offences (if any) and, by refusing to take her back, had put himself in desertion. This case could have been decided on the ground that the husband had unreasonably refused to take his wife back, without reference to condonation. It cannot be said that the subject of condonation in reference to desertion is anything like settled yet.

(ii) *Revocation of an order on the resumption of cohabitation*

Section 8 (2) of the Act of 1960 provides that on proof that the parties have resumed cohabitation, the court shall revoke the order.

Section 7 (1) provides (*a*) that no order shall be enforceable and no liability shall accrue thereunder until the parties have ceased to cohabit, and (*b*) that if in the case of a matrimonial order they continue to cohabit for a period of three months beginning with the date of the making of the order, the order shall cease to have effect at the expiration of that period.

Section 7 cannot be applicable to cases of desertion, since no order can be made if the parties are cohabiting, because an essential element in the offence would be lacking.

Section 8, however, is applicable and the complainant would have to prove that cohabitation has been resumed, that is to say, that amount of cohabitation that would put an end to desertion.

B. Offer to return

A genuine offer by a deserting spouse to the other, to be reconciled and to resume cohabitation, puts an end to the desertion. More than this, if the other spouse refuses, then the tables are turned, and the deserted spouse becomes the deserter. In other words, by taking appropriate action, the deserter can purge his or her fault, and the other party refuses to accept the new situation at his or her peril. This, however, is only true with qualifications. Assuming the husband is the deserter, and this offer is made in good faith, then his offer must be reasonable, that is to say, not subject to any unreasonable conditions. In a case of simple desertion, then the wife must accept or take the consequences; that is, by refusing, she will become the deserter.

There are, however, cases where the deserted spouse is justified in refusing the offer. The desertion, or the married life of the parties, may have aggravating features such as adultery or cruelty, which would entitle the deserted spouse to say "I am not going back to that sort of life, or the risk of it," or "I am not going to condone your adultery."

1. *The offer*

The leading case is *Pratt* v. *Pratt* [1939] A.C. 417. In this case the parties were married in 1933, and a year later the wife left the matrimonial home and never returned. She was thus guilty of desertion without just cause. In 1936 she wrote letters to her husband, in which she asked him to meet her with a view to a reconciliation. He was not, however, responsive, and subsequently filed a petition for divorce, which was undefended. The judge who tried the case thought that the letters had put an end to the desertion, and the appeal to the Court of Appeal was dismissed. Lord Romer, in giving the leading judgment in the House of Lords, relied on the case of *Thomas* v. *Thomas* [1924] P. 194, and said that there could be no doubt that the offer contained in the wife's letter was genuine. It was contended by counsel for the petitioner that mere letters, however sincere, could never put an end to the respondent's desertion, but Lord Romer said he was wholly unable to accede to this contention. It was argued that it was necessary, in order to put an end to her desertion, that she should take some active steps towards returning to the matrimonial domicile. This was true, but in fact she did take such a step when she wrote the letters. Whether the meeting for which she asked would have brought about a reconciliation is a question that must ever remain unanswered, but in view of his refusal to allow a meeting to take place, her continued absence thereafter from the matrimonial home could not, without utter misuse of language, be called desertion. Lord Macmillan, in the same case at p. 420, went somewhat further and said: —

"What is required of a petitioner for divorce on the ground of desertion is proof that throughout the whole course of the three years the respondent has without cause been in desertion. . . . If on the facts it appears that a petitioning husband has made it plain to his deserting wife that he will not receive her back, or if he has repelled all the advances which she may have made towards a resumption of married life, he cannot complain that she has persisted without cause in her desertion."

It is doubtful whether this is the law in England, as there is no doctrine of "adherence" as there was in the law of Scotland.

In *Joseph* v. *Joseph* [1939] P. 385 a wife left her husband and announced she would not return. Six months later she wrote offering to return, but the husband rejected her offer. She applied for restitution of conjugal rights, and it was held she had remedied her wrong and was entitled to an order. Langton, J., at p. 386, said: —

". . . the decision of the House of Lords in *Pratt* v. *Pratt* [1939] A.C. 417 confirms me in the view that in a matter of this kind, a spouse who is initially in the wrong can put himself or herself right by taking the proper steps. I am satisfied that she took such steps, and that by making a bona fide offer to return, remedied the wrong."

Sir Raymond Evershed, M.R., in *Perry* v. *Perry* [1952] P. 203, at p. 211, said that if the deserting spouse genuinely desires to return, his or her partner cannot refuse reinstatement, and that it was against public policy that a party desiring a resumption of cohabitation should be embarrassed in his efforts for reconciliation. Furthermore, in order to give proper scope to the policy of promoting reconciliation, casual acts of intercourse do not amount to "condonation" or put an end to the desertion. See *Mummery* v. *Mummery* [1942] P. 107, and s. 42 of the Matrimonial Causes Act, 1965.

In *Storey* v. *Storey* (1962), 106 Sol. J. 429, the husband left the wife and there was no further cohabitation, but the husband, by himself and his solicitors, had offered a reconciliation which the wife had ignored. The husband petitioned for divorce on the ground of desertion, and the wife by her answer denied desertion and cross-petitioned on the same ground. The judge dismissed both the petition and the cross prayer, finding that the husband did not leave his wife with the intention to terminate cohabitation for all time, and that the wife was not prepared to live with her husband apart from her parents. The husband appealed. The Court of Appeal (Willmer, Donovan and Davies, L.JJ.) allowed the appeal. The wife's refusal to entertain the husband's offers of reconciliation made her the deserting party, and the wife had not set up any complaints which constituted just cause for not taking him back.

Another case on the same subject is *Parker* v. *Parker* (1962), 106 Sol. J. 592, D.C. (Karminski and Baker, JJ.), where a husband appealed from the decision of magistrates who held him in desertion in spite of five letters written by the husband to the wife suggesting reconciliation. The wife ignored some letters and replied to others in hostile terms, refusing either to meet him or return to him. The magistrates took the view that the offers were not bona fide, and that there had been no offer which the wife could reasonably be expected to accept.

The Divisional Court held that the issue was one of fact, and there was evidence to support the finding. Karminski, J., however, gave a warning that the court was not for all time putting the husband in a state of desertion, and the wife was not entitled to adopt an obdurate attitude if the husband made further attempts at reconciliation.

2. *Offer to return when the parting is by consent*

In *Gallagher* v. *Gallagher* [1965] 2 All E.R. 967, C.A., there was a consensual separation and the husband offered to return but the wife would not consider it. The husband's petition for divorce on the ground of desertion was dismissed but allowed on appeal, it being held that both in the case of a deserting spouse and in the case of spouses living apart consensually the offer which was made must at least be considered by the other spouse, who was not entitled to ignore it or refuse it as distinct from declining to accept it on proper consideration.

3. *Repentance*

It is sometimes said that the deserter must repent as a condition for reinstatement. For instance, Scrutton, L.J., in *Bowron* v. *Bowron* [1925] P. 187, at p. 195, said: —

> "But where there was original cruelty and expressed intention to force the wife to leave, I do not think that the fact that there is no cruelty or expressed intention after she leaves prevents the desertion from continuing. The intention is presumed to continue unless the husband proves genuine repentance and sincere and reasonable attempts to get his wife back."

There can be little doubt that repentance is important in establishing whether the offer is a genuine one or not, but it is possible for the deserting spouse, at any rate in a simple case of desertion, to be quite unrepentant but nevertheless make a bona fide offer to return, which should be accepted if that spouse is prepared to undertake all the obligations of a spouse. This was decided in the case of *Price* v. *Price* [1951] P. 413. In that case, the wife left the husband and petitioned for a divorce, alleging cruelty, but the petition was dismissed. She subsequently offered to return to her husband, but she stated she did this in the interests of the children, that she did not love him and, in fact, that she hated him and she did not express any repentance. The husband refused to accept her on the ground that it was not a bona fide offer. The judge, however, came to the conclusion that it was a bona fide offer, and his decision was upheld on appeal. Somervell, L.J., said at p. 416: —

> "This was simply a question of fact: was this offer a genuine offer? Her expressions of dislike of her husband were no doubt very relevant in coming to a conclusion on that matter. But, once the judge had come to the conclusion that this was a genuine offer in the circumstances, there seems to me to be an end of the case. I say, ' in the circumstances,' because, as has been pointed out, there may be a case where the deserting spouse has ill-treated the deserted spouse, or the other way round, and there may be cases where a mere offer to return without the assurance of a change of habits may not be enough. . . ."

and Hodson, L.J., said at p. 420: —

> "The law is very clearly set out in this well-known passage in the judgment of Lord Reading, C.J., in *Jones* v. *Newtown*

and Llanidloes Guardians [1920] 3 K.B. 384: 'There is no doubt that at common law if a wife chooses wilfully and without justification to live away from her husband she cannot, so long as she continues absent, render him liable for necessaries supplied to her, or for her maintenance by the union, for the reason that she has of her own free will deprived herself of the opportunity which the husband was affording her of being maintained in the home. But the relief of the husband from the obligation of maintenance continues only so long as she voluntarily remains absent. Her absence, although wrongful, does not affect the relationship of husband and wife. She is entitled after however long a period of absence to return at any time.'

That passage draws attention to something which, I think, is perhaps not always clearly remembered, namely, that the husband's obligation to maintain his wife is prima facie complied with by providing a home for her. A wife has no right to separate maintenance in a different home unless she can justify the fact that she is living apart from her husband. If a woman, as the wife in this case has done, leaves her husband, the right to separate maintenance is not destroyed but suspended, and as soon as she expresses her willingness to go back, if that offer is rejected, that suspension comes to an end. It seems to me to follow from that that, although the question does not directly arise, in that case, on the bare facts, as I have stated them, from that moment onwards the boot is on the other leg and the party who is approached and rejects the approach becomes the deserter, and that that is the effect of the decision of the Divisional Court in *Thomas* v. *Thomas* [1946] 1 All E.R. 170. . . .

. . . If the offer was an offer in the true sense of the word, and was rejected, then in my view the judge's decision stands, and I find it a little difficult to understand counsel's additional argument that, even if an offer were a good one, yet the husband was not bound to have her back because, as I understood him to put it, she said she hated him and no man can be expected to have a woman back who has said that she hates him. I do not think it possible for the courts to investigate matters of emotion of that kind. . . ."

This case was followed in *Dyson* v. *Dyson* [1954] P. 198. A husband had presented a petition for divorce on the grounds of his wife's cruelty and adultery. The charges of dirtiness, so the trial judge said, were a grave reflection on the wife but they were exaggerated and distorted, and another charge, of neglecting the child so as to endanger its life, was quite untrue. Adultery was not proved, though the judge said the wife's conduct had been utterly reprehensible as she had been caught kissing and cuddling the co-respondent. The husband took only the issue of adultery to appeal, but this was dismissed. Four days later, he wrote to his wife offering to make a fresh start. Her solicitors, replying, said she had just cause for refusing, in view of the charges he had made against her. Some months later, she issued a summons under s. 23 of the Matrimonial Causes Act, 1950. Barnard, J., dismissed the summons because he held the wife was not justified in refusing the husband's offer. The husband had not been guilty of a matrimonial offence, or of conduct so grave and weighty as to make married life quite impossible. Referring to *Price* v. *Price* [1951] P. 413, he said at p. 207: —

" . . . I think that that decision makes it perfectly clear, that an offer, to be genuine, does not carry the implication that the person who makes it is really desirous of having the other party back, provided that he is honest in saying that he will receive the other spouse back."

4. *Lack of sincerity*

If a spouse offers to submit to the obligations of married life, one cannot expect more. You cannot make one love the other (*Price* v. *Price* [1951] P. 413). There is no reason why a wife, whose adultery has been condoned, should not be capable of making a bona fide offer to resume married life where the husband had left the matrimonial home. In *Wells* v. *Wells* [1954] 1 W.L.R. 1390, the wife confessed to adultery, but the husband condoned this by having intercourse with her. He later left her. She begged him to go back, but he refused to do so. In her application for restitution of conjugal rights, it was held that since her offer was sincere, she was entitled to a decree.

5. *Change of heart*

Sir Raymond Evershed, M.R., in *W.* v. *W.* (*No.* 2) [1954] P. 486, at p. 502, said: —

" The question, then, is: What is sufficient to break the period, the course of conduct, called desertion? It has been laid down in one of the passages I shall presently quote that once a spouse has deserted (that is to say, once he or she has evinced the intention of treating the marriage relationship as at an end) then, prima facie, if he or she remains away from the other in fact, he or she continues in desertion.

Merely writing a letter or expressing an intention to come back, or to invite the other party back without anything more is not enough. There must go with the expression, and be illustrated and evinced by it, a real change of heart. . . .

In cases in which the offending spouse has been guilty of some matrimonial offence in addition to desertion, for example, cruelty, it is, I think, true that the . . . injured spouse may reasonably expect a much greater manifestation, a much greater proof, of real change of heart extending both to the other offence and to the desertion, than in a case in which the only matter at issue is desertion. . . .

Treating it as a matter of fact, I think that clearly the commissioner had evidence before him which entitled him to conclude that the true character of these letters . . . was that they were manœuvres in what I will call, without meaning the phrase offensively, the legal game. I do not think that they did in fact represent any change of heart. . . ."

6. When justified in refusing

The duty of the deserted spouse to take back the deserter without qualification arises only in cases of simple desertion. Where there are aggravating circumstances, the deserted spouse may be justified in refusing to accept the offer. This was considered in the case of *Thomas* v. *Thomas* [1924] P. 194. The husband had been guilty of a long series of acts of insulting cruelty to his wife, and eventually expelled her from the matrimonial home. The next day he repented, and asked her to go back, but she refused. The justices found he was in desertion, and the desertion was upheld by the Divisional Court and the Court of Appeal. Pollock, M.R., said at p. 198: —

" It is contended for the husband that his so-called repentance must be accepted as the outstanding feature of his conduct during some eight or nine months, even though he might not be entitled to an order for restitution of conjugal rights in accordance with the principles laid down in *Russell* v. *Russell* [1895] P. 315, as interpreted in *Oldroyd* v. *Oldroyd* [1896] P. 175. Why so? It must be a question for those who have to decide upon the evidence before them what weight and emphasis is to be given to and placed upon his cruelty, his indifference, his determination to get rid of his wife, his attempt to alarm her, and his sorrow when he realised the need of her. . . . No doubt desertion can be put an end to by cohabitation; but it is very different a proposition to say that a husband can obliterate his previous conduct by subsequent offers, as to the genuineness of which the wife may, upon reasonable grounds, entertain doubts."

Warrington, L.J., said at p. 200: —

" The Divisional Court have held, affirming the view of the justices, that the question whether desertion continues is one of fact to be determined in view of the circumstances of the particular case, and that it having been proved to the satisfaction of the justices that before deserting his wife he had frequently ill-treated her, she was justified in refusing to comply with his request to return, and therefore the desertion had not been effectually determined. In my opinion this decision is correct. . . .

The learned judges of the Divisional Court do not decide, nor do I, that where there is nothing but a turning away of the wife, followed by a genuine expression of a desire on the husband's part for her return, the desertion would continue notwithstanding. . . ."

In *Trevor* v. *Trevor* (1965), 109 Sol. J. 574, the husband left the wife on nine occasions. The wife then got an order on the ground of desertion from the magistrates. The husband offered to return and she refused. Her petition for divorce was dismissed, but on appeal this was reversed, the Court of Appeal holding that she was entitled to refuse on account of his previous conduct.

Other examples to justify refusal to accept the offer are as follows: —

7. *Offer merely a stratagem*

In *Ware* v. *Ware* [1942] P. 49, the wife told her husband that she was in love with another man and wanted to be divorced, and she left him. The husband wrote to the wife asking her to return, but she would not do so; but about a year later she wrote to him and asked him to wipe out the past and consider the future together. The husband did not reply. Bucknill, J., said that in his view the offer was merely a stratagem, and that the case of *Pratt* v. *Pratt* [1939] A.C. 417 must not be used to support a stratagem to defeat a petition.

8. *Conduct may make desertion unforgiveable*

The deserting spouse's conduct may have been such that the other spouse may be justified permanently in refusing an offer to return. A husband and wife had parted by consent and the husband wrote suggesting a new start but the wife wrote implicitly refusing the offer. Three years later the husband petitioned for divorce and his petition was dismissed, but the Court of Appeal allowed his appeal (*Gallagher* v. *Gallagher* [1965] 2 All E.R. 967). At p. 971 Willmer, L.J., said: "Unless she was to make herself a deserter, she was bound in one form or another to show willingness to live once again with the husband; and that is precisely what this wife failed, and indeed refused, to do." What that conduct must be cannot be stated precisely; it is a matter of degree.

Lord Merriman, P., described it in this way, in *Edwards* v. *Edwards* [1948] P. 268, at p. 272: —

". . . let it be plainly understood that in every case, whether of ordinary desertion or constructive desertion, it is a question of degree what amends a husband must be prepared to make before he can suggest that his wife should take him back. In the ordinary simple case of desertion all he has to do is to return to the matrimonial home. Where he has driven his wife away by some cruel conduct, the case is different: it is a question of degree. There may be some conduct so gross that no woman could be expected ever to resume cohabitation with him. The point is that every case must be dealt with on its merits, and if his merits are so slight that the husband has very little hope of ever being taken back, that is one of the consequences of his own conduct, and it ought not to affect the result of the case."

The next year, the President repeated these words which he had uttered in the Divisional Court, in *Everitt* v. *Everitt* [1949] P. 374, at p. 385, in the Court of Appeal: —

"It follows, therefore, in my opinion, that, if, for example, the husband is offering to resume cohabitation but has been guilty of adultery which is uncondoned as in *Lodge* v. *Lodge* (1890), 15 P.D. 159, or of cruelty of so atrocious a character that the wife could not possibly be expected to subject herself to a risk of a recurrence, then in the words of Warrington, L.J., in *Thomas* v. *Thomas* [1924] P. 194: 'The actual separation must continue to have the quality of desertion by the husband; otherwise I see no alternative except to regard the wife as deserting him, which would be impossible.' But that is precisely what was done in *Lodge* v. *Lodge*."

He goes on to approve the judgment of Lord Penzance in *Basing* v. *Basing* (1864), 3 Sw. & Tr. 516, where that judge had said that the petitioner was not bound to condone her husband's adultery and take him back.

It goes without saying that if a husband is living with another woman, and offers to take his wife back, she is justified in refusing (*Edwards* v. *Edwards* (1893), 62 L.J.P. 33) even though that association had come to an end (*Graves* v. *Graves* (1864), 3 Sw. & Tr. 350) and even if the adultery has been condoned, if it has been revived for instance by a short period of desertion (*Everitt* v. *Everitt* [1949] P. 374).

In *Burton* v. *Burton* (1969), 113 Sol. J. 852, the husband had a violent temper and after treatment in hospital during which cortisone was prescribed his temper became more violent and frequent. The wife left and the husband wrote genuine and contrite letters asking for a reconciliation. The justices held that the wife was justified in refusing to return. Sir J. Simon, P., said that it had been argued that the husband had to have the intention to bring cohabitation to an end. The most that could be said was that the husband had to have intent to do the acts complained of and the foresight of probable consequences. The wife had reasonable grounds for refusing to return to her husband in view of the previous history.

9. *Offer unreasonable*

(a) *As husband or wife in name only*

In *Wily* v. *Wily* [1918] P. 1 the husband offered to live under the same roof with his wife, each party being free from molestation by the other. Hill, J., said that this was not an offer of matrimonial cohabitation. He said that willingness to live under the same roof was not sufficient. There must be something more and the wife must be treated as a wife.

In *Casey* v. *Casey* [1952] 1 All E.R. 453, the husband deserted his wife by refusing to allow her to enter the house. A fortnight later he asked her to return to look after the children. He said he would not sleep with her, or take her out. The magistrates dismissed the wife's summons for desertion, holding that she should have accepted the offer, but the Divisional Court (Lord Merriman, P., and Karminski, J.) allowed the appeal, and said that the offer was not a reasonable one, and the wife was not bound to accept it. Lord Merriman, P., said at p. 454:—

" This is not a case where there is any sort of physical impediment, or any moral reason for refusing to live with her as man and wife. He is in the forties and she is in the thirties, and they have a young family. It would need very strong evidence of some overriding reason or obstacle to persuade me that in those circumstances a reconciliation which did not involve readiness and willingness to cohabit in the ordinary sense of the word is a reconciliation which this wife is bound to accept."

In *Slawson* v. *Slawson* [1942] 2 All E.R. 527, the wife left her husband on the ground of dislike of marital intercourse. He invited her to return, and she said she was willing to do so but only as a housekeeper. Bucknill, J., at p. 528, said: —

" It seems to me that on the cases . . . a spouse who is proved to have deserted the other can bring the desertion to an end by making an honest proposal to come back and lead the ordinary married life of a husband and wife, but if the offer is something less than that—if it is an offer to return merely as a housekeeper and to impose a condition on the husband which is unreasonable, then it is not an offer to return which terminates the desertion. Whether or not the offer is unreasonable is a question of fact in each case. I have to consider the circumstances of the case, and it seems to me that I ought to go no further than this: that in this case it is quite unreasonable for the wife to impose such a condition on her husband. There was no question of health or age, or danger of childbirth, or anything of that sort. It is just that the wife did not intend, or wish, to carry out her duty as a wife, and I think the husband was entitled to say: ' No, that is not an offer which I ought to be expected to accept '."

So too, in *Hutchinson* v. *Hutchinson* [1963] 1 W.L.R. 280 (D.C.), a wife's refusal to accept a husband's offer to return was held to be justified since he insisted on the unreasonable condition that there should be no sexual relations between them.

(b) *Living with mother-in-law*

In *Millichamp* v. *Millichamp* (1931), 146 L.T. 96, the parties, while engaged, agreed to live with the husband's mother. After the marriage, differences arose between the wife and her mother-in-law, and the wife left. The wife summoned her husband for wilful neglect to maintain, and the husband offered to take her back to his mother's house, which was all he could afford. The wife succeeded before the magistrates, and this decision was upheld by the Divisional Court. Lord Merrivale, P., said that the husband's first duty was to his wife. The justices had come to the conclusion that by reason of the differences about his mother, he failed in that duty because he put his mother first, instead of putting his wife first.

Contrasting with this case is *Jackson* v. *Jackson* (1932), 146 L.T. 406, where the husband provided a house next door to his mother, but Lord Merrivale said that in this case it was not unreasonable.

(c) Not to take back children

In May, 1936, a wife was living separate from her husband and applied to the magistrates for maintenance on the grounds of desertion and wilful neglect to maintain. The summonses were dismissed because she refused a genuine offer to resume cohabitation. Twelve months later the wife, not having done anything, again issued similar summonses, and this time the justices made an order on the ground of wilful neglect to maintain. The justices decided that the husband was telling the truth when he made his offer. Apparently, he was willing to take his wife back, but not to take back her children with her. On appeal the Divisional Court (Sir Boyd Merriman, P., and Langton, J.) dismissed the appeal, holding that the magistrates were entitled to come to a fresh determination as the position in 1937 could not be the same as in 1936 (*Balchin* v. *Balchin* [1937] 3 All E.R. 733).

In *Barrett* v. *Barrett* [1948] P. 277, the husband petitioned for divorce on the ground of desertion. In consequence of friction between the husband and the daughters of the marriage, the wife left with the daughters. He asked his wife to return, and she was willing to do so with the daughters, but the husband refused to have her back if she brought the daughters. The Court of Appeal held that it was reasonable for the wife to refuse to abandon her daughters in the prevailing war conditions, and she was not guilty of desertion. Tucker, L.J., said that the whole case turned on whether the condition thus imposed was reasonable or unreasonable, and he approved of a dictum of Butt, J., in *French-Brewster* v. *French-Brewster* (1889), 62 L.T. 609–611: —

" If the husband has left her for a time but is willing to return, and the wife refuses to receive him back except upon conditions she has no right to impose, she cannot set up his continued absence as desertion."

Chadwick v. *Chadwick* (1964), *The Times*, 24th October (D.C.), decided that there is no general rule that a man must put his wife before his child by an earlier marriage if the wife so insisted; the question is what is reasonable in the circumstances. See *Fraser* v. *Fraser* [1969] 3 All E.R. 654.

(d) No home

In *Harris* v. *Harris* (1866), 15 L.T. 448, the parties were married in 1857, and the husband left his wife a few weeks later. Shortly afterwards, he telegraphed her to come to London, where they stayed for two or three days in an hotel. The husband then sent her back to her father, saying he could not support her. Two years later he sent a note that he did not want to have anything to do with her or her family, but a few months later he called on her father and said he wanted her back, but he had no home to take her to. Wilde, J.O., said: —

" It has been established that in these cases the real question is whether the court is satisfied, from what a man has said, written or done, that he was really desirous and intended to take his wife back. It is not sufficient that a man should write a letter and say to his wife: ' Come back,' or that he should say to a third person that he is willing to take her back. The court must look to the whole of his conduct and say that he intended to take his wife back for the purpose of sharing the home with him."

(e) Unfounded charges not withdrawn

In *Sayers* v. *Sayers* (1929), 93 J.P. 72, the parties had lived happily together for thirteen years, and then, on grounds which were quite insufficient, the husband became possessed of an idea that his wife was carrying on with some other man, and in abusive terms asked her to leave the house. She left. The husband then expressed himself ready to take her back, but did not wholly withdraw the charges. Hill, J., said: —

" Here we have a stupid husband who makes false charges, and a stupid wife who will not be reconciled. There was desertion by the husband in compelling the wife to leave. Treating the husband's offer to let by-gones be by-gones as genuine, we have to consider if it can be regarded as adequate. The husband has not fully withdrawn the charges, and the magistrates have rightly directed this."

10. *Offer not unreasonable*

If a deserting husband fails to comply with a reasonable condition insisted upon by his wife as the basis for a reconciliation, desertion will continue (*Gibson* v. *Gibson* (1859), 23 J.P. 535; *Pizzala* v. *Pizzala* (1896), 68 L.J.P. 91*n*, and *Slawson* v. *Slawson* [1942] 2 All E.R. 527). If the condition is unreasonable, desertion will not continue (*Dallas* v. *Dallas* (1874), 43 L.J. P. & M. 87; *Dickinson* v. *Dickinson* (1889), 62 L.T. 330, and *Fletcher* v. *Fletcher* [1945] 1 All E.R. 582).

Where a wife had applied for a separation on the ground of cruelty, which had failed, and subsequently offered to resume cohabitation, Jones, J., in *Thory* v. *Thory* [1948] P. 236 (a husband's petition for divorce), said, about the wife's offer to resume cohabitation and the fact that she had earlier applied for a judicial separation alleging cruelty: —

". . . I do not think there is anything there which suggests that her conduct was so outrageous that it would be completely unreasonable to expect the petitioner to take her back."

(a) *To endure the rigours of the English climate*

In *Powell* v. *Powell* (1957), *The Times*, 22nd February, the petitioner married a Greek girl in Athens in 1946, and then they came to live in England. In 1949 she went to Greece for a four or five months holiday, and she never returned, saying that her health could not withstand the rigours of the English climate. She invited him to go and live in Greece, but he refused to do so. Mr. Commissioner Wrangham refused the petitioner a divorce, but the decision was reversed by the Court of Appeal, Hodson, L.J., saying that the court must consider whether the wife was justified in leaving her husband and not returning because of her health. The husband had kept the home open for three or four years, and he was ready and anxious for her to come back. It was impossible to say that the wife had just cause because of her health, since her letters showed that she was living an active life in Athens. Moreover, since she had not defended the suit, she had not put that excuse before the court. She had stayed away against the husband's will.

(b) *Refusing accommodation at the matrimonial home*

In *McGowan* v. *McGowan* [1948] 2 All E.R. 1032, the parties married in 1945 and, on the husband's demobilisation, went to live with his parents. Three days later the wife left the house, saying she would not live with his parents. In 1947 the wife secured a flat and asked him to join her there, but he refused to do so and she took out a summons for desertion. The magistrates found that she had no good reason for leaving the parents' home, but said the husband was unreasonable in not joining her at the flat. They dismissed the summons for desertion, but made an order on the ground of wilful neglect to maintain. On appeal to the Divisional Court, it was held that since the wife was unreasonable in leaving the matrimonial home, she was in desertion, and in finding accommodation which he was unwilling to accept, she had not proved he was not fulfilling his obligations to her.

This case is similar to the case of *Millichamp* v. *Millichamp* (1931), 146 L.T. 96, but the court distinguished this case on the ground that there the husband had put his mother first, and that it was unreasonable to expect the wife to live under these conditions.

(c) *Being neurotic*

The mere fact that a husband was suffering from a neurosis is not sufficient excuse for a wife to refuse to take him back. In *Leng* v. *Leng* [1946] 2 All E.R. 590, the husband, who was neurotic, was alleged to have told his wife to go, and she subsequently got an order on the ground of desertion. He then wrote and asked her to come back, but the magistrates, although holding it was a bona fide offer, held that she was justified in refusing because of his neurotic conduct, saying that he would have difficulty in making decisions and the health of the wife and child might be affected. Lord Merriman, at p. 591, after saying that if the appeal was dismissed the wife could get a divorce in due course, which would make neurosis a ground for divorce, said: —

"I decline to be a party to any such judgment. Let it be considered for one moment with what restrictions divorce for insanity is hedged around, and then let it be considered whether any court has the right to say that the neurotic condition of the husband, and nothing else, is ground for refusal by a wife to live with her husband so that he is to be held to be a deserter. The thing has only to be stated to be seen to be nonsense."

11. *Turning the tables*

The effect of a refusal of a bona fide offer to resume cohabitation, in a case where it is reasonable that it should be accepted, is not merely to put an end to the deserter's desertion, but to transpose the position of the parties so that the deserted spouse becomes the deserter. Lord Merriman, in *Everitt* v. *Everitt* [1949] P. 374, said at p. 385: —

". . . the only possible conclusion from Warrington, L.J.'s judgment in *Thomas* v. *Thomas* [1924] P. 194 is that the unjustified refusal by the spouse who has been deserted to resume cohabitation not merely terminates the desertion but also reverses the process: it turns the tables—puts the boot on the other leg; and it is immaterial whether the case is one of mere desertion which is terminable by a simple offer on the part of the deserter to return or one of constructive desertion terminable, with more difficulty no doubt, by appropriate repentance and appropriate assurance of amendment of such a kind, according to the invidual circumstances, as the aggrieved spouse is not justified in refusing. To that, of course, must be added the qualification that at the end of his judgment Warrington, L.J., said: ' In each case the question must be determined on its own merits '."

This subject was dealt with at length by the Divisional Court (Lord Merriman, P., and Hodson, J.) in *Thomas* v. *Thomas* [1946] 1 All E.R. 170, where it was held that a mere withdrawal from cohabitation by a wife, unaccompanied by any other marital misconduct, entitled her to an order for maintenance if there was repentance and a genuine desire to resume married life, even though such separation on her part had been unjustified in the first instance.

By the same process, a refusal by a spouse to accept a genuine offer to resume cohabitation turned that spouse into a deserter. Lord Merriman said at p. 173: —

" I wish to make it clear that I am dealing only with the class of case in which there is a mere separation, uncomplicated by misconduct other than withdrawal from cohabitation. We are not, for example, dealing with the case of a wife who has committed adultery, a case which stands in a peculiar position, nor are we dealing with the case of a husband, who has driven his wife from home by cruel conduct. There again, special considerations apply. We are dealing with a case where there is a mere separation, assumed to be unjustified on the part of the wife, in the first instance. With regard to such a case, it is clear beyond the slightest doubt that at any time the wife can repent, and by a mere repentance and an expression of a genuine desire to resume married life, can restore herself at once to the position in which the husband is again bound to maintain her. . . ."

and in another passage:

" I am bound to say that I can see no logical reason why the process which re-establishes her right to maintenance should not also establish her right to assert that the husband in his turn becomes the deserter, and in my opinion that is the inevitable conclusion from the well-known passage in the judgment of Warrington, L.J., in *Thomas* v. *Thomas* [1924] P. 194."

12. *Offer by letter*

The offer to return may be made orally or by letter, but the court, in deciding whether the offer is genuine, is more ready to accept a letter which is written by the party himself or herself, spontaneous, uninfluenced and uninspired.

Lord Romer, in *Pratt* v. *Pratt* [1939] A.C. 417, at p. 427, said: —

" The appellant indeed concedes that the writing of the letters was a spontaneous act on the part of the respondent, and not one done upon the advice or at the instigation of her legal advisers. Nor does he suggest that the letters were written for the purpose of being used by her in any legal proceedings."

Similarly, in *Dyson* v. *Dyson* [1954] P. 198, at p. 208, Barnard, J., said: —

" I feel convinced that when the husband sat down, without any legal advice or assistance, and wrote this letter to his wife, he really meant what he said."

So also when solicitors wrote in rather formal terms asking a wife to return to her husband, the court held, having regard to all the circumstances including the fact that when he saw her he either ignored her or made insulting gestures, that the letter was not bona fide (*Martin* v. *Martin* (1898), 78 L.T. 568).

In *Re Duckworth* (1889), 5 T.L.R. 608, when solicitors wrote to a wife that her husband was willing to have her back and " find a house " for her, and that the offer would be used in evidence against her if she did not accede to it, it is not surprising that this was held not to be a bona fide offer.

On the other hand, in *Price* v. *Price* [1951] P. 413, a solicitor's letter was held to be a bona fide offer.

A letter written by one of the parties before legal advice is bound to be more convincing, as showing a genuine desire to have a reconciliation, rather than a manœuvre to put that party in the right and the other in the wrong. Much depends on the contents of the letter, and the surrounding circumstances. Some persons find writing a letter a difficult matter, and it would be natural to seek the assistance of a solicitor.

When a husband wishes to have his wife back, the procedure should not be treated as a commercial contract where offer and acceptance are the appropriate terms. *Amour propre*, wounded pride, hurt feelings have to be considered. The woman has to be wooed, and a solicitor's letter is not usually considered the most appropriate method of wooing.

13. *The best test of a bona fide offer*

Denning, L.J., in *Pike* v. *Pike* [1954] P. 81, at p. 89, referred to the unreported case of *Barnard* v. *Barnard*, 18th November, 1952 (Final) List of Appeals No. 17, where the Court of Appeal said that the best way of seeing whether the offer is genuine is to accept it and see whether he will take her in.

14. *Genuineness is a question of fact*

This has been laid down in many cases such as *Kershaw* v. *Kershaw* (1887), 51 J.P. 646, and *Martin* v. *Martin* and *Re Duckworth* referred to above. In *Gaskell* v. *Gaskell* (1963), 108 Sol.J. 37, the Divisional Court suggested a husband whose offer to return had been rejected might establish his bona fides by seeking the aid of some reconciliation agency such as the Marriage Guidance Council. See *Fraser* v. *Fraser* [1969] 3 All E.R. 654.

In *Dunn* v. *Dunn* [1965] 1 All E.R. 1043 this subject was considered at length by a Divisional Court (Sir Jocelyn Simon, P., and

Scarman, J.). The husband left the wife because, he said, she had told him to go. She wrote three letters asking him to return. The justices on the hearing of the wife's summonses for desertion, persistent cruelty and wilful neglect, found the wife's overtures not genuine. On appeal it was held that although it might be prudent to test by acceptance an offer to return there was no rule of law that such offer must be so tested. The court referred to three cases which are set out in footnotes to this report, namely *Barnard* v. *Barnard* (1952), [1965] 1 All E.R. at p. 1050, *Turpin* v. *Turpin* (1960), at p. 1051 and *Storey* v. *Storey* (1962), at p. 1052, all in the Court of Appeal. In *Barnard's* case Singleton, L.J., said he was not surprised that the magistrates had found that the wife's offer to return was not genuine since at that time she was accusing him of cruelty and asking for an order on that ground. Denning and Hodson, L.JJ., while holding in this case the offer was not genuine, still thought the best test is to accept the offer and see what happens.

In *Turpin* v. *Turpin* the Commissioner had thought there was a difference between *Price* v. *Price* (q.v.) and *W* v. *W* (*No.* 2) (q.v.), but the Court of Appeal held they were not inconsistent. Writing a letter was not enough. There had to be something more to show sincerity.

In *Storey* v. *Storey* the wife had ignored the husband's letters asking for a reconciliation and therefore could not successfully contend his offers were not genuine.

In *Ogden* v. *Ogden* (1969), 113 Sol.J. 585, the Court of Appeal held that the husband's offer of reconciliation was genuine, although both the magistrates and a Divisional Court had held otherwise.

C. The effect of adultery

In the High Court this is a subject of some importance, but it can rarely if ever be applicable in the magistrates' court.

Adultery by the deserted spouse does not automatically put an end to the desertion of the other. Whether the adultery terminates the other's desertion depends on whether the deserter knew of the adultery and whether it had any influence on his or her mind. In *Herod* v. *Herod* [1939] P. 11, at p. 24, Sir Boyd Merriman said: —

" If the intention permanently to break up the matrimonial home is established either by the wrongdoer's own declarations or because his conduct has been such as to lead to the conclusion that he must have intended that result, it seems to me he has been guilty of desertion; and that he continues to be so, notwithstanding that the other spouse has been guilty of a breach of the matrimonial obligations which is proved to have had no influence on his intentions."

The burden of proof is on the petitioner, and if it is left in doubt whether the respondent knew of the adultery, or if known, whether his or her conduct was affected by it, the petitioner fails.

Herod was approved by the Court of Appeal [1939] 2 All E.R. 698, where it was held that the petitioner's adultery had not influenced the mind of the respondent and the period of desertion had, therefore, not been interrupted (see also *Williams* v. *Williams* [1943] 2 All E.R. 746 (C.A.); *Richards* v. *Richards* [1952] P. 307 (C.A.); *Dryden* v. *Dryden* [1952] 2 All E.R. 533 (C.A.); *Parrock* v. *Parrock* [1956] 1 W.L.R. 270 and *Day* v. *Day* [1957] P. 202). In the last mentioned case the adultery took place before the desertion.

The important point is that the deserter's mind has to be shown to be influenced by the adultery. In the magistrates' court this is quite irrelevant. If a wife takes out a summons for desertion against her husband, then it is sufficient for the husband to prove that the complainant has committed an act of adultery during the subsistence of the marriage, which he has not condoned or connived at, or by wilful neglect or misconduct conduced to (Act of 1960, s. 2 (3) (*b*)) and if he does that the magistrates cannot make an order in favour of the wife on the ground of desertion; and if a wife has an order on the ground of desertion (or any other ground) the court must revoke the order on the application of the husband on proof of adultery (s. 8 (2)).

D. The effect of insanity

What is the effect of the respondent's insanity on desertion? The court's answer to this has varied, but the House of Lords has settled the matter in the leading case of *Crowther* v. *Crowther* [1951] A.C. 723. In that case the husband left his wife in 1946. In 1948 he was admitted to hospital under a reception order under the Lunacy and Mental Treatment Acts, 1890–1930, and detained as a person of unsound mind. It was held by Ormerod, J., and the Court of Appeal that there was an irrebuttable presumption that he was incapable of the mental and moral activity necessary for an intention to desert, and the period of desertion was wholly interrupted. Four of the law lords, Lords Porter, Normand, Reid and MacDermott, said that it was open to the petitioner to show that the respondent was capable of an intention to desert, but if she did not establish this, or there was no evidence on the subject at all, the court could not draw an inference of continued desertion after the date of certification. Lord Oaksey was prepared to hold that since the respondent was in desertion, the onus was on him to prove an intention to resume cohabitation.

This latter view was adopted by s. 2 of the Divorce (Insanity and Desertion) Act, 1958, but this Act was applicable only to the High Court, and so far as magistrates are concerned, the law remains as stated by the majority of the House of Lords in *Crowther* v. *Crowther*.

In his opinion, Lord Porter referred to the argument that the desertion of a husband sent to prison is not terminated or even suspended while he remains in prison (*Drew* v. *Drew* (1888), 13 P.D. 97), but he pointed out that if the husband formed an intention to return, expressed that intention, and took such steps as an imprisoned person could to carry out his resolve, that might put an end to his desertion. *Drew's* case depended on physical incapacity, and not on intention. He said that the cases of *Cohen* v. *Cohen* [1940] A.C. 631 and *Bowron* v. *Bowron* [1925] P. 187 decided that where there was an original intention to desert, it continues until it is brought to an end. Lord Reading in *Jones* v. *Newtown and Llanidloes Guardians* [1920] 3 K.B. 381 had said: —

> " Here the wife has become a lunatic and continues to be insane. She is therefore unable to exercise any judgment. She cannot elect to return home."

Lord Porter distinguished this case because it was under a different statute with a different purpose, but he adopted the view of Bucknill, J., in *Bennett* v. *Bennett* [1939] P. 274 that the question in issue was: " Did the wife during the time she was insane intend to desert her husband? " This raises a rebuttable presumption that the wife's desertion has come to an end, and the deserted spouse may prove, if he can, that she was capable of retaining an intention to desert and did retain that intention.

Lord Reid thought that an intention was bound to come to an end if the person no longer has a mind capable of entertaining it, but as there are many degrees of mental incapacity, the petitioner ought to be allowed to prove, if he or she can, that the respondent had a mind capable of entertaining an *animus deserendi*.

The result is that insanity, of a certified person, does not automatically put an end to that person's desertion, but that the onus is on the person alleging the desertion to prove the insane person has the mental capacity for desertion.

The same would apply to a voluntary patient under the Mental Treatment Act, 1930 (*Monckton* v. *Monckton* [1942] P. 28), a feeble-minded person under s. 1 of the Mental Deficiency Act, 1927 (*Brown* v. *Brown* [1947] P. 95, and see *More* v. *More* [1950] P. 168) and now to the corresponding categories of patients under the Mental Health Act, 1959.

In *Keeley* v. *Keeley* [1952] 2 T.L.R. 756, the Court of Appeal held that a wife in a mental home had the capacity to form an intention to desert, and her refusal to come home at her husband's request amounted to desertion. The medical superintendent gave evidence that she was capable of making a reasonable decision on this subject. The court said, however, that proof that her illness, physical or mental, compelled her to stay in hospital would (and the fact that it was the public interest which compelled the wife to remain in hospital might) have afforded a good defence. The court followed the decision in *Wickens* v. *Wickens* [1952] 2 All E.R. 98, where the husband had been a voluntary patient in a mental hospital for twenty years, and was quite happy to stay there and not return home. The Court of Appeal held he was capable of forming the intention to desert, but Morris, L.J., added: " It is inevitable that there is a natural reluctance in any court to come to a conclusion that a patient in a mental hospital has been guilty of desertion."

Keeley v. *Keeley* [1952] 2 T.L.R. 756 was distinguished in the case of *Clark* v. *Clark* [1956] 1 W.L.R. 345. The parties were married in 1939 and in 1943 the wife entered a mental home as a voluntary patient. The husband did not write, but in answer to a letter from his solicitors, the medical superintendent wrote that the wife did not wish to go back to her husband but wished to remain in hospital. This was in 1952. The husband petitioned for a divorce, which was defended by the wife through a guardian, and she pleaded just cause, in that she was not fit to run a home or look after a husband.

Barnard, J., said that the parting was by consent since the husband had consented to her going into hospital. This case differed from *Keeley* v. *Keeley* because, in that case, the husband had visited his wife and wanted her to come home, and in this case he had not. Furthermore, there was no home for her to go to and even if there had been, the husband had not found anyone to look after his wife, and therefore she had just cause for not returning.

Although cases involving insanity are more likely to be heard in the High Court, where the continuance of desertion for two years is important, and are comparatively rare before magistrates, yet the point can arise as is shown by *Snell* v. *Snell* [1960] C.L.Y. 983. In January, 1955, the husband threatened to murder his wife, and was forcibly removed to a mental hospital and certified. He struck her when she visited him, and also when on parole. The wife issued summonses for desertion and wilful neglect to maintain, more than six months after the last assault. The magistrates dismissed the summonses, holding that his conduct had not been wilfully aimed at the wife with a view to causing her to leave him. The Divisional Court (Lord Merriman and Collingwood, J.) allowed the wife's appeal, holding that if she was justified in leaving and refusing to return because of what had happened in the past, and an apprehension of its repetition, she was entitled to relief on the grounds alleged.

Of course, the complainant's mental illness is no excuse for the respondent leaving. Thus, where a wife who suffered from a mental illness and went into a mental home was left by her husband who only visited her for a time and then disappeared, she was entitled to a divorce on the ground of his desertion (*Sotherden* v. *Sotherden* [1940] P. 73).

In *Perry* v. *Perry* [1964] 1 W.L.R. 91, a wife left her husband. At some time previously she had been certified as insane. She accused her husband, both before and after leaving, that he was associating with other women and that he was attempting to murder her. There was medical evidence that she was suffering from paranoid psychosis, and that although when she left she knew what she was doing, she had a strong conviction of her husband's violent intentions towards her. Lloyd-James, J., dismissed the husband's petition for divorce on the ground of desertion because the husband had failed to prove his wife had the mental capacity to form an intention to desert him. The judge considered *Williams* v. *Williams* [1964] A.C. 698, but said that it did not directly bear on the problem, as it was a case of cruelty and wholly different considerations applied.

This was a case of actual desertion. The wife left the husband and it was held she was incapable of the *animus deserendi*. Supposing the husband had left the wife, because her accusations had become intolerable. This could be a case where there are all the elements of cruelty except injury to health. However such a case is decided, an anomaly would be bound to result.

If it were held to be desertion, then the question of whether an *animus deserendi* existed would depend on which party left the house. On the other hand if it were said that it was not desertion, it would be difficult to reconcile with *Williams* v. *Williams* (see p. 219).

Perry's case was distinguished in *Kaczmarz* v. *Kaczmarz* [1967] 1 All E.R. 416 by Cairns, J. The husband petitioned for divorce on the ground of the wife's desertion. She had stated that she would never return to her husband. She had become a mental patient and suffered from a delusion that to have had sexual intercourse with her husband was a sin. The judge held that the defendant had sufficient mental capacity to form the intention not to return to her husband, and even if she had lost this capacity subsequently desertion continued under s. 1 (2) of the Matrimonial Causes Act, 1965, which replaced the Matrimonial Causes Act, 1963, s. 2 (2), but has itself been repealed by the Divorce Reform Act, 1969.

The judge also held that if the wife without delusions thought her husband had committed a grave sin it was not just cause for refusing cohabitation.

E. Supervening consent

Where one spouse has deserted the other, and they enter into an agreement to live apart, desertion is terminated (*Long* v. *Long* [1940] 4 All E.R. 230). See section on Consent, p. 61 et seq.

F. Non-cohabitation clause or judicial separation

The magistrates have power to make an order that the complainant shall be no longer bound to cohabit with the defendant, and such a provision has the effect of a decree of judicial separation (Act of 1960, s. 2 (1) (*a*)).

This provision should never be inserted in cases of desertion because it has the effect of bringing desertion to an end, and therefore prejudiced a spouse who was seeking a divorce on the ground of three years' desertion (*Harriman* v. *Harriman* [1909] P. 123).

If this clause has been left in by mistake, it can be deleted by the magistrates and desertion may be deemed to have run as though the clause had never been inserted (*Cohen* v. *Cohen* [1947] P. 147 and *Thory* v. *Thory* [1948] P. 236).

G. The presentation of a petition for divorce or nullity

The question was posed by Lord Romer in *Cohen* v. *Cohen* [1940] A.C. 631, at p. 635, whether the presentation of such a petition, and the service thereof on the other spouse, necessarily terminates the other's desertion. He answered it by saying that it was a question of fact depending on the circumstances of the particular case, and referring to the particular case said at p. 646: —

> " It was never disproved, and there is nothing in the history of this case that even remotely suggests that the petition while it was on the file deterred the respondent in the very least from taking steps to end his desertion."

In *W.* v. *W.* (*No.* 2) [1954] P. 486 the Court of Appeal held that the making of a decree nisi of nullity did not necessarily put an end to desertion.

V. CONSTRUCTIVE DESERTION AND CRUELTY

1. Magistrates are not infrequently faced with the situation where the complainant has issued two summonses, one for persistent cruelty and the other for desertion, being really constructive desertion. The question is whether they can dismiss the summons

for persistent cruelty, and yet find for the complainant on the summons for desertion.

2. Sometimes the complainant issues a summons for persistent cruelty and having had this dismissed, then tries again with a summons for desertion, being constructive desertion. The question here is whether the magistrates can try the case and, if so, find for the complainant, in spite of their previous decision or the decision of other magistrates dismissing the summons for persistent cruelty.

3. There is a third alternative where a summons for desertion, being constructive desertion, is dismissed and the complainant tries again with a summons for persistent cruelty.

The answers to these questions are largely to be found in two cases in the Divisional Court: *Foster* v. *Foster* [1954] P. 67 and *Cooper* v. *Cooper* (*No.* 2) [1955] P. 168.

In *Foster* v. *Foster* the wife took out a summons for persistent cruelty, alleging physical violence over a period of ten years and association with other women. This summons was dismissed. Later, in another district, she took out a summons for desertion, alleging the same complaints as previously and, in addition, that she had left home because her husband said he had finished with her, and an order was made in her favour. The husband appealed on the ground that, the cruelty charge having been disposed of, she could not be heard to say that the same allegations were sufficient to constitute grave and weighty conduct sufficient for just cause for her to leave, and reliance was placed on *Pike* v. *Pike* [1954] P. 81 and *Barker* v. *Barker* [1949] P. 219. Lord Merriman, P., and Collingwood, J., said that the second bench of magistrates were justified in making the order. Lord Merriman, after saying that it was said for the husband that this was an attempt to build up a case of constructive desertion by what was really a case of unproved cruelty, said at p. 77: —

> "But in my opinion the wife was not bound to put the charge of desertion before the Dorking justices under the penalty of being estopped from afterwards alleging that she had been deserted before the date of that hearing.
> The matter can, perhaps, best be tested by supposing, for the sake of argument, that those steps had been taken, and that there had been before the justices at Dorking on 17th September, 1952, both a charge of cruelty brought up to 29th

August, 1952, and a charge of desertion from 4th September, 1952. Would the Dorking justices, having found that the charge of cruelty had not been proved, have been bound to dismiss the charge of desertion because it was an attempt to build up a charge of constructive desertion by what was really a case of unproved cruelty? In my opinion they would not, because of the evidence which (I am assuming for the purposes of the argument) the wife would have given, as she gave it at Sutton, about the husband telling her that he had finished with her. In other words, I am not prepared to hold that a court could not find that a husband who had admittedly smacked his wife in the face many times because he said he was sick of being nagged by her about his going out and neglecting her, and who ' did not remember ' having threatened her, as she alleged, but said that if he did so he did not mean it seriously, ought not to be taken to mean what he says if he tells his wife at the end of it all that he had finished with her, even though he said that he would not actually turn her out, but coupled his statement that he had finished with her with the assertion that he would go out more than he did before, thereby implying that things would be worse than they had been before if she remained in the matrimonial home."

In his judgment, Collingwood, J., referred to the criticisms of the judgment of Hodson, J., in *Barker* v. *Barker* made by Bucknill, L.J., in *Edwards* v. *Edwards* [1950] P. 8.

This case answers clearly the questions 1 and 2 above. The President takes it as self-evident that magistrates may dismiss a summons for persistent cruelty and at the same time find constructive desertion on the same facts; and in the case of a summons for desertion following a dismissed summons for persistent cruelty, that the evidence in the former case may be used in the latter.

In *Cooper* v. *Cooper* the wife took out a summons for persistent cruelty and gave evidence about assaults, and produced two notes from her husband telling her to " get out " and " clear out." This summons was dismissed and the complainant took out summonses for desertion and wilful neglect. At the outset of the case, because the wife was relying on the same evidence as before, the magistrates dismissed the case on the ground that she was estopped by the previous decision. An appeal to a Divisional Court (Lord Merriman, P., and Karminski, J.) was allowed, *Foster* v. *Foster* being followed. In the meantime, there had been a decision by Willmer, J., in *Bright* v. *Bright* [1954] P. 270, who had held that a wife's petition for constructive desertion which followed a dismissed petition based on cruelty, and where the allegations were the same in both cases, could not be heard on the ground that the wife was estopped and that not only evidence which had been given, but evidence which could have been given, was not admissible.

The Divisional Court in *Cooper* v. *Cooper* disapproved of part of Willmer, J.'s judgment and their disapproval is best summarised in the words of Karminski, J. [1955] P., p. 177, where he said: —

> " I would say at once I agree with my lord, that if Willmer, J., meant that the dismissal of a cruelty charge in effect operated to estop the wife from using any of the same facts as evidence of desertion, then that is in flat contradiction of this court in *Foster* v. *Foster*."

As to the third question, the answer would appear to be given by Hodson, J., in *Pike* v. *Pike* [1954] P. 81, at p. 88, where he says: —

> ". . . no injustice could possibly be done to her, because if she has a case of cruelty any finding of this court that she has not made out a case of desertion does not operate as an estoppel in any cruelty proceedings which she may, if so advised, bring in the future."

He added that he hoped nothing he had said would encourage her to take such a step, and Denning, L.J., said at p. 89: —

> " It is open to her, no doubt, to bring another petition now charging cruelty, but I certainly would not wish to encourage it."

Assuming this is correct, then such a summons would be bound to fail, if based on the same facts. In constructive desertion where the complainant seeks to prove conduct in the nature of cruelty, she must show that it was so grave and weighty that she was justified in leaving. If that fails, how can it possibly be said that the same conduct was so grave and weighty as to amount to legal cruelty? In other words, the greater includes the less.

The converse is not true. In constructive desertion, in addition to a course of conduct, one has to prove the *factum* of separation, and facts such as words of expulsion would be more cogent on the issue of desertion than they would be in a trial for cruelty.

The following cases may be consulted on this subject but they were more relevant to High Court proceedings than those before magistrates.

Dixon v. *Dixon* [1953] P. 103, where Davies, J., found difficulty in reconciling *Pike* v. *Pike* with *Edwards* v. *Edwards* and *Butland* v. *Butland* (1913), 29 T.L.R. 729, and also the words of Lord Greene in *Buchler* v. *Buchler* [1947] P. 25, when he said that conduct short of an actual matrimonial offence would be sufficient just cause.

Hill v. *Hill* [1954] P. 291: Davies, J., held that a wife was estopped from pleading just cause and cross petitioning for constructive desertion in reply to a husband's petition for desertion, when a previous petition by her for cruelty had been dismissed, the trial judge holding that the incidents complained of were extremely trivial and that she had entirely failed to prove a matrimonial offence of any kind.

Thompson v. *Thompson* [1957] P. 19: the subject of estoppel *per rem judicatam* was considered at length, and it was held that the court had an overriding duty which it could use at its discretion to go into the facts again and, per Hodson and Morris, L.JJ., that estoppel did not apply where the subject of litigation was not the same, e.g., a petition for divorce on the ground of desertion after a petition for maintenance under s. 23 of the Matrimonial Causes Act, 1950, for wilful neglect to maintain had been dismissed.

Estoppel

The subject of estoppel in matrimonial cases was considered by the Court of Appeal in *Thoday* v. *Thoday* [1964] 2 W.L.R. 371, and most of the relevant cases were considered.

The facts were that the wife petitioned for divorce on the ground of cruelty. The husband did not give evidence and relied on his counsel's submission. Collingwood, J., dismissed the petition, holding the cruelty not proved, particularly having regard to the absence of satisfactory evidence of injury to the wife's health.

Subsequently the husband petitioned for divorce on the ground of desertion, and the wife in her answer pleaded just cause for leaving and cross prayed on the ground of constructive desertion. The wife's particulars covered a good deal of the ground in her cruelty petition but went substantially beyond this. On an appli-

cation to strike out these paragraphs, the Court of Appeal, allowing
an appeal from Hewson, J., held that the power to strike out a
pleading was only to be exercised in a plain and obvious case and
that as the allegations raised new issues of just cause and constructive desertion which had not been decided in the previous
suit there was no estoppel *per rem judicatam*.

Diplock, L.J., pointing out that by s. 4 of the Matrimonial
Causes Act, 1950, the court was required to exercise a quasi-
inquisitorial function, which was not easy to adapt to the concept
of estoppel *inter partes*, said at p. 384: —

> " 'Estoppel' merely means, that under the rules of the
> adversary system of procedure upon which the common law
> of England is based, a party is not allowed in certain circum-
> stances to prove in litigation particular facts or matters which,
> if proved, would assist him to succeed as plaintiff or defendant
> in an action."

He then indicated at pp. 384–385 that estoppel *per rem
judicatam*, that is an estoppel created by the decision of a court,
includes two species: —

> " 1. ' Cause of action estoppel ' which prevents a party
> to an action from asserting or denying, as against the other
> party, the existence of a particular cause of action, the non-
> existence or existence of which has been determined by a
> court of competent jurisdiction in previous litigation between
> the parties.
>
> 2. ' Issue estoppel ' which is restricted not to the cause of
> action but an issue in such action. This has to be distinguished
> from ' fact estoppel.' The determination by a court of com-
> petent jurisdiction of the existence or non-existence of a fact,
> the existence of which is not in itself a condition the fulfilment
> of which is necessary to the cause of action which is being
> litigated before that court, but which is only relevant to
> proving the fulfilment of such a condition, does not estop
> at any rate *per rem judicatam* either party in subsequent
> litigation from asserting the existence or non-existence of the
> same fact contrary to the determination of the first court."

" Cause of action estoppel " in the divorce court would be
" matrimonial offence estoppel," and in this case the wife did
not seek to allege the same matrimonial offence, i.e., cruelty, as
she unsuccessfully alleged in the previous litigation. " Just cause "
and " constructive desertion " involve an issue which was identical

with cruelty. According to Diplock, L.J., in cruelty two conditions must be fulfilled: (1) serious ill-treatment of the spouse, and (2) adverse effect on the health of the other spouse or reasonable apprehension thereof.

To establish the defence of just cause for separating, condition (1) alone need be fulfilled. To establish constructive desertion, condition (1) must be fulfilled and also something else, viz., the ill-treatment must be accompanied by expulsive words or amount in itself to expulsive conduct, or perhaps it is better to say misconduct caused the parting.

As Collingwood, J., had made no specific finding as to the ill-treatment there was no estoppel.

Willmer, L.J., gave the leading judgment and his views may be summarised as follows: —

(1) Estoppel *per rem judicatam* applies to matrimonial cases subject to the duty of the court imposed by s. 4 of the Matrimonial Causes Act, 1950 (*Thompson* v. *Thompson* [1957] P. 19; *Laws* v. *Laws* [1963] 1 W.L.R. 1133).

(2) In a case where the cause of action or plea in defence in the second action is precisely the same as raised in the previous case, and has been the subject of full examination and adjudication, the party seeking to re-open the matter will be estopped (*Holland* v. *Holland* [1961] 1 W.L.R. 194; *Warren* v. *Warren* [1962] 1 W.L.R. 1310).

(3) Where the cause of action or plea in defence is different from that put forward in the previous suit, a party will not normally be estopped (*Fisher* v. *Fisher* [1960] P. 36; *Bohnel* v. *Bohnel* [1964] 1 W.L.R. 179; *Foster* v. *Foster* [1954] P. 67 and *Cooper* v. *Cooper* (*No.* 2) [1955] P. 168).

(4) There may be cases where a party may be estopped from raising particular issues, if they are precisely the same as those previously adjudicated upon. If it is not clear that this issue has been specifically dealt with there will be no estoppel (*Dixon* v. *Dixon* [1953] P. 103).

If the court held the party was not a credible witness so that it was not satisfied the event related did not take place he would be estopped; similarly, if it were held the conduct was not of a grave and weighty nature (*Bright* v. *Bright* [1954] P. 270 and *Hill* v. *Hill* [1954] P. 291).

If, however, it had been held that the conduct was grave and weighty but had not caused injury to health, evidence of it would be admissible in the second suit (*Edwards* v. *Edwards* [1950] P. 8).

CHAPTER 3

CRUELTY

I. INTRODUCTION

THE Act of 1960, s. 1 (1) (*b*), provides that a married woman or a married man may apply by way of complaint to a magistrates' court for an order under this Act against the other party to the marriage, on the ground that the defendant has been guilty of persistent cruelty to—

    (i) the complainant;

    (ii) an infant child of the complainant; or

    (iii) an infant child of the defendant who, at the time of the cruelty, was a child of the family.

A. History

Cruelty *simpliciter* is a matrimonial offence for which there were remedies in the High Court. It is an offence which the courts dealing with matrimonial affairs have recognised for many hundreds of years. The ecclesiastical courts had jurisdiction to grant a divorce *a mensa et thoro*, that is to say, a judicial separation on the ground of cruelty. When the Matrimonial Causes Act, 1857, transferred the jurisdiction in divorce to the High Court, it continued the remedy for cruelty by way of judicial separation, and it also made it a ground for divorce by a wife if she proved adultery in addition. After 1937 either party could get a divorce on the ground of cruelty (Matrimonial Causes Act, 1965, s. 1 (1) (*a*) (iii)), until the Divorce Reform Act, 1969 when the whole basis for divorce was changed.

The Summary Jurisdiction (Married Women) Act, 1895, gave a wife, for the first time, a summary remedy in the magistrates' court for persistent cruelty and now, as shown above, the Act of 1960 has extended the remedy to both spouses. The Act of 1895 provided that the wife had to show that the cruelty had caused her to leave and live separate and apart from her husband. This requirement was abolished by the Summary Jurisdiction (Separation and Maintenance) Act, 1925, s. 1 (1).

Until 1870, the only cruelty recognised by the courts was physical violence, but in that year it was decided in *Kelly* v. *Kelly* (1870), 2 P. & D. 59, that there could be cruelty in the absence of physical violence, that is to say, there could be cruelty by a course of conduct, as where a husband tyrannises over his wife and tries to bend her to his will although he uses no physical force. This is sometimes known as mental cruelty.

The next milestone was *Russell* v. *Russell* [1897] A.C. 395, which decided that injury to health, or a reasonable apprehension thereof, was an essential element in cruelty. This was decided by the House of Lords by a majority of five to four.

The latest developments are that intention to hurt is not an essential element (*Gollins* v. *Gollins* [1964] A.C. 644 (H.L.)) and insanity is not necessarily a defence (*Williams* v. *Williams* [1964] A.C. 698 (H.L.)).

Under the new system of divorce the concept of cruelty has been abolished, but by s. 1 (2) (*b*) of the Matrimonial Causes Act, 1973, replacing the Divorce Reform Act, 1969, s. 2 (1) (*b*), one way of proving that the marriage has irretrievably broken down is to show that the respondent has behaved in such a way that the petitioner cannot reasonably be expected to live with the respondent. This behaviour on behalf of the respondent may be described as intolerable conduct or in other words misconduct without any reference to its effect on the health of the petitioner.

The following cases are relevant:—

Fuller v. *Fuller* [1973] 2 All E.R. 650 (C.A.), where the wife went back as a lodger but nevertheless was entitled to a decree.

Bradley v. *Bradley* [1973] 3 All E.R. 750 (C.A.), where the wife swore that she had no alternative but to be in a bedroom with the husband and to cook his meals for she was too frightened to do anything else. She lost her case at first instance but the Court of Appeal ordered a new trial, holding that she was entitled under the section to show that she could not reasonably be expected to live with him although she had been forced to do so.

Ash. v. *Ash* [1972] Fam. 135, Bagnall, J. The wife claimed that she could not reasonably be expected to live with her husband due to his acts of violence and intoxication. It was held that the court had to consider fully the respondent's behaviour and the petitioner's character and a decree was granted.

Katz v. *Katz* [1972] 1 W.L.R. 955, Sir George Baker, P. A similar petition by the wife. The husband showed signs of mental illness, constantly criticised his wife and made objectionable remarks about her. He accused his wife of misdoing and called her a tramp and a slut. It was held that the behaviour of the husband was conduct by one spouse which affected the other and a decree was granted.

Pheasant v. *Pheasant* [1972] Fam. 202. The husband petitioner relied on the Divorce Reform Act, 1969, s. 2 (1) (*b*), now the Matrimonial Causes Act, 1973, s. 1 (2) (*b*). He contended that the wife had been unable to give him the spontaneous demonstrative affection that his nature demanded, that he could not be reasonably expected to continue to live with her and that the marriage had irretrievably broken down. Ormrod, J., dismissed the petition, holding that the test was closely similar to but not necessarily identical with that formerly applied to constructive desertion, and was whether it was unreasonable to expect the petitioner to put up with the respondent's behaviour, bearing in mind their characters and their difficulties.

The last three cases were considered in *Livingstone-Stallard* v. *Livingstone-Stallard* [1974] 3 W.L.R. 303, and at p. 307 Dunn J. said: —

" Mr. Reece, for the husband, has referred me to the cases— all of which have been so far decided at first instance—*Ash* v. *Ash, Pheasant* v. *Pheasant* and *Katz* v. *Katz* and has submitted that incompatibility of temperament is not enough to entitle a petitioner to relief, that the behaviour must be of sufficient gravity so that the court can say that it would, under the old law, have granted a decree of divorce on the ground of constructive desertion. Mr. Reece has submitted that the best approach is to apply the test which was applied in the constructive desertion cases, bearing in mind that the parties are married and that the conduct must be sufficiently grave to justify a dissolution of the marriage; weighing the gravity of the conduct against the marriage bond or, as Mr. Reece put it, against the desirability of maintaining the sanctity of marriage. I have in the past followed the reasoning of Ormrod, J., in *Pheasant* v. *Pheasant* but, on reflection and with respect, I am not sure how helpful it is to import notions of constructive desertion into the construction of the

Matrimonial Causes Act, 1973. Nor, speaking for myself, do I think it helpful to analyse the degree of gravity of conduct which is required to entitle a petitioner to relief under section 1 (2) (*b*) of the Act. As Lord Denning, M.R., has emphasised in another context, the Act of 1973 is a reforming statute and section 1 (2) is in very simple language which is quite easy for a layman to understand. Coming back to my analogy of a direction to a jury, I ask myself the question: Would any right-thinking person come to the conclusion that this husband has behaved in such a way that this wife cannot reasonably be expected to live with him, taking into account the whole of the circumstances and the characters and personalities of the parties? It is on that basis that I approach the evidence in this case."

It will be seen that the judges had not yet given a definitive interpretation of the words " the respondent has behaved in such a way that the petitioner cannot reasonably be expected to live with the respondent." It is by no means certain that this means grave and weighty misconduct as formerly was required in cruelty and constructive desertion. The difference in approach in the High Court and divorce county court and the magistrates' court and the standards required has now become very striking and emphasises the necessity of bringing the law in the magistrates' court into line with the other courts. It is also suggested that having regard to the modern approach to these problems as mentioned by Lord Denning, M.R., in *Wachtel* v. *Wachtel* [1973] Fam. 72, 91 (C.A.), the magistrates should not ignore this change in outlook.

B. Cruelty and legal cruelty

The popular idea as to what is cruelty (the Shorter Oxford Dictionary defines cruelty as " The quality of being cruel; disposition of inflicting suffering; delight in or indifference to another's pain; mercilessness, hard-heartedness ") does not necessarily coincide with such cruelty as will entitle a spouse to a remedy in law. The latter is sometimes called " legal cruelty."

It is true that Shearman, J., in *Hadden* v. *Hadden* (1919), *The Times*, 5th December, said: —

> " I do not think there is such a thing as ' legal cruelty ' as distinct from actual cruelty; cruelty means ' cruel conduct,' whether in legal language or the vernacular."

But this expression, however, is exceptional and in general the courts do make a distinction between the two.

Lord Herschell in *Russell* v. *Russell* [1897] A.C. 395, at p. 445, said: —

> "It was conceded by the learned counsel for the appellant and is indeed, beyond controversy, that it is not every act of cruelty in the ordinary and popular sense of the word which amounted to *saevitia*, entitling the party aggrieved to a divorce; that there might be many wilful and unjustifiable acts inflicting pain and misery in respect of which that relief could not be obtained."

Then there is the rather extraordinary statement of Sir Francis Jeune, P., in *Jeapes* v. *Jeapes* (1903), 89 L.T. 74: —

> "To leave a wife to starve is undoubtedly cruelty, but I was not certain it could be construed into legal cruelty."

More recently, in *Jamieson* v. *Jamieson* [1952] A.C. 525, at p. 544, Lord Merriman had this to say about legal cruelty and cruelty in its popular sense: —

> "But it is important to bear in mind that in determining 'what elements were treated as essential to the constitution of the *saevitia*, or cruelty, which entitled to a divorce,' Lord Herschell was careful to point out that judges had not infrequently, when speaking of acts as 'cruel,' 'used that word in its popular sense, and not as indicating that the acts were cruel in the legal acceptance of the term—that is to say such as would entitle to a divorce' ([1897] A.C. 395, 449), and he quoted pronouncements both of Lord Stowell and of Sir John Nicholl in that sense to illustrate the risk of confusion arising from the use of the words 'cruelty' and 'cruel' in the popular sense. Therefore, when the legal conception of cruelty is described as being conduct of such a character as to cause danger to life, limb or health, bodily or mental, or to give rise to a reasonable apprehension of such danger, it is vital to bear in mind that it comprises two distinct elements; first, the ill-treatment complained of, and secondly, the resultant danger or the apprehension thereof. Thus it is inaccurate and liable to lead to confusion, if the word 'cruelty' is used as descriptive only of the conduct complained of, apart from its effect on the victim."

The courts have never fixed the line which divides those acts which they consider "legal cruelty" from those which they think do not, for that line must necessarily be a fluctuating one depending on the ideas prevalent in each generation. In this sense, what is "legal cruelty" is in some measure a test of our civilisation.

There is a tendency, albeit a gradual one, to relax the requirements of what is necessary to prove "legal cruelty" and our ideas are less rigid or hard-boiled than those of our fathers or forefathers. Lord Stowell said in *Evans* v. *Evans* (1790), 1 Hagg. Con. 35, at p. 37: —

"... it is the duty of the courts and consequently the inclination of the courts to keep the rule extremely strict. The causes must be grave and weighty and such as to show an absolute impossibility that the duties of married life can be discharged."

Then as late as 1919 Scrutton, L.J. (*The Times*, 11th December) said that the law of cruelty in divorce must be closely watched against a tendency to take a too lenient view of what constituted "legal cruelty," and after agreeing with Lord Stowell's words about "grave and weighty," he added: —

"It is not every conduct that causes injury to health which could be considered cruelty."

An examination of modern cases shows that the courts will find conduct as "legal cruelty" which would hardly have been held to be such in former times. See, for example, *Lauder* v. *Lauder* [1949] P. 277, where a husband sulked and ignored his wife, seriously affecting her nervous stability, which was held by the Court of Appeal to be cruelty.

From recent dicta it would appear that while "popular cruelty" may not amount to "legal cruelty," yet "legal cruelty" must contain the ingredient of "popular cruelty." Thus in *Le Brocq* v. *Le Brocq* [1964] 1 W.L.R. 1085, Harman, L.J., at p. 1089, said: —

"'Cruel' means 'cruel' . . . I think moreover that 'cruel' is not used in any esoteric or 'divorce court' sense of that word, but that the conduct complained of must be something which an ordinary man—or a jury: I suppose this court sits as a jury—would describe as 'cruel' if the story were fully told."

Pearson, L.J., at p. 1093, used similar language and quotes Lord Evershed in *Gollins* v. *Gollins* [1964] A.C. 644, at p. 670: —

"The question in all such cases is, to my mind, whether the

acts or conduct of the party charged were ' cruel ' according to the ordinary sense of that word . . ."

And Salmon, L.J., uses almost identical language at p. 1096.

As against these views, it must be pointed out that five judges in *Gollins* would have dismissed the wife's summons on the ground that the conduct complained of was not cruelty in the ordinary sense of the word; and yet five judges (whose views prevailed) held that the husband was guilty of legal cruelty.

Davies, L.J., in the Court of Appeal ([1964] P. 32) quoted from the judgment of the Divisional Court, at p. 59: —

" They (the justices) did not ask themselves whether the conduct amounted to cruelty in the ordinary sense of that term . . . we do not consider that the husband's conduct, however reprehensible, can properly be stigmatised by the word ' cruelty ' in its ordinary acceptation."

Davies, L.J., continued: —

" This seems with all respect a dangerous test."

Judging from the division among the judges in this case it certainly seems to be an uncertain one. His view was that any conduct, by one spouse to the other, provided that it can properly be described as ill-treatment and provided that it is sufficiently grave and weighty and not merely trivial, can amount to cruelty, if such conduct causes injury to health or a reasonable apprehension thereof.

Lord Reid in *Williams* v. *Williams* [1964] 3 A.C. 698, at p. 721, said: —

" So the law cannot just take ' cruelty ' in its ordinary or popular meaning because that is too vague."

Lord Pearce does not deal directly with this point, but he says in *Gollins* (*supra*), at p. 695: —

". . . when reprehensible conduct or departure from the normal standards of conjugal kindness causes injury to health or an apprehension of it, it is, I think, cruelty if a reasonable person, after taking due account of the temperament and all the other particular circumstances, would consider that the conduct complained of is such that this spouse should not be called on to endure it."

Nothing about cruelty in its ordinary sense here.

Gollins decided that intention was not a necessary ingredient in cruelty. It is submitted that in the popular sense, intention, or malignity, or deliberation, or at the least callousness, is. (It is interesting to note that Dr. Johnson in his Dictionary defines Cruel (referring to persons), as—" Pleased with hurting others; inhuman; hard-hearted; without pity; without compassion; savage; barbarous; unrelenting.") Here lie the seeds of confusion, which magistrates will have to guard against.

If it is understood that the expression, " cruel means cruel," is just another way of saying that the conduct must be grave and weighty, no harm will be done; but if it is understood that the conduct, *in addition* to being grave and weighty, has to be cruel in its popular or ordinary meaning (as is apparently suggested by Sir Jocelyn Simon, P., in *Mulhouse* v. *Mulhouse* [1964] 2 All E.R. 50, at p. 65) then difficulties will arise.

It is submitted that one can only say with certainty that legal cruelty has two positive ingredients: (1) the misconduct must be grave and weighty, and (2) it must cause injury to health or a reasonable apprehension thereof (Diplock, L.J., in *Thoday* v. *Thoday* [1964] 2 W.L.R. 371, at p. 385, and Scarman, J., in *Noble* v. *Noble* [1964] 2 W.L.R. 349, at p. 351).

II. DEFINITION OF CRUELTY

In *Russell* v. *Russell* [1897] A.C. 395, the House of Lords by a majority adopted the definition of cruelty laid down by Lopes and Lindley, L.JJ., in the Court of Appeal in the same case ([1895] P. 315), namely that: —

> " There must be danger to life, limb or health (bodily or mental) or a reasonable apprehension of it " (see [1897] A.C. 399).

In this case, the wife had circulated false charges of an unnatural offence against her husband, and had persisted in them when she knew them to be false, but there was no evidence that his health had been thereby affected. The argument for the husband by Sir Robert Reid, Q.C., was briefly this ([1897] A.C., at p. 408): —

> " These are the elements you have to consider—danger to health, physical injury, and so forth. But there are exceptional cases. The question is, do cases like the present come within the category of minor cases of annoyance, or do they rather

come within the class of case Lord Stowell described as making the consortium absolutely impossible."

By the narrow majority of five to four the House of Lords rejected this argument. In the words of Lord Davey (at p. 467): —

" The general idea which, I think underlies all those decisions is that, while declining to lay down any hard and fast definition of legal cruelty, the courts acted on the principle of giving protection to the complaining spouse against the actual or apprehended violence, physical ill-treatment, or injury to health."

Cruelty which does not cause injury to health, or apprehension of it, must be rare, and in practice it is not difficult to produce medical evidence that the complaining spouse has in fact suffered physical injury, or that there is a danger of it, or that he or she is suffering from a nervous disorder, varying from nervous debility to neurasthenia.

The definition of Lopes and Lindley, L.JJ., is, of course, not really a definition at all. It prescribes a necessary ingredient, without which conduct is not cruelty, but it does not go on to say that conduct which causes injury to health, or a reasonable apprehension of it, is necessarily cruelty; and since *Russell* v. *Russell* more than one judge has emphasised that to prove " legal cruelty," mere proof of injury to health is not sufficient (*Baker* v. *Baker* (1919), *The Times*, 11th December (C.A.); *Horton* v. *Horton* [1940] P. 187).

No judge has formulated a comprehensive definition of cruelty. Lord Halsbury, Q.C., in *Russell* v. *Russell* [1897] A.C. 395, at p. 424, said: —

" As no judge has ever affected to define what cruelty is exhaustively, so no judge has in my view ever affected to prescribe what individual elements would go to make up cruelty."

Lord Simon's observations in *Watt or Thomas* v. *Thomas* [1947] 1 All E.R. 582, at p. 585,* are typical of many judges in their cautious approach to this subject: —

". . . the leading judicial authorities in both countries who have dealt with this subject are careful not to speak in too precise and absolute terms, for the circumstances which might

* The report in [1947] A.C. 484 does not contain this passage.

conceivably arise in an unhappy married life are infinitely various. Lord Stowell, for example, in *Evans* v. *Evans* (1 Hagg. Con. 37, 38), avoids giving a ' direct definition,' while insisting that ' mere austerity of temper, petulance of manners, rudeness of language, want of civil attention and accommodation, even occasional sallies of passion, if they do not threaten bodily harm, do not amount to legal cruelty.' "

The Judge Ordinary in *Hudson* v. *Hudson* (1863), 33 L.J. P.M. & A. 5, at p. 6, said: —

" Pehaps exact definition is to be distrusted where all is degree and circumstance. Certainly great precision in the rule serves only to beget laxity in its application."

Lord Tucker, in the House of Lords in *Jamieson* v. *Jamieson* [1952] A.C. 525, at p. 550, gave a salutary warning about defining cruelty as follows: —

" My lords, judges have always carefully refrained from attempting a comprehensive definition of cruelty for the purposes of matrimonial suits, and experience has shown the wisdom of this course. It is in my view equally undesirable—if not impossible—by judicial pronouncement to create certain categories of acts or conduct as having or lacking the nature or quality which render them capable or incapable in all circumstances of amounting to cruelty in cases where no physical violence is averred.

Every such act must be judged in relation to its attendant circumstances, and the physical or mental condition or susceptibilities of the innocent spouse, the intention of the offending spouse and the offender's knowledge of the actual or probable effect of his conduct on the other's health (to borrow from the language of Lord Keith in 1951 S.C. 286, 300) are all matters which may be decisive in determining on which side of the line a particular act or course of conduct lies."

There are, too, the words of Lord Reid in *King* v. *King* [1953] A.C. 124, at p. 146, on the difficulty of formulating a definition to cover all kinds of cruelty: —

" I do not intend to try and define cruelty. I doubt whether any definition would apply equally well to cases where there has been physical violence and to cases of nagging, or to cases where there has been a deliberate intention to hurt and to cases where temperament and unfortunate circumstances have caused much of the trouble. But in cases like the present, the wife's conduct must at least be inexcusable, after taking everything into consideration."

The same learned law lord in *Gollins* v. *Gollins* [1964] A.C. 644, at p. 658, said: —

"No one has ever attempted to give a comprehensive definition of cruelty and I do not intend to try to do so. Much must depend on the knowledge and intention of the respondent, on the nature of his (or her) conduct and on the character and physical or mental weaknesses of the spouses, and probably no general statement is equally applicable in all cases except the requirement that the party seeking relief must show actual or probable injury to life, limb or health."

And at p. 660, he said: —

"I would try to reduce tests, rules and presumptions to a minimum."

For Lord Pearce's definition, see p. 165.

An objective test which is very useful in practice was suggested by Sir John Nicholl in *Westmeath* v. *Westmeath* (1827), 2 Hagg. Eccl. Supp. 61, at p. 71, when he said that while cruelty was impossible to define with precision, the test should be rather the effects produced than the acts done.

A. Injury to health

As we have seen, it is an essential element in legal cruelty that the health of the complaining spouse has been affected, or that there is a reasonable apprehension that it will be affected. It is common, therefore, in trying cruelty cases, for the court to consider the question of injury to health first, for if this cannot be established the complaint must fail. Injury to health, or its probability, need not be proved by medical evidence, but it frequently is. If, for instance, there is evidence of black eyes, it does not require a doctor to say that this is an injury to health. The doctor who as a rule can give the best evidence is the doctor who has regularly attended the complainant, especially where the complaint is not of assaults but of a course of conduct undermining the complainant's health. Wallington, J., criticised a specialist who had seen a husband on one occasion, and from his answers to questions had formed an opinion which he gave to the court. The learned judge said that he had usurped the function of the court. The Court of Appeal in *Barker* v. *Barker* (1957), *The Times*, 1st November, said these criticisms were unjustified. The doctor had done what any doctor would have done in the circumstances, but on the other hand it was futile to call a doctor who had seen the patient only once, after the spouses had parted company, to speak about his health when they were together.

In *Fromhold* v. *Fromhold* [1952] 1 T.L.R. 1522 (C.A.), the trial judge sought to make a distinction between particular injuries such as black eyes and bruises and injury to general health. Not surprisingly, the Court of Appeal rejected this distinction.

Singleton, L.J., said, at p. 1525: —

" If the judge is satisfied . . . that a man kicks his wife in the way this wife says she was kicked, and bruises her in the way that she said she was bruised . . . I should have thought it was something which most people would regard as cruelty."

Hodson, L.J., said, at p. 1527: —

" With regard to the direction on the matter of injury to health, the evidence given by the wife was to the effect that she was injured on various parts of her body. The judge seems quite clearly to have misdirected the jury in saying that since there was no evidence of injury to her general health, particular injuries of the nature described were immaterial."

Where there have been physical assaults there is no need to prove general injury to health. In *Hudson* v. *Hudson* [1965] 2 All E.R. 82 the magistrates had dismissed a summons for persistent cruelty although there was evidence of physical assaults and bruising. The Divisional Court (Sir J. Simon, P., and Faulks, J.) held that the justices were wrong if they had held that cruelty could not be proved unless general injury to health was shown. Where there was evidence of physical violence, medical evidence of injury to health was not essential. The court approved *Mulhouse* v. *Mulhouse* [1964] 2 All E.R. 50, at p. 56, where Sir J. Simon, P., had said: " Of course if there is violence between the parties the court will not stop to inquire whether there is general injury to health. . . ."

There can be injury to health without cruelty. In *Sapier* v. *Sapier* (1964), 108 Sol. J. 338, Scarman, J., found that both parties suffered injury to health due to their own inadequacies. He held there had been no cruelty by either party though the marriage had broken down.

When can it be said that there is a reasonable apprehension that health will suffer? If, after a long course of conduct, health has not been affected, can it be said that it will be affected in the future? The Court of Appeal thought not in *Jillings* v. *Jillings* (1958), *The Times*, 11th December. This was a case of nagging over a period of years, but the husband remained a strong and healthy man. Hodson, L.J., said the test was not wholly subjective, and when one talked about a reasonable apprehension of injury to health, it was necessary to apply an objective test.

B. Grave and weighty

While, as we have seen, judges have repeatedly referred to the impossibility of defining cruelty, at the same time there has been a constant search for a formula, or a touchstone, whereby it can be recognised. On the positive side, it is now accepted that—

1. the conduct must have caused injury to health or a reasonable apprehension thereof;
2. the misconduct must be of a grave and weighty nature;
3. the misconduct must be the cause of the injury to health, etc.; and
4. the test is not that of the reasonable man, but the effect on this spouse of this conduct, or misconduct.

The phrase " grave and weighty " is now a time-honoured one, having been used in the courts for at least 150 years. Thus Lord Stowell in *Evans* v. *Evans* (1790), 1 Hagg. Con. 35, said, at p. 37: —

> " the causes must be grave and weighty and show an absolute impossibility that the duties of married life can be discharged."

(See the discussion at pp. 20 and 75 in connection with Constructive Desertion.)

The phrase is a vague one, but this must necessarily be so, since we are dealing with matters of degree. There is no clear demarcation line dividing cruel conduct from non-cruel conduct, and therefore the court has a discretion. There can be no absolute standard but the court has to make up its mind what conduct a spouse should not be expected to tolerate. On one side of the line are the petty irritations, which must always occur when two people are living in close intimacy; and on the other serious matters of complaint. It is not necessary to know exactly where the line is as long as the court can decide on which side the conduct falls. No better phrase than " grave and weighty " has yet been discovered,

to describe the serious conduct for which there is a remedy, unless
it be the one word " intolerable."

In *Saunders* v. *Saunders* (1964), 108 Sol. J. 605, the court considered that the departure from normal standards of conjugal
kindness referred to by Lord Pearce in *Gollins* v. *Gollins, supra,*
was not sufficient. The conduct must be grave and weighty.

See also *McEwan* v. *McEwan* (1964), 108 Sol. J. 198, and *Le
Brocq* v. *Le Brocq* [1964] 1 W.L.R. 1085 (C.A.).

III. PERSISTENT CRUELTY

Section 1 of the Act of 1960 provides a remedy for *persistent*
cruelty. The Act of 1960 has therefore retained the anomaly (more
apparent than real) that a higher degree of cruelty is required
in the magistrates' court, for a separation and maintenance order,
than was required in the High Court for a divorce (see *Barker* v.
Barker [1949] P. 219, where a Divisional Court disapproved a
contrary view by Denning, J., in *Perks* v. *Perks* [1945] 2 All E.R.
491).

Cruelty in the expression " persistent cruelty " means the same
thing as cruelty has always meant in the divorce court until the
Divorce Reform Act, 1969, but with the addition of the element
of persistence. This was said by Evans, P., in *Cornall* v. *Cornall*
(1910), 74 J.P. 379, which was approved by Lord Merriman, P.,
in *Jamieson* v. *Jamieson* [1952] A.C. 525, at p. 543. See also
Donkin v. *Donkin* [1933] P. 17.

One act of cruelty which might formerly have been sufficient
for a decree of dissolution of the marriage is insufficient for an
order under this section (*Rigby* v. *Rigby* [1944] P. 33). There must
be a minimum of two acts (*Simcock* v. *Simcock* [1932] P. 94) and
if they occur on one day it will be persistent cruelty. As Barnes, J.,
trenchantly said in *Broad* v. *Broad* (1898), 78 L.T. 687: —

> " If there is cruelty on one day, why should it not amount to
> persistent cruelty? Is the wife to wait until she is half
> murdered? "

In *Goodman* v. *Goodman* (1931), 95 J.P. 95, Lord Merrivale
thought persistent cruelty meant cruelty continued over a period of
time and persevered in, and added: " It does not mean a sudden
act of violence or a sudden quarrel," but obviously, while one
can agree with both these assertions, they give no guidance as to

conduct which is less than the one or more than the other. This case really turned on condonation and therefore the expressions are obiter.

The following year the Divisional Court held that an assault in June, 1931, followed by one in October, 1931, after the parties had separated, was sufficient evidence of persistent cruelty (*Simcock* v. *Simcock*, *supra*; and see *Waters* v. *Waters* [1967] 3 All E.R. 417, where cruelty took place during non-cohabitation).

In a later case the husband assaulted his wife in 1928, followed by another assault in March, 1931, and a third in July, 1932 (*Donkin* v. *Donkin*, *supra*). There was also evidence of drunkenness and threats. The court thought there was sufficient evidence of a course of conduct which amounted to persistent cruelty.

The result is that a wide discretion is left to the justices, for their decision is largely one of fact. The decision often depends on the impression made by the parties in the witness-box, rather than on the number of assaults. Some justices are inclined to interpret " wear and tear " of married life as " rough and tumble " and allow considerable latitude to husbands, particularly if the parties come from the poorer classes.

In practice, the element of persistence does not make much difference. It is true that one act of cruelty could be sufficient to establish cruelty in the High Court, whereas in the magistrates' court there must be at least two acts, but even in the magistrates' court there are now remedies for single acts where the defendant has been convicted (s. 1 (1) (c)).

In *Brewster* v. *Brewster* [1971] 2 All E.R. 993 a wife summoned her husband for persistent cruelty, and although her evidence was unchallenged by her husband and was corroborated by her son the complaint was dismissed. A Divisional Court allowed the appeal, holding that the justices were wrong if they had held that acts before the six months could not be taken into account and also if they had held that the breakdown of the marriage had been caused by other causes than the husband's cruelty. Sir J. Simon, P., at p. 998, said: —

> "In a case of persistent cruelty, later conduct can only be evaluated in the light of earlier conduct, whether good or bad. The relevance of temporal remoteness is twofold: where the ground of the complaint is in the distant past, the court should scrutinise the evidence all the more narrowly, and the

further past it is, the more likely it is to have been condoned and less easy it is to be revived by subsequent misconduct."

He referred to *Richardson* v. *Richardson* [1949] 2 All E.R. 330 (see p. 309) and approved *Bond* v. *Bond* [1964] 3 All E.R. 346.

Particulars of cruelty in the magistrates' court

It was argued in *Frith* v. *Frith* [1962] 1 W.L.R. 1436, D.C. (Sir J. Simon, P., and Scarman, J.), that the rule which provides that particulars of adultery, or reasonable belief in adultery, must be given prior to the hearing should also apply to cruelty and constructive desertion based on conduct in the nature of cruelty. This was not so. Courts of summary jurisdiction were designed to provide immediate relief free from formality.

The true rule was that where there was a complaint to justices, if a matrimonial offence was alleged, the defendant could apply to the complainant before the date of the hearing for particulars. If such a request was not complied with and, as a result, a matter arose in the course of the hearing which the defendant was unable to deal with, his proper course was to ask for an adjournment, and justices had the power to grant an adjournment when the justice of the case required it.

Practitioners should note this direction, as it is the first indication that it is proper to ask for particulars in cruelty and constructive desertion cases, and the complainant refuses the particulars at the risk of the proceedings being delayed by an adjournment.

IV. TWO KINDS OF CRUELTY

Cruelty cases divide themselves readily into two kinds: —

  (*a*) the crude, brutal kind and
  (*b*) cases where there is no physical violence or hardly any, but the conduct of the defendant is such as to affect the complainant's health.

A. Physical violence

These are cases of direct physical violence. The question here is one of quantum, that is to say, has the physical injury inflicted by the respondent or defendant been sufficient to amount to cruelty in law?

As a rule, these cases cause little difficulty. The defendant, usually the husband, behaves like a brute and assaults his wife violently from time to time.

What then is the minimum which will establish " legal cruelty "? It was established that one isolated act would be sufficient in the divorce court but this is most unusual.

Sir John Nicholl in *Westmeath* v. *Westmeath* (1827), 2 Hagg. Eccl. Supp. 61, at p. 71, said: —

> " The law does not require that there should be many acts; for if one act should be of that description which should induce the court to think that it is likely to occur again, and to occur with real suffering, there is no rule that should restrain it from considering that to be fully sufficient to authorise its interference."

In *Grossi* v. *Grossi* (1873), L.R. 3 P. & D. 118, Hannen, J.O., held that cruelty was established when there was one act of violence by the husband, who had been bound over by the magistrates to keep the peace for twelve months.

In *Reeves* v. *Reeves* (1862), 3 Sw. & Tr. 139, the husband demanded money from his wife, swore at her, said he did not want her, attempted to strike her and kicked her on the leg. Sir Cresswell Cresswell held that this was sufficient to justify a decree (see also *Saunders* v. *Saunders* (1847), 1 Rob. Eccl. 549: spitting in the wife's face, accompanied by pushing and dragging her about a room, and the admission by the husband that he had once slapped her face).

In *Smallwood* v. *Smallwood* (1862), 5 L.T. 324, Sir Cresswell Cresswell refused to grant a decree where the husband sprang on his wife, threw her down and nearly strangled her. The wife withdrew from cohabitation, but continued to live under the same roof until the husband left some time later.

The distinction the courts seem to make is that regard must be had to the circumstances under which the isolated blow is given, and also to the character of the person giving it. If the violent act was committed during unusual excitement, and without producing any considerable injury to the person, it is not cruelty, but if the blow is a serious one, and the court is of the opinion that the injured spouse would be in danger of further ill-usage, then it will be sufficient.

Acts which, if taken by themselves, may be trivial, when considered cumulatively may amount to cruelty (*Jamieson* v. *Jamieson* [1952] A.C. 525; *Waters* v. *Waters* [1956] P. 344).

The following two cases are examples of the fact that in certain circumstances one act of cruelty was sufficient to prove cruelty for the purposes of a divorce.

In *Railton* v. *Railton* (1962), *The Times*, 25th May, Wrangham, J., granted a decree nisi of divorce on the ground of cruelty where there was one serious assault only, and the Court of Appeal in *Edwards* v. *Edwards* (1962), 106 Sol. J. 590, allowed an appeal from a commissioner who refused to grant a divorce where the act of cruelty occurred when the husband was cutting sandwiches with a bread knife when a quarrel arose, and the husband rushed at his wife, knife in hand and stuck the knife in the wall. The wife's health was so affected that she was unable to work for a month as a result of a neurosis. The commissioner had held that the husband had had no intention of injuring his wife, though doubtless he put her in fear. Danckwerts, L.J., with whom Diplock, L.J., agreed, said that he disagreed with the commissioner that this isolated incident was insufficient to amount to cruelty. Ormerod, L.J., agreed but added that other incidents which had been condoned had been revived by the knife incident.

In *Hudson* v. *Hudson* [1965] 2 All E.R. 82 and *Mulhouse* v. *Mulhouse* [1964] 2 All E.R. 50 it was decided that where there was evidence of physical violence there was no need to prove general injury to health.

B. Course of conduct

Cruelty by a course of conduct presents considerable difficulties because of the great variety of circumstances encountered.

Channell, B., in *Kelly* v. *Kelly* (1870), L.R. 2 P. & D. 59, at p. 61, said: —

" It is obvious that the modes by which one of two married persons makes the life or health of the other insecure are infinitely various, but as often as perverse ingenuity may invent a new manner of producing the result, the court must apply the remedy by separating the parties. The most frequent form of ill-usage which amounts to cruelty is that of personal violence, but the courts have never limited their jurisdiction to such cases alone."

There have been many cases of cruelty by a course of conduct before the courts, and to detect a consistent stream of principle flowing through them is not easy. We are often told each case must depend on its own facts, which is not very helpful. It is, however, clear that individual acts, not in themselves cruel, might by accumulation amount to cruelty.

Thus Shearman, J., in *Hadden* v. *Hadden* (1919), *The Times*, 5th December, said: —

> "It has been urged by Mr. Holman Gregory, that this act and that act did not amount to cruelty. It is the old dilemma of the Greek philosophers, that as the addition of one grain of millet to another could not constitute a heap, a heap could never be formed. But the true test is that laid down in *Kelly* v. *Kelly* [*supra*]: 'Many acts which are venial in themselves, become reprehensible when they take their place as parts of a system'."

Barnes, J., in *Walker* v. *Walker* (1898), 77 L.T. 715, at p. 717, said: —

> "There were many acts which perhaps did not amount to cruelty but which were nevertheless admissible as evidence of general conduct."

and Wilde, J.O., in *Power* v. *Power* (1865), 4 Sw. & Tr. 173, at p. 177: —

> "But cruelty . . . lies in the cumulative ill-conduct which the history of the married life discloses."

On the other hand one should bear in mind the warning of Sir C. Robinson (*Westmeath* v. *Westmeath* (1827), 2 Hagg. Eccl. Supp. 61), who said that it must always be remembered that a natural test of injuries of this kind is the sense in which they are received. If they are not resented at the time as injuries the court might not view them as cruelty.

See also *Benton* v. *Benton* [1958] P. 12, where a wife's allegations of sodomy were held not to revive condoned cruelty because the husband did not resent the allegations.

The very important case of *Jamieson* v. *Jamieson* [1952] A.C. 525 settled a number of important questions on the subject of cruelty by a course of conduct where no personal violence was involved.

The wife complained that the husband had attempted to impose his will on her; that he provided her with insufficient housekeeping money; had told her that he hated the sight of her, that he was frequently rude and threatening in the presence of the children and greatly humiliated her; that he had not entertained her, and refused to share his life with her or discuss his business with her; that he ignored her, caused her great grief and had caused a serious breakdown in her health. It was held that if all this was proved it would amount to cruelty.

The following points were made: —

(1) Mental cruelty was well recognised as a ground for a separation for a long time (Lord Normand, at p. 533).

(2) Conduct must be judged up to a point by reference to the victim's capacity for endurance, in so far as that capacity is or ought to be known to the guilty spouse (Lord Normand, at p. 535).

(3) Where the cruelty is mental cruelty the guilty spouse must either intend to hurt the victim or at least be unwarrantably indifferent as to the consequences to the victim (ibid.).

(4) " Actual intention to hurt " is a circumstance of peculiar importance because conduct which is intended to hurt strikes with a sharper edge than conduct which is the consequence of mere obtuseness or indifference (ibid.).

(5) What on paper may seem to be a number of pinpricks may present a very different aspect when developed in evidence (Lord Normand, at p. 536).

(6) A specific intention to injure is not necessary to prove cruelty (Lord Merriman, P., at p. 540).

(7) In matrimonial causes, it is right to use the time-honoured maxim that a man is presumed to intend the natural consequences of his acts so long as it is understood that the presumption is not irrebuttable and that it is only to be applied in connection with conduct which can fairly be described as ill-treatment (Lord Merriman, P., at p. 541).

(8) Relief to the wife is based on past behaviour and is not

withheld if it is not proved that further acts of cruelty will be committed (Lord Merriman, P., at pp. 542 and 546).

(9) Before the magistrates cruelty is the same as in the divorce court with the addition of the element of persistence (Lord Merriman, P., at p. 543).

(10) Cruelty must be judged by the conduct of the respondent and its effect on the complainant.

(11) ". . . there can hardly be a more grave matrimonial offence than to set out on a course of conduct with the deliberate intention of wounding and humiliating the other spouse and making his or her life a burden and then to continue in that course of conduct in the knowledge that it is seriously affecting his or her mental and physical health. Such conduct may consist of a number of acts each of which is serious in itself, but it will be even more effective if it consists of a long-continued series of minor acts no one of which could be taken as serious if taken in isolation. Once it is established that physical violence is not a necessary ingredient of cruelty . . . then I can see no justification in principle for requiring that the deliberate acts of the defender must be of a certain character . . ." (Lord Reid, at p. 548).

(12) It is undesirable to make categories of acts which amount to cruelty. "Every such act must be judged in relation to its attendant circumstances, and the physical or mental condition or susceptibilities of the innocent spouse, the intention of the offending spouse and the offender's knowledge of the actual or probable effect of his conduct on the other's health . . . are all matters which may be decisive in determining on which side of the line a particular act or course of conduct lies" (Lord Tucker, at p. 550).

1. *Tyrannical conduct*

It is cruel for a husband to try to dominate his wife and break her spirit. *Jamieson* v. *Jamieson* [1952] A.C. 525 is a good example of such conduct. But the leading case is *Kelly* v. *Kelly* (1870), L.R. 2 P. & D. 59, which has stood the test of time. The husband was obsessed with an idea that, on religious grounds, it was his duty to make his wife completely subservient to him, and that she should be kept under strict discipline. Accordingly, he refused to sit at meals with her, insisted on occupying a separate room, put a control on the money he allowed her, censored her correspondence and so on; he also called her a vile traitor and apostate and said that she had given her confidence to another man, all of which resulted in the deterioration of the wife's health. The court, while agreeing the husband had no intention of hurting his wife, held that this conduct amounted to legal cruelty.

This case emphasises that neither physical violence nor a deliberate intention to hurt are necessary for " legal cruelty."

It has been repeatedly followed, as, for instance, in *Mytton* v. *Mytton* (1886), 11 P.D. 141 (quoted with approval in *Lauder* v. *Lauder* [1949] P. 277), where the husband used harsh and irritating language and tyrannical conduct, and without using physical violence made the wife's life intolerable and injured her health; and Butt, J., said at p. 143: —

> " Although I am not aware that there were any blows, still if the conduct of the husband is such as to endanger the life or even the health of the wife that is cruelty in every sense of the word whether we talk of ' legal cruelty ' or anything else."

In *Bethune* v. *Bethune* [1891] P. 205, the husband refused to share a bed with his wife, told her he loathed being in the same room with her and that he hated her presence, and habitually neglected her. On one occasion only he gave her a violent push; and this conduct was held to be cruelty.

In more recent times we have the case of *Sleightholme* v. *Sleightholme* (1956), *The Times*, 17th February, where the whole course of conduct of the husband was to dominate his wife or alternatively to drive her into a mental home. The magistrates found that he had tried to break his wife's spirit and their decision was upheld by the Divisional Court (Lord Merriman, P., and Collingwood, J.).

2. *Abusive and violent language*

The earlier cases seem to suggest that language alone (apart from threats) could never be cruelty.

Sir Wm. Scott in *Kirkman* v. *Kirkman* (1807), 1 Hagg. Con. 409, said that mere words of abuse, however reproachful, could not be cruelty. Dr. Lushington said the same of disgusting language in *Chesnutt* v. *Chesnutt* (1854), 1 Sp. Ecc. & Ad. 196.

This hard doctrine has not been steadily followed in later cases. Harsh and irritating language, together with tyrannical conduct, was held to be cruel (*Mytton* v. *Mytton* (1886), 11 P.D. 141). It is also an element in *Bethune* v. *Bethune* [1891] P. 205, *Waddell* v. *Waddell* (1862), 2 Sw. & Tr. 584, and *Pritchard* v. *Pritchard* (1920), 37 T.L.R. 104. Wilde, J.O., in *Knight* v. *Knight* (1865), 4 Sw. & Tr. 103, thought the husband's unrestrained violence of language an important part of the husband's cruel course of conduct.

Finally, we come to the modern case of *Atkins* v. *Atkins* [1942] 2 All E.R. 637 (see also *Usmar* v. *Usmar* [1949] P. 1, where Willmer, J., used similar language in a similar case) where the cruelty consisted solely of a long history of nagging. Henn Collins, J., said at p. 638: —

> " One knows that dropping water wears away the stone. Constant nagging will become completely intolerable, and though in the case of married life you may be able to point to no single instance which could possibly be described as in common parlance ' a row,' yet nagging may be of such a kind, and so constant, that it endangers the spouse on whom it is inflicted."

3. *Threats*

" If a man keeps his wife in fear and subjection by threats he is guilty of cruelty " (Lord Merrivale, in *Donkin* v. *Donkin* [1933] P. 17).

The court has always acted on the principle that it is not necessary to wait until the blow falls before it will afford protection. After all, the mere offer of a blow is a crime; and when a person is in bodily fear of a named person, and the court finds that there is reasonable ground for such fear, the defendant can be made to enter into a bond and even find sureties for his good behaviour. See Stone's Justices' Manual, 1974, pp. 414–416. The divorce court and the domestic court similarly protects a spouse, usually the wife.

The words of Lord Stowell are often quoted: —

> " I have heard no one case cited in which the court has

granted a divorce without proof of a reasonable apprehension of bodily hurt. I say an apprehension, because assuredly the court is not to wait till the hurt is actually done; but the apprehension must be reasonable: it must not be an apprehension merely from an exquisite and diseased sensibility of mind."

(*Evans* v. *Evans* (1790), 1 Hagg. Con. 35, at p. 40; approved in *Curtis* v. *Curtis* (1858), 1 Sw. & Tr. 192; *Kelly* v. *Kelly* (1870), L.R. 2 P. & D. 59; *Russell* v. *Russell* [1897] A.C. 395). For other cases of threats see *Bostock* v. *Bostock* (1858), 1 Sw. & Tr. 221; *Kirkman* v. *Kirkman* (1807), 1 Hagg. Con. 409; *Knight* v. *Knight* (1865), 4 Sw. & Tr. 103; *D'Aguilar* v. *D'Aguilar* (1794), 1 Hagg. Eccl. 773.

4. *False and true accusations*

False accusations, particularly of infidelity, have readily been held to be cruelty. Sir Francis Jeune, P., in *Jeapes* v. *Jeapes* (1903), 89 L.T. 74, doubted whether leaving a wife to starve was " legal cruelty," but he had no doubt in the same case that charging her falsely with infidelity was. Barnes, J., in *Walker* v. *Walker* (1898), 77 L.T. 715, said that he could conceive nothing more abominable and degrading than for a husband to make an unfounded charge of infidelity against his wife, and he was not sure the cruelty would not be equally great if the charge were true and the husband had condoned it, afterwards repeating the accusation. See also *Knight* v. *Knight* (1865), 4 Sw. & Tr. 103.

In *Otway* v. *Otway* (1813), 2 Phillim. 109, the husband followed his wife from room to room abusing her and accusing her of adultery and incest, and this was held to be cruelty. It is difficult to reconcile this case with *Gale* v. *Gale* (1852), 2 Rob. Eccl. 421, where Sir John Dodson said at p. 423: —

" Undoubtedly the charge of having committed incest is not *per se* sufficient to constitute legal cruelty."

though he had added that coupled with averments of a substantial character it might form part of the libel.

A charge of incest, which did not affect the health of the other spouse, would not amount to cruelty, and in all these cases it must be understood that the conduct complained of only amounts to cruelty when the health of the spouse is thereby affected. In the famous case of *Russell* v. *Russell* [1897] A.C. 395 where the wife circulated unfounded charges of homosexuality, the court would have found this conduct to be cruel if the husband's health had been affected.

A modern case is *Davis* v. *Davis* (1929), *The Times*, 1st November, where the wife had circulated false accusations of her husband's adulterous intercourse with members of his congregations whilst Wesleyan minister in various places, and his health had suffered. Lord Merrivale granted a decree for judicial separation.

See also *Williams* v. *Williams* [1964] A.C. 698, where the husband's false accusations of infidelity were readily accepted as cruel.

A wife married her husband knowing he was impotent. Nevertheless she nagged about it during the marriage and his health was injured in consequence. Payne, J., held this to be cruelty (*J.* v. *J.* (1967), 111 Sol. J. 792).

5. *Adulterous associations*

An adulterous association or flagrant infidelity does not in itself amount to cruelty, but for a husband to obtrude his infidelity on his wife's attention, to flaunt his adultery before her, to force his paramour on his wife's company or to debauch his servants in the same house as he is residing with his wife might be cruelty, if his wife's health is thereby affected. Flirting with a woman to the wife's distress, the wife being in delicate health (*Barrett* v. *Barrett* (1903), 20 T.L.R. 73), introducing the wife to loose women (*Fenwick* v. *Fenwick* (1922), 38 T.L.R. 603), bringing a paramour home and sleeping with her in the same house as his wife (*Litton* v. *Litton* (1924), 40 T.L.R. 272), installing his mistress in his house (*Le Couteur* v. *Le Couteur* (1896), *The Times*, 2nd March) where his wife's health was affected have all been held to be cruelty. As a wife can now get an order on the ground of adultery alone, without the necessity of proving cruelty as well, the discussion under this head is largely academic.

Nevertheless a recent case has shown that this subject still has some practical importance. In *Walker* v. *Walker* [1962] P. 42, a Divisional Court (Lord Merriman, P., and Lloyd-Jacob, J.) held that ill-treatment consisting of a persistent course of conduct on the part of one spouse deliberately inducing in the mind of the other spouse the reasonable belief that adultery was being committed and resulting in injury to health, mental and physical, or a reasonable apprehension of danger thereof, amounted to cruelty.

In *Windeatt* v. *Windeatt* [1962] 1 All E.R. 776 (C.A.), a husband associated with another woman, but no sexual impropriety was alleged. The wife was a sensitive, highly strung woman and this conduct affected her health. It was held that cruelty was proved, and that it was a question of fact and degree to be judged on the facts as a whole, and that intention to injure could be inferred. Per Willmer, L.J., at p. 785: ". . . it has been well established that any course of conduct, even if it is not consciously aimed at the other spouse, may nevertheless amount to cruelty if it is intentionally pursued with a callous indifference to the feelings of the other spouse . . ."; and at p. 787: "I do not accept that only in such circumstances (i.e., where association with another woman was flaunted before the wife) could association with another woman be regarded as ill-treatment by a husband or a wife, because, as I indicated during the argument, I can think of no course of conduct more calculated to cut at the root of matrimonial life than that, or anything more calculated to hurt and distress a sensitive wife."

Condoned adultery can be relied upon as cruelty, and evidence of it can be given as part of the history of the marriage and the conduct complained of (*Chalcroft* v. *Chalcroft* [1969] 3 All E.R. 1172).

6. *Indifference, neglect and boorishness*

Although it has been said that mere coldness or lack of affection cannot amount to cruelty, yet indifference and neglect may reach such a degree that it makes the married life of the other spouse intolerable, and if it affects that spouse's health, may amount to cruelty. The following are a few examples: —

(1) A husband took no notice of his wife and child; never went out with them; seldom spoke to them and on one occasion struck his wife in the face when she complained about him coming home late (*Fenwick* v. *Fenwick* (1922), 38 T.L.R. 603).

(2) Husband selfish; went and came as he liked; did not tell wife; attitude of indifference and dislike; no weekly allowance (*Hadden* v. *Hadden* (1919), *The Times*, 5th December).

(3) Husband refused to share bed with wife. Told her he loathed being in the same room with her and hated her presence. Habitually neglected her and refused to take her out (*Bethune* v. *Bethune* [1891] P. 205).

(4) Husband refused to occupy the same room as his wife; gave her insufficient money for the household expenses; never went anywhere with her; ceased to speak to her; took no notice of the child (*Walmesley* v. *Walmesley* (1893), 69 L.T. 152).

(5) Husband ignored wife completely. Would not speak to her. In company he treated her as though she did not exist, and habitually " looked through " her (*Hamilton* v. *Hamilton* (1948), York Assizes (unreported)).

(6) Wilful neglect to maintain and indifference to wife's financial difficulties (*Gollins* v. *Gollins* [1964] A.C. 644).

(7) But where the husband was of a retiring and submissive nature, silent and morose, with no interest in family life, the Court of Appeal reversed the commissioner who found cruelty (*Le Brocq* v. *Le Brocq* [1964] 1 W.L.R. 1085 (C.A.)).

A similar case, where taciturnity was held by the Court of Appeal not to be cruelty was *McEwan* v. *McEwan* (1964), 108 Sol. J. 198.

The leading case in this line is *Lauder* v. *Lauder* [1949] P. 277, where the husband was subject to moods and fits of depression during which he sulked and ignored his wife for many days on end, with serious effect to her health. All the judges in the Court of Appeal, Lord Merriman, Singleton, L.J., and Pearce, J., agreed that " sending a wife to Coventry " would be cruelty, but Singleton, L.J., thought mere moodiness and sulkiness when the husband ignored his wife for periods, even if it hurt her health, was not cruelty. He thought a spouse ought to take the other for better or worse, but on that basis there would be no divorce at all. Lord Merriman said there were two essential elements to be proved in a charge of cruelty: (*a*) something which could be called misconduct on the part of the husband, and (b) danger, actual or apprehended, to the health of the wife.

Since then, there have been a number of cases which have underlined the principles laid down in *Lauder* v. *Lauder,* as follows: —

Simpson v. *Simpson* [1951] P. 320, where the wife summoned the husband for persistent cruelty, and her allegations included keeping her short of money, and that he humiliated her by closing her account at the stores where she dealt, kept food bought for himself in a garage, refused to take her for a holiday or out in his new car, neglected her by staying out of the house, was taciturn, unfriendly, and had told her to go on several occasions. Her health was affected. In general, her complaints were of stinginess, lack of affection and attention, callous indifference, taciturnity and selfishness. The magistrates made an order in favour of the wife. On appeal to the Divisional Court (Lord Merriman, P., and Karminski, J.) it was said for the husband that there was an unwarrantable extension of the principles laid down in *Lauder* v. *Lauder, supra,* that his alleged misconduct was nothing more than the " development and manifestation of his character, acting so to speak in its own sphere " and that it was no more " aimed at " his wife than her conduct was aimed at him. The Divisional Court held that the husband had entered on a course of conduct which was calculated to break his wife's spirit and, if possible, to induce her to leave the matrimonial home, and it amounted to persistent cruelty.

Karminski, J., in *Eastland* v. *Eastland* [1954] P. 403, where the husband failed to make provision for his wife, and was irresponsible and shiftless, found that this case was on the other side of the line from *Simpson* v. *Simpson*; even though the wife's health had been affected, he refused to grant a decree in an undefended divorce case, and referred to *Kaslefsky* v. *Kaslefsky* [1951] P. 38, to which this case had certain similarities, in that the husband's conduct was " negative." He thought that the conduct constituting cruelty must be taken as being capable of being aimed at or directed or impinging upon the petitioning wife, which in this case he did not think it did. Both *Eastland* and *Kaslefsky* were overruled by *Gollins* v. *Gollins* [1964] A.C. 644.

In *Waters* v. *Waters* [1956] P. 344 the wife brought a summons against her husband for persistent cruelty, which was dismissed by the magistrates at the end of the wife's case. Lord Merriman, P., said that although the justices had a right to throw out a case if they thought there was nothing in it, without listening to the other side, generally speaking, particularly in cruelty cases, it was unwise to do so. It is all-important in this type of case to hear the whole story. The wife's case was that the husband was extremely boorish, unbearably taciturn, that he deliberately refused to co-operate in the running of the house, and his personal uncleanliness was so bad and persisted in, in spite of her protests, that it became nauseating, and that he was callously indifferent and offensive when she was injured in an accident. She said she was heading for a nervous breakdown. It was said for the husband that his conduct was a manifestation of his character (based on *Horton* v. *Horton* [1940] P. 187) but, as Lord Merriman pointed out, this was an excuse that did not succeed either in *Kelly* v. *Kelly* (1870), L.R. 2 P. & D. 59, or *Lauder* v. *Lauder, supra.*

Lord Merriman said he would not attempt the task, which was difficult if not impossible, of reconciling the cases in the Court of Appeal. He referred to *Jamieson* v. *Jamieson* [1952] A.C. 525, which decided that actual intention was not necessary if the respondent was unwarrantably indifferent to the consequences. He also cited *Lang* v. *Lang* [1955] A.C. 402, which he said applied to cases of mental cruelty just as much as to cases of constructive desertion, saying: —

> " If a reasonable man . . . would know, and this husband did know, that continuance in the course of conduct complained of would have an injurious effect on his wife's mental health, what more is necessary? "

The court ordered a rehearing of the case.

The authorities were reviewed by the Divisional Court in *Cade* v. *Cade* [1957] 1 W.L.R. 569. The wife summoned the husband for persistent cruelty alleging that he had shown callous indifference to her, that he stayed out late leaving the wife with the children in spite of her protests, and persisted in this when the birth of the third child was imminent, even though he knew she was frightened to be left alone in this condition. He refused to sleep with her and told her he had lost interest in her and wanted a separation. Her health was affected. The magistrates found persistent cruelty proved. The husband appealed. It was argued for him that his conduct was passive and there was no evidence of a deliberate intent to hurt his wife. Collingwood, J., referred to *Simpson* v. *Simpson*, *Waters* v. *Waters* and *Jamieson* v. *Jamieson*, *supra*, which controvert these arguments. It was also argued that the allegations were really of desertion, and that desertion could not be an ingredient of cruelty, for which *Carpenter* v. *Carpenter* [1955] 1 W.L.R. 669 was cited. Collingwood, J., held that simple desertion could be cruelty, and that in constructive desertion it was impossible to draw the line between conduct which constitutes expulsive conduct and conduct which constitutes an ingredient in cruelty.

7. *Unnatural conduct*

Unnatural conduct by one spouse to the other, without that other's consent, can be cruelty. The difficulties are to prove the conduct, as corroboration is difficult to obtain; and to prove absence of consent. Greer, L.J., for instance, thought that sodomy could never be an act of cruelty, because it could not be done without the other's consent (*Statham* v. *Statham* [1929] P. 131, at p. 145).

Attempted sodomy would be cruelty. Indeed, the Court of Appeal in *Moss* v. *Moss* [1916] P. 155, at p. 158, described such acts as " gross cruelty." The onus of proving consent, where sodomy was admitted or proved to have been committed on a wife, was on the husband (*Keogh* v. *Keogh* [1962] 1 W.L.R. 191, Wrangham, J.), and a wife who so consents without fraud is barred from relief on that ground (*Tickler* v. *Tickler* (1962), *The Times*, 15th November, Wrangham, J.). Similarly, if a husband forces a wife to masturbate him, that will be cruelty (*Raw* v. *Raw* [1947] W.N. 96).

Holborn v. *Holborn* [1947] 1 All E.R. 32 was a case of constructive desertion, but it is submitted that the reasoning applies equally to cruelty. Therefore, where a spouse persists in making sexual demands which are known to be regarded by the other spouse as inordinate or revolting, such persistent lack of consideration may be so grave and weighty as to amount to cruelty. In *Lawson* v. *Lawson* [1955] 1 W.L.R. 200 (C.A.) it was decided in a case of persistent cruelty, where the wife made allegations of sodomy, that if she was believed that she was not a consenting party, then she could not be regarded as an accomplice, and therefore corroboration was not necessary. No one can doubt that in all such cases it is desirable.

If a woman persists in unnatural relations with other women, in spite of the protests of her husband, and her conduct causes a breakdown in his health, this is cruelty (*Gardiner* v. *Gardiner* [1947] 1 All E.R. 630). The result will be the same even if Lesbianism is not proved, if the association between the wife and another woman is such as to give the husband grave anxiety as to the nature of the association, and is persisted in against the husband's entreaties (*Spicer* v. *Spicer* [1954] 1 W.L.R. 1051).

In *Coffer* v. *Coffer* (1964), *The Times*, 16th May, Payne, J., held that homosexual activities between the wife and another woman, or a reasonable suspicion of them, can amount to cruelty. In this case the court exercised its discretion in regard to the husband's adultery with the same woman.

8. *Crime*

The fact that one spouse commits criminal offences is not cruelty in itself, but the conduct may amount to cruelty. The following are illustrations: —

Thompson v. *Thompson* (1901), 17 T.L.R. 572.—The husband was convicted of indecent assaults on a number of young women and was sentenced to twelve months' imprisonment. His wife's health was shattered. Jeune, P., found cruelty proved.

Bosworthick v. *Bosworthick* (1901), 18 T.L.R. 104.—This was a case of a number of indecent assaults and also indecent exposure. The husband was sent to prison and the wife's health was affected. Barnes, J., followed the decision in *Thompson* v. *Thompson*, above. Both these cases were undefended divorces.

Boyd v. *Boyd* [1955] P. 126.—The husband was sent to prison for five years for incest with his daughter, and after his release was convicted for an indecent assault on a girl of twelve. Bucknill, J., held this was cruelty.

Warburton v. *Warburton* (1953), *The Times*, 10th July.—The husband had been to prison for burglary before the marriage, and after was sent to prison for two years for stealing. Mr. Commissioner Latey found cruelty had been proved, but the Court of Appeal reversed this decision. It was pointed out that there was only one conviction since the marriage. Somervell, L.J., said that prima facie a conviction for crime was not necessarily cruelty, though it was a shock to the wife. Jenkins, L.J., said he would not lay down a general rule that in no circumstances could a course of conduct amount to cruelty. It was easy to imagine cases where the criminal career of the husband involved or implicated the wife—if, for example, the matrimonial home was made a receptacle for stolen goods. Hodson, L.J., said there must be some evidence either of an intention to injure the other spouse, or of facts from which such an intention could be inferred. He was not saying that in no circumstances could persistence in a course of criminal conduct against a protesting spouse be the basis of a charge of cruelty.

Woollard v. *Woollard* [1955] P. 85.—Mr. Commissioner Latey, who tried this case, distinguished it from *Warburton* v. *Warburton, supra*. The husband was convicted of fraudulent conversion in 1939, theft in 1941, and obtaining money by fraud in 1951. Money obtained by fraud had been paid into his wife's account without her knowledge. He had been bound over for the first offence and sent to prison for the next two. The wife's remonstrances had been met with resentment and her health had been affected. Held that cruelty was proved.

Cooper v. *Cooper* (*No.* 1) [1955] P. 99.—The husband had been convicted of an indecent assault upon the child of the marriage. Based upon this and other complaints, the wife took out a summons for persistent cruelty, which was dismissed by the magistrates. The Divisional Court (Lord Merriman, P., and Karminski, J.) sent the case back for a re-hearing. The court approved of *Thompson* v. *Thompson, Bosworthick* v. *Bosworthick* and *Boyd* v. *Boyd, supra*, and quoted with approval the following passage from the judgment of Denning, L.J., in *Kaslefsky* v. *Kaslefsky* [1951] P. 38, at p. 46: —

> " Such an intention (i.e., to hurt the wife) may readily be inferred from the fact that it is the natural consequence of the conduct, especially when the one knows, or it has been brought to his notice, what the consequences will be, and nevertheless he does it, careless and indifferent whether it distresses the other or not."

Karminski, J., said at p. 114: —

> ". . . one . . . cannot help but infer . . . that a man in these circumstances who did what apparently he did to his small child must have assumed or known, if he thought about it, that it would cause the greatest distress and possibly severe injury to health to the mother of the child, his wife."

Karminski, J., then considered *Jamieson* v. *Jamieson* (see p. 177), emphasising that in mental cruelty there must be either intent to hurt the victim, or unwarrantable indifference as to the consequences, and to the danger of putting acts into compartments to see if they are relevant to cruelty, and added at p. 122: —

> "It is essential, as Lord Tucker pointed out, to judge every act in relation to its attendant circumstances, the condition or susceptibilities of an innocent spouse, the intention of the offending spouse, and no less the offender's knowledge of the actual or probable effect of his conduct on the other's health."

Ivens v. *Ivens* [1955] P. 129 (C.A.).—A husband, the respondent in divorce proceedings, had committed indecent assaults on the wife's daughter by a previous marriage. The husband promised his wife he would not repeat this conduct, but he did and his wife's health was affected. The commissioner who tried the case dismissed the petition on the ground that the husband's conduct was not aimed at the wife, but this was reversed by the Court of Appeal, approving the decision in *Cooper* v. *Cooper*, *supra*. Lord Goddard, C.J., said he could not imagine anything which would be more likely to undermine the woman's health than the knowledge that her husband was indecently assaulting her child, and he could conceive nothing more calculated to justify the court in saying that the husband knew perfectly well what the effect of his conduct would be upon his wife's health. Hodson, L.J., quoted the commissioner: " I do not find that he did it to hurt his wife; it was to satisfy his own unnatural, reprehensible feelings "! Quite true, but this did not mean that it was not cruel to the wife.

Crawford v. *Crawford* [1956] P. 195; [1955] 3 All E.R. 592. —The husband pleaded guilty to indecent exposure and asked for six other cases to be taken into account. There was also evidence of bullying. The magistrates found persistent cruelty proved, and this finding was upheld by the Divisional Court. The headnote in the All England Reports summarises the principles in cases of mental cruelty as follows: —

    (i) cruelty may be inferred from the whole facts and atmosphere disclosed by the evidence;

    (ii) actual intention on the part of the husband to injure the wife is an important but not an essential factor;

   (iii) it is impossible to create categories of facts or conduct which do or do not amount to cruelty;

   (iv) sexual offences directly relevant to the husband's conjugal obligations may constitute ill-treatment of the wife;

    (v) mental ill-treatment may be coupled with physical ill-treatment in order together to found a charge of persistent cruelty.

Spitalnick v. *Spitalnick* (1956), *The Times*, 24th March.—The husband before his marriage carried on criminal activities but this was unknown to his wife. Four hours after the wedding he was arrested and, on conviction, received sentences of four years' and seven years' imprisonment to run concurrently. The wife's health was affected. The commissioner said there was no doubt about the cruelty, but had there been cruelty since the marriage? He found there was.

Watson v. *Watson* (1957), *The Times*, 11th April.—The husband who was a clerk in Holy orders pleaded guilty to a number of indecent assaults on boys and his wife's health was affected. Willmer, J., held that whether the husband had intended it or not, he had been extremely cruel to his wife.

Priestley v. *Priestley* (1958), *The Times*, 7th November.—The husband had been a criminal before his marriage, but he had led his wife to believe he was of good character. After the marriage, he told her about his criminal activities. She was shocked but her health was not affected. Subsequently she left him and, desperately anxious to find her and having no money, he broke into a house in her parents' village and was subsequently sentenced to three years' imprisonment. Wrangham, J., held that as he was not living with his wife at the time, his crime did not amount to cruelty. This decision was upheld in the Court of Appeal, mainly on the ground that there was no evidence of injury to health.

Ingram v. *Ingram* [1956] P. 390.—A wife was convicted of espionage. The husband, whose health had been affected by her conduct, was entitled to a divorce on the ground of her cruelty, since the conduct was so serious that, considered against the background of the marriage, it struck at the roots of the matrimonial relationship and it was pursued by the wife regardless of the hurt it might do to the husband, and thereby was shown to have been intended to injure him.

Stanwick v. *Stanwick* [1970] 3 All E.R. 983.—The wife had adopted a persistent course of irresponsibility and dishonesty with regard to money matters and had been convicted of forgery and false pretences. The husband's health had been affected. His petition for divorce on the ground of cruelty was dismissed but this was reversed by the Court of Appeal. Davies, L.J., said this was a worse case than *Gollins* and also referred to *Crump* v. *Crump* [1965] 2 All E.R. 980, where the wife had a mania about cleanliness for fear of cancer and Cairns, J., held this to be cruel conduct although she could not help herself. He also referred to *Cade* v. *Cade* [1957] 1 All E.R. 609, where Lord Merriman had held that desertion in itself could be cruelty.

9. *Drunkenness*

Persistent drunkenness after warnings that such a course is inflicting pain on the other spouse, certainly if it is known to be injuring the other's health, may, of itself, amount to cruelty (*Baker* v. *Baker* [1955] 1 W.L.R. 1011).

The evidence was that the husband was a persistent and heavy drinker, and that his drinking had broken up the marriage. Davies, J., had no doubt that his conduct amounted to cruelty.

In *Renwick* v. *Renwick* (1960), *The Times*, 9th March, the husband had too much to drink too often. On one occasion he insisted on driving his wife in his car while drunk. She tried to stop him and took away the ignition key, and he smacked her face. Wrangham, J., held that his insistence on driving with her as a passenger when it was dangerous, was cruel.

In *Parmenter* v. *Parmenter* (1962), *The Times*, 13th October, the husband was a chronic alcoholic, and his doctor had seen him drunk on a number of occasions and had warned him that he was endangering his wife's health and, indeed, she had to have medical treatment as a result of his conduct. Willmer, L.J., with whom Harman and Davies, L.JJ., agreed, said the question was purely one of fact, and he was quite satisfied that the requirement of the matrimonial offence of cruelty had been proved. He thought it was cruelty in one of its worst forms. The wife, who had to put up with this sort of behaviour week after week, suffered more than the wife whose husband occasionally knocked her about and bruised her. Harman, L.J., said that drunkenness in the ordinary way was not cruelty, but a long-continued state of drunkenness, resulting in the kind of behaviour described, even though not intended directly in any conscious way, must have been known to him to have the effect which the doctor said it had.

The extraordinary feature of this case is how the commissioner came to the conclusion that cruelty had not been proved. It appears that he relied on the decision of the Divisional Court in *Gollins* v. *Gollins* [1964] P. 32. The Court of Appeal held that in any event this decision was not applicable, and as it happens, it has since been overruled ([1964] A.C. 644). Presumably the learned commissioner was influenced by the comments of the Divisional Court in *Gollins* v. *Gollins* to the effect that the husband's conduct was not aimed at the wife, and was merely a development of his character and so forth. This illustrates once more how such tests are misleading. Harman, L.J., said that those who continued to direct themselves in cases of cruelty by what happened in other cases of cruelty were following a will-of-the-wisp. In other words, it is more a question of common sense than pedantic hairsplitting.

See also *Hall* v. *Hall* [1962] 1 W.L.R. 1246 (considered at pp. 22 and 106), a case on constructive desertion arising out of drunkenness.

10. *Coitus interruptus; contraceptives; refusal of sexual intercourse*

(a) *By husband*

The persistent refusal of a husband to have intercourse other than by *coitus interruptus* will be cruelty if this practice causes injury to the wife's health. Willmer, J., in *White* v. *White* [1948] P. 330, at p. 340, said: —

> " I feel that a husband must take his wife as he finds her, and if she is a woman of a type who needs the full and natural completion of the act, then to persist in withholding it from her in the face of her repeated complaints and objections, is in itself an act of cruelty, of cold calculated cruelty . . ."

This case was followed by Wallington, J., in *Walsham* v.

Walsham [1949] P. 350 (who held, however, that mere abstention from sexual intercourse could not amount to cruelty, even though it might injure the wife's health) and Hodson, J., in *Cackett* v. *Cackett* [1950] P. 253. In all these three cases, the husband had been warned by the wife's doctor of the consequences to her health if the practice was persisted in.

In *Knott* v. *Knott* [1955] P. 249, this element of the doctor's warning was absent. In this case the wife complained that the husband practised *coitus interruptus* against her will, and would not let her have a child. She would not accept contraceptives. Her health was affected. Sachs, J., reviewed all the cases. He relied on the speech of Lord Tucker in *Jamieson* v. *Jamieson* [1952] A.C. 525 that in cases of cruelty, the judge had to consider the physical or mental condition or susceptibilities of the innocent spouse, and then said at p. 255: —

> " I am not prepared to hold that his wife's deterioration in health was due to an active intent to injure her. I do hold that in his determination to continue with *coitus interruptus* and to refuse to let the wife have children he was ' reckless ' of the effect upon his wife and that his conduct in that respect was ' inexcusable '—to use adjectives adopted by Lord Normand in *King* v. *King* [1953] A.C. 124, at pp. 129–130. . . .
> I would hold that for a man deliberately and without good reason permanently to deny to a wife with a normally developed maternal instinct a fair opportunity of having even a single child is of itself criminal when injury to her health results—at any rate where the husband adopts a course which preserves to himself a measure of sexual enjoyment."

In *P.* v. *P.* [1964] 3 All E.R. 919 a commissioner had refused a decree to a wife because her husband had refrained from sexual intercourse through lack of desire, holding that this could not be cruelty although the wife's health had been affected. This decision was criticised by Cairns, J., in *Crump* v. *Crump* [1965] 2 All E.R. 980, at p. 984, saying: " I am bound to say that if conduct, otherwise cruel, cannot necessarily be excused on the ground of insanity, I find it difficult to see how it can be excused on the ground of inclination or disinclination."

However the Court of Appeal in *B.* (*L.*) v. *B.* (*R.*) (1965), 109 Sol. J. 831, followed *P.* v. *P.*, *supra*, where the husband had lacked enthusiasm for sexual intercourse, Davies, L.J., saying that the evidence had not shown that the husband had pursued a callous course of conduct calculated to injure the wife's health. It would be interesting to see whether deliberately refraining from sexual intercourse whether from a general disinclination or lack of enthusiasm resulting in disappointment to the other spouse would amount to intolerable conduct under the Act of 1973.

The Court of Appeal in *Sheldon* v. *Sheldon* [1966] P. 62 held that a husband's persistent refusal of sexual intercourse without explanation over a long period of time which had caused injury to the wife's health amounted to cruelty and justified her in leaving home. See also *Hughes* v. *Hughes* (1966), 110 Sol. J. 349.

(b) By wife

Cairns, J., held that the conduct of a wife, in particular her refusal of sexual intercourse, was unjustified and a grave and weighty matter which adversely affected the husband's health and amounted to cruelty (*Evans* v. *Evans* [1965] 2 All E.R. 789).

The case of *Fowler* v. *Fowler* [1952] 2 T.L.R. 143 (C.A.) at first gives the impression that if a wife refuses to bear children, and refuses intercourse except with contraceptives, this is not cruelty even if the husband's health is affected unless she does it deliberately to hurt him. It will be seen, however, that in that case the commissioner found that the husband's anxiety state could not be attributed to the wife's attitude. Two members of the Court of Appeal stressed the wife's fear of childbirth. The passages about intention must now be considered in the light of *Jamieson* v. *Jamieson* [1952] A.C. 525, which was decided subsequently in the House of Lords. The whole position is considered by Mr. Commissioner Latey, Q.C., in *Forbes* v. *Forbes* [1956] P. 16 (where the wife deliberately refused to have children, and insisted on contraceptives with the knowledge of the injurious effect her conduct was having on the health of her husband), and he said at p. 23 : —

> " I am satisfied that the injury to his mental health was caused in the main by his wife's persistent refusal to be a wife to him in the full sense, (a) by her insistence on contraceptives, and (b) by refusing him the chance of a child.
>
> Quite apart from the exhortation in the solemnization of matrimony that, first, Christian marriage was ordained for the procreation of children, I cannot ignore the fact that it is a natural instinct in most married men to propagate the species and to bear the responsibilities, and enjoy the comforts, of

their own children. If a wife deliberately and consistently refuses to satisfy this natural and legitimate craving, and the deprivation reduces the husband to despair, and affects his mental health, I entertain no doubt that she is guilty of cruelty within the definition on which this court always acts."

He referred to the admirably succinct and epigrammatic statement of Shearman, J., in *Hadden* v. *Hadden* (1919), *The Times*, 5th December: " I do not question . . . that he had no intention of being cruel . . . but his intentional acts amounted to cruelty," and added: " That, to my mind, is the shortest way in which any judge has put the principle—and the clearest—that is to be acted upon."

It would seem, therefore, that in the matter of sexual intercourse and the use of contraceptives, and the refusal to have a child, the law is the same for husband and wife with this possible exception, that fear of childbirth may be a relevant matter. In *Forbes* v. *Forbes*, *supra*, the wife had no fear of childbirth.

(c) *Husband wishing to be a woman*

If a man dresses up as a woman, and expresses his desire to live as a woman, is this cruelty to the wife?

In *Williams* v. *Williams* (1958), *The Times*, 15th March, the parties married in 1947 and in 1952 the husband told his wife that since boyhood he had wished to be a woman, prayed he would change, and suggested they should live as sister and brother. He dressed as a woman and continued to do so even after she had told him this was distressing to her, and affecting her health. The culmination arrived when her family made a visit and he dressed up as a woman. The wife then left. Collingwood, J., held this amounted to cruelty.

A very similar case was *Dolling* v. *Dolling* (1958), *The Times*, 23rd May, and Davies, J., came to the same conclusion.

The Court of Appeal in *Bohnel* v. *Bohnel* [1960] 1 W.L.R. 590 supported the commissioner who found that cruelty was not proved where a man dressed up as a woman, but did not disapprove *Williams* v. *Williams* which was quoted in argument. The distinguishing feature was that, whereas in the two cases quoted above the husband had flaunted his " womanliness," in *Bohnel* v. *Bohnel* he tried hard to conceal it, and it was only by accident that on two occasions the wife discovered this propensity and practice.

On the first occasion she had a terrible shock and a nervous breakdown, but she was not affected on the second occasion and continued to live with him for a further eight months. Willmer, L.J., at p. 595, said: —

". . . In these circumstances, I think the commissioner directed himself correctly in asking himself the question whether, in pursuing his abnormal course of conduct, the husband was doing something which, as a reasonable man, he ought to have foreseen was likely to cause injury to the wife. If so, there is good authority for saying that such conduct might amount to cruelty, so as to warrant the court in granting relief to the wife. But the question is one that it is rarely easy to answer, and, in the case of conduct such as is in question in this case, it is always a matter of difficulty to decide on which side of the line it falls. I do not think that the law, as it applies to a case of this class, can be better or more succinctly stated than it was by Lord Tucker in *Jamieson* v. *Jamieson* [1952] A.C. 525, when he said, at pp. 550–551: —
  'Every such act must be judged in relation to its attendant circumstances, and the physical or mental condition or susceptibilities of the innocent spouse, the intention of the offending spouse, and the offender's knowledge of the actual or probable effect of his conduct on the other's health (to borrow from the language of Lord Keith) are all matters which may be decisive in determining on which side of the line a particular act or course of conduct lies."

Applying this test, it seems to me that, in order to found a charge of cruelty on the conduct of the husband in continuing to practise his abnormal tendency after 1955, it would have to be shown (*a*) that there was some real probability of the wife finding out about it, (*b*) that if she did find out it would probably cause her another serious shock, and (*c*) that such shock would be likely to cause further injury to her health, as it did in 1955. So long as the husband succeeded in concealing his continued practice of the abnormal tendency from the wife, it is clear that it could do her no hurt."

See also *T.* v. *T.* (1961), 105 Sol. J. 933.

11. *Husband inducing belief in his adultery*

Where the husband persists in a course of conduct deliberately inducing in his wife a reasonable belief in his adultery, which results in injury to her health, this is cruelty. In *Walker* v. *Walker* [1962] P. 42, the Divisional Court (Lord Merriman, P., and Lloyd Jones, J.) considered this question in an appeal from the magistrates. The husband formed an association with a woman living next door, and spent much of his time with her so that the wife came to believe that he was committing adultery. He had been seen by the wife and by his son on different occasions to kiss the woman, and the wife had seen him with the woman on his knee. She issued summonses for desertion, adultery and persistent cruelty. The magistrates found there was no desertion because they were living in the same house, and they also found that adultery had not been proved, but they made an order on the ground of persistent cruelty. Lord Merriman, P., said that the principle laid down in *Glenister* v. *Glenister* [1945] P. 30 (see p. 96) had been approved in the Court of Appeal and was at first a defence in the case of desertion, and then in wilful neglect to maintain, and that in *Baker* v. *Baker* [1954] P. 33 it was held that if a wife left her husband because he had induced in her a belief that he was carrying on an adulterous association, that amounted to constructive desertion and, in his view, this was equally true on the same facts for persistent cruelty. At p. 46 he said: —

> " It has been argued that adultery itself, let alone a reasonable belief in adultery, cannot amount to persistent cruelty unless, it is said, there is some substantial degree of misconduct on top of, or outside, the actual impropriety of the association. Those are very fine resounding words but, in my opinion, they fit this case exactly because when an association with the woman who lives in the next house, which is owned by the husband, is being carried on and flaunted in the face of the wife, and with the deliberate pretence, at any rate, that the husband has taken the woman away for a particular week-end and so forth, I should say that that is undoubtedly a substantial degree of misconduct on top of the impropriety of the association itself. In other words, I think that there is ample evidence of ill-treatment—grave conjugal unkindness— in connection with this association which, coupled with the undoubted results on the wife's mental health as found by the justices, satisfies the legal description of cruelty, and of persistent cruelty in this case, which necessitates proof not only of the ill-treatment but of the resulting injury, actual or apprehended."

12. *The individual reaction*

Especially in " course of conduct " cases a good deal depends on the reaction of the particular individual. What might be nothing more than mildly irritating to one person, might be torture to a more sensitive person. In this class of case the law is not concerned with the normal person, but with a particular individual.

Lord Merriman said of sexual malpractices of one spouse with the other, that the test of just cause of one leaving the other was "the known reaction" of one spouse to the other's actions (*Holborn* v. *Holborn* [1947] 1 All E.R. 32).

Bucknill, J., in *Barrett* v. *Barrett* (1903), 20 T.L.R. 73, gives another example: —

> "If a wife suffered from heart disease, to the knowledge of her husband, and he gave her a sudden shock, through which she might be in danger of death, such an act was not necessarily an act of actual violence, yet if the wife was so constituted as to be thereby made sickly or ill . . . the husband's act would amount to cruelty."

Pearce, J., in *Lauder* v. *Lauder* [1949] P. 277, at p. 308, expresses it neatly: —

> ". . . the question is whether *this* conduct by *this* man to *this* woman or vice versa is cruelty."

Lord Normand in *Jamieson* v. *Jamieson* [1952] A.C. 525, at p. 535, said he was inclined to accept the view "that the conduct alleged must be judged up to a point by reference to the victim's capacity for endurance, in so far as that capacity is or ought to be known to the guilty spouse." He cites the high authority of Lord Watson in *Mackenzie* v. *Mackenzie* [1895] A.C. 384, at p. 405, for the proposition that much depends in each case upon its circumstances and in particular upon the victim's capacity for endurance.

The reaction of the individual, his or her sensitivity or susceptibilities, are particularly important in sexual cases. See p. 194.

13. *Miscellaneous*

Other examples of conduct amounting to cruelty are, damage to other spouse's property (*Forth* v. *Forth* (1867), 16 L.T. 574; *Horton* v. *Horton* [1940] P. 187); conduct with the deliberate intention of driving the other spouse away (*Litton* v. *Litton* (1924), 40 T.L.R. 272); threats of suicide (*Baker* v. *Baker* (1919), *The Times*, 11th December (C.A.)); violent temper (*Martin* v. *Martin* (1860), 2 L.T. 118); excessive sexual demands resulting in numerous miscarriages (*Rodwell* v. *Rodwell* (1948), York

Assizes, unreported); violent banging and moaning and driving the wife almost to the verge of suicide (*Weatherill* v. *Weatherill* (1947), Leeds Assizes, unreported); extorting money (*Baker* v. *Baker* (1919), *The Times*, 11th December; *Le Couteur* v. *Le Couteur* (1896), *The Times*, 2nd March; *Bertram* v. *Bertram* [1944] P. 59); persistently living on wife's means, pawning her property and continuously making her miserable (*Bertram* v. *Bertram* [1944] P. 59).

In *Dunn* v. *Dunn* [1962] 1 W.L.R. 1480, the Divisional Court (Sir J. Simon, P., and Karminski, J.) held that wilful neglect to maintain could be cruelty, and was in fact cruelty in this case.

The husband had been guilty of persistent cruelty, which the wife had condoned. Thereafter, from October to December, 1961, he gave her no money with a small exception. The wife applied to the magistrates for an order on the ground of persistent cruelty. The magistrates held that this wilful neglect to maintain was not sufficient to revive the cruelty, and dismissed the complaint.

The President said that a false accusation of adultery, or failure to maintain, could in certain circumstances revive earlier condoned cruelty. It was a question of fact in each case whether the conduct was of sufficient gravity to have this effect. He cited *Beard* v. *Beard* [1946] P. 8 (C.A.). The learned President went on to say that not only was wilful neglect in this case sufficient to revive the condoned cruelty, but was in itself an act of cruelty.

The President, while not deciding the matter, seemed to indicate that if the conduct which revived the cruelty did not itself amount to cruelty, then the wife might be precluded from bringing a summons for persistent cruelty if the condoned cruelty had occurred more than six months before the summons was taken out, and that this was the effect of s. 104 of the Magistrates' Courts Act, 1952, which provides that a magistrates' court shall not hear a complaint unless the complaint was made within six months from the time when the matter of complaint arose. Karminski, J., thought the section should be construed strictly. This is a highly questionable proposition. It is submitted that the conduct reviving the cruelty must be looked at as a whole with the condoned cruelty. Nor is it easy to see why a statute of this nature should be construed to shut out a proper complaint. Any doubt or ambiguity should be resolved in favour of the complainant.

If condoned cruelty plus conduct less than cruelty amounts to
persistent cruelty, and the last conduct took place within six
months of the complaint, how can it be said that the matter of
the complaint did not arise within six months? It has never been
held that " complaint " means the whole of the complaint.

In *Hawell* v. *Hawell* (1964), *The Times*, 10th June, a wife's
obsession with cleanliness was held to be cruel.

V. INTENTION

A. Malignancy

At one time it was said that malignancy, or a deliberate intention
to be cruel, was an essential element in legal cruelty (*Astle* v.
Astle [1939] P. 415; *Horton* v. *Horton* [1940] P. 187; *Atkins* v.
Atkins [1942] 2 All E.R. 637).

These were followed by Finnemore, J., in *Squire* v. *Squire*
(1947), 63 T.L.R. 572. Its history goes further back as will be
seen from the argument of Sir Edward Clarke in *Beauclerk* v.
Beauclerk [1891] P. 189, who said: —

> " If the acts of the husband are done without the intention of
> being cruel, they do not constitute legal cruelty."

The Court of Appeal in that case, deciding on another point,
made no comment on this argument.

The question came up in clear-cut form in *Squire* v. *Squire*
[1949] P. 51 in the Court of Appeal. The cruelty alleged was that
the wife systematically for nights on end prevented the husband
from sleeping, so that his health was affected. She herself was in
bad health and her conduct was largely caused by this, and not
with the intention of hurting her husband. At first instance,
Finnemore, J., after referring to *Astle* v. *Astle*, *Horton* v. *Horton*
and *Atkins* v. *Atkins*, had said (63 T.L.R. 572, at p. 575): —

> " All these cases emphasise, as I think the cases before 1937
> laid down, the fact that cruelty must be deliberate, malignant
> and intended—whatever precise words you like to use."

This statement of the law was unanimously rejected by the
Court of Appeal, which held that a person is presumed to intend
the natural consequences of his acts, adopting the pithy sentence
of Shearman, J., in *Hadden* v. *Hadden* ((1919), *The Times*, 5th
December): —

"I do not question the evidence of the husband that he had
no intention of being cruel to her, but I hold that his
intentional acts amounted to cruelty."

This had been, indeed, said long before. Lord Penzance had
said in *Kelly* v. *Kelly* (1870), L.R. 2 P. & D. 59, at p. 72: —

"He, the husband, says that he does not desire to injure her,
and it has never been asserted that he does. But still she has
nothing to hope for, for Mr. Kelly is acting in the discharge of
a religious duty."

and the court held there was cruelty. This emphasises that the
motive is immaterial, so long as the conduct injures the other
spouse. Lord Stowell in *Holden* v. *Holden* (1810), 1 Hagg. Con.
453, had said it was not necessary to inquire from what motive the
treatment proceeded. "If bitter waters are flowing, it is not necessary to inquire from what source they spring"; and then in
Kirkman v. *Kirkman* (1807), 1 Hagg. Con. 409, the same judge
said that if the safety of the spouse was endangered it was unnecessary to show that it proceeded from malignity; and in *Hall* v. *Hall*
(1864), 3 Sw. & Tr. 390, the Judge Ordinary said "with danger to
the wife in view, the court does not hold its hand to inquire into
motives and causes," but he makes a saving with regard to
madness, dementia or positive diseases of the mind.

In view of all these authoritative statements and the well-known
principle that a person is presumed to intend the natural consequences of his acts (see per Lord Merriman in *Edwards* v. *Edwards*
[1948] P. 268), it is difficult to see how the aberration crept in.
The answer may be that, in most cases, the respondent is malignant
and does intend to hurt the petitioner; or, at any rate, he or
she knows that the conduct complained of does hurt the spouse,
and nevertheless persists in it. It is an easy step to regard an
element that occurs in most cases as an essential element in all.

Then there are cases where malignity is important. The quality
of an act can be affected by the intention behind it. Everyone
knows that a slight blow given with hostile intent can cause suffering, while hearty blows given in fun or play are disregarded. The
court in *Squire* v. *Squire* was alive to this consideration, and
Evershed, L.J., said ([1949] P., at p. 60): —

"I do not say that proof of such an intention [i.e., a spiteful
or malignant intention] may not be an important or, in some
cases, even an essential consideration."

B.   Aimed at

Two cases in the Court of Appeal, *Westall* v. *Westall* (1949), 65
T.L.R. 337, and *Kaslefsky* v. *Kaslefsky* [1951] P. 38, laid down
that for conduct to be cruel it must be " aimed " at the other
spouse. This dubious doctrine has been criticised on various
grounds but in particular that it was really the discredited doctrine
of malignancy in another form. (See articles by the present writer
in 17 *Modern Law Review*, p. 344, at 441 et seq. and Sir Carleton
Allen, Q.C., in 73 L.Q.R., at p. 525.)

Kaslefsky v. *Kaslefsky, supra,* and *Eastland* v. *Eastland* [1954]
P. 403, where the husband's shiftless and irresponsible conduct
caused the wife great distress (this decision was criticised in App.
II of the 1st edition of this book) were overruled by the House
of Lords in *Gollins* v. *Gollins, supra.*

What was meant by " aimed at " was by no means clear, and
led to arbitrary distinctions, which made the law difficult to apply.
Lord Reid thought this was too vague a test, and it is to be noted
that while their lordships were divided as to the result of the case
they were unanimous in rejecting the test of " aimed at."

C.   Gollins v. Gollins and Williams v. Williams

Until these two cases were decided in 1963 by the House of
Lords, whether intention was a necessary element in cruelty, and
if so to what extent, was by no means clear. It was recognised that
an intention to be cruel may be a vital element in determining
whether the conduct complained of was cruel or not, yet it was
clear there could be cases where cruelty could be established
without proof of this intention.

The case of *Gollins* v. *Gollins* [1964] A.C. 644 is of great
importance and must be considered in detail. The facts were that
the husband was an unsuccessful farmer and ran into debt. He
borrowed money from his wife, and when she ran a guest house he
did little or nothing to help her. He was incorrigibly lazy. In
Harman, L.J.'s expressive phrase, he just hung his hat in the
hall. He was constantly dunned for debts. There was no suggestion
that he was deliberately trying to hurt his wife. There were no
violent quarrels. What worried her and made her ill was his
refusal to try to help her or earn money and clear his debts. The
result was that the wife, an active and capable woman, was

brought to a state of ill health where she could no longer earn her own living or maintain her children because of the shiftless and selfish conduct of her husband.

The proceedings had a curious history. In the first place the wife succeeded on a summons alleging wilful neglect to maintain and a maintenance order was made. Later she wished for a separation order and for this purpose took out a summons for persistent cruelty. The magistrates found this proved and made a separation order. From this decision the husband appealed successfully to a Divisional Court, but this decision was reversed by the Court of Appeal, by a majority, two judges to one, and this decision was upheld in the House of Lords by three law lords to two.*

In the result it will be seen that five judges held the husband's conduct to be cruel (and this view prevailed), but five held his conduct was not cruel. In the Divisional Court, Sir Jocelyn Simon, P., and Cairns, J., decided for the husband because they said his conduct was not aimed at the wife, and in any case his conduct could not be said to be cruel in the ordinary acceptation of that word. Harman, L.J., dissented in the Court of Appeal on the latter ground. This, too, was the view of Lord Morris of Borth-y-Gest, at p. 677: —

> ". . . in the end it must be shown as a question of fact that the conduct is such that it can properly and rationally be stigmatised by the word ' cruelty ' using that word in its ordinary acceptation."

Lord Hodson said that he had formed a clear opinion that in this case the conduct of the husband could not justly be called cruel. The majority view is set out in the following extracts: —

> Lord Reid (at p. 658): " The question is whether the law of England requires that these two shall continue to live together and would regard her as guilty of the matrimonial offence of desertion if she left him. If that is the law then she must be told that it is her legal duty as a wife to sink into poverty and ill-health and become with her children a charge on the State. But does the law not permit us to say that such conduct in such circumstances amounts to persistent cruelty?"

* On the authority of *Gollins* v. *Gollins*, *supra*, Karminski, J., in *Gollins* v. *Gollins (No. 2)* (1964), 108 Sol. J. 941, granted the wife a decree nisi on the ground of cruelty.

(at p. 659): " This appears to me to be a plain uncomplicated case of a husband fully responsible for his conduct, knowing that it was injuring his wife's health and yet persisting in it, not because he wished or intended to injure her but because he was so selfish and lazy in his habits that he closed his mind to the consequences . . . So the question must be whether his conduct was of a kind which can in law be called cruel and whether the law requires an intention to injure before there can be cruelty."

(at p. 662): " Why should we have to drag in intention at all? It seems to me a very poor defence to say ' I know the disastrous effect on my wife of what I have been doing. Probably I could have resisted temptation if I had really tried. But my conduct is innocent because I have not the slightest desire or intention to harm my wife. I have acted throughout from pure selfishness '."

(at pp. 666–667): " If the conduct complained of and its consequences are so bad that the petitioner must have a remedy, then it does not matter what was the state of the respondent's mind . . . In other cases the state of his mind is material and may be crucial."

Lord Evershed (at p. 610): ". . . I am unable to accept the premise that ' cruelty ' in matrimonial proceedings requires or involves of necessity the element of malignity—though I do not of course doubt that if malignity be in fact established it would be highly relevant to a charge of cruelty . . . and if this view be right it follows . . . that the presence of intention to injure on the part of the spouse charged or (which is, as I think, the same thing) proof that the conduct of the party charged was ' aimed at ' the other spouse is not an essential requisite for cruelty. The question in all such cases is, to my mind, whether the acts or conduct of the party charged were ' cruel ' according to the ordinary sense of that word, rather than whether the party charged was himself or herself a cruel man or woman. . . . The case where one party to a marriage sets out by deliberate means to injure the other is no doubt simple; but equally it is, I should think, relatively rare. More frequent (and in its effects more often hurtful and insidious) is such a case as the present where the ' intention ' of the party charged, if it exists at all, is no more and no less than an ' intention ' to gratify his or her purely selfish inclinations."

Lord Pearce, after referring to *Jamieson* v. *Jamieson* [1952] A.C. 525; *Kelly* v. *Kelly* (1870), L.R. 2 P. & D. 59, and *Hadden* v. *Hadden* (1919), *The Times*, 5th December, said: —

" Thus in all the opinions there appears the view that intention, though it may be a deciding factor in some doubtful cases, is not essential to cruelty."

The result of the decision in *Gollins* may be summarised as follows: —

1. Intention to injure on the part of the spouse charged is not an essential element in cruelty.
2. There may be cases where the presence of such an intention will make conduct cruel which otherwise would not be.
3. Such tests as " Was the conduct aimed at the other spouse? " or " Was the conduct negative in character? " are unnecessary and unhelpful.
4. In view of the foregoing, it was unnecessary to resort to such notions as " a man is presumed to intend the natural consequences of his acts."

While this case decided that a specific intention to injure was unnecessary, it left open the question, whether an intention to do the acts complained of was necessary. This was dealt with in the case of *Williams* v. *Williams* [1964] A.C. 698. This case is considered more particularly at p. 218 et seq., but so far as intention is concerned the House of Lords decided that the test whether one spouse has treated another with cruelty is wholly objective and, therefore, proof of insanity is not necessarily an answer to the charge.

The following cases, prior to *Gollins*, are, it is submitted, still good law.

Cooper v. *Cooper* (*No.* 1) [1955] P. 99 was a case where the husband was convicted of an indecent assault upon the child of his marriage, and the wife complained of persistent cruelty. At p. 104, Lord Merriman, P., said that *Jamieson* v. *Jamieson* [1952] A.C. 525 was not an authority for the proposition that an actual intention to injure is essential in every case, and it was held that the magistrates had misdirected themselves in holding it was. Of course, in a doubtful case, an intention to injure may be of decisive importance, but conduct which is the consequence of mere obtuseness or indifference may, none the less, be cruelty.

Similarly, in *Waters* v. *Waters* [1956] P. 344 (which was a case of boorishness, and the magistrates had dismissed the wife's complaint on the ground that the husband had had no intention of being cruel), the Divisional Court (Lord Merriman, P., and

Wallington, J.) said that it was not sufficient to say that the husband had had no intention of being cruel. His conduct would be just as reprehensible if he could be said to be at least unwarrantably indifferent as to the consequences to the victim.

A good example is *Welsford* v. *Welsford* (1959), *The Times*, 9th October, which was a husband's petition on the ground of cruelty. The husband and wife had become friendly with the co-respondent and his wife, and the wife and the co-respondent formed an affection for one another with the result that the wife became cold to the husband generally, and in her sexual relations with him. She told him she was in love with the co-respondent and would like to marry him. Eventually she refused to have sexual intercourse with her husband, and he became distracted and unhappy, and his health was affected. Wrangham, J., said that there was no doubt that the marriage came to an end because the wife rejected her husband as a husband, and that rejection was a breach of a fundamental conjugal duty. The fact that she had not wished to injure her husband would not affect the matter. In the absence of evidence to the contrary, the doer of an act must be taken to foresee the natural consequences of that act, even though the consequences were not desired. Her conduct in rejecting her husband in the sense in which she did reject him had intentionally, although perhaps regretfully, inflicted upon him an injury necessarily involved in such rejection, and as the husband's health had been affected, this amounted to cruelty in law.

D. Character

It is sometimes suggested that if the conduct alleged to be cruel is merely the manifestation of a person's character, then it cannot be cruelty. This proposition deserves examination, because it has a germ of truth in it but is more apt to be misleading.

In *Horton* v. *Horton* [1940] P. 187, a husband petitioned for divorce on the ground of his wife's cruelty. The wife had, out of jealous spite, damaged the husband's masonic regalia and scratched his glasses, assaulted him and nagged him and, as the judge found, had acted with malevolence and an evil, unwifely spirit, and the husband had suffered in health in consequence. The husband was granted a decree. Bucknill, J., at p. 193, said: —

" Mere conduct which causes injury to health is not enough. A man takes the woman for his wife for better or for worse. If he marries a woman whose character develops in such a way as to make it impossible for him to live happily with her, I do not think he establishes cruelty merely because he finds life with her is impossible. He must prove that she has committed wilful and unjustifiable acts inflicting pain and misery upon him and causing him injury to health. In this case, the husband's health was not injured merely by the development and manifestation of the wife's character acting so to speak in its own sphere. It was injured by her wilful and unjustifiable conduct to him, which was an intrusion and did violence to his own mode of living. . . ."

The confusion which arises from this statement is that her conduct was a manifestation of her character. She was a spiteful person. The question for the court was—" Was her conduct cruel?" Does the intrusion of the question of character assist this inquiry or not? Does it matter what the cause of her conduct was? It is submitted that it does not.

It is true that if a man marries a woman and finds that her character develops in a way he does not like so that he loses affection for her, and becames unhappy, she may not be guilty of cruelty. If, however, her conduct exceeds a certain limit (or rather an uncertain and undefined limit) then it will amount to cruelty. Lord Stowell's statement in *Evans* v. *Evans* (1790), 1 Hagg. Con. 35, at p. 38, supports this: —

" Mere austerity of temper, petulance of manners, rudeness of language, a want of civil attention and accommodation, even occasionally sallies of passion, *if they do not threaten bodily harm*, do not amount to cruelty."

It is suggested that the operative words are those italicised.

Wilde, J.O., in *Forth* v. *Forth* (1867), 16 L.T. 574, said: —

" When a man marries an ill-tempered woman, he must put up with her humour, but the moment she steps beyond that mark and lifts her hand to her husband, and subjects him to personal violence then the court must interfere."

Moreover, personal violence is not necessary, if the extent of her temper is of such a degree as to affect the husband's health.

The depraved conduct cases are examples of defect of character, but were still held to be cruelty. In *Boyd* v. *Boyd* (1939), noted at [1955] P. 126, Bucknill, J., held that incest followed by indecent

assault which had affected the wife's health amounted to cruelty.
Lord Merriman in *Edwards* v. *Edwards* [1948] P. 268 remarked
that Boyd was being " his nasty self." Is not that to say that
his behaviour was the " manifestation of his character acting
in its own sphere," or, in other words, he did what he did because
it was his character to do so, and as Scott, L.J., said in *Bertram*
v. *Bertram* [1944] P. 59, at p. 60: —

> " Cruelty of character is bound to show itself in conduct and
> behaviour."

Having a nasty character is no excuse for cruel behaviour; on
the contrary, bad conduct arising from bad character is more
likely to be repeated in the future.

In *Ivens* v. *Ivens* [1955] P. 129 (C.A.), a commissioner held that
a husband who indecently assaulted his wife's child had not been
guilty of cruelty, the commissioner saying, " I do not find that he
did it to hurt his wife; it was to satisfy his own unnatural, reprehensible feelings." The Court of Appeal, not surprisingly, reversed
this decision.

In a sense, all cruelty springs from defects in character. A cruel
person is a person whose character is defective in that respect.
Cruelty may arise from selfishness, spite, meanness, greed, lust or
sadism, all of which are defects of character. Whatever the cause
it is the impact on the victim which is important.

What the judge may have meant—and no one can quarrel with
this—was that there is certain conduct which a spouse has to
put up with; it is part of the ordinary wear and tear of married
life. A spouse may be short-tempered, or fond of drinking, or
gambling, or going to the club too much, and so on, activities
which might cause unhappiness to the other spouse, but which
have to be borne; but if the short temper leads to blows; or the
drinking to drunkenness and disgusting conduct, such as habitual
fouling of the bed; or the gambling becomes persistent and
ruinous, then that is conduct for which the spouse may have a
remedy; but all this is a question of degree, and to ask, " Is this
a development of the husband's character in its own sphere? "
does not conspicuously help the inquiry.

The point was well made by Lord Penzance in *Hall* v. *Hall*
(1864), 3 Sw. & Tr. 347, when he said: —

> " With danger to the wife in view, the court does not hold

its hand to inquire into motives and causes. The sources of
the husband's conduct are, for the most part, immaterial . . ."

Some support for the " character no cruelty " doctrine is given
by Denning, L.J., in *Timmins* v. *Timmins* [1953] 1 W.L.R. 757,
when he said, at p. 760: —

> " But the judge has expressly found that her breakdown was
> not due to any ' wrongful conduct ' on the part of the
> husband. Having regard to his other findings, this must mean,
> I think, that the domineering conduct of the husband was
> not done with any intent to injure or inflict misery on the
> wife. It was simply a defect of temperament manifesting
> itself in a most unpleasant way. . . ."

Contrast this with the language of Lloyd-Jacob, J., in the same
case (at p. 764): —

> " The preservation of her sanity is, in my judgment, a grave
> and weighty matter, and for the husband to behave in an
> overbearing, domineering and dictatorial manner when he has
> once appreciated the consequences of such behaviour to her
> state of mind would no longer be an exercise of his frailty,
> but a wickedly cruel matrimonial offence. The husband's
> conduct in relation to the removal of his second child from
> the mother's custody, and his rejection of his wife's offer to
> return to the matrimonial home for a few days, illustrate such
> lack of consideration as to satisfy me that a return under an
> order of the court might be fraught with the gravest peril.
> I could not be a party to such a consequence."

The language of Denning, L.J., is inconsistent with the decisions
in *Evans* v. *Evans* (1790), 1 Hagg. Con. 35, *Forth* v. *Forth* (1867),
16 L.T. 574, and *Kelly* v. *Kelly* (1870), L.R. 2 P. & D. 59, at p. 72,
where Lord Penzance said: —

> " He, the husband, says he does not desire to injure her, and it
> has never been asserted that he does. But still she has nothing
> to hope for, for Mr. Kelly is acting in discharge of a religious
> duty."

In *Kelly* v. *Kelly*, as in *Bethune* v. *Bethune* [1891] P. 205 and
Mytton v. *Mytton* (1886), 11 P.D. 141, the court has not hesitated
to grant a decree where the cruelty consisted of tyrannical conduct
arising out of the domineering character and temperament of
the husband. With all due respect, it seems the height of absurdity
for a man to be acquitted of cruel conduct because he says, " Well,

I can't help it; that is how I am made. It is part of my character and temperament: I am just being my nasty self."

If the conduct was criminal, he would get short shrift. One fails to see why he should get less for a matrimonial offence. It not only flies in the face of good sense, but is contrary to long established authority.

Of course, there is a sense, when a spouse's character has to be taken for better or worse. As Lord Asquith said in *King* v. *King* [1953] A.C. 124, at p. 147: —

> "It is true that, generally speaking, a man marries at his peril as the character of his wife may disclose. She may develop on quite unexpected lines. She may prove, contrary to all expectations, touchy, perverse, cross-grained and temperamental. She may make wild unfounded charges against him, and he may, in the circumstances, have no remedy. But it does not follow from this that the indefinite repetition of false charges, however frequent the repetition, and wounding the charges, may not reach a point at which it passes into the realm of cruelty, affording a ground for divorce. Indeed, it has often been held to be so."

In short, it is conduct, not character that counts in considering cases of cruelty and constructive desertion.

This view is strongly reinforced by *Gollins* v. *Gollins* [1964] A.C. 644 and *Williams* v. *Williams* [1964] A.C. 698.

It was emphasised in *Gollins* that the husband's conduct was due to his selfishness and laziness; and that it is more common for cruelty to consist in the gratification of purely selfish inclinations and the effects in such cases are often more hurtful and insidious than in cases of deliberate cruelty. The matter is summed up by Lord Pearce as follows at p. 694: —

> "Nor do I think that the attempt in *Horton's* case ([1940] P. 187) to exclude from cruelty acts caused merely by the natural development of a spouse's character within its own sphere is helpful. Allowances must always be made for temperament and mere temperamental disharmony simpliciter is not cruelty. But if a temperament which naturally tends to unkindness or selfishness or callousness develops to a point at which its acts are cruel, whether intentionally or not, it cannot be right to say that the other spouse must endure it without relief. Nor can one helpfully say that development of character is within its own sphere if its emanations affect

and cause injury to the other spouse. Marriage by its nature causes one party to be affected by most of the reprehensible conduct on the part of the other, and usually it is obvious that it will be so."

VI.   CLASS DISTINCTIONS

The law recognises that there are different classes of society. In considering what necessaries a husband is liable for, his economic position is taken into account. There is also authority for recognising this distinction in cruelty cases. Sir J. Nicholl in *Westmeath* v. *Westmeath* (1827), 2 Hagg. Eccl. Supp. 61, at p. 73, says: —

"A blow between parties in the lower conditions and in the highest stations of life bears a very different aspect. Among the lower classes blows sometimes pass between married couples who are in the main very happy and have no desire to part; amidst very coarse habits such incidents occur almost as freely as rude or reproachful words: a word and a blow go together. Still even amongst the very lowest classes there is generally a feeling of something unmanly in striking a woman . . ."

and now the learned judge becomes very eloquent: —

". . . if a nobleman of high rank and ancient family uses personal violence to his wife, his equal in rank, the choice of his affection, the friend of his bosom, the mother of his off-spring—such conduct in such a person carries with it something so degrading to the husband and so insulting and mortifying to the wife as to render the injury far more severe and unsupportable."

Life in this country has become much more democratic and egalitarian since 1827, and while there are still wide disparities in wealth, it may be doubted whether the code of conduct is very different between the highest and lowest in the land. See *Buchler* v. *Buchler* [1947] P. 25, a case of desertion, where the Master of the Rolls deplored conduct based on class distinctions. This theme of class distinction in cruelty is noticeably absent from modern cases. A truer test is, perhaps, that suggested in the same judgment of Sir J. Nicholl in *Westmeath* v. *Westmeath*, namely, as to whether the conduct was resented at the time. There are some people who regard horseplay as a natural part of married life, and some wives who regard an occasional thrashing as a sign of their husband's affection.

VII. DEFENCES

A. Provocation

In *Waring* v. *Waring* (1813), 2 Hagg. Con. 153, at p. 154, Sir William Scott (later Lord Stowell) said: " . . . if the conduct of the wife . . . provokes the just indignation of the husband, and causes danger to her person, she must seek the remedy for that evil, so provoked, in the change of her manners."

Provocation may be a defence to a charge of cruelty, but if the acts of the provoked party are disproportionately severe to the provocation, then provocation is no excuse. Sir Herbert Jenner Fust, in *Dysart* v. *Dysart* (1847), 1 Rob. Eccl. 470, said at p. 476, quoting Dr. Swabey in *Best* v. *Best* (1823), 1 Add. 411: —

" It has been repeatedly laid down in these courts that no wife can solicit their interference with effect to protect her from ill-treatment which she has drawn upon her by her own mis-conduct: she must first at least seek a remedy in the reform of her own manners. If, however, it would appear that even mis-conduct on the wife's part has produced a return from the husband, *wholly* unjustified by the provocation and *quite* out of proportion to the offence, it might still be the duty of the court to interfere judicially . . ."

and later

" I am to remember that if the conduct of the husband tended to produce bodily injury and harm to the wife it is not necessary that her conduct should be altogether free from blame. . . ."

The question was considered in *King* v. *King* [1953] A.C. 124 and resulted in a considerable difference of judicial opinion. A husband complained of nagging and complaints of adultery as a result of which his health was affected, and Barnard, J., granted him a decree nisi. On appeal this was reversed (Denning and Hodson, L.JJ., Somervell, L.J., dissenting). The House of Lords [1953] A.C. 124 (Earl Jowitt, Lords Normand and Oaksey; Lords Reid and Asquith of Bishopstone dissenting) dismissed the appeal. The view of the majority may be summed up in the words of Lord Normand, at p. 129: —

" The general rule in all questions of cruelty is that the whole matrimonial relations must be considered, and that rule is of special value when the cruelty consists not of violent acts but of injurious reproaches, complaints, accusations or taunts. Wilful accusations may be made which are not true and for which there are no probable grounds, and yet may not amount to cruelty. To take an obvious example, they may have been provoked by the cruel conduct of the other spouse."

In this case, the wife had been provoked by her husband's adultery, for which she forgave him, and by the odd circumstance that her husband's mistress had then married her husband's brother, who was his partner, so that the parties came into contact with one another. The wife could not resist making nasty remarks, which was the basis of the husband's complaint.

The Times on 9th June, 1955, reported some observations of Singleton, L.J., in the Court of Appeal in a case which is not named. He said: —

" If a wife is left alone at night wondering where her husband is, becoming suspicious as time goes on, is it surprising that sometimes when he comes in she says, ' Where have you been? '

It might be thought that if a wife is neglected in that sense, her only weapon is her tongue and though no one would encourage nagging, a husband, who has brought about a rift in the marriage, by his loss of affection for his wife, can scarcely be heard to complain if his wife complains of his treatment of her."

Similarly, a nagging wife may drive her husband to violence, and this would not amount to cruelty. In *Douglas* v. *Douglas* (1958), *The Times*, 20th November, the Divisional Court considered a case where the magistrates had dismissed a wife's complaint of persistent cruelty, on the ground that her nagging had justified the husband's violence. Lord Merriman quoted Lord Normand in *King* v. *King, supra*, and said the wife was the author of her own wrong. It had been argued that words could never justify violence, but he did not agree with that. The whole of the circumstances had to be considered.

Adultery by the wife does not justify a husband in attacking her savagely (Wrangham, J., in *McKenzie* v. *McKenzie* (1959), *The Times*, 5th June).

The Divisional Court considered the matter again in *Yuen* v. *Yuen* (1950), *The Times*, 11th November, where the wife had been attacked by her husband who had kicked her, bruised her arms, legs and body and ripped her clothes off. The magistrates had dismissed her summons for persistent cruelty on the ground that she had provoked her husband. The Divisional Court ordered a new trial, and referred the magistrates to the words of Sir Herbert Jenner Fust, quoted above, and advised that if the violence is out of proportion to the provocation, it would amount to cruelty.

A useful observation on this subject is by Davies, J., in *Baker* v. *Baker* [1955] 1 W.L.R. 1011, at p. 1016, where he said: —

> " If a wife is provoking her husband by associating with another man to his knowledge, and against his wishes; or indeed, if in consequence of such an association, even if unknown to her husband, she is either deliberately or because she cannot help it, adopting a cold and provocative attitude to her husband, that may well explain or excuse conduct on the part of the husband which would otherwise be inexcusable."

It is possible for each party to be cruel to the other. Wrangham, J., so held in *Kelly* v. *Kelly* [1968] 1 W.L.R. 152, where each party was violent to the other, inflicted injuries on each other, and each behaved unreasonably. There were cross petitions for divorce and the judge granted each a decree. In the magistrates' court if such a position arose, the wife would be successful on her summons but the justices could take into account her conduct when assessing maintenance.

Karminski, J., applied *Waring* v. *Waring, supra*, in *Stick* v. *Stick* [1967] 1 All E.R. 323 and held the provocation must bear direct relation to acts of retaliation alleged to constitute cruelty. In this case the wife withdrew from sexual intercourse, but the husband's reaction was altogether too violent, including two black eyes, seizure by the throat and locking her in her room. She was granted a decree on the ground of his cruelty.

When a husband accused of cruelty to his wife pleaded that he had been provoked by her misconduct with other men Rees, J., said: " To constitute a valid defence provocation must be such as to deprive a reasonable man of his self control " (*Rhodes* v. *Rhodes and Hayes* (1965), 109 Sol. J. 213).

B. Consent

A spouse cannot complain of cruelty if he or she consents to the acts complained of. Whether one says that the complainant is the author of her or his own wrong, or whether it is said to be analogous to *volenti non fit injuria*, or that a party cannot approbate and reprobate, it amounts to the same thing. This defence applies particularly in cases of complaints of a sexual nature. It is common in practice to find that a wife who has fallen out with her husband drags up all matters of abnormal sexual practices against her husband, when at the time she was a willing party. Cruelty must consist of an act or acts against the will of the other party.

Greer, L.J., in *Statham* v. *Statham* [1929] P. 131 (C.A.), at p. 145, said that it was impossible, where a husband and wife committed sodomy, that either could complain. What, however, is consent? Both Karminski, J., in *Davidson* v. *Davidson* [1953] 1 W.L.R. 387 (D.C.) and Hodson, L.J., in *Bampton* v. *Bampton* [1959] 1 W.L.R. 842 (C.A.), pointed out that the assent of a wife, especially a young wife, must not readily be taken as a true assent. Such acts could be forced on her or obtained by fraudulent persuasion such as that such things were a normal incident of married life.

Similarly in *Raw* v. *Raw* [1947] W.N. 96, where one of the complaints of the wife was that she was made to masturbate her husband, it was held that though she did it, she did it unwillingly and it revolted her and her husband knew it, and it was therefore cruel, there being no real consent; following *Holborn* v. *Holborn* [1947] 1 All E.R. 32.

For a husband to have himself sterilised would be an act of cruelty to his wife (per Evershed, M.R., and Hodson, L.J., in *Bravery* v. *Bravery* [1954] 1 W.L.R. 1169, at p. 1172), but her consent would be a complete defence. Denning, L.J., dissented in this case, holding that even if there was consent, it did not preclude her from complaining when her health in later years was affected.

A doctor, who gave his wife drugs so that she became an addict, could not complain if in consequence she committed acts of cruelty to him. He was the author of his own wrong (*Colbert* v. *Colbert* (1955), *The Times*, 21st April, C.A.), but in a case where the wife became a drug addict and obtained drugs by forging doctors' certificates, cruelty was found (*Sabin* v. *Sabin* (1959), *The Times*, 5th February).

C. Self defence

The fact that acts are committed in self defence may be a

defence to allegations of cruelty. In *Threadgold* v. *Threadgold* (1959), *The Times*, 1st May, a wife petitioned for divorce on the ground of cruelty and alleged that her husband kept silent for long periods of time. Karminski, J., said that it was true that deliberate, prolonged silences designed to overcome the other spouse's resistance could be cruelty just as much as nagging or abuse, but in order to constitute cruelty there must be an offensive use of silence and not a defensive one. In this case, the husband had used silence defensively as a shield.

D. Insanity or mental illness

Before the case of *Williams* v. *Williams* [1964] A.C. 698, it was generally believed that certain forms of insanity could be a defence to a charge of cruelty, and that if it were shown on behalf of the respondent that due to disease of the mind he did not know the nature and quality of his acts, or if he did know, that he did not know that what he was doing was wrong (the *McNaghten* rules (1843), 10 Cl. & Fin. 200) the petitioner could not succeed in getting relief.

The House of Lords has now decided in *Williams* that the test whether one spouse has treated another with cruelty is wholly objective and, therefore, proof of insanity is not necessarily an answer to the charge, the question being whether, in all the circumstances of the case, one spouse has treated the other with cruelty. This was the decision of the majority but the Lords were unanimous in rejecting the *McNaghten* rules as a test in cruelty cases.

The earlier history of this subject may be briefly described. In *Hanbury* v. *Hanbury* [1892] P. 22 and on appeal (8 T.L.R. 559) stress was laid on the respondent knowing and understanding the nature of his acts and their consequences. This case was followed by *Astle* v. *Astle* [1939] P. 415 and *Kellock* v. *Kellock* [1939] 3 All E.R. 972. In *White* v. *White* [1950] P. 39, Denning, L.J., was prepared to hold that insanity could never be a defence, which was one of the recommendations of the majority of the 1956 Royal Commission (Cmd. 9678, para. 256), but Bucknill and Asquith, L.JJ., held that the first limb of the *McNaghten* rules applied, and this was followed by the Court of Appeal in *Swan* v. *Swan* [1953]

P. 258. *Palmer* v. *Palmer* [1955] P. 4 went one step further, the Court of Appeal there deciding that both limbs were applicable.

As the *McNaghten* rules were devised to deal with criminal cases they were difficult to apply to divorce cases, especially as the meaning of "wrong" in that connection could not clearly be defined.

The decision in *Williams* renders all these cases obsolete. The facts were that the husband suffered from paranoid schizophrenia. The wife in her petition complained of cruelty, her main complaint being that he unjustly accused her of misbehaviour with other men. The medical evidence was to the effect that the respondent knew what he was doing but did not know that what he was doing was wrong.

It was agreed that the husband's conduct was cruel. The question was, whether his insanity provided a defence.

Lord Reid, after considering all the cases, and rejecting the *McNaghten* rules as not applicable to cruelty cases, considered what is meant by "cruel." He pointed out that sometimes the word connoted blameworthiness and sometimes not. He continued: —

> "So the law cannot just take 'cruelty' in its ordinary or popular meaning because that is too vague...."

He went on to say that there were people not insane who for one reason or another, sickness, selfishness, stupidity and the like, could not appreciate or foresee the harm they were doing, nor were they able to control their acts or form a rational decision about them. Yet these are the cases where the other spouse stands in greatest need of protection. If culpability is to be the test it would be necessary to deem these people to have qualities and abilities that they do not possess.

At p. 723 he says: —

> "... decree should be pronounced against such an abnormal person, not because his conduct was aimed at his wife, or because a reasonable man would have realised the position, or because he must be deemed to have foreseen or intended the harm he did, but simply because the facts are such that, after making all allowances for his disabilities and for the temperaments of both parties, it must be held that the character and gravity of his acts were such as to amount to cruelty. And if that is right for an abnormal person, I see no

good reason why the same should not apply to an insane person."

Lord Pearce at p. 762 put it thus: —

"In my opinion, insanity should, like temperament and other circumstances be one of the factors that may be taken into account in deciding whether a wife is entitled to relief.

Where, therefore, the conduct in question is such that it would not amount to cruelty in the absence of an actual intention to hurt, an insane man who could form no such intention would not be held to have treated his wife with cruelty. Where, however, the conduct would be held to be cruelty regardless of motive or intention to be cruel, insanity should not bar relief."

Cairns, J., followed Lord Reid's words above in *Crump* v. *Crump* [1965] 2 All E.R. 980 in granting a decree to a husband who complained of his wife's cruelty. She screamed from time to time and had outbursts of temper. She had a mania for cleanliness and had a ritual for wiping everything. This was caused by a morbid obsessional psychoneurosis. She knew what she was doing but could not control herself. The husband's health was affected. Cairns, J., held that though her cruelty was due to her mental condition, it was cruelty sufficient in law for him to grant a decree.

Cairns, J., also criticised *P.* v. *P.* [1964] 3 All E.R. 919 where a commissioner had refused a decree to a wife because the husband had refrained from sexual intercourse due to lack of desire, holding this could not be cruelty even though the wife's health was affected. At p. 984 in *Crump* v. *Crump, supra*, Cairns, J., commented: "I am bound to say that if conduct, otherwise cruel, cannot necessarily be excused on the ground of insanity I find it difficult to see how it can be excused on the ground of inclination or disinclination."

See also *Priday* v. *Priday,* referred to at length on p. 221.

E. Conduct due to illness

Is illness a sufficient excuse for cruel conduct by one spouse to another? Finnemore, J., in *Squire* v. *Squire* (1947), 63 T.L.R. 572, thought it was.

The Court of Appeal ([1949] P. 51), relying on views of Sir William Scott in *Holden* v. *Holden* (1810), 1 Hagg. Con. 453, 458, and in *Kirkman* v. *Kirkman* (1807), 1 Hagg. Con. 409, 410, held that illness (not amounting to insanity) was no excuse. Lord Simon in *Watt* (*or Thomas*) v. *Thomas* [1947] 1 All E.R. 582, at p. 586, had already expressed a similar view: —

> " Neither can the husband's right to a decree for cruelty be denied on the ground of the wife's pathological condition, which was producing increased nervous irritability."

(This part of Lord Simon's speech does not appear in the Law Reports [1947] A.C. 484.)

As Evershed, L.J., pointed out [1949] P. 51, at p. 62, all cruelty, not proceeding from malevolence, must proceed from some sickness or disorder of the mind, though in many cases falling short of insanity. On the other hand, Tucker, L.J., at p. 58, was careful to make the reservation that the state of health of the parties was a relevant consideration, and that there was a duty of a spouse to care for the other in sickness as well as in health.

As to mental illness see p. 218.

The difficulty of deciding when illness is a good defence to charges of cruelty, or not, is well illustrated by the case of *Priday* v. *Priday* [1970] 3 All E.R. 554. The wife developed schizophrenia. As a result she performed household duties inadequately. She became incapable of social communication and frustrated attempts by her husband to make her take tablets prescribed for her. As a consequence the husband suffered from depression. He petitioned for divorce on the ground of her cruelty. Cumming Bruce, J., dismissed the petition holding that the strains, stresses and ensuing depression suffered by the husband were not dissimilar from those endured by the spouse of a passive invalid struck down by physical disease whose behaviour could not be characterised as cruelty.

The learned judge referred to *Williams* v. *Williams*, which he purported to follow, and he repeated Lord Reid's opinion that the law cannot mean cruelty in its ordinary and popular meaning since that was too vague, but he emphasised that for one spouse to be guilty of cruelty to the other the word " treated " is of importance, and a passive condition due to illness could not be said to be " treating." He interpreted *Le Brocq* v. *Le Brocq* [1964] 3 All E.R. 464, where the husband was unsociable and taciturn, as a case where the conduct of the husband had not been sufficiently grave and weighty. *Saunders* v. *Saunders* [1965] 1 All E.R.

838 could be distinguished. The test of impossibility to live with the other spouse did not apply to every case. He said: —

> " As I contemplate the spectrum of the manifestations of insanity I observe (1) at one end dangerous violence with the consequence of actual or apprehended cruelty; in such cases the matrimonial law relieves the sane partner from the dangerous duty of cohabitation; (2) at the other end, chronic invalids whose insanity has reduced them to total and vacant passivity, devoid of memory or recognition and free from any propensity which could induce anyone to suggest that the sane spouse has been treated with cruelty. Between these two extremes are an infinite variety of situations on one or the other side of the border line."

F. Neurosis as cruelty

In *Alway* v. *Alway* (1961), *The Times*, 1st August, Judge Leslie, sitting as a special commissioner, tried the husband's petition for divorce on the ground of his wife's cruelty. The wife had developed a compulsive neurosis as a result of which she became obsessed with the need to have everything abnormally clean and hygienic. She took so long to get ready for bed at night that the husband was deprived of sleep. The suit was undefended, but the Queen's Proctor had been called in, and he made the following submissions: —

(1) that the state of the wife's health was a relevant consideration on the question whether her behaviour constituted legal cruelty;

(2) that a spouse could not be held guilty of cruelty if he or she were insane within the *McNaghten* rules (but see *Williams* v. *Williams* [1964] A.C. 698);

(3) that there was no halfway house between sanity and insanity, analogous to the condition of diminished responsibility in homicide cases in the criminal law;

(4) that no impulse could be regarded as irresistible unless the person concerned was insane within the *McNaghten* rules;

(5) that the presence of a malignant intent was not an essential ingredient in legal cruelty.

The learned commissioner accepted all these propositions and found that although the wife's conduct was due to illness, it was not due to insanity. She must have known that her actions would have a deleterious effect on her husband's health. While she did not intend to harm her husband, they were intentional acts which were likely to harm him and did, in fact, do so, and therefore her conduct amounted to cruelty in law.

G. Bona fide offer to return in cruelty cases

In *Wilkins* v. *Wilkins* (1962), 106 Sol. J. 433, the magistrates found persistent cruelty proved and made an order including a non-cohabitation clause. The Divisional Court (Sir Jocelyn Simon, P., and Karminski, J.) said that the non-cohabitation clause must be removed, as reconciliation was possible. The husband was given an opportunity of making a bona fide offer to remedy his conduct, which the wife would have to consider at her peril of being found in desertion.

It is believed that this is the first reported case to lay down the doctrine that a bona fide offer by a husband to remedy his conduct can expunge the offence of persistent cruelty. In this brief report there is nothing to show that the court laid down any principles as to the conditions under which a wife must accept such an offer, or be found in desertion, or when she is entitled to refuse. Much would depend on the severity of the cruelty and the likelihood of repetition.

VIII. CRUELTY TO CHILDREN

The Act of 1960, s. 1 (1) (*b*) (ii) and (iii), provides that persistent cruelty to an infant child of the complainant, or an infant child of the defendant who, at the time of the cruelty, was a child of the family (which is defined by s. 16 as any child of both parties, or any other child of either party who has been accepted as one of the family by the other party) shall be a ground for obtaining an order.

Before this Act, the courts had decided that cruelty to a child of the marriage could be cruelty to the wife if her health was affected, and that it was unnecessary to prove an express intention to injure the wife's health. A wife had to prove that what was done to the child was unreasonable and unjustifiable, and must prove facts from which the court should infer that the husband knew or must have known that his conduct would, or would be likely to, injure his wife's health (*Wright* v. *Wright* [1960] P. 85 (C.A.)).

Cruelty to children may still amount to persistent cruelty to the wife. It is submitted that under the above section, it is unnecessary to prove injury to the wife's health, or apprehension of such injury. All that is required is proof of cruelty to the child, and not the wife. It will be necessary to prove unreasonable and unjustifiable conduct towards the child, as a result of which the child's health has been or may be affected.

The Court of Appeal in *Wright* v. *Wright, supra,* overruled *Birch* v. *Birch* (1873), 28 L.T. 540, which had decided that cruelty to a child could not be cruelty to the mother unless it could be proved that the conduct to the child was with the express purpose by the husband of injuring the wife, and criticised dicta in *Kaslefsky* v. *Kaslefsky* [1951] P. 38 which seemed to support that view. It was pointed out that there was a line of cases beginning in 1901 which had decided that indecent assaults on a child of the marriage and sexual offences against third parties may amount to cruelty to the innocent spouse even though in committing those acts the husband had no intention to injure his wife, and in the view of the court, there was no difference in principle between the cases of indecent assault on a child of the marriage and cases of ill-treatment by beating.

CHAPTER 4

MISCELLANEOUS OFFENCES

I. ASSAULTS

THE Act of 1960 provides by s. 1 (1) (c) that a husband or wife may apply for an order against the other who has been found guilty—

   (i) on indictment, of any offence which involved an assault upon the complainant; or

  (ii) by a magistrates' court, of an offence against the complainant under s. 20, s. 42, s. 43 or s. 47 of the Offences against the Person Act, 1861, being, in the case of the said s. 42, an offence for which the defendant has been sentenced to imprisonment or any other form of detention for a term of not less than one month; or

 (iii) of, or of an attempt to commit, an offence under any of ss. 1–29 of the Sexual Offences Act, 1956, or under s. 1 of the Indecency with Children Act, 1960, against an infant child of the complainant, or against an infant child of the defendant who, at the time of the commission of or attempt to commit the offence, was a child of the family.

The offences tried in the magistrates' court, referred to above, are as follows: —

Offences against the Person Act, 1861—

  s. 20: unlawfully and maliciously inflicting grievous bodily harm, with or without a weapon;

  s. 42: common assault or battery;

  s. 43: aggravated assault upon a female;

  s. 47: assault occasioning actual bodily harm.

Actual bodily harm includes any hurt calculated to interfere with health or comfort. It need not be permanent or amount to grievous bodily harm. It is sufficient if it causes an hysterical and nervous condition (*R.* v. *Miller* [1954] 2 Q.B. 282).

Sections 1 to 29 of the Sexual Offences Act, 1956, include rape, intercourse with young girls, and with defectives and imbeciles,

225

incest, unnatural offences, and indecent assaults; and s. 1 of the Indecency with Children Act, 1960, refers to gross indecency with an infant child, but it is to be noted the offence has to be against an infant child of the complainant or an infant child of the defendant who, at the time of the commission of or attempt to commit the offence, was a child of the family.

Formerly, the court could only make an order on a summary conviction for aggravated assault, or where on indictment the husband was convicted for assault and was fined £5 or more, or sent to prison for a term exceeding two months. Owing to various technical difficulties, very little use was made of this remedy (which, incidentally, was the first summary remedy accorded to a wife by the Matrimonial Causes Act, 1878) and there are few reported cases.*

Where the offences are relatively not serious, the spouses are protected against an order for, by s. 12 (1) of the Criminal Justice Act, 1948, it is provided that a probation order under s. 3 and an absolute or conditional discharge under s. 37 of that Act is to be deemed not a conviction for any purpose other than the purpose of the proceedings in which the order is made. *Cassidy* v. *Cassidy* [1959] 1 W.L.R. 1024 was a case where a husband pleaded guilty to causing grievous bodily harm and was given a conditional discharge, and bound over for twelve months. The magistrates held that this was not a conviction by reason of s. 12 (1) of the Criminal Justice Act, 1948, and their decision was upheld by the Divisional Court.

The Act of 1960 uses the expression " found guilty " instead of the phrase " on conviction " found in the Act of 1895. It is submitted that the change in phraseology is of no consequence since a conviction is complete as soon as the person charged is found or pleads guilty. See Stroud's Judicial Dictionary, p. 636, and the cases there cited.

II. HABITUAL DRUNKARD OR DRUG ADDICT

The Act of 1960, s. 1 (1) (*f*), provides that either spouse may have an order on the ground that the other spouse " is for the time being an habitual drunkard, or a drug addict."

According to s. 16 (1) an " habitual drunkard " means a person

* See the author's article on Aggravated Assault, 107 L.J. News. 165.

(not being a mentally disordered person within the meaning of the Mental Health Act, 1959) who, by reason of habitual intemperate drinking of intoxicating liquor—

(*a*) is at times dangerous to himself or to others, or incapable of managing himself or his affairs; or

(*b*) so conducts himself that it would not be reasonable to expect a spouse of ordinary sensibilities to continue to cohabit with him.

A " drug addict " means a person (not being a mentally disordered person within the meaning of the Mental Health Act, 1959) who, by reason of the habitual taking or using, otherwise than upon medical advice, of any drug to which any of the provisions of the Dangerous Drugs Act, 1951, for the time being applied—

(*a*) is at times dangerous to himself or to others, or incapable of managing himself or his affairs; or

(*b*) so conducts himself that it would not be reasonable to expect a spouse of ordinary sensibilities to continue to cohabit with him.

Habitual drunkenness was first made a matrimonial offence by s. 5 of the Licensing Act, 1902, and was extended to include drug addiction by s. 3 of the Summary Jurisdiction (Separation and Maintenance) Act, 1925.

The Act of 1960 reproduced these provisions, but whereas, under the earlier legislation, relief was only granted when it was proved that by reason of habitual intemperate drinking of intoxicating liquor (or in the case of drugs, by reason of the habitual taking or using of drugs, otherwise than under medical advice) the defendant is at times dangerous to himself or to others or incapable of managing himself or his own affairs, there is now added the further provision that by drugs or drink he so conducts himself that it would not be reasonable to expect a spouse of ordinary sensibilities to continue to cohabit with him.

" Habitual " is a question of fact (*Robson* v. *Robson* (1904), 68 J.P. 416).

The fact that the defendant is able when sober to manage his own affairs is not a defence (*Eaton* v. *Best* [1909] 1 K.B. 632).

In *B.* v. *B.* (1962), 106 Sol. J. 573, D.C., the magistrates had made an order on the ground of desertion, and had given custody of the child of the marriage to the wife. It appears that the wife was a drug addict and, in 1961, had been in hospital for this addiction, and also had committed offences relating to drugs. While still under treatment, she had visited her husband who had refused her admission. A doctor had given evidence that she was fit and free of her problem.

Karminski, J., said that since, on the medical evidence, the wife was a drug addict within the meaning of s. 1 of the Matrimonial Proceedings (Magistrates' Courts) Act, 1960, the husband could not reasonably be expected to live with her. Baker, J., said that it was in the child's interest that the court should not take a chance, and accordingly the order for custody was discharged, but a new trial was ordered on the issue of desertion.

III. COMPELLING WIFE TO SUBMIT TO PROSTITUTION

The Act of 1960, s. 1 (1) (g), provides that a wife may have an order if her husband has compelled her to submit to prostitution or has been guilty of such conduct as was likely to result and has resulted in her submitting herself to prostitution. This provision is a re-enactment of s. 1 (2) (c) of the Summary Jurisdiction (Separation and Maintenance) Act, 1925.

There are no reported cases on this offence.

IV. VENEREAL DISEASES

A married woman or a married man may apply by way of complaint to a magistrates' court for an order under the Matrimonial Proceedings (Magistrates' Courts) Act, 1960, against the other party to the marriage if the defendant, while knowingly suffering from a venereal disease, has insisted on, or has without the complainant being aware of the presence of that disease permitted, sexual intercourse between the complainant and the defendant (s. 1 (1) (e)).

The communication of a venereal disease may be the result of an isolated act. It is a matrimonial offence and also an example of legal cruelty where one spouse wilfully and recklessly communicates a venereal disease to the other spouse, or has intercourse with the other spouse even if the disease is not inflicted, and against the will of the complainant who knows of his affliction (*Foster* v.

Foster [1921] P. 438). The mere innocent communication of the disease does not amount to cruelty (*Butler* v. *Butler* [1917] P. 244).

Under the Act of 1960 it must be proved that the defendant—
   (1) knew he was suffering from a venereal disease,
   (2) has insisted on sexual intercourse with the complainant (on the strict words of the section the complainant's knowledge is here immaterial),
   (3) or has permitted sexual intercourse with the complainant, who did not know of the presence of the disease.

The Act specifies sexual intercourse, and therefore an attempt at sexual intercourse would not be sufficient for the purpose of this section, but an attempt by the defendant to have intercourse knowing he is suffering from a venereal disease may amount to cruelty apart from this Act (*Popkin* v. *Popkin* (1794), 1 Hagg. Eccl. 765n).

A medical practitioner is bound to give evidence about his treatment of the patient if required to do so (*Garner* v. *Garner* (1920), 36 T.L.R. 196), and it is also his duty, if called upon by the party suffering from the disease, to give information to this party or to anyone, if the patient authorises him to do so, at any rate when this information is required for use in court, because assisting the course of justice is even more important than secrecy or the confidential relationship between doctor and patient (per Lewis, J., with the approval of Lord Merriman, P., in *C.* v. *C.* [1946] 1 All E.R. 562).

In *Chesnutt* v. *Chesnutt* (1854), 1 Sp. Ecc. & Ad. 196, wilful communication of " crabs " has been held to be cruelty.

CHAPTER 5

ADULTERY

I. INTRODUCTION

ADULTERY is a matrimonial offence with which the domestic court is concerned in the following ways: —

    A. As a ground for making an order, on the complaint of either spouse.

    B. As a defence to any complaint in respect of any matrimonial offence for which the Act gives a remedy.

    C. As a ground for revoking an order already made.

The provisions under the Act of 1960 are as follows: —

A. As a ground for an order (s. 1 (1))

A married woman or a married man may apply by way of complaint to a magistrates' court for an order under this Act against the other party to the marriage on any of the following causes of complaint arising during the subsistence of the marriage, that is to say, that the defendant:

*　　　　*　　　　*

    (*d*) has committed adultery.

But the Act provides by s. 2 (3) (*a*) that it is a defence if the court is satisfied that the complainant has condoned or connived at, or by wilful neglect or misconduct conduced to that act of adultery.

B. As a defence (s. 2 (3))

The court hearing a complaint under section one of this Act shall not make a matrimonial order containing a provision such as is mentioned in paragraph (*a*), (*b*) or (*c*) of subsection (1) of this section:

*　　　　*　　　　*

    (*b*) where the complainant is proved to have committed an act of adultery during the subsistence of the marriage,

230

unless the court is satisfied that the defendant has condoned or connived at, or by wilful neglect or
misconduct conduced to, that act of adultery.

C. As a ground for revoking an order (s. 8 (2))

Where on a complaint for the revocation of a matrimonial
order it is proved that the party on whose complaint the order
was made during the subsistence of the marriage committed
an act of adultery, the court shall revoke the order:
Provided that:

* * *

(b) the court shall not revoke the order by reason of such
an act of adultery as aforesaid:
(i) except at the request of the person who was
the defendant to the proceedings in which the order
was made; or
(ii) if the court is of the opinion that the person
aforesaid has condoned or connived at, or by wilful
neglect or misconduct conduced to, that act of
adultery,
and shall not be bound by reason of that act of adultery
to revoke any provision of the order included therein
by virtue of paragraphs (d) to (h) of subsection (1) of
section two of this Act.

An unusual case on revocation was *Baker* v. *Baker* [1963] 3 All
E.R. 901, where a wife had obtained a maintenance order on the
ground of desertion in 1959. In 1960 she divorced her husband on
the ground of cruelty, the decree being made absolute on 24th
January, 1961. In 1962 the husband applied to the magistrates to
revoke the maintenance order on the ground of her adultery,
relying on the fact that she had given birth to a child on 24th
December, 1960. The husband said he had not had intercourse
with his wife since 1958, while she deposed that he had, between
December, 1959, and March, 1960. The wife did not disclose this
to the divorce court. The magistrates dismissed the application on
the ground that the husband had not satisfied the onus of proof.

The Divisional Court held that the magistrates were right in
investigating the husband's allegations since public policy was no
more offended by allowing the husband to allege adultery than by

allowing her to allege she had had sexual intercourse with him since 1958. The case was however remitted to a new bench of magistrates to re-try the issue of adultery, as the previous bench had misdirected themselves on the evidence.

D. Time limit

There is a time limit (s. 12 (1)) for the bringing of proceedings which is as follows: —

> A complaint under section one of this Act on the ground of the commission of an act of adultery by the defendant may be heard if it is made within six months of the date when that act of adultery first became known to the complainant.

There are also provisions for safeguarding the interests of sailors and members of H. M. Forces.

It follows that this time limit only applies to a complainant who is applying for an order on the ground of adultery, and does not apply where adultery is set up as a defence or as a ground for revoking an order.

An important change with regard to the time in which a summons can be issued by a spouse in respect of the other spouse's adultery is that formerly it had to be proved that the last act of adultery took place within six months of the issue of the summons (*Teall* v. *Teall* [1938] P. 250). In the 1960 Act this is altered so that the time limit of six months is measured from the date when the act of adultery first became known to the complainant.

E. History

Adultery was first made a ground for obtaining maintenance summarily in 1937 by the Matrimonial Causes Act, 1937, s. 11. Subsection (1) added adultery to the grounds on which a wife might apply for an order. Subsection (2) gave the husband the power to apply for an order on the ground of adultery, while subs. (3) read as follows: —

> On any application made by virtue of this section, the court shall not make an order unless it is satisfied that the applicant has not condoned, or connived at, or by his or her wilful neglect or misconduct conduced to the adultery, and that the application is not made or prosecuted in collusion with the other party to the marriage or any person with whom it is alleged that the adultery has been committed.

Section 11 was repealed by the Act of 1960. It will be noticed that under the later Act the reference to collusion was omitted.

Adultery has always been a matrimonial offence, and in the ecclesiastical courts it was a ground for divorce *a mensa et thoro*. The Act of 1857 made it a ground for divorce by a husband, and also by a wife if in addition she proved two years' desertion, or cruelty; or incestuous adultery; or bigamy coupled with adultery.

The Matrimonial Causes Act, 1923, gave the right to the wife to divorce her husband on the ground of adultery alone, and this provision was re-enacted in the Matrimonial Causes Act, 1937; and later by the statute which consolidated the law with regard to matrimonial causes in the High Court, namely the Matrimonial Causes Act, 1950, it was provided by s. 1 (1) (*a*) that adultery committed by either party since the celebration of the marriage is a ground for divorce. This was repeated in s. 1 of the Matrimonial Causes Act, 1965, but repealed by the Divorce Reform Act, 1969.

Under the Act of 1895, s. 6, it was provided that no order should be made on the application of a married woman if it should be proved that she had committed an act of adultery, provided it had not been condoned or connived at or conduced to by the husband. Section 7 gave the court the power to revoke the order made on the ground of the wife's adultery, but did not include the proviso about condonation, connivance or conduct conducing. It was therefore held in the Court of Appeal in the case of *Marczuk* v. *Marczuk* [1956] P. 217 that a husband could get an order revoked on the ground of his wife's adultery, even though he had condoned that adultery. The Act of 1960, however, has in effect overruled *Marczuk* v. *Marczuk*.

Under the Divorce Reform Act, 1969, the sole ground for obtaining a divorce was the irretrievable breakdown of the marriage and this has been re-enacted in the Matrimonial Causes Act, 1973. Adultery by itself is now no longer a ground for divorce, nor is it by itself proof that the marriage has broken down irretrievably. By s. 1 (2) (*a*) the court has to be satisfied that the respondent has committed adultery and that the petitioner finds it intolerable to live with the respondent. There is still some judicial difference whether this means that the petitioner finds it intolerable to live with the respondent because of the adultery or the intolerable conduct arises from another cause or causes. See

Goodrich v. *Goodrich* [1971] 2 All E.R. 1340; *Roper* v. *Roper* [1972] 3 All E.R. 668 and *Cleary* v. *Cleary* [1974] 1 All E.R. 498. The Court of Appeal favoured the former interpretation but in *Carr* v. *Carr* [1974] 1 All E.R. 1193 the Court of Appeal inclined to the latter view. The matter is discussed in a Note in the *Law Quarterly Review*, vol. 90, p. 292, July 1974.

II. DEFINITION
A. The act

Adultery is consensual sexual intercourse between a married person and a person of the opposite sex (per Singleton, L.J., in *Dennis* v. *Dennis* [1955] P. 153: he also said that in his view there was no distinction between adultery and carnal knowledge in criminal law, so far as the sexual intercourse is concerned: in other words, the quality and extent of sexual intercourse is the same in both cases).

In *Dennis* v. *Dennis*, *supra*, it was held that there must be some penetration of the woman by the man, although the act of sexual intercourse need not have been complete. Therefore an attempt at sexual intercourse which did not achieve any penetration is not sufficient. It rarely happens, of course, that the court has to investigate with any minuteness what actually happened, and where opportunity and inclination are proved, adultery is presumed, but when the issue is directly raised, in a contested case, that the acts of familiarity between the parties did not amount to adultery, the court has to go into the matter and consider whether there was any penetration. For instance, in *Sapsford* v. *Sapsford and Furtado* [1954] P. 394, the respondent wife and the co-respondent admitted manual satisfaction and gross indecency, but denied adultery. Karminski, J., said at p. 399: —

> ". . . I do not think that it can be said . . . that manual satisfaction can by itself amount to adultery. On the other hand it has been said many times that an act of adultery need not be such a complete act of intercourse as is required to consummate a marriage. . . ."

He went on to consider *Thompson* (*otherwise Hulton*) v. *Thompson* [1938] P. 162, where a woman, who on examination was found to be a virgin, had shared a bedroom with the respondent over long periods and Langton, J., had found there was mutual intercourse amounting in law to adultery, " mutual intercourse " meaning, according to Karminski, J., that there has to be intercourse in which both the man and the woman play what may be described as their normal role. The learned judge found that although the acts of indecency referred to did not amount to adultery, they were evidence from which adultery could be inferred.

B. Consent of defendant essential

If a woman is raped, then she is not guilty of adultery (*Clarkson* v. *Clarkson* (1930), 46 T.L.R. 623) but the man is (*Coffey* v. *Coffey* [1898] P. 169). Once intercourse has taken place, this is prima facie adultery and the onus then shifts to the wife in such a case to establish that it took place against her will. *Redpath* v. *Redpath and Milligan* [1950] 1 All E.R. 600 was a case where a wife alleged that she had been raped, and the co-respondent was prosecuted, but was acquitted. On a petition for divorce by the husband alleging adultery, Pilcher, J., held that the onus was on the husband to prove that the wife's intercourse was voluntary, but this was reversed by the Court of Appeal, Bucknill, L.J., saying at p. 600: —

> " Sexual intercourse is normally a consensual act, that is to say, it requires the consenting minds and bodies of both parties. In my view, once the act of intercourse is established, the burden is on the wife to show that that act was one to which she was forced against her will. I do not think a husband can be expected to prove the state of the wife's mind when the sexual intercourse took place."

See also *Clark* v. *Clark* (1954), *The Times*, 3rd June (C.A.), where rape was not proved and adultery was found.

Similarly, a person who through insanity is incapable of appreciating the culpability of the act cannot be found guilty of adultery. In *S.* v. *S.* [1962] P. 133, the intervener, who was a mental patient, was dismissed from the suit because she was ignorant that her act was wrongful. Mr. Commissioner Latey, Q.C., accepted the argument that the *McNaghten* rules applied ((1843), 10 Cl. & Fin. 200) so that where it is proved that at the time of committing the offence the party accused was labouring under such a defect of reason, from disease of the mind, as not to know the nature and quality of the act he was doing; or, if he did know it, that he did not know what he was doing was wrong, he cannot be found guilty of adultery. See also *Stead* v. *Stead* [1968] P. 538.

In *Goshawk* v. *Goshawk* (1965), 109 Sol. J. 290, the wife petitioned for divorce on the ground of her husband's adultery; she admitted she had a child of whom the husband was not the father, but she said she was drunk when it was conceived and therefore she was not a consenting party. The judge said this was not conclusive and exercised his discretion. Apparently a woman could be so drunk in these circumstances as to make her not a consenting party.

C. One act of adultery sufficient

The Act of 1960 simply uses the words " has committed adultery " as a ground of complaint, but in s. 2 and s. 8 the reference is to " an act of adultery." Apart from the wording of the Act it is generally accepted that one act of adultery is sufficient. In *Gipps* v. *Gipps* (1864), 11 H.L. Cas. 1, 28, Lord Chelmsford said : —

"It must be borne in mind that the offence of adultery is complete in a single instance of guilty connection with a married woman."

This was quoted with approval in *Douglas* v. *Douglas* [1951] P. 85 (C.A.), at p. 96.

Lord Merrivale, P., used to insist that there had in certain cases, such as hotel cases, to be shown an adulterous inclination, either generally or towards one woman, or an adulterous tendency (*Farnham* v. *Farnham* (1925), 41 T.L.R. 543), but this view was overruled by the Court of Appeal in *Woolf* v. *Woolf* [1931] P. 134.

D. Adultery after divorce

Before the Act of 1960, magistrates were sometimes faced with the problem of determining whether adultery had taken place after the parties had been divorced, for the purpose of deciding whether an order in the magistrates' court should be revoked, having regard to the fact that a maintenance order, obtained before the magistrates while the marriage was subsisting, continues in force after the divorce (*Bragg* v. *Bragg* [1925] P. 20). Happily, magistrates are now spared solving this problem, since by s. 8 (2) the only adultery in respect of which an order can be revoked is adultery which has taken place during the *subsistence of the marriage.*

The law which was formerly contained in *Chorlton* v. *Chorlton* [1952] P. 169 and *Abson* v. *Abson* [1952] P. 55 which decided that sexual intercourse by the wife after the decree absolute amounted to adultery if it was with a married man, but not if it was with a single man, need no longer be considered by magistrates, since such adultery would be after the marriage had terminated and not during its subsistence. See also *Baker* v. *Baker* [1963] 3 All E.R. 901, discussed on p. 231.

III. PROOF

Adultery, more than any other matrimonial offence, presents great difficulties of proof. It is an offence which invariably is committed in secret; where direct evidence of its commission is rarely available, and if it is, is seldom trusted or accepted. The proof, in most cases, is arrived at by inference, from the inclination of the parties, and their opportunities. Questions, therefore, arise as to the standard of proof, the probative value of confessions, the acceptability of evidence given by one of the parties to the alleged adultery, and the desirability of corroboration, and what evidence raises a presumption of guilt.

A. General principle

This is set out by Lord Buckmaster in *Ross* v. *Ellison* (*or Ross*) [1930] A.C. 1, at p. 7: —

" Adultery is essentially an act which can rarely be proved by direct evidence. It is a matter of inference and circumstance. It is easy to suggest conditions which can leave no doubt that adultery has been committed, but the mere fact that people are thrown together in an environment which lends itself to the commission of the offence is not enough unless it can be shown by documents, e.g., letters and diaries, or antecedent conduct, that the association of the parties was so intimate and their mutual passion so clear that adultery might reasonably be assumed as the result of an opportunity for its occurrence."

This principle is really a matter of common sense. That great judge, Sir William Scott, said in *Chambers* v. *Chambers* (1810), 1

Hagg. Con. 439, that where a young woman is estranged from her husband, and lives together with a young officer for months at different places, though under the flimsy disguise of separate beds, that courts of justice should not put upon such intimacy the construction which everybody else would put upon it, would be monstrous. If persons place themselves in a compromising situation, from which the world at large would infer adultery, they must not be surprised if courts do the same.

B. Presumption

Where there is proof of attachment, criminal intention, and opportunity, there is a presumption that adultery has been committed (*Davidson* v. *Davidson* (1856), Dea. & Sw. 132). See too *Greville-Bell* v. *Greville-Bell and Primo de Rivera* (1958), *The Times*, 21st November. Indecent familiarities raise a strong presumption of adultery (*Elwes* v. *Elwes* (1794), 1 Hagg. Con. 269, 276). In *Farnham* v. *Farnham* (1925), 41 T.L.R. 543, Lord Merrivale said at p. 544: —

> ". . . the inference of adultery arises when there is proof of a disposition of parties to commit adultery together with the opportunity for committing it."

In this case the President accepted the evidence of the manageress of the hotel that the husband and the woman seemed very friendly, and she took them for husband and wife, that they took a room with a double bed, and afterwards it looked as though it had been slept in. In those days, when adultery was the only ground for a divorce, there was a temptation, where the parties wanted a divorce, to arrange either collusively or otherwise a sham appearance of adultery, for the respondent and a woman to stay at an hotel and provide the bill to the petitioner. Now that there are a number of other grounds for divorce, this temptation has largely disappeared. So far as magistrates' courts are concerned, such an arrangement would be pointless, and perhaps it is for this reason that collusion has disappeared from the Act.

C. Inclination

Inclination without opportunity is not sufficient. In *Cox* v. *Cox* [1958] 1 W.L.R. 340 (D.C.), the wife had embraced a workmate, at work, in the presence of other workers, and had aroused him sexually. But adultery was not proved because there had been no opportunity.

Opportunity without inclination is, as a rule, not enough; see *Corke* v. *Corke and Cooke* [1958] P. 93, where the co-respondent was a lodger with the respondent, and there was no evidence of any familiarity. See also *Gibbons* v. *Gibbons* (1932), 96 J.P. 247, a housekeeper case.

There are cases, however, where the absence of inclination is of no consequence. In *Gower* v. *Gower* [1950] 1 All E.R. 804 the wife, while separated from her husband, met a married man, Mr. *C*, who was living apart from his wife. They moved together to different addresses, and she was known as Mrs. *C*, and occupied the same bedroom as he did. Barnard, J., who heard the husband's petition, did not find adultery proved on the ground that there was no evidence of inclination. Bucknill, L.J., said at p. 805: —

> " I venture to think that the learned judge misdirected himself there. The vital question is: Where were these people sleeping during the time that they were together? If the evidence points almost irresistibly to the fact that they were sleeping in the same room, one does not want any further evidence than that. There is no need for evidence of kissing and that sort of thing."

In other words, the elements of inclination and opportunity are helpful in drawing the inference that adultery has taken place, but they are not the only ways of proving adultery (*Rutton* v. *Rutton* (1796), 2 Hagg. Con. 6n). In *Gower's* case, it is difficult to see how the learned judge could say there was not a scrap of evidence of inclination. One would have thought the fact that they slept in the same room was the most cogent evidence of inclination. What he meant presumably was that there was no evidence of inclination, apart from the fact that they were sharing the same bedroom, but as Buckley, L.J., said, what more do you want than that?

D. Presumption rebuttable

Though inclination and opportunity raise a presumption of guilt, this presumption may be rebutted. In *England* v. *England* [1953] P. 16, the wife and the man concerned admitted that they were attracted to one another and had planned to get married when they could, and had even discussed having sexual intercourse together, that he had been a constant visitor to her room for months, and that he had spent one night in her room but they both gave evidence that, on that night, she had been ill and he had sat on a chair looking after her. The justices dismissed the husband's summons to revoke a maintenance order, and the Divisional Court on appeal upheld the justices. It was agreed there was ample evidence on which adultery could have been found proved, but there was no irrebuttable presumption, nor any estoppel. After referring to *Woolf* v. *Woolf* [1931] P. 134, which was an undefended case, Lord Merriman, P., said at p. 21: —

> " I decline to hold that there is any rule of law that the conjunction of strong inclination with evidence of opportunity (and the same facts may be evidence of both) leads to an irrebuttable presumption that adultery has been committed. That it affords very strong prima facie evidence is indisputable, but that is quite another thing."

E. Onus of proof—reasonable doubt

The difficulty of this subject was illustrated in the case of *Christian* v. *Christian* (1962), 106 Sol. J. 430, where the Court of Appeal was divided. The wife alleged adultery with a girl aged fourteen. There were a number of amorous letters from the husband to the girl and, on one occasion, the wife had found them in bed together. He had further pleaded guilty to two acts of indecent assault upon the girl for which he had been sent to prison for twelve months. The husband, in a statement under caution, denied adultery but said that he had done everything else. There was medical evidence that an examination had shown no evidence of sexual intercourse, the hymen being intact, a condition consistent with some possibly manual, but not complete, penetration. The husband did not defend the petition and, after submissions by the Queen's Proctor, the judge dismissed the petition, holding there was a reasonable doubt.

The majority in the Court of Appeal (Donovan and Davies, L.JJ.) held that the petitioner had not displaced the onus of proof. Willmer, L.J., dissenting, said there was abundant evidence of inclination and opportunity. The medical evidence was neutral, and there was nothing to displace the inference which normally would have been irresistible that adultery had taken place.

F. Hotel cases

A common type of case in the divorce court (less common now than it used to be) but rather exceptional in magistrates' courts, is where one of the parties—usually the husband—sends the other spouse a hotel bill with an indication that he had stayed one or more nights at a hotel with a person of the opposite sex. If we take the typical case where the husband is the respondent, he stays at a hotel with a woman, and the chamber maid serves breakfast while they are in bed together and later gives evidence of this fact. The name of the lady is usually not disclosed. Before 1931 the divorce court was very sensitive about these cases, as it was suspected in many cases that the set up was a sham, and a device for the parties to get a divorce, collusively or otherwise, or to mislead the court into supposing there had been adultery in the hotel to cover up real adultery between a husband and his paramour, whom he wished to protect.

A typical example is *Farnham* v. *Farnham* (1925), 41 T.L.R. 543, where a hotel bill had been provided by the husband to his wife. Lord Merrivale suspected this was merely a device, and adjourned the case for further enquiries, but was satisfied when the manageress gave evidence that she had seen the couple, that they seemed very friendly, that she took them for husband and wife, and that when she saw the double bed the next day it had obviously been slept in. In this type of case, Hill, J., insisted on the practice of causing a letter to be written to the husband, asking for the name and address of the lady concerned.

In *Townend* v. *Townend* (1928), *The Times*, 7th June, Lord Merrivale uttered dire threats against solicitors in respect of framed hotel cases. In *Woolf* v. *Woolf* [1931] P. 134, he rejected a petition in a hotel case, after calling in the King's Proctor. This was reversed by the Court of Appeal (Lord Hanworth, M.R., Lawrence and Romer, L.JJ.), Lord Hanworth, M.R., saying at p. 143: —

". . . The President seems to have thought it was the duty of the petitioner to prove something more. He says: ' It is quite true that if the respondent had shown an adulterous inclination generally, or an adulterous inclination with regard to one woman, or an intimate association with one woman, and she had been identified or there was reason to believe she was the woman in question, what seems to me to be the missing link would be supplied.' That, I think, is a ruling of law not justified by the authorities. The petitioner is under no obligation to show adulterous inclination generally on the part of the respondent. In my opinion, if evidence is given in good faith which under all but the most unusual circumstances is clear evidence of adultery, it is the duty of the court to act upon it, unless the King's Proctor can bring forward cogent evidence to rebut the obvious presumption.

In *Loveden* v. *Loveden* (1810), 2 Hagg. Con. 1, 2, Sir William Scott said that it was not necessary to prove the direct fact of adultery, for ' if it were otherwise, there is not one case in a hundred in which that proof would be attainable: it is very rarely indeed that the parties are surprised in the direct fact of adultery. In every case almost the fact is inferred from circumstances that lead to it by fair inference as a necessary conclusion; and unless this were the case, and unless this were so held, no protection whatever could be given to marital rights.' That passage has been quoted with approval in the Court of Appeal by Lopes, L.J., in *Allan* v. *Allan* [1894] P. 248, 252, where he says: ' To lay down any general rule to attempt to define what circumstances would be sufficient and what insufficient upon which to infer the fact of adultery, is impossible. Each case must depend on its own particular circumstances.'

It seems to me that, human nature being what it is, adultery must be inferred here. The husband was twenty-five, and no more, and he had been married, and there is no reason to assume that his sexual appetite was less than that of a normal healthy man. I think that to say that an adulterous inclination should be proved is to lay an unjustifiable burden on the petitioner. The case is one of an innocent woman proving opportunity for adultery, and the fact that the parties spent two nights in the same bedroom. In my opinion, in this case the court ought to be satisfied that adultery has been proved."

The court, of course, is entitled to know the background in each case, and if that indicates, for instance, that the hotel interlude was a screen to cover an adulterous association with another woman, it is not bound to find adultery proved in the hotel (*Raspin* v. *Raspin* [1953] P. 230).

G. Direct evidence

This can be of three kinds: —

    (*a*) by detectives;

    (*b*) by other eye witnesses;

    (*c*) by a party to the adultery.

(*a*) It is very common to use detectives in adultery cases, mainly for the purpose of obtaining confessions from the parties, but they are also used to watch the parties for evidence of association and intimacy. Sometimes they give evidence of actually having seen the parties in the act of adultery, in motor cars, or through peeping through bedroom windows, or in the open air, and so on. The courts always regard this evidence with great suspicion. In *Sopwith* v. *Sopwith* (1859), 4 Sw. & Tr. 243, where the evidence of a private detective was not accepted, the Judge Ordinary described them as a class of most dangerous agents, because they were people whose living depended on making discoveries for those who employ them.

(*b*) When witnesses say they have seen parties in the act of adultery, the court scrutinises their evidence very carefully. They may be servants who are acting out of spite, or other persons who have some corrupt motive. When the party impugned is of blameless character and good reputation, the court is slow to accept the evidence of people who say they saw the act of adultery. In *Alexander* v. *Alexander* (1860), 2 Sw. & Tr. 95, it was alleged that a married woman who had been married twenty years without any suspicion, and who had a number of children, was seen to have committed adultery with the groom. The evidence was that they had been seen through a window where the blind was not drawn, and in a washhouse when the door was open. The Judge Ordinary said the evidence to satisfy the court, against a woman of character, must be most cogent, and added: "No woman's character would be safe, if it would be destroyed under the circumstances proved in this case."

(*c*) When a party to the adultery gives evidence of that adultery, he or she should be regarded as an accomplice, and the rules relating to accomplices in criminal cases should be applied. This involves the question of corroboration.

H. Standard of proof

In deciding whether or not adultery has been committed, the court must be satisfied beyond reasonable doubt. The most authoritative exposition is that of Lord MacDermott in *Preston-Jones* v. *Preston-Jones* [1951] A.C. 391, at p. 417, where he said: —

". . . The evidence must, no doubt, be clear and satisfactory, beyond a mere balance of probabilities, and conclusive in the sense that it will satisfy what Lord Stowell, when Sir William Scott, described in *Loveden* v. *Loveden* (1810), 2 Hagg. Con. 1, 3 as ' the guarded discretion of a reasonable and just man '; but these desiderata appear to me entirely consistent with the acceptance of proof beyond reasonable doubt as the standard required.

. . . I am unable to subscribe to the view which, though not propounded here, has had its adherents, namely, that on its true construction the word ' satisfied ' is capable of connoting something less than proof beyond reasonable doubt. The jurisdiction in divorce involves the status of the parties and the public interest requires that the marriage bond shall not be set aside lightly or without strict inquiry. The terms of the statute recognise this plainly and I think it would be quite out of keeping with the anxious nature of its provisions to hold that the court might be ' satisfied,' in respect of a ground for dissolution, with something less than proof beyond reasonable doubt. I should, perhaps, add that I do not base my conclusions as to the appropriate standard of proof on any analogy drawn from the criminal law. I do not think it is possible to say, at any rate since the decision of this House in *Mordaunt* v. *Moncreiffe* (1874), L.R. 2 Sc. & Div. 374, that the two jurisdictions are other than distinct. The true reason, as it seems to me, why both accept the same general standard —proof beyond reasonable doubt—lies not in any analogy, but in the gravity and public importance of the issues with which each is concerned."

Mordaunt v. *Moncreiffe*, to which the learned law lord referred, decided that proceedings with regard to adultery were civil proceedings, and not criminal. Nevertheless, the standard of proof is the same, not because adultery is a criminal matter, but because status is involved and the issues are grave, of public importance, and of considerable consequence to the parties involved.

The Court of Appeal in *Ginesi* v. *Ginesi* [1948] P. 179 decided that adultery must be proved with the same degree of strictness as is required for the proof of a criminal offence. Tucker, L.J., said at p. 181: —

"I am satisfied that Hodson, J., was correct when he said that adultery must be proved with the same degree of strictness as is required for the proof of a criminal offence, and I limit my observations to cases of adultery. Adultery was regarded by the ecclesiastical courts as a quasi-criminal offence, and it must be proved with the same strictness as is required in a criminal case. That means that it must be proved beyond all reasonable doubt to the satisfaction of the tribunal of fact."

The facts of the case were that the wife was living apart from her husband, and had obtained a maintenance order for herself and children. She had the lifelong friendship of a Mr. Birkett, who was a widower. He took her out to the pictures, dances, etc. The husband had her watched by three teams of detectives. She was also employed by Birkett first as a shop assistant and then as secretary. The evidence of the detectives was relied on only as to two nights, when the wife and Birkett were together alone in the middle of the night, once in his car and the other at his office for an hour. On this the stipendiary magistrate of Bradford found adultery, but this was reversed by the Divisional Court, whose decision was upheld by the Court of Appeal.

In the case of *Preston-Jones* v. *Preston-Jones, supra,* the real issue was whether adultery was proved when a child was born 360 days after the husband last had access to his wife. The question of proof in the ordinary case of adultery, where adultery is inferred from the conduct and inclination of the parties, was not in point. In *Gower* v. *Gower* [1950] 1 All E.R. 804, Bucknill, L.J., at p. 805, said this: —

> " Counsel for the wife laid great emphasis on the fact that this is a charge of adultery. He said that adultery is a quasi-criminal offence and must be proved as such. I have never quite understood what that meant. The standard of proof required in a criminal case is higher than the standard of proof in a civil action because in a civil action a matter may be proved on a balance of probabilities and the court may decide one way or the other on a very small margin of preference, while, on the other hand, in a criminal case the matter must be proved beyond any reasonable doubt. To put it in another way, if the the case for the prosecution is based on circumstantial evidence, the evidence must be such as to be inconsistent with any reasonable hypotheses other than the guilt of the accused. If the accused gives any reasonable explanation which is consistent with innocence, the matter is not proved beyond any reasonable doubt."

Denning, L.J., who agreed, cast doubt on the correctness of *Ginesi* v. *Ginesi,* and doubted whether the Court of Appeal was committed to the view that adultery must be regarded as a criminal charge to be proved beyond all reasonable doubt.

Bater v. *Bater* [1951] P. 35 was a case of cruelty, but the Court of Appeal said that the petitioner must prove her case beyond reasonable doubt. Denning, L.J., said this expression was apt for civil as well as criminal cases, but that because of our high regard for the liberty of the individual, a doubt may be regarded as reasonable in the criminal courts which would not be so in the civil courts. See also *Davis* v. *Davis* [1950] P. 125 (C.A.), and *Miller* v. *Minister of Pensions* (1947), 63 T.L.R. 474.

In *Galler* v. *Galler* [1954] P. 252, the Court of Appeal said that in divorce, as in crime, the court has to be satisfied beyond reasonable doubt. So the matter rests at present. So far as adultery is concerned, a balance of probabilities will not do. Nor if there is an innocent explanation of the facts can there be said to be no reasonable doubt.

The proper approach in these matters is the one suggested by Sir William Scott in *Loveden* v. *Loveden* (1810), 2 Hagg. Con. 1, at p. 3, which has often been quoted and approved: —

> " The only general rule that can be laid down upon the subject is, that the circumstances must be such as would lead the guarded discretion of a reasonable and just man to the conclusion . . ."

The principles are the same both in criminal and civil cases, but the stringency of proof depends largely on the subject-matter, so that in civil proceedings, allegations of crime require a high standard of proof. Adultery is not criminal, but has affinities to crime, and therefore strict proof is required. The standard of proof of adultery on the intervention of the Queen's Proctor is the same as on the original petition (*Rudman* v. *Rudman and Lee* [1964] 1 W.L.R. 598).

The subject of standard of proof in adultery was considered in the Court of Appeal in *Bastable* v. *Bastable and Sanders* [1968] 3 All E.R. 701. The husband alleged his wife had committed adultery with the co-respondent, who was a close friend; there was no evidence of affectionate behaviour nor had they been caught in compromising situations, but the husband called other evidence which he alleged indicated she had committed adultery with the co-respondent. The wife denied these allegations, but the trial judge found adultery proved. The Court of Appeal allowed the wife's appeal, holding that the standard of proof had to be high, that

" in proportion as the offence is grave so ought the proof to be clear," that the onus of proof had not been satisfied in this case and that suspicion was not enough. The above cases were reviewed.

I. Confessions

Provided it is genuine and made bona fide, a confession is accepted by the court as evidence of adultery, even if there is no other evidence to support it. The court's approach to confessions is one of caution, and corroboration is preferred. In *Robinson* v. *Robinson* (1859), 1 Sw. & Tr. 362, the court (Cockburn, C.M., Wightman, J., and Cresswell, J.O.) said that if there was evidence, not open to exception, of admissions of adultery, it would be the duty of the court to act on those admissions even if there was no other evidence to support them. The court, if after looking at the admission with distrust and vigilance it came to the conclusion that it was trustworthy, that it amounted to a distinct, clear and unequivocal admission, should have no hesitation in acting upon it. The court added that the admission of a party charged with a criminal or wrongful act has at all times, and in all systems of jurisprudence, been considered a most cogent and conclusive proof.

This was followed in *Williams* v. *Williams and Padfield* (1865), L.R. 1 P. & D. 29, where the wife, on being told by a neighbour of her suspicions, fell on her knees and begged that her husband be not told, and on the neighbour saying she would tell, the wife left home and wrote several letters admitting her adultery and begging for forgiveness. The court accepted the admissions, which were the only evidence. A husband's confession in a criminal trial of his adultery was held to be sufficient in divorce proceedings (*Hartley* v. *Hartley and Fleming* (1919), 35 T.L.R. 298).

The rule laid down in *Russell* v. *Russell* [1924] A.C. 687 that neither spouse could give evidence which would tend to bastardise their issue was a complicating factor in confessions, but that rule has now disappeared as a result of s. 32 (1) of the Matrimonial Causes Act, 1950 (now s. 48 (1) of the Act of 1973). Cases such as *Warren* v. *Warren* [1925] P. 107, *Roast* v. *Roast* [1938] P. 8, *Ettenfield* v. *Ettenfield* [1940] P. 96 (C.A.), and *Frampton* v. *Frampton and Bushell* [1941] P. 24, where confessions tended to bastardise the issue, and it was held that the admissions were still evidence of adultery and admissible, are now obsolete in so far as they refer to the *Russell* rule, but they do indicate the readiness with which confessions are now accepted.

The headnote in *Getty* v. *Getty* [1907] P. 334 reads: —

> " Although it is the general practice in matrimonial cases not to act and grant relief upon uncorroborated confessions of adultery, there is no absolute rule of practice and no rule of law precluding the court from acting upon such uncorroborated evidence. The true test seems to be whether the court is satisfied from the surrounding circumstances in any particular and exceptional case that the confession is true."

This may be an unexceptional statement of the law, but it has little relation to the case reported. The wife wrote a letter admitting adultery nineteen years before. The judge, Bucknill, J., called a solicitor who had been acting for her and made him answer certain questions, to which he had replied that the wife had admitted her adultery to him, but had refused to name the man because of possible consequences to him. The judge said this was strong corroboration, and without it he would have had great difficulty in acting on the confession.

A confession is, of course, only evidence against the party making it, and not against the other party with whom the adultery is alleged to have taken place. Viscount Birkenhead, L.C., in *Rutherford* v. *Richardson* [1923] A.C. 1, at p. 6, said: —

> "...*A*, a husband brings against his wife *B* a petition for divorce, on the grounds of her adultery with a named co-respondent *C*. There is some independent evidence against both *B* and *C*, but not sufficient to justify a positive adverse conclusion. *B*, however, makes full confession. Here the court may very reasonably pronounce a decree against *B*, while concluding that the matter is not established as against *C*. Indeed, to hold otherwise would be to lay it down that the admission or confession of *B*—which may be quite untrue, and which may be induced by hidden and private motives— is to be treated as good evidence against *C*. And so it happens that the court may quite reasonably conclude that it is proved that *B* has committed adultery with *C*, but not that *C* has committed adultery with *B*. The law of England does not technically recognise a verdict of ' not proven,' but substantially this is the nature of the verdict which in the circumstances supposed exculpates *C*.
>
> But still another case requires consideration. Supposing that the case presented and the impression made by *C* upon

the court is of such a character that the judge, summarising his impression, may record it in this way:

'Not only has *C* convinced me that I must give him the benefit of the doubt, because the admissions are not evidence as against him, but he has positively satisfied me that no adultery was ever committed at all between the parties charged.'

Such a conclusion, if plainly reached by a judge or a jury, makes it impossible for any purpose whatever to act upon the admissions which would otherwise have been a reliable guide in relation to him or her who made them. For in the cause supposed, that which has been proved by *C* is, as my noble and learned friend, Lord Dunedin, suggested in the course of the argument, absolutely destructive of the case made by *B* and, therefore (*inter alia*), of the admissions upon which and upon which alone that case depended. These observations apply equally to the converse case where *A* is the wife petitioning for divorce, *B* being the husband the respondent, and *C* the intervener."

J. Corroboration

Corroborative evidence is evidence which tends to support or confirm other evidence in the case. It must be evidence of some material particular tending to show that the accused committed the acts charged, which affects the accused by connecting or tending to connect him with what he is charged (*R.* v. *Baskerville* [1916] 2 K.B. 658).

1. *Accomplice*

In matrimonial cases where adultery is alleged, the party with whom the adultery is alleged to have taken place is in the same position as an accomplice. In *Ginger* v. *Ginger* (1865), L.R. 1 P. & D. 37, the court declined to accept the uncorroborated evidence of the woman with whom the husband was alleged to have committed adultery, though the emphasis was on the fact that she was a woman of loose character, rather than on the fact that she was an accomplice. More recently, the Court of Appeal in *Galler* v. *Galler* [1954] P. 252 laid down that a witness who gives evidence that he or she has committed adultery with a party to the proceedings is in the same position as an accomplice in a criminal case, and a warning must accordingly be given before such evidence is accepted without corroboration. The facts were that the husband was charged with adultery in divorce proceedings,

and the only evidence against him was that of a nurse of the
children, who alleged numerous acts of adultery with the husband
while living in his house. The husband denied the adultery, and
in spite of the absence of corroboration, her evidence was
accepted by the commissioner. Hodson, L.J., at p. 255, said: —

> " It is not the law that the court cannot act on the evidence
> of a person in the position of the witness in this case without
> corroboration, but it is the law that it is unwise so to do,
> and that juries must be directed that it is unsafe to act on
> uncorroborated evidence of this nature, although they are
> at liberty to do so if they feel sure."

He pointed out that when a man is in a house with a housekeeper, charges of adultery are easy to make and hard to rebut.
He referred to *Fairman* v. *Fairman* [1949] P. 341, where the
Divisional Court held that such a witness must be treated with
the same circumspection as an accomplice in criminal courts.

Corroboration is not required as a matter of law, but as a
matter of precaution.

The nature of corroboration in matrimonial cases has been discussed in cases where the wife has accused the husband of sodomy.
In *Statham* v. *Statham* [1929] P. 131, it was said that in such a
case the same cogent evidence is required to overcome the presumption of innocence as in a criminal case, and the court ought
to warn itself of the dangers of finding the offence proved on the
uncorroborated evidence of an accomplice. In *B.* (*D.*) v. *B.* (*W.*)
[1935] P. 80, where the wife accused the husband of abnormal
sexual practices, Sir Boyd Merriman, P., said at p. 83: —

> ". . . it is advisable that the justices should look for some
> corroboration on the part of the wife . . . if there was not a
> reasonably strict rule in this respect, one spouse would be so
> easily at the mercy of the other in relation to things which
> from their nature must happen in private. But when that has
> been said it is admitted that the necessity for corroboration
> is not an absolute rule of law. Justices should direct them-
> selves, just as a judge should direct a jury, that it is safer to
> have corroboration, if possible; but when the warning has
> been given, and given in the fullest form, then there is no
> rule of law which prevents the tribunal finding the matter
> proved in the absence of corroboration."

2. *Corroboration by other spouse*

In the great majority of cases heard by the magistrates, evidence is given by both spouses. It has been laid down time and again that it is inadvisable for justices to come to a decision without hearing both parties, and therefore submissions of no case are rarely likely to succeed. It therefore happens from time to time that one side, particularly in cross-examination, provides corroboration of the other's allegations, either by admissions, or providing evidence of facts which tend to substantiate the allegations. An example is *Marjoram* v. *Marjoram* [1955] 1 W.L.R. 520, where the wife gave evidence that her husband had told her that he had been associating with a Mrs. *B*, before he went to live at her house, and that he had been sleeping with her. The husband, in evidence, said he agreed with his wife's evidence about associating with Mrs. *B* but he denied adultery. Lord Merriman, P., said that the husband's evidence was corroboration of the wife's evidence.

The headnote in *Curtis* v. *Curtis* (1905), 21 T.L.R. 676, reads: —

" As a general rule of practice the court will not act upon the uncorroborated evidence of the petitioner but there is no rule of law which prohibits it from acting on such evidence if it is satisfied that the story put forward is a true one and that there is no collusion."

The report of the case shows, however, that there was corroboration since the husband, in evidence, admitted that he had been to houses of ill fame and that he had written a confession. His assertion that he had written the confession under his wife's compulsion, and his denial of adultery, were more than lame, and it is not suprising that the judge found he was a liar.

In *Riches* v. *Riches and Clinch* (1918), 35 T.L.R. 141, the court accepted the uncorroborated evidence of the petitioner that he had found the wife in bed with the co-respondent, that he had thrashed him, and that the police had been sent for to protect the co-respondent.

Lord Merrivale, P., found strong corroboration of a confession in *Simpson* v. *Simpson* (1931), 146 L.T. 47, in the fact that in making it, the wife had everything to lose.

In *Ramsdale* v. *Ramsdale* (1945), 109 J.P. 239, the wife had obtained an order for maintenance on the ground of desertion. The husband had defended the case and had made allegations of adultery against a named man, but the justices did not find

adultery proved. Subsequent to the order, he applied to revoke
it on the ground of adultery with the same man. It was held that
the justices should hear evidence of the nature of the association
both before and after the date of the order, even if it meant a
repetition of what was said in the court at the previous hearing.
Lord Merriman, P., at p. 240, said: —

> " This was not a case in which the party charged had been
> taken in adultery, or in which there was direct evidence of
> that adultery. On the contrary, it was the familiar case where
> it is sought to infer adultery from an association of an affec-
> tionate, illicit character, coupled with evidence, within the
> relevant period of opportunity for indulging that affection.
> It ought to go without saying, but unfortunately it does not,
> that to deal properly with such a case, the court must have
> before it all the evidence of association and not only that part
> of it which happens to relate to events later than a certain
> date. . . . Manifestly, the whole of the evidence which she
> could give about the nature of the association, both before
> and after the making of the order, was relevant to the
> charge."

In both *Boddy* v. *Boddy* (1860), 30 L.J.P.M. & A. 23, and *Wales*
v. *Wales* [1900] P. 63, evidence of adultery after the acts of
adultery complained of was held to be admissible. See also *Roberts*
v. *Roberts* [1954] P. 472.

In *Jensen* v. *Jensen and Howard* [1964] 1 W.L.R. 859, Cairns,
J., held that the answers of the wife and co-respondent in their
memoranda of appearance that they did not intend to defend the
case, taken together with the husband's evidence of association
between them and her admission to him that she had committed
adultery, constituted sufficient proof of adultery.

K. Virginity

If the woman concerned in the alleged adultery can prove by
medical evidence that she is *virgo intacta*, it is not a complete
answer to the charge, but it makes the proof of adultery much
more difficult.

In *Hunt* v. *Hunt* (1856), Dea. & Sw. 121, a husband alleged
adultery against his wife. He admitted the marriage had not been
consummated, and the wife pleaded and proved by medical
evidence that she was *virgo intacta*. The evidence of adultery was
that she had visited a man on a number of occasions, and the

blinds had been pulled down. It was held adultery was not proved.

In *Hallam* v. *Hallam and Gould* (1930), 47 T.L.R. 207, the wife charged the husband with adultery with a maid in the house, and she and her sister gave evidence against the husband. Two doctors certified that the maid was a virgin, and Hill, J., said that while this did not dispose of the case, it threw the greatest doubt on the evidence of the petitioner and her sister, and dismissed the petition.

In *Rutherford* v. *Richardson* [1923] A.C. 1, the intervener produced medical evidence which established there had been no penetration, and the appearance of the organs was not consistent with an effective attempt at penetration. Viscount Birkenhead, in the course of his speech, said at p. 11: —

" Some suggestion was made in argument in this House that this condition, even though inconsistent with penetration, was not inconsistent with some lesser act of sexual gratification. If there were evidence of such an act, it cannot be doubted that, whatever view may have been taken in past ages in the ecclesiastical courts, a decree based on adultery might issue."

This view has not found favour, and some degree of penetration is necessary for sexual intercourse to amount to adultery (see p. 234). This matter was considered by Langton, J., in *Thompson* (*otherwise Hulton*) v. *Thompson* [1938] P. 162, who held that the facts of certificates of virginity, though not conclusive on the issue of adultery, made the burden of proof very considerably heavier on the petitioner, but in spite of the strong presumption in favour of the alleged adultress, he found adultery proved.

L. Venereal disease

Where a spouse proves that he or she has venereal disease, and that he or she has not had intercourse with anyone else, there is prima facie proof that the other spouse has committed adultery. It is not too easy to establish who is the guilty party where both are suffering from venereal disease. In *Gliksten* v. *Gliksten and Deane* (1917), 116 L.T. 543, the wife alleged the husband had communicated venereal disease to her. He admitted that he had venereal disease but he said he had got it from her. The medical evidence was that the husband had gonorrhea, but that it was not established whether the wife had it or not. Hill, J., held that the wife could not rely on the fact that the husband had venereal disease to establish adultery. In *Anthony* v. *Anthony* (1919), 35 T.L.R. 559, there were similar allegations, and it was held that the petitioner, the wife, by adducing evidence that she had contracted syphilis by living with the husband and had never had intercourse with any other man, had made out a prima facie case. In this case, a claim of privilege by the Crown in respect of Army medical sheets was upheld by the court, even though the man asked for their production. Army records are admissible under the Evidence Act, 1938 (*Andrews* v. *Cordiner* [1947] K.B. 655).

It was held in *Stead* v. *Stead* (1927), 71 Sol. J. 391, that where the husband was suffering from " crabs " this was prima facie evidence of adultery.

In *Ramsdale* v. *Ramsdale* (1945), 109 J.P. 239, it was sought to prove adultery by proving that the wife had contracted syphilis some time after being separated from her husband. A doctor was called who had made a blood test which was positive, but it was held that while this was sufficient proof that she had contracted the disease, in order to establish that it was a primary infection caused by sexual intercourse, and the approximate date thereof, it was not competent for this doctor to refer to the records of other doctors, but first-hand evidence should be given by the doctors concerned.

M. Birth of child

A child born in wedlock is presumed to be legitimate. It may, however, be shown that, owing to the interval of time between coition and the birth, either because it is too long or too short, the husband could not be the father, and therefore adultery must be inferred. The difficulties which arose through the rule in *Russell* v. *Russell* [1924] A.C. 687 have now gone, and therefore either spouse can give evidence which might tend to bastardise issue of the marriage.

The normal period of pregnancy is 275–280 days, but it is recognised that there may be variations. No one would doubt, if a child was born to the mother say two years after the husband had gone abroad, that she had committed adultery. Similarly if a child was born only a few weeks after the husband had coition, and it was proved he could not have had intercourse with her before, or for a very long time before, the same inference would be drawn. The following are the cases on the subject: —

Gaskill v. *Gaskill* [1921] P. 425, where the period was 331 days. Viscount Birkenhead, who tried the case, called in the Attorney-General who called three eminent gynaecologists, who said such an interval was not impossible. Since there was no other evidence of adultery, Viscount Birkenhead dismissed the petition.

Wood v. *Wood* [1947] P. 103, which was an appeal from magistrates who had refused to find adultery where a period of 346 days was involved. There was no medical evidence. Lord Merriman, P., said that the line must be drawn somewhere, but while one could say when a case was on the right side or the wrong side, in most cases it was not easy to say where the line was. He was not prepared to hold that 346 was on the wrong side in the absence of medical evidence.

Hadlum v. *Hadlum* [1949] P. 197, in which the Court of Appeal upheld a finding of no adultery when 349 days was involved. There was medical evidence on behalf of the wife that this was possible.

M-T. v. *M-T.* [1949] P. 331, in which Ormerod, J., held that a child was illegitimate where the period was 340 days. Here the wife had been divorced on the ground of her adultery, and there was some evidence that the adultery took place in July, and the child was born the following April. Furthermore, an eminent gynaecologist, Sir Eardley Holland, gave evidence that since *Gaskill* v. *Gaskill* [1921] P. 425, medical knowledge on this subject had advanced and it was possible to say that 340 days was an impossibly long period.

Preston-Jones v. *Preston-Jones* [1951] A.C. 391. Here a normal healthy child was born 360 days after the husband went abroad. There was no other evidence of adultery. A doctor gave evidence that it would be very extraordinary if a child was conceived over 300 days before birth. The House of Lords held that the onus of proof did not extend to the husband proving the scientific impossibility of his being the father of the child, and that on the whole evidence the wife's adultery had been proved beyond a reasonable doubt. Lord Simonds said that where the interval diverges largely from the normal, the onus of proof on the husband is light and easily discharged. If the only evidence had been the 360 days, that would not have been sufficient to prove the adultery beyond reasonable doubt. It was the medical evidence which made all the difference.

In the converse case, it was held in *Clark* v. *Clark* [1939] P. 257 that a child was legitimate when born 174 days after coition, because the evidence was that the child was premature, but when the medical evidence was that the child was perfectly normal at birth, 188 days after coition was not sufficient and the presumption of legitimacy was displaced (*Re S. B., B.* v. *B.* [1949] Ch. 108).

The presumption of legitimacy is displaced if the date of birth shows that the child was conceived after a decree of judicial separation, or after a separation order has been made by magistrates (*Andrews* v. *Andrews and Chalmers* [1924] P. 255; *Ettenfield* v. *Ettenfield* [1940] P. 96).

The birth of a child can be proved by the production of a certified copy of the register, with evidence that the signature of the informant in the original register is in the handwriting of the respondent (*Best* v. *Best and McKinley* [1920] P. 75).

In *Jackson* v. *Jackson and Pavan* [1964] P. 25, the signature of the wife in the register was identified. The father of the child had signed the register pursuant to s. 10 of the Births and Deaths Registration Act, 1953, but there was no evidence of identification. It was held that the entry was prima facie evidence of an admission of adultery by the child's father, and the evidence before the court, which the co-respondent had not contested, was sufficient to show that the man who signed the register and the co-respondent were the same man.

In *Mayo* v. *Mayo* [1949] P. 172, the entry of birth made by a wife who omitted to give information of the name, etc., of the father, was held to be an admissible admission of adultery. This was not followed in *Perring* v. *Perring and Simpson* [1949] 2 All E.R. 334, apparently because it conflicted with *Russell's* case, but as that decision is now abrogated the decision in *Perring* v. *Perring* may be ignored.

The presumption of legitimacy is not necessarily rebutted by the fact that a spouse used contraceptives during intercourse (*Francis* v. *Francis* [1960] P. 17, applying *Cotton* v. *Cotton* [1954] P. 305 and *Watson* v. *Watson* [1954] P. 48).

N. Notice of adultery alleged

As we have seen, the issue of adultery can arise in three ways before the magistrates, namely, a complaint of either party of the other's adultery, a defence to any summons claiming maintenance on the ground of a matrimonial offence, and an application to revoke an order on the ground of adultery. In the first and third cases, the respondent would be served with a summons which would give some particulars of the complaint. In the second case, there would be no summons by the respondent. In all three cases it is essential that the other side be notified, with particulars of the adultery alleged. It is an ordinary requirement of the administration of justice (*Broadbent* v. *Broadbent* (1927), 43 T.L.R. 186, per Lord Merrivale). The notice should contain, where possible, the place, the time and the name of the person with whom the adultery is alleged to have been committed (*Boston* v. *Boston* (1928), 92 J.P. 44). Ormerod, J., in *Duffield* v. *Duffield* [1949] 1 All E.R. 1105, at p. 1107, said that he could not emphasise too strongly that in cases where adultery is alleged, whatever the circumstances in which it is alleged, full particulars must be given.

IV. THE PRIVILEGE AGAINST SELF-INCRIMINATION

Until 1968, where proceedings were instituted in consequence of adultery, no party or witness was liable to be asked or bound to answer any question tending to show that he or she had been guilty of adultery, unless in the same proceedings this witness or party had given evidence in disproof of his or her adultery. The enactment governing evidence in the magistrates' court on this matter was s. 3 of the Evidence Further Amendment Act, 1869.

Paradoxically there was no such privilege where the proceedings were not instituted in consequence of adultery. It took nearly 100 years to remove this anomaly, which was done by s. 17 (5) of the Civil Evidence Act, 1968, reading as follows:

" A witness in any proceeding instituted in consequence of adultery, whether a party to the proceedings or not, shall not be excused from answering any question, by reason that it tends to show that he or she has been guilty of adultery; and

accordingly the proviso to section 3 of the Evidence Further
Amendment Act 1869, and, in sections 43 (2) of the Matrimonial Causes Act 1965, the words from ' but ' to the end of
the subsection shall cease to have effect,"

i.e., this privilege is also cancelled in the High Court.

CHAPTER 6

WILFUL NEGLECT TO MAINTAIN

I. INTRODUCTION

THE Act of 1960, s. 1 (1), provides as follows: —

"A married woman or a married man may apply by way of complaint to a magistrates' court for an order under this Act against the other party to the marriage on any of the following causes of complaint arising during the subsistence of the marriage, that is to say, that the defendant—

*   *   *

(h) being the husband, has wilfully neglected to provide reasonable maintenance for the wife or for any child of the family who is, or would but for that neglect have been, a dependant; or

(i) being the wife, has wilfully neglected to provide, or to make a proper contribution towards reasonable maintenance for the husband or for any child of the family who is, or would but for that neglect have been, a dependant, in a case where, by reason of the impairment of the husband's earning capacity through age, illness or disability of mind or body, and having regard to any resources of the husband and the wife respectively which are, or should properly be made available for this purpose, it is reasonable in all the circumstances to expect the wife so to provide or contribute."

Wilful neglect to maintain by itself was first made a matrimonial offence in 1895,* and a remedy was provided in the magistrates' court by s. 4 of the Summary Jurisdiction (Married Women) Act, 1895, which provided that a wife could obtain an order for maintenance against her husband if he wilfully neglected to provide reasonable maintenance for her or her infant children whom he was legally liable to maintain, and it was also a necessary condition that this neglect had caused the wife to live separate and

* Coupled with desertion it was made an offence by the Married Women (Maintenance in the Case of Desertion) Act, 1886.

apart from him. This condition was repealed by s. 1 of the Summary Jurisdiction (Separation and Maintenance) Act, 1925.

The High Court was given jurisdiction to entertain applications by a wife for maintenance on the ground of wilful neglect to provide reasonable maintenance by s. 5 of the Law Reform (Miscellaneous Provisions) Act, 1949, now s. 27 of the Matrimonial Causes Act, 1973.

The Act of 1960 differs from the old Acts in that the remedy is available in certain circumstances to the husband as well as the wife, and also the remedy is extended to a child who is a child of the family and who is or would have been but for the neglect a dependant, and is not limited to a child of the wife, whom the husband was legally liable to maintain.

II. THE DUTY TO MAINTAIN

This may be considered under three heads: —
  (A) at common law;
  (B) under the Act of 1960;
  (C) under the National Assistance Act, 1948.

A. Husband's duty to maintain wife at common law

The right of a wife to maintenance as against her husband is not contractual in nature. It is true that she can enter into a separation agreement with her husband which is valid and enforceable, but, as will be seen, even this cannot override the husband's common-law duty, which is incident to the status of matrimony. This is summarily expressed in Bacon's Abridgement (7th ed., vol. 1, *tit.* " Baron and Feme," p. 713): —

> "A husband is obliged to maintain his wife, and may by law be compelled to find her necessaries, as meat, drink, clothes, physic, etc., suitable to the husband's degree, estate, or circumstances."

(quoted in *Dewe* v. *Dewe* [1928] P. 113 by Lord Merrivale, P., at p. 118).

A husband is not bound to support an adulterous wife (*R.* v. *Flintan* (1830), 1 B. & Ad. 227, at p. 230) or one in desertion, but whereas the former has forfeited all rights to maintenance the right of the latter is only suspended, and can be revived by appropriate action on her part, such as by making a bona fide offer to resume cohabitation (*National Assistance Board* v. *Wilkinson* [1952] 2 Q.B. 648 (D.C.)).

The position of a wife who has deserted her husband is explained in the judgment of the Earl of Reading, C.J., in *Jones* v. *Newtown and Llanidloes Guardians* [1920] 3 K.B. 381, at p. 384: —

" There is no doubt that at common law if a wife chooses wilfully and without justification to live away from her husband she cannot, so long as she continues absent, render him liable for necessaries supplied to her, or for her maintenance by the union, for the reason that she has of her own free will deprived herself of the opportunity which the husband was affording her of being maintained in the home. But the relief of the husband from the obligation of maintenance continues only so long as she voluntarily remains absent. Her absence, although wrongful, does not affect the relationship of husband and wife. She is entitled after however long a period of absence to return at any time."

A husband may show that he is excused the duty of maintenance in various ways. Hill, J., in *Papadopoulos* v. *Papadopoulos* [1930] P. 55, at p. 68, gave the following instances: —

" . . . he may show that his wife has been guilty of adultery, neither condoned nor connived at, nor conduced to by the husband, or that she had deserted him and was continuing to desert him, or that there is a subsisting binding contract performed and not repudiated by him that she should not claim maintenance otherwise than as provided by the contract, or that a court of competent jurisdiction in a proceeding between husband and wife had already determined the rights of the wife in respect of maintenance and that he had fulfilled the obligations so imposed on him. But the onus is on the husband to prove the excuse."

The passage about agreements has to be modified in the light of later cases (see p. 269 et seq.), but this passage has been referred to with approval by Bucknill, J., in a Divisional Court in *Richardson* v. *Richardson* (1942), 167 L.T. 260, at p. 261.

B. Husband's duty to maintain wife under the Acts relating to matrimonial proceedings

The Act of 1895 gave the wife a new remedy, which as we have seen has been continued to the present day, though modified from time to time, to claim periodical maintenance in the courts of summary jurisdiction when the husband has wilfully neglected to provide reasonable maintenance for her and/or her children.

" Wilful " in this connection means "deliberate" with no excuse (per Lord Goddard, C.J., in *National Assistance Board* v. *Prisk* [1954] 1 W.L.R. 443).

The duty to maintain under these Acts has been described in a number of cases. A husband's obligation to maintain his wife is prima facie complied with by providing a home for her. A wife has no right to separate maintenance in a different home unless she can justify the fact that she is living apart from her husband (per Hodson, L.J., in *Price* v. *Price* [1951] P. 413, at pp. 420–421, quoted with approval by Lord Merriman in *Marjoram* v. *Marjoram* [1955] 1 W.L.R. 520, at p. 528).

In *Weatherley* v. *Weatherley* (1929), 94 J.P. 38, where the justices made an order for wilful neglect, the husband was a police constable and had made an ample allowance to his wife out of his earnings of £4 18s. per week; Lord Merrivale said (p. 39): —

> " What seems requisite, before a husband can be found to be guilty of a wilful breach of his duty to maintain his wife, is that there must be a refusal to maintain, which has no explanation reasonable in common sense and good faith. I am not going to try to define the state of things in which it might arise, but I will say where upon proved facts, the husband against whom the charge is maintained is shown to have done his duty to the best of his ability, and never wilfully have failed in his duty to discharge his marital obligations taking them generally as the relations of husband and wife, there is very great difficulty in conceiving a case where a woman can disclaim her proper obligations to her husband, and, having failed to be maintained separately by her disclaimer, make herself a complainant in law on the ground of her own wrong."

Similarly in the same year, in *Burrow* v. *Burrow* (1930), 143 L.T. 679, where a wife had left her husband for ten years and, without having any communication with him, issued a summons for wilful neglect and the justices made an order, the learned President said, at p. 680: —

> " The law is that if a wife lives with her husband or is prevented by her husband from living with him, he must provide for her maintenance and that duty is immediate and unconditional. If, on the other hand, the wife leaves the husband and has no communication with him, the duty is latent. It could be revived to be made immediately operative by proper action on the wife's part, unless there is some

impediment to the enforcement or making of an order for maintenance. In this case the wife for ten years before the summons was made, had made no communication with her husband, had not demanded maintenance, did not propose to return to him, and was not seeking to live with him. In that state of things the liability to maintain was not immediately operative, it was in a state of suspense."

Where a husband is ignorant of his wife's needs, it cannot be said he is guilty of wilful neglect to maintain her (per Lord Merriman, P., in *Jones* v. *Jones* [1959] P. 38, where the husband had been ordered to make a weekly payment to his wife under s. 42 of the National Assistance Act, 1948, and had paid punctually, but his wife took out a summons for wilful neglect to maintain). Lord Merriman, P., at p. 41, said: —

"It is well settled that punctual payment under an agreement (and I think the same thing applies to punctual payment under an order) is of very strong evidential value that the amount so ordered or so agreed is a reasonable amount; but it is not conclusive. Circumstances may have changed, and it is with regard to a case in which circumstances have changed that what was said by Denning, L.J., in *National Assistance Board* v. *Parkes* [1955] 2 Q.B. 506, 517, is so important . . . 'The principle of *Tulip* v. *Tulip* [1951] P. 378 applies . . . just as much when there is an agreement to pay nothing as when a fixed sum is to be paid; and it overrides anything said previously in *Baker* v. *Baker* [1950] W.N. 29 and *Chapman* v. *Chapman* (unreported).' . . . What is important are the words that follow. Denning, L.J., went on: 'But so long as the husband is ignorant of the new situation he is under no such duty, and is not guilty of wilful neglect to maintain her. That is, I think, the effect of the decision in *Stringer* v. *Stringer* [1952] P. 171.' . . . *Stringer* v. *Stringer* . . . is a case in which stress was laid on the point that the husband had not had it brought to his notice that the circumstances had changed since the original parting . . . Likewise, on the line of authorities— *Starkie* v. *Starkie* (*No. 2*) [1954] 1 W.L.R. 98 . . . *Whittaker* v. *Whittaker* [1939] 3 All E.R. 833, *Diggins* v. *Diggins* [1927] P. 88, *Jones* v. *Jones* (1930), 46 T.L.R. 33, and others—which have laid down that the element of misconduct is implicit in the words 'Wilful neglect to provide reasonable maintenance,' I think this wife has failed to prove her case. . . ."

The Court of Appeal (Ormerod, Danckwerts and Diplock, L.JJ.) dismissed an appeal from Cairns, J., in *Smith* v. *Smith*

(1962), 106 Sol. J. 611, holding that where a wife had an order for maintenance in the magistrates' court, she could not apply to the High Court under s. 23 of the Matrimonial Causes Act, 1950, if the husband was making his payments regularly, for the simple reason that it would be impossible to say that the husband was wilfully neglecting to pay his wife reasonable maintenance. Different considerations might apply if there were a change of circumstances. The court was not going to encourage what would virtually be appeals to the High Court in this manner.

Would failure to provide reasonable maintenance for the child of the marriage give jurisdiction to make a maintenance order in favour of a wife who would not otherwise be entitled? This was the question asked and answered by the Divisional Court in *Young* v. *Young* [1964] P. 152 (see also *Vaughan* v. *Vaughan* [1965] P. 15). If the husband is to blame for the separation, then unless the wife has sufficient means of her own, an order must be made in her favour. If the parting is consensual without any stipulation exonerating the husband from maintaining the child, it is open to the court to make a maintenance order in favour of the wife. Where the wife has committed adultery which has not been condoned, connived at or conduced to, the wife is not entitled to an order for herself. When the wife has been guilty of cruelty or desertion, the position is the same.

It is to be noted that the order of a court of summary jurisdiction for payment of a weekly sum by the husband to his wife, where there is no order for separation, is no bar to the common-law rights of the wife to pledge her husband's credit for necessaries (*Sandilands* v. *Carus* [1945] 1 K.B. 270).

C. Maintenance under the National Assistance Act, 1948

By s. 42 (1) of this Act it is provided: —

> For the purposes of this Act—(a) a man shall be liable to maintain his wife and children and (b) a woman shall be liable to maintain her husband and her children.

and by s. 43 (1) and (2): —

> Where assistance is given or applied for by reference to the requirements of any person . . . the Board . . . may make a complaint to the court against any other who for the purposes of this Act is liable to maintain the person assisted . . . On a complaint under this section the court shall have

regard to all the circumstances and in particular to the resources of the defendant, and may order the defendant to pay such sum, weekly or otherwise, as the court may consider appropriate.

The obligation to maintain in s. 42 is not absolute, and certain defences are available. A man is not liable to maintain an adulterous wife (*National Assistance Board* v. *Wilkinson* [1952] 2 Q.B. 648) nor one in desertion (*National Assistance Board* v. *Prisk* [1954] 1 W.L.R. 443). Doubtless, cruelty, too, would be a defence. The question arose in *National Assistance Board* v. *Parkes* [1955] 2 Q.B. 506 whether an agreement whereby a wife covenanted that she would not claim maintenance from her husband was one of the circumstances the court should take into account when the National Assistance Board claimed reimbursement from the husband. The Court of Appeal answered this question in the negative on two grounds. The first was that in any event such a covenant did not prevent a wife claiming maintenance: a wife cannot barter away her right to maintenance; and secondly, even if this were not so, as the Act has been interpreted, the only defences open to a husband were matrimonial offences by the wife, and an agreement not to claim maintenance did not come into that category.

III. THE ELEMENT OF MISCONDUCT IN WILFUL NEGLECT TO MAINTAIN

Magistrates are sometimes under the impression that if a husband does not maintain his wife, in any circumstances, this amounts to wilful neglect to maintain. In *Jones* v. *Jones* (1929), 94 J.P. 30, Hill, J., said at p. 30: —

" Justices shrink from finding desertion or cruelty but since the Act of 1925 they tend to find wilful neglect rather lightly."

There has to be a breach of duty on the part of the husband. His non-payment must be wrongful. In the same case Lord Merrivale, P., said that the husband's failure to pay must amount to misconduct. This was stressed by Lord Merriman in *Whittaker* v. *Whittaker* [1939] 3 All E.R. 833. There the parties were separated under an agreement and the husband had got into arrears. The wife sued in the county court and the husband pleaded that she had committed adultery, which the county court judge held to be proved. The wife then attempted to get maintenance in the magistrates' court, and the real question was whether the magistrates were bound by the finding of the county court judge. The magistrates thought they were not so bound, but this was reversed by a Divisional Court (Lord Merriman, P., and Henn Collins, J.), but the learned President took the opportunity of saying, at p. 838: —

> "That he had not provided it [reasonable maintenance] is . . . common ground, but wilful neglect means more than that, it means there has been some wrongful default. . . ."

Where the parties had parted by consent and there was no agreement, express or implied, to pay maintenance, the learned President again invoked the doctrine of misconduct to excuse the husband's non-payment (*Baker* v. *Baker* (1949), 66 T.L.R. (Pt. 1) 81).

The word " misconduct " is not always apt, in this connection, because " misconduct " usually denotes some moral delinquency, which is quite clear in cruelty or even desertion. Failure to maintain may sometimes be morally wrong, but at other times it may amount to a breach of duty, where there is nothing morally wrong. Harman, J., pointed out in his dissenting judgment in *Tulip* v. *Tulip* [1951] P. 378, at p. 393, that a man who punctually pays under a separation agreement can hardly be said to be guilty of misconduct, but the majority of the court held that he may still be found guilty of wilful neglect to maintain.

It was this confusion over the meaning of the word " misconduct " which led Lord Merriman, P., astray in *Lilley* v. *Lilley* [1960] P. 158. In this case the wife had got an order on the ground of desertion, which was later revoked on her refusal to live with her husband. She later applied for maintenance on the ground of wilful neglect to maintain. The facts were that she suffered from a neurosis, and the medical evidence was that if she lived with her husband, whose presence she found repugnant, her health would get worse. She was however quite sane, and she wrote to her husband that she could not live with him, nor would she ever do so. The stipendiary magistrate found she was in desertion, but in any event, she was not entitled to maintenance because there had been no misconduct on the part of the husband. On her appeal, the Divisional Court (Lord Merriman, P., and Hewson, J.) held that she was not in desertion, but because there had been

no misconduct on the part of the husband, she was not entitled
to maintenance.

One can see that this was a hard case for the husband. He
wanted his wife's society, and she refused to live with him. If
she was not in desertion, and she could not live with him for reasons
of health only, then the husband was exactly in the position of
one whose wife had a physical injury and was confined to hospital,
and a man must keep his wife not only in health but in sickness.

The Court of Appeal held that she was in desertion, but if she
had not been, the husband would have been liable to maintain
her. Hodson, L.J., giving the judgment of the court, said, at p.
180: —

> " The wrongdoing may, however, consist of the very fact of a
> failure to maintain. There need be no other matrimonial
> offence imputed to the husband."

All that misconduct means, then, is a breach of duty to maintain.
The court, therefore, must enquire what the duty to maintain
was, and whether in the circumstances the husband has some
excuse, such as the wife's adultery or desertion, for not carrying
it out, or whether in the circumstances the maintenance he had
supplied was adequate.

In *Kent* v. *Kent* (1962), 106 Sol. J. 192; (1962), *The Times*, 9th
February, a husband reduced his payments to his wife to pay
his solicitors' costs. Ormerod and Danckwerts, L.JJ., held the
duty to maintain his wife came first. Willmer, L.J., dissented, and
said that wilful neglect to maintain imputed an element of matrimonial misconduct. It would have been wrong for the husband
to have defaulted on his liabilities to his solicitors, and in these
circumstances it would be contrary to all justice and an affront to
common sense to say the husband was guilty of wilful neglect.

IV. WILFUL NEGLECT AND DESERTION

> " In most cases where the spouses are living apart from one
> another the question of whether there has been a wilful
> neglect to maintain the wife depends on the same facts as the
> question whether or not there has been desertion on the part
> of either, and there is no point in taking proceedings on both
> grounds " (*Lilley* v. *Lilley* [1960] P. 158, at p. 178).

These two offences have much in common and in general the

defences to desertion are equally applicable to wilful neglect.
There are two exceptions: —

    1. When the parties are cohabiting but the husband is
either not maintaining his wife and/or children at all, or not
adequately.

    2. Where the parties are living apart, but the parting is
consensual.

Apart from these two exceptions, the defences to a summons
for desertion are equally applicable to wilful neglect. Thus
adultery, or desertion by the other spouse, or all the other defences
under " just cause," such as the *Glenister* line of cases, refusal of
a bona fide offer to resume cohabitation, cruelty or grave and
weighty conduct which justifies the husband in not living with his
wife, are defences to wilful neglect as to desertion (see p. 116 et
seq.).

As has been pointed out, justices tend to find husbands guilty
of wilful neglect more readily than they will find desertion,
adultery or cruelty, possibly because there is not the same moral
stigma, but as the Divisional Court has frequently pointed out, an
order should not be made unless the wilful neglect was wrongful.

The following are some examples: —

Ellis v. *Ellis* (1929), 93 J.P. 175. A wife obtained an order on
the ground of desertion, which was revoked on her refusal to
return to her husband. Nevertheless, when the wife applied for
an order on the ground of wilful neglect to maintain, on the
same evidence the justices made an order. The evidence was that
the husband had a home waiting for her and wanted her back.
She refused to go. Lord Merrivale said, at p. 176: —

> " Such a claim must be founded on an obligation to maintain.
> The obligation is suspended if the wife wilfully lives apart
> from the husband."

On the other hand, where a summons for wilful neglect had
been dismissed because the husband had offered a home with his
mother which the wife had refused, and then subsequently the
wife offered to return and the husband would not have her,
it was held that if the justices found the wife's offer was genuine
then she would be entitled to an order (*Markovitch* v. *Markovitch*
(1934), 98 J.P. 282; *Grubb* v. *Grubb* (1934), 98 J.P. 99).

Similarly it was decided in *Holborn* v. *Holborn* [1947] 1 All
E.R. 32, where a wife left her husband because of his revolting

sexual activities, that if the wife was justified in withdrawing from cohabitation, and the husband had failed to maintain her after she had left him, the justices were justified in finding that there had been wilful neglect to maintain her.

Bucknill, J., in *Richardson* v. *Richardson* (1942), 167 L.T. 260, said it was obvious common sense that a wife who was in desertion was not entitled to maintenance, and it would be an obvious injustice if she could claim; and this is so whether the desertion was simple or constructive, as in *Winnan* v. *Winnan* [1949] P. 174, where the wife had driven the husband out by keeping large numbers of cats.

Yet another example of justices dismissing a summons for desertion and wrongly finding wilful neglect to maintain, is *Browne* v. *Browne* (1963), 107 Sol. J. 96 (D.C.), where a wife continued working after marriage and supported her husband. She became pregnant, ceased working and went to stay with her mother. The husband continued to live in the matrimonial home, and only occasionally visited his wife when he asked for money. The wife collected her things from the matrimonial home, did not inform her husband of the birth of the child, refused his offer to return, denied him access to her and did not answer his letters. On appeal, Sir Jocelyn Simon, P., said there was no evidence that the parting was consensual. The mere fact that the parties were living apart by consent did not automatically entitle the wife to support. The onus was on her to show an express or implied term of agreement that the husband would support her. There was neither here. The wife was in desertion and not entitled to maintenance.

Howard v. *Howard* [1962] 3 W.L.R. 413 is another case where justices wrongly dismissed a summons for desertion but found wilful neglect to maintain.

V. WHERE THE PARTIES HAVE PARTED BY CONSENT

" . . . where there is a separation deed containing provisions for the support of the wife she will not be left to sue her husband under the deed if he defaults in payment, but can apply for an order on the ground of his wilful neglect to maintain her. Even if he complies with his obligations under the deed, the wife may show a change of circumstances since

the execution of the deed and apply for an order. . . ."
(*Lilley* v. *Lilley* [1960] P. 158, at p. 178).

This extract states the law, when the husband has taken upon himself the obligation to maintain his wife under the agreement or deed.

This position was not reached easily, and the cases show a gradual development.

A. Failure to pay under agreement

The first step was taken when the husband did not meet his financial commitments under the agreement. Thus, in *Diggins* v. *Diggins* [1927] P. 88 the husband agreed to pay his wife 30s. a week, but ceased payment after two weeks. The magistrates made an order for maintenance on the ground of wilful neglect to maintain, which was upheld by a Divisional Court (Lord Merrivale, P., and Bateson, J.), who decided that the deed did not exclude the jurisdiction of the magistrates, but that the wife's right to maintenance was subject to the proper interpretation of the deed, and in that case the deed did not either expressly or by implication deprive her of that or effectually limit it.

Fletcher v. *Fletcher* (1928), 92 J.P. 94, was a similar case where the husband had failed to keep up an oral agreement to pay his wife a weekly sum.

In *McCreanney* v. *McCreanney* (1928), 92 J.P. 44, there was a difference. The husband agreed to pay 17s. 6d. a week and the wife undertook not to sue for more. He did not keep up his payments, and the wife issued a summons for wilful neglect, which was dismissed, the magistrates accepting the argument that the wife's only remedy was in the county court. The Divisional Court (Lord Merrivale, P., and Hill, J.) allowed the wife's appeal, and held that the magistrates had jurisdiction to make an order, at any rate up to 17s. 6d. a week, Lord Merrivale adding at p. 45: —

> " Taking the language used in the statutes in its ordinary everyday meaning, and noting the manifest intention of the Act of 1925 to simplify for the classes of married women who come within its terms, we consider that so admirable a course should not be defeated by argumentative subtleties."

B. Wife claims in bankruptcy

The question then arose—what is the position if the husband

goes bankrupt, and the wife proves in the bankruptcy and accepts a dividend on her capitalised claim? Is she entitled to an order for wilful neglect to maintain? A Divisional Court (Lord Merrivale, P., and Bateson, J.) in *Dewe* v. *Dewe* [1928] P. 113 answered this question in the affirmative. Lord Merrivale pointed out that the alternative would be that it would turn an agreement to live apart with maintenance into an agreement to live apart without maintenance. The wife's right to maintenance was not contractual, but was an incident in the status or estate of matrimony.

C. Where agreement carried out

Lord Merrivale was curiously hesitant in *Burton* v. *Burton* (1929), 142 L.T. 165, on the effect of the 1925 Act on an agreement by the wife not to seek maintenance, but in *Iles* v. *Iles* (1931), 95 J.P. 136, he said that the right of a married woman to maintenance was independent of any specific contract and antecedent to any statutory provisions, and as the deed in question did not expressly or by implication exclude the wife's rights, she was entitled to an order.

It was in *Matthews* v. *Matthews* [1932] P. 103 that he first enunciated the principle that a clause in an agreement of separation whereby the wife undertook not to institute proceedings for maintenance did not oust the jurisdiction of the summary courts. The deed was of merely evidential value and not an estoppel.

D. Morton v. Morton

The persistence of Mrs. Morton in pursuing her claims for maintenance has resulted in two reported cases, and though she herself got no satisfaction at all, and indeed may be considered unfortunate in the extreme in her litigation, she has helped to remove some obscurities in the law on this subject. In 1930 she took out summonses for desertion and persistent cruelty in the magistrates' court, but at the court she agreed with her husband to accept £1 a week for herself and 10s. for their child. The husband paid the £1 regularly but stopped the 10s. when the child started work. The wife thereupon took out a summons for wilful neglect to maintain, which failed. Then she sued in the county court for arrears of maintenance under the agreement, and failed again. In 1941 she took out a further summons for wilful neglect, and this time she succeeded, a stipendiary magistrate awarding her 30s. a week. This was her only success, and it was shortlived because a Divisional Court (Lord Merriman, P., and Hodson, J.) reversed this decision (*Morton* v. *Morton* [1942] 1 All E.R. 273). Lord Merriman, at p. 274, said he agreed with the view of Lord Merrivale in *Jones* v. *Jones** that the phrase " wilful neglect to provide reasonable maintenance " imports some element of matrimonial misconduct, and goes on to say at p. 276: —

> " The existence of an agreement is not a bar to the jurisdiction of the magistrates, neither on the question whether the offence has been committed, nor on the point of amount; but I think it is desirable to emphasise, as applied to the circumstances of this case, how high a value such an agreement should have had in guiding the magistrate in the exercise of his jurisdiction, which unquestionably remains notwithstanding the agreement."

He then refers to *Diggins* v. *Diggins* [1927] P. 88 and approves Lord Merrivale's words to the effect that the evidential value of an agreement which provides for periodical payments, which have been punctually paid, is very high.

Finally, the court held that because the payments had been punctually paid, there was no evidence that there had been wilful neglect to maintain.

Twelve years later, the indefatigable Mrs. Morton tried again, and this time in the High Court under s. 23 of the Matrimonial Causes Act, 1950, but once more she failed, and she appealed to the Court of Appeal where she lost for the last time (*Morton* v. *Morton* [1954] 1 W.L.R. 737).

What had happened was that in 1951 the Court of Appeal had given its decision in *Tulip* v. *Tulip* [1951] P. 378 (discussed fully below), where the court had held that where a husband had paid regularly under a deed of separation, and the wife's financial position had deteriorated, and the husband's improved, the court had jurisdiction to determine whether the maintenance was reasonable in spite of the deed and his payments under it.

Mrs. Morton was only getting her £1 a week and 27s. from National Assistance, while her husband's financial position had improved. Singleton, L.J., referred to the headnote in the earlier

---

* N.B.—The reference in [1942] 1 All E.R. for this case as [1924] P. 203 cannot be right because Lord Merrivale was not in that case and it was on a different point, and the reference should be (1929), 46 T.L.R. 33.

Morton case " . . . as its terms had been carried out, the husband could not be said to be guilty of an offence of wilful neglect to maintain, and there was no ground on which the magistrate could make an order," and said: —

> " It may be that the latter part of that which I have read goes too far in view of the decision of this court in *Tulip* v. *Tulip.* . . ."

The decision of the Divisional Court was probably wrong because although the law had been stated correctly, it had not been applied correctly, and too much emphasis had been put on the agreement, the financial provisions of which were then out of date.

However, the reason why Mrs. Morton lost her case in the Court of Appeal was because the husband had offered to pay £2 10s. a week, and she had refused.

E. Tulip v. Tulip

This case marks a turning point in the law on this subject. The facts were that in 1932 the husband agreed in a separation deed to pay his wife £156 per annum, and made his payments regularly. The wife covenanted to support herself. In 1949 the wife asked for an increase on the ground that her financial position had deteriorated through illness, whereas the husband's financial position had improved.

The wife applied to the High Court for maintenance on the ground of wilful neglect to maintain (now s. 27 of the Matrimonial Causes Act, 1973) and Barnard, J., held ([1951] P. 223) that as the husband had faithfully carried out his agreement he could not be held to be guilty of wilful neglect, which he said imports some element of matrimonial misconduct. He distinguished *Matthews* v. *Matthews* [1932] P. 103 (which was the only case to date where it had been held that a husband could be liable although he had carried out his undertakings by paying a lump sum, and that the agreement had very little evidential value as the wife would get very little benefit from it), and he found support in *Morton* v. *Morton* [1942] 1 All E.R. 273.

On appeal ([1951] P. 378) the Court of Appeal, Lord Asquith of Bishopstone and Birkett, L.J. (Harman, J., dissenting) reversed Barnard, J.'s decision and held that the existence of the deed did

not preclude the wife's application, and that the court had jurisdiction to determine whether, at the time of that application, the
husband was providing maintenance for the wife which was
reasonable in the circumstances.

It was admitted that the husband had not been guilty of any
matrimonial offence unless the refusal to increase his payments
constituted the offence of wilful neglect to provide reasonable
maintenance. The argument for the wife was that the only
importance of the deed was its evidential value. For instance,
where a wife made an application the day after she had entered
into a deed with independent advice, the evidential value would
be overwhelming, whereas after an interval of twenty years, it
might be of little or no value. This argument was accepted.

Birkett, L.J., quoted at length from Lord Merriman's judgment
in *Morton* v. *Morton* [1942] 1 All E.R. 273 and purported to found
his decision on that case. In fact, *Tulip* v. *Tulip* differs from that
case as was shown by Singleton, L.J., in *Morton* v. *Morton* [1954]
1 W.L.R. 737. What the learned President was saying in *Morton*
v. *Morton* [1942] 1 All E.R. 273 was that in spite of the agreement,
and of the fact that it had been regularly carried out, the court
had jurisdiction to deal with the application, but this decision was,
as interpreted by Barnard, J., that although in theory that was the
position, where the husband had carried out the terms of the
agreement, he could not possibly be found guilty of wilful neglect
since there had been no misconduct on his part. On this, Birkett,
L.J., said at p. 388: —

> "I am of the opinion that in so deciding Barnard, J., was
> wrong. With great respect to him, he seems to have ignored
> several essential matters. He seems to have decided that a
> sum for maintenance, agreed to in 1932, was unalterable
> so long as the husband continued to pay it, and was willing
> to go on paying it. But the real question for his determina-
> tion was not that, but whether at the time the application was
> made to him, the husband had wilfully neglected to provide
> reasonable maintenance. That must mean reasonable at the
> time of the application in the light of all the circumstances
> then existing . . . In a word, he said that once a sum for
> maintenance had been fixed by mutual agreement, and
> embodied in a separation agreement, it must be considered
> to be reasonable maintenance for all time. In my view, this
> way of deciding the application was wrong . . ."

In arriving at this conclusion, Birkett, L.J., relied to some extent on the fact that the wife in this case had not covenanted not to apply for maintenance in the future. As will be seen, later cases show that this consideration is of no importance. The real principle is referred to by Birkett, L.J., in a quotation from *Hyman* v. *Hyman* [1929] A.C. 601, at p. 629, where Lord Atkin said: —

> " In my view, no agreement between the spouses can prevent the court from considering the question whether in the circumstances of the particular case it shall think fit to order some reasonable payment to the wife. . . . The wife's right to future maintenance is a matter of public concern, which she cannot barter away."

F. Where the wife contracts or covenants not to sue

A common clause in separation agreements provides that if the husband faithfully carries out his obligations, the wife will not sue for more maintenance. Such a clause is valueless, and does not prevent a wife successfully pursuing a summons for wilful neglect, if the circumstances show the maintenance is insufficient.

This was decided in *Dowell* v. *Dowell* [1952] 2 All E.R. 141, where a husband agreed to pay certain sums for the maintenance of his wife and child, and the wife undertook not to take proceedings for maintenance if his payments were punctually made. The payments were punctually paid, but owing to ill-health the wife asked the husband for more maintenance, which he refused. On a summons before the justices, an order was made on the ground of wilful neglect and this was upheld in the Divisional Court, Lord Merriman, P., saying that the jurisdiction is absolute, and cannot be bargained away, but it is a question for the discretion of the court in each case, taking all the circumstances into account, whether there has been wilful neglect to provide reasonable maintenance in spite of the punctual performance of the agreement. An important point in this case was that the wife's application was only two years after the agreement had been entered into.

G. Where the husband does not agree to maintain his wife

It happens from time to time that a married couple part by consent, and there is no express or implied agreement by the husband to maintain the wife. The wife may even agree that her husband should not maintain her. She prefers to be independent and keep herself. Can the husband be guilty of wilful neglect to maintain her in such circumstances? This question arose for decision in *Baker* v. *Baker* (1949), 66 T.L.R. (Pt. 1) 81. The wife contended that the husband had been guilty of constructive desertion, because she had left him on the ground that he had made life impossible for her. Her summons for desertion was dismissed, but the justices made an order for wilful neglect. Lord Merriman, P., in the Divisional Court said, at p. 82: —

> " There is no law in this case; it is merely an application of the principle that, if a wife is living separate and apart from her husband, it is not enough for her to give evidence that her husband had money and she needed maintenance. The question is: What was the nature of the parting? If the wife can prove desertion, she is of course, entitled to maintenance on that ground. If the separation was consensual, then, if she can prove . . . that this was on the basis, express or implied, that the husband undertook to be responsible for her maintenance, she is entitled either to an agreed amount (if there was an agreed amount), or to a reasonable amount under the section, although she is living apart from her husband. But unless she can show, where the separation was consensual, that the husband had accepted a liability, expressed or implied, to maintain her, she has no case at all."

Later on in his judgment, the learned President added: —

> " I know of nothing to prevent the wife from putting herself right tomorrow, and if she is content to do so then her rights might be very different."

Baker v. *Baker* was followed by *Stringer* v. *Stringer* [1952] P. 171 in the Divisional Court (Lord Merriman, P., and Karminski, J.). Lord Merriman pointed out that this was not one of the exceptions referred to by Hill, J., in *Papadopoulos* v. *Papadopoulos* [1930] P. 55, and that the onus was on the wife and not on the husband, as said by Hill, J., with regard to the other exceptions. He also referred to the unreported case of *Chapman* v. *Chapman* in the Court of Appeal (4th April, 1951), and at p. 179 said that Asquith, L.J., with the concurrence of Harman, J., had said: —

> "Often two such summonses [for desertion and wilful neglect] do so [i.e., stand or fall together], and if the wife fails on desertion, she automatically fails on wilful neglect to maintain, but that is not necessarily or inevitably so. Sometimes, where, for instance, the evidence is that the separation was consensual, she may fail on desertion and win

on maintenance; in cases, that is, where the consensus impliedly includes a term that the wife should be entitled to some support from the husband."

Starkie v. *Starkie* (*No.* 2) [1954] 1 W.L.R. 98 was to the same effect.

The Divisional Court next considered this question in *Pinnick* v. *Pinnick* [1957] 1 W.L.R. 644, but in the meantime the Court of Appeal had expressed its views on the subject in *National Assistance Board* v. *Parkes* [1955] 2 Q.B. 506. This was a case under the National Assistance Act, 1948, where the parties had separated, and the wife had covenanted that she would not at any future time claim maintenance. Later, she became destitute, and obtained assistance from the National Assistance Board, which then proceeded under s. 43 of the Act to recover the maintenance paid to the wife. Apart from the liability under the Act, the court considered the question of a husband's obligation to maintain his wife.

Denning, L.J., said that where a wife covenanted not to claim any maintenance that did not *ipso facto* destroy the husband's obligation to maintain her. He pointed out that if a husband paid under the deed, he was fulfilling his duty to maintain, but if new circumstances arose and she brought them to his notice, and he had the means to pay more, then he was under a duty to increase the sum, notwithstanding the prior agreement (*Tulip* v. *Tulip* [1951] P. 378; *Dowell* v. *Dowell* [1952] 2 All E.R. 141 and *National Assistance Board* v. *Prisk* [1954] 1 W.L.R. 443) and at p. 517 he said: —

" The principle of *Tulip* v. *Tulip* applies, I think, just as much when there is an agreement to pay nothing as when a fixed sum is to be paid: and it overrides anything said previously in *Baker* v. *Baker* and *Chapman* v. *Chapman*. But so long as the husband is ignorant of the new situation, he is under no such duty, and is not guilty of wilful neglect to maintain her. That is, I think, the effect of the decision in *Stringer* v. *Stringer*. . . .

The truth is that, on a separation by consent, the existence of an agreement for fixed maintenance, or for no maintenance, does not oust the duty of the husband to maintain his wife. As Lord Atkin said in *Hyman* v. *Hyman*—in another connection, but I think his words are apposite here also— ' The wife's right to future maintenance is a matter of public concern, which she cannot barter away.' In the great majority of cases, the husband by fulfilling his agreement, fulfils his duty; but circumstances may arise when the wife is in need and the husband knows of it and can and ought to pay for her. The private agreement of the parties must then give place to the overriding duty of a man to maintain his wife. His duty only ceases when she has been guilty of a grave fault, such as adultery or desertion, by which she forfeits her right to maintenance."

Birkett, L.J., also said at p. 523 that he could see no distinction in principle between a separation agreement, where a sum had to be paid, and one where nothing has to be paid, if later conditions alter and the wife is in need.

The Divisional Court in *Pinnick* v. *Pinnick* [1957] 1 W.L.R. 644 considered the matter in the light of these observations. The facts were that the parting was consensual, and there was no agreement, express or implied, as to maintenance. The justices made an order for maintenance on the ground of wilful neglect. The husband's appeal was allowed by the Divisional Court (Lord Merriman, P., and Collingwood, J.) who found that there was no inherent conflict between *Baker* v. *Baker* and *Tulip* v. *Tulip*, because the question on what financial terms the parting had taken place, and the question whether some fresh need of the wife and notice thereof to the husband had occurred so as to find wilful neglect to maintain in spite of those terms, are two separate and distinct questions, and in the case in question there had been no change of circumstances.

In *Jones* v. *Jones* [1959] P. 38 a Divisional Court considered the question once more. A husband was ordered to make weekly payments under s. 43 of the National Assistance Act, 1948, and punctually obeyed the order. The wife, whose financial needs were not covered by it, applied for and was granted an order on the ground of wilful neglect to maintain. It was held on appeal that as the husband was ignorant of his wife's needs, he could not be said to have been guilty of a wilful neglect to maintain her, for such neglect imports an element of misconduct.

Lord Merriman, P., said he realised, as a matter of realism, that this could not be the end of the story, but he was only concerned with the case as it stood. This means presumably that if the wife issued another summons for wilful neglect, the husband could not then put forward his ignorance of her needs as a defence, and since the magistrates had already found he could pay more, the effect of the appeal was merely to postpone the order for payments on the ground of wilful neglect.

H. Summary

Where there is a separation agreement, the law now appears to be as follows: —

(1) Where a husband undertakes to pay maintenance to his wife and defaults, she can ignore the agreement and apply to the magistrates for an order on the ground of wilful neglect.

(2) Where he punctually pays under the agreement, this does not amount to an estoppel, but the agreement is merely of evidentiary value. The court will have jurisdiction to deal with the application, and the evidentiary value of the agreement will depend partly on the lapse of time, change of circumstances of either or both parties, and the husband's knowledge of his wife's needs.

(3) An undertaking by the wife not to sue will not oust the jurisdiction of the magistrates.

(4) If the agreement does not expressly or impliedly provide for the maintenance of the wife the husband is not liable for her maintenance, but if the wife can show a change in her circumstances, and that she has given notice of this fact to her husband, the magistrates can make an order.

VI. MAINTENANCE AGREEMENTS

The position of spouses who had entered into a separation agreement was not satisfactory, and the Maintenance Agreements Act, 1957, was passed " to make provision with respect to the validity and alteration by the court of financial arrangements in connection with agreements between the parties to a marriage. . . ."

This Act was replaced by ss. 13–15 of the Matrimonial Proceedings and Property Act, 1970, which have now been replaced by ss. 34–36 of the Matrimonial Causes Act, 1973.

Section 34 provides that any provision in such an agreement restricting the right to apply to a court shall be void, but otherwise the financial arrangements shall be binding. It applies to agreements made before or after this Act. An application may be made to a magistrates' court (s. 35). The court has power to alter or vary such agreements where there has been a change in the circumstances or where there have been omissions, and where it does not contain proper financial arrangements for any child of the family.

A magistrates' court shall not entertain any application unless both parties are resident in England or Wales and at least one party is resident in the petty sessions area for which the court acts, and shall not have power to make any order except—

(a) in a case where the agreement includes no provision for periodical payments by either party, an order inserting provision for the making by one of the parties of periodical payments for the maintenance of the other party or for the maintenance of any child of the family;

(b) in a case where the agreement includes provision for the making by one of the parties of periodical payments, an order increasing or reducing the rate of, or terminating, any of those payments.

The case of *Ewart* v. *Ewart* [1959] P. 23 decided that where the deed was made for the purpose of resuming cohabitation, and not for the purpose of living separately, the court had no jurisdiction under the statute to vary it. Under the 1957 Act only agreements for the purposes of the parties living separately came within the Act, but this is not so under the 1973 Act. *Ewart's* case is not therefore applicable to the 1973 Act.

K. v. *K.* [1961] 1 W.L.R. 802 was a case under s. 1 (3) (*a*) of the Act of 1957, which is now s. 35 (2) of the Act of 1973, and the Court of Appeal had to consider the meaning of the words of this section. The court held that there was one question which the court had to decide, namely, whether by reason of a change in the circumstances in the light of which the financial arrangement in the agreement was made, it should be altered so as to make different financial arrangements, and that the expression " circumstances in the light of which " meant circumstances which influenced the parties and within their contemplation, and included anticipated events. Holroyd Pearce, L.J., at p. 810, said the powers of the court are different from varying a maintenance order, and he thought the legislature did not intend to remove entirely the stability of agreements, but only when injustice was caused by a change in circumstances.

This was followed and approved in *Ratcliffe* v. *Ratcliffe* [1962] 1 W.L.R. 1455, where the court held that, though there had been a change in the circumstances, before there should be an alteration it must be satisfied that the agreement had become unjust by reason of the change of circumstances. It also held that the section should not be construed in such a way as to undermine the sanctity of a perfectly good maintenance agreement voluntarily entered into for good consideration.

In the case of *Gorman* v. *Gorman* [1964] 1 W.L.R. 1440, C.A., the agreement provided for maintenance of the children only, with provision of a house for the wife and children. The wife covenanted to support herself and not by judicial proceedings or otherwise to compel the husband to maintain her. Subsequently the wife had to give up work due to ill health and the husband's income rose from £1,000 p.a. to £4,000 p.a. The husband made a voluntary payment to her of £6 a week. She sought to have the agreement varied. The court held there was a change of circumstances which gave the court jurisdiction to alter the agreement, but declined to do so, apparently influenced by the voluntary payment. There was much discussion whether the test of " circumstances in the light of which " should be subject to a subjective test or an objective test. Willmer, L.J., thought there was room for both approaches to the problem, that is to say to consider what the parties thought at the time and what they contemplated and also what reasonable persons would have thought and contemplated at the time. Pearson, L.J., favoured an objective test, that is, what reasonable people would have thought and taken into consideration at the time.

VII. MAINTENANCE—CONDUCT OF THE PARTIES

Until recently it was generally accepted that the conduct of the parties was a circumstance of importance to be taken into account when assessing the financial consequences when one party proved that the other had committed a matrimonial offence for which a court order for maintenance could be made. The *locus classicus* of this subject is *Wood* v. *Wood* [1891] P. 272. Lindley, L.J., at p. 276, said: —

" The circumstances which have to be taken into account are
(1) Conduct of the parties;
(2) The position in life and the ages and the respective
    means;
(3) The amount of the provision actually made;
(4) The existence or non-existence of children and who is
    to have the care and custody of them;
(5) Any other circumstances which may be important in
    any particular case."

Scarman, J., in *Kirke* v. *Kirke* [1961] 1 W.L.R. 14 said that
this was as good a guide as any. This case was followed in *Courtney* v. *Courtney* [1968] P. 523, D.C. In *Tumath* v. *Tumath* [1970]
P. 78, C.A., Salmon, L.J., at p. 85, said: —

" It is well settled that in exercising discretion in proceedings
for permanent maintenance it is of the utmost importance for
the court to have regard to the conduct of the parties (*Restall*
v. *Restall* [1930] P. 189). Indeed in *Wood* v. *Wood* [*supra*]
Lindley, L.J., places it first."

It will be seen that so far the courts have placed considerable
emphasis on the conduct of the parties in deciding upon the
amount to be awarded.

The passing of the Divorce Reform Act, 1969, now consolidated
in the Matrimonial Causes Act, 1973, has brought a new approach
to the whole question of the conduct of the parties when considering maintenance where a marriage has broken down. Section
25 of the Act of 1973 (see Appendix IV) sets out the considerations
which should be applied in proceedings in the High Court Family
Division and the divorce county court in dealing with the financial
position of the parties. Strictly speaking this section has no
application to the magistrates' court, nor is the Act of 1960
mentioned. Nevertheless by analogy it forms a useful guide to
magistrates in these circumstances. Seven matters are specifically
enumerated and the section then goes on " . . . and so to exercise
those powers as to place the parties, so far as it is practicable and,
having regard to *their conduct*, just to do so, in the financial
position in which they would have been if the marriage had not
broken down," etc.

From this the Court of Appeal has inferred that the conduct of
the parties is of lesser importance than the items specified, and
can be largely ignored unless the conduct of one party is gross
(*Wachtel* v. *Wachtel* [1972] Fam., at p. 89). The following

passage from the judgment of Lord Denning, M.R., is worth quoting:

" The conduct of the parties.

When Parliament in 1857 introduced divorce by the courts of law, it based it on the doctrine of the matrimonial offence. This affected all that followed. If a person was the guilty party in a divorce suit, it went hard with him or her. It affected so many things. The custody of the children depended on it. So did the award of maintenance. To say nothing of the standing in society. So serious were the consequences that divorce suits were contested at great length and at much cost.

All that is altered. Parliament has decreed: 'If the marriage has broken down irretrievably, let there be a divorce.' It carries no stigma, but only sympathy. It is a misfortune which befalls both. No longer is one guilty and the other innocent. No longer are there long contested divorce suits. Nearly every case goes uncontested. The parties come to an agreement, if they can, on the things that matter so much to them. They divide up the furniture. They arrange the custody of the children, the financial provision for the wife, and the future of the matrimonial home. If they cannot agree, the matters are referred to a judge in chambers.

When the judge comes to decide these questions, what place has conduct in it? Parliament still says that the court has to have 'regard to their conduct': see section 5 (1) of the Act of 1970. Does this mean that the judge in chambers is to hear their mutual recriminations and to go into their petty squabbles for days on end, as he used to do in the old days? Does it mean that, after a marriage has been dissolved, there is to be a post mortem to find out what killed it? We do not think so. In most cases both parties are to blame—or, as we would prefer to say—both parties have contributed to the breakdown.

It has been suggested that there should be a 'discount' or 'reduction' in what the wife is to receive because of her supposed misconduct, guilt or blame (whatever word is used). We cannot accept this argument. In the vast majority of cases it is repugnant to the principles underlying the new legislation, and in particular the Act of 1969. There will be many cases in which a wife (though once considered guilty or blameworthy) will have cared for the home and looked after the family for very many years. Is she to be deprived of the benefit otherwise to be accorded to her by section 5 (1) (f) because she may share responsibility for the breakdown with her husband? There will no doubt be a residue of cases where the conduct of one of the parties is in the judge's

words . . . 'both obvious and gross,' so much so that to
order one party to support another whose conduct falls into
this category is repugnant to anyone's sense of justice. In
such a case the court remains free to decline to afford financial
support or to reduce the support which it would otherwise
have ordered. But, short of cases falling into this category,
the court should not reduce its order for financial provision
merely because of what was formerly regarded as guilt or
blame. To do so would be to impose a fine for supposed
misbehaviour in the course of an unhappy married life. Mr.
Ewbank disputed this and claimed that it was but justice that
a wife should suffer for her supposed misbehaviour. We do
not agree. Criminal justice often requires the imposition of
financial and indeed custodial penalties. But in the financial
adjustments consequent upon the dissolution of a marriage
which has irretrievably broken down, the imposition of financial penalties ought seldom to find a place."

This case has been followed in the Court of Appeal in *Harnett*
v. *Harnett* [1974] 1 W.L.R. 219. In the divorce court, therefore,
the conduct of the parties is the *last* consideration to be taken
into account, whereas in the magistrates' court it would appear
to be the *first* consideration to be taken into account. No doubt in
due course the Act of 1960 will be amended and this anomaly will
be corrected, but until that time it is suggested that the magistrates
should give effect as far as possible to the new climate of opinion
in this respect.

To view the matter in perspective, a spouse, usually the wife,
can only obtain an order for maintenance in the magistrates'
court if she can prove a specified matrimonial offence by the
other spouse, usually the husband, but where there are children
an order can be made for their maintenance against either the
complainant or the defendant (see s. 2 (1) (*h*) of the Act of 1960)
so long as they are children of the family (as to who is a child
of the family, see p. 292).

There is one absolute statutory bar to an order being made in
favour of a wife personally, namely that she has committed
adultery: see s. 2 (3) (*b*), which provides as follows: —

"The court . . . shall not make an order . . . (*b*) where
the complainant is proved to have committed an act of
adultery during the subsistence of the marriage, unless the
court is satisfied that the defendant has condoned, or connived
at, or by wilful neglect or misconduct conduced to, that act
of adultery."

There are two other instances of absolute bars which are not statutory, namely a wife in desertion (see *Naylor* v. *Naylor* [1962] P. 253) and also if she has been guilty of cruelty (see *Young* v. *Young* [1962] 3 W.L.R. 946).

What is the position, then, when the court makes an order under s. 2 (1) (*h*) or for wilful neglect of the children only or persistent cruelty to the children only, where the wife has disentitled herself to an order for herself because of her adultery, desertion, or cruelty, or where by agreement she has agreed not to claim maintenance for herself? These matters have been the subject of a number of authorities.

In *Kinnane* v. *Kinnane* [1954] P. 41 a Divisional Court held that where the only legitimate finding was that the husband had wilfully neglected to maintain the children whom he was legally liable to maintain, the justices had power to make an order for maintenance of the wife. This was followed in *Starkie* v. *Starkie* (*No.* 2) [1953] 2 All E.R. 1519 where the justices held that the parties had parted by consent and they made an order in favour of the wife, but in respect of the child only, of the then maximum of £1 10s. per week. The Divisional Court held that the proper award was in addition a nominal order for 1s. per week for the wife. These cases and the following case—*Naylor* v. *Naylor* [1962] P. 253—were tried when the law applicable was the law before the enactment of the 1960 Act. The court held that, while the only statutory bar for the recovery of maintenance was adultery by the wife, a deserting wife was also in the same position, citing *Jones* v. *Guardians of Newton, etc.* [1920] 3 K.B. 381 and *National Assistance Board* v. *Parkes* [1955] 2 Q.B. 506. The court also held that in the circumstances an order could not be made in favour of the wife for wilful neglect by the husband to provide reasonable maintenance in respect of the children.

In *Young* v. *Young* [1962] 3 W.L.R. 946 the law applicable was the 1960 Act. The wife complained of persistent cruelty and wilful neglect to maintain herself and her child. The justices dismissed the complaint of persistent cruelty but made an order in favour of the wife and child in respect of wilful neglect. The husband appealed so far as the order was in favour of the wife. The Divisional Court held that because the wife was in desertion she was not entitled to an order for herself, and Sir Jocelyn Simon, P., said at p. 953:

" . . . where the wife has been guilty of desertion or cruelty. The husband cannot be guilty of wilful neglect to provide reasonable maintenance for her in those circumstances: he could however be guilty of wilful neglect to provide reasonable maintenance for the child of the family. Is it open for the court to make an order for the wife in such circumstances? In my view the answer is *NO*."

If there had been a consensual separation which did not specifically exonerate the husband from maintaining his wife an order made on the ground of his neglect to maintain a child may include provision for the maintenance of the wife.

The latest case is *Northrop* v. *Northrop* [1968] P. 74. The justices dismissed a complaint of desertion by the wife and held in effect that the parting was by consent. They held that the husband had been guilty of wilful neglect to maintain his wife and child and made an order accordingly. The Court of Appeal held that, on proof that the husband had wilfully neglected to maintain her or the child, if she had committed no offence, she could be awarded maintenance for herself and the child. The amount to be awarded for maintenance was that which was reasonable in all the circumstances including the effect on the wife's earning capacity of having to care for and provide accommodation for an infant child and whether or not she herself was guilty of a matrimonial offence.

Diplock, L.J., protested that the courts had introduced esoterism into this branch of the law where Parliament intended only simplicity. At that time there was a limitation on the amounts which the magistrates could award, namely £7 10s. for a wife and £2 10s. for a child. Subject to these limitations, Diplock, L.J., pointed out that the only limitation on the power to order maintenance was that the sum should be such " as the court considers reasonable in all the circumstances of the case."

The position has been radically altered by the Maintenance Orders Act, 1968, which has removed all the financial limitations so that there is no limit to what magistrates can award in any particular case provided that this is reasonable. The importance of this Act is greater than is generally recognised. The common sense of the matter is that if a wife has the custody of a child or children, the children have to be fed, clothed, housed, and so on, but in order to do this properly then the wife herself must have sufficient maintenance to be fit to carry out her parental duties. If the law precludes her from an order in her favour because of her matrimonial offences then the sensible thing for the magistrates to do is to include in the amount awarded to the child sufficient to cover the wife's maintenance.

This would be in line with the judgment of Lord Denning in *Wachtel* v. *Wachtel, supra.*

VIII. MEANS

When a married couple separate, there is bound to be hardship for both parties. If their financial resources are solely the earnings of the husband, then to split those earnings between two establishments means that both will go short. The far from easy task of the magistrates is to divide the husband's earnings in an equitable manner that will be fair to both parties. If sympathy for the wife (and usually she has the children too) leads to awarding her such a sum that the husband is unable to keep the payments up, the husband, faced with an impossible task, does not pay, and sending him to prison is no good for him, his wife or the State. The magistrates should bear in mind the words of Lord Merrivale in *Church* v. *Church* (1933), 97 J.P. 91, at p. 95: —

> " They [the justices] must see what evidence there is of the husband's actual earnings and his capacity to earn a livelihood under existing conditions in that neighbourhood, also of the earning capacity of the wife, and they must take care, if they make an order which is capable of being enforced by imprisonment, that it is clearly within the faculties of the husband."

It should go without saying that the justices must have evidence of the husband's means (see *Clews* v. *Clews* (1932), 96 J.P. 91), and they must be satisfied either that he has actual earnings in his possession, or that he has the capability of earning money. If he could earn money, but wilfully abstains from doing so, that would be enough to establish wilful neglect to maintain (*Earnshaw* v. *Earnshaw* [1896] P. 160, and see *Stirland* v. *Stirland* [1960] 1 W.L.R. 18, where the husband was capable of working). A similar decision is *Jacobson* v. *Jacobson* (1961), 105 Sol. J. 991, where it was held that potential earning capacity could be taken into account in fixing the *amount* of the order. A naval seaman, by stopping his wife's allotment, may be guilty of neglect to maintain (*Snow* v. *Snow* (1932), 96 J.P. 477).

It has been said that the conventional standard in the divorce court (derived from the old ecclesiastical courts), that one-third of the joint incomes should be awarded to the wife, is very difficult to apply to a man earning wages and a woman able to earn money (per Lord Merrivale in *Jones* v. *Jones* (1929), 94 J.P. 30). The effect would be in some cases to make the wife better off than the husband, and where the husband's earnings are precarious, to leave him with nothing at all. In that case the husband earned £3 and the wife earned ten shillings to fifteen shillings a week and lived rent free. The magistrates made an order of £1 a week, which the Divisional Court reduced to ten shillings. Nevertheless, although the one-third rule is not as a matter of law applicable in the magistrates' court, it does afford a rough guide to magistrates in arriving at their decision.

According to Hodson, J., in *Scott* v. *Scott* [1951] P. 245, at p. 248: —

> " . . . the question of what is reasonable maintenance for the wife and the children has to be considered with reference to the husband's common-law liability to maintain his wife and children, and the word ' reasonable ' no doubt has to be interpreted against the background of the standard of life which he previously maintained."

If, of course, the husband's means have increased then the wife should get some of the benefit of this. There is no duty on a wife to work in order to reduce the husband's liability to maintain her (Barnard, J., in *Le Roy-Lewis* v. *Le Roy-Lewis* [1955] P. 1). Nevertheless, the wife's earnings are a relevant circumstance to be taken into account, and also her ability to earn (*Church* v. *Church, supra*).

Where a relation of the husband had offered to pay £1 a week for the wife, the justices ordered the husband to pay that amount. In the Divisional Court (*Walton* v. *Walton* (1900), 64 J.P. 264), Jeune, P., said at p. 264: —

> " If the husband is lucky enough to have some relatives who can help him, so much the better for him. If at any time the husband finds he cannot pay the allowance, he can apply to have it reduced."

In *W.* v. *W.* [1962] P. 124, Scarman, J., set out the criteria

whereby maintenance should be assessed. The husband's ability
to pay must be judged in the light of all his circumstances, and
not by a mere cash calculation. Absence of regular income
was not decisive. One must look at his mental and physical
resources, including his health and age, the money at his disposal,
his capital position and the rate of his current expenditure, and
his debts. It was better to make a small order that would be paid
than a large one which the husband would fail to honour.

In *Brandon* v. *Brandon* (1964), 108 Sol. J. 201 (D.C.), a magistrates' court having rejected a submission that there was no case
to answer, made an order for maintenance on the ground of desertion without calling for evidence as to the husband's means. The
Divisional Court held that it was the advocate's duty to remind
magistrates, if appropriate, that they had not had evidence of
means.

It is quite common for husbands in giving evidence of their
means to produce a pay packet, or refer to their standard earnings
and not their average earnings, omitting to mention for instance,
overtime. The Divisional Court in *Elleman* v. *Elleman* (1964), 108
Sol. J. 220, held that magistrates should call for a certificate of
earnings from the employers or for wage packets over a period
which would show the true position.

It was held in *Williams* v. *Williams* [1964] 3 W.L.R. 832 that
the cost of a son's education was a prior charge to maintenance
to a wife.

IX. QUANTUM

The following are some examples from modern cases on the
considerations the justices should have in mind in arriving at the
quantum of maintenance.

Kershaw v. *Kershaw* [1964] P. 13.—Order on the ground of
the husband's desertion. He earned £14 a week from a regular
job and a varying amount as a variety artist. He said he averaged
£6 a week. She said £14-£15 a week. Justices assessed this at £10
a week and made an order of £7 10s. for the wife and £2 10s. for
the child. The Divisional Court dismissed the husband's appeal.
They also decided that the power under s. 60 (1) of the Magistrates'
Courts Act, 1952, to order an investigation of means by a pro-

bation officer should not be used unless it was the only reasonable
way of ascertaining the facts. Sir J. Simon, P., thought that it
was a general principle that the standard of living of the
wife should not be lowered more than is inherent in the
circumstances of the separation.

Stead v. *Stead* [1968] P. 538.—A wife obtained an order against
her husband and subsequently divorced him. Four years later she
became pregnant to another man and on this account the husband
subsequently had the order revoked, but a Divisional Court
reversed this decision, Willmer, L.J., pointing out that s. 8 (2) of
the Act of 1960 referred to adultery during the subsistence of the
marriage. The court was not concerned with the wife's morals
(*Miller* v. *Miller* [1961] P. 1).

Ashley v. *Ashley* [1968] P. 582.—A magistrates' court awarded
maintenance of 15s. a week for the wife and 7s. 6d. for the child
because the wife was on National Assistance, so that the Board
would get the money. A Divisional Court held this was irrelevant,
but that the order should not reduce the husband below subsistence
level, and awarded in this case £5 and 30s. respectively out of net
earnings of £14 5s., citing *Stone* v. *Stone* [1957] P. 168 and *Slater*
v. *Slater* [1962] P. 94.

Attwood v. *Attwood* [1968] P. 591.—In this case the award to
the wife for herself and child together with her own earnings came
to more than half of the joint incomes. A Divisional Court reduced
the order.

Sir Jocelyn Simon, at p. 595, said: —

> " In my view, the general considerations which should be
> borne in mind in this type of case are as follows: —(1) In
> cohabitation a wife and the children share with the husband a
> standard of living appropriate to his income, or, if the wife is
> also working, their joint incomes. (2) Where cohabitation has
> been disrupted by a matrimonial offence on the part of the
> husband, the wife's and children's maintenance should be so
> assessed that their standard of living does not suffer more
> than is inherent in the circumstances of separation; though
> the standard may be lower than theretofore, since the income
> or incomes may now have to support two households in place
> of the former one where household expenses were shared.
> (3) Therefore, although the standard of living of all parties
> may have to be lower than before there was a breach of
> cohabitation, in general the wife and children should not be

relegated to a significantly lower standard of living than that which the husband enjoys. As to the foregoing, see *Kershaw* v. *Kershaw* [1966] P. 13 and *Ashley* v. *Ashley* [1968] P. 582. (4) Subject to what follows, neither should the standard of living of the wife be put significantly higher than that of the husband, since so to do would in effect amount to imposing a fine on him for his matrimonial offence, and that is not justified by the modern law. (5) In determining the relevant standard of living of each party, the court should take into account the reasonable expenses of each party, especially, though not exclusively, expenses of earning an income and of maintaining any relevant child. (6) If the wife has an income, or if she has what should in all the circumstances be considered as a potential earning capacity, that must be taken into account in determining the relevant standards of living: see *Rose* v. *Rose* [1951] P. 29 and *Levett-Yeats* v. *Levett-Yeats*. (7) Where a wife is earning an income, that ought generally to be brought into account, unless it would be reasonable to expect her to give up the source of the income: *Levett-Yeats* v. *Levett-Yeats* (1967), 111 Sol. J. 475. (8) Where the wife is earning an income, the whole of this need not, and should not ordinarily, be brought into account so as to enure to the husband's benefit: *Ward* v. *Ward* [1948] P. 62 and *J.* v. *J.* [1955] P. 215. (9) This consideration is particularly potent where the wife only takes up employment in consequence of the disruption of the marriage by the husband, or where she would not reasonably be expected to be working if the marriage had not been so disrupted. (10) At the end of the case, the court must ensure that the result of its order is not to depress the husband below subsistence level: *Ashley* v. *Ashley, supra.* (11) An appellate court will not interfere with an award of maintenance unless, to use the words used in *Ward* v. *Ward*, ' it is unreasonable or indiscreet '; that is to say, that the justices are shown to have gone wrong in principle or their final award is otherwise clearly wrong."

Roberts v. *Roberts* [1970] P. 1.—The husband left his wife and child and went to live with Mrs. *B.* and her three children. The wife lived on Social Security. The husband kept Mrs. *B.* and her children. The justices ordered £1 10s. for the wife and £1 for the child.

On appeal a Divisional Court said that the justices should not have preferred the husband's obligations to Mrs. *B.* and her family to those owed to his wife and child. Moral obligations came before immoral obligations.

X. CHILD OF THE FAMILY

A child of the family is defined by s. 16 of the Act of 1960 as follows: —

" (a) any child of both parties; and
(b) any other child of either party who has been accepted as one of the family by the other party."

This definition can be contrasted with the definition in the Matrimonial Causes Act, 1973, s. 52, where (b) reads as follows: —

"any other child, not being a child who has been boarded-out with those parties by a local authority or voluntary organisation, who has been treated by both of those parties as a child of their family."

This definition in the Act of 1973 applies in the High Court and the divorce county court but not in the magistrates' court, which is governed by the Act of 1960. It will be seen that there are two main differences. In the magistrates' court a child of the family if not a child of both parties must be a child of one of them, which is not so in the other courts. Furthermore the child must be " accepted " as one of the family by the other party whereas in the other courts it must be " treated " as one of the family by both parties.

Whether a child is a child of the family is important in the magistrates' court for three reasons: —

1. By s. 1 (1) (b) (iii) of the Act of 1960 it is a matrimonial offence and a cause for complaint if the defendant has been guilty of persistent cruelty to a child of the family.

2. By s. 1 (1) (h) and (i) of the 1960 Act it is similarly a cause of complaint if the defendant has wilfully neglected to maintain a child of the family.

3. By s. 2 (5) of the same Act in considering whether any or what provision should be included in a matrimonial order for a child of the family who is not a child of the party paying, the court shall have regard to the extent, if any, to which that party had, on or after the acceptance of the child as one of the family, assumed responsibility for the child's maintenance and to the liability of any person other than a party to the marriage to maintain the child.

The following cases have been decided on the subject of children of the family so far as concerns magistrates' courts: —

Bowlas v. *Bowlas* [1965] P. 450, C.A.—Wife had two children by a former marriage. After the marriage her husband refused to live with her and left her after four days. The justices made an order for maintenance for the wife and her children on the grounds of desertion and wilful neglect to maintain her and her children. A Divisional Court dismissed the husband's appeal, but the Court of Appeal sent it back for a new trial because under s. 2 (5) it was for the justices to determine the extent to which the husband had assumed liability and the liability of the father of the children who lived in the U.S.A. and against whom there was an order which he had ignored.

Caller v. *Caller* [1968] P. 39.—When the marriage took place the wife was pregnant to another man and this was known to the husband, who prior to the marriage had agreed to accept the child as the child of the family. Three weeks before the birth the husband left the wife. The justices found desertion and made an order in respect of wife and child. The Divisional Court held the child was a child of the family but ordered a rehearing as to maintenance of the child, the wife to seek out the putative father and bring affiliation proceedings against him.

R. v. *R.* [1969] P. 414.—The husband divorced his wife who had committed adultery. The child was not his and he immediately disowned the child. The husband was granted a divorce on the ground of this adultery. An issue arose whether the child was a child of the family. The statute was the Matrimonial Causes Act, 1965, ss. 34 and 36 (2), which used the word " accepted " as in the 1960 Act and not " treated " as in the 1973 Act. It was held that a child of one party could not be held to have been accepted by the other party unless he consented expressly or impliedly to receive the child as one of the family, and that consent must be given with knowledge of the material facts.

Snow v. *Snow* [1971] Fam. 74, C.A.—The wife, previously married and divorced, went to live with *X* by whom she had two children. In 1968 she married the husband and brought her children to the matrimonial home. Three months later she left the husband and went to live with *X*. The wife applied in the magistrates' court for an order on the ground of desertion and wilful neglect to maintain her and the children, claiming the children as children of the family. The court made an order of

£1 15s. per week. Until the marriage X had paid £3 a week for the children. The wife could have applied for an affiliation order but did not. The husband had applied for income tax allowance for the children. So did X. The Inland Revenue suggested an apportionment. At the hearing in the magistrates' court counsel for the husband accepted that the children were children of the family. This admission was withdrawn before the Divisional Court, who adjourned the case for the wife to take affiliation proceedings against X, who was ordered to pay £1 5s. for each child, and in the hearing that immediately followed the magistrates made an order against the husband for £1 15s.

On the question whether the husband had accepted the children as children of the family the court thought the test was that laid down by Salmon, L.J., in *Bowlas* v. *Bowlas, supra*: —

> ". . . did this man on the day that he married, marry this woman on the basis that he was then accepting the children as children of the family? "

There had to be mutual acceptance.

The Court of Appeal dismissed the appeal.

CHAPTER 7

CONDONATION; CONNIVANCE AND CONDUCT CONDUCING

I. INTRODUCTION

WHERE the complaint is of adultery the court has to be satisfied that the complainant has not condoned or connived at, or by wilful neglect or misconduct conduced to, that act of adultery; or where the complainant is proved to have committed an act of adultery during the subsistence of the marriage it has to be satisfied that the defendant has condoned or connived at, or by wilful neglect or misconduct conduced to that act of adultery, before the court can make an order for maintenance, or a separation order (s. 2 (3) of the Act of 1960). Similarly, proof of no condonation, etc., is required for revocation of an order by reason of adultery (s. 8 (2)).

II. CONDONATION

Condonation applies to adultery and cruelty and possibly other matrimonial offences except desertion (see p. 119 et seq.). It does not depend on the wording of the Act of 1960 or its predecessor the Act of 1895, but on the common law (*Williams* v. *Williams* [1904] P. 145 (D.C.)). " Condonation " is a strictly technical word (Sir Cresswell Cresswell in *Dent* v. *Dent* (1865), 4 Sw. & Tr. 105, at p. 107), and relates to the blotting out of the offence by the innocent party. It is an act of generosity by the innocent party and in general is an act of forgiveness during good behaviour (but as to adultery, see s. 42 (3) of the Matrimonial Causes Act, 1965). There is no comprehensive definition, but the following are generally regarded as authoritative: —

> "I think that the forgiveness which is to take away the husband's right to a divorce must not fall short of reconciliation, and that this must be shown by the reinstatement of the wife in her former position, which renders proof of conjugal cohabitation, or the restitution of conjugal rights,

necessary " (Lord Chelmsford, L.C., in *Keats* v. *Keats and Montezuma* (1859), 1 Sw. & Tr. 334, at p. 357).

" Condonation in connection with the law of divorce has been defined in a variety of phrases in many previous judgments. The essence of the matter is (taking the case where it is the wife who has been guilty of the matrimonial offence) that the husband with knowledge of the wife's offence should forgive her and should confirm his forgiveness by reinstating her as his wife. Whether this further reinstatement goes to the length of connubial intercourse depends on the circumstances, for there may be cases where it is enough to say that the wife has been received back into the position of wife in the home, though further intercourse has not taken place. But where it has taken place, this will, subject to one exception, amount to clear proof that the husband has carried his forgiveness into effect " (Lord Simon, L.C., in *Henderson* v. *Henderson and Crellin* [1944] A.C. 49, at p. 52).

The Royal Commission on Marriage and Divorce (1956), Cmd. 9678, para. 237, defines condonation: —

" An offence is condoned where the injured spouse, with knowledge of the material facts, forgives the other spouse and confirms that forgiveness by reinstatement in the matrimonial home . . . a matrimonial offence which has been condoned may be revived by the commission of a further matrimonial offence."

The various elements in these definitions or descriptions must now be considered.

A. Forgiveness

Although the word "forgiveness" is frequently used in describing condonation, and though in general that is what it amounts to, nevertheless the expression must be understood in a special sense.

1. *Words are not sufficient*

This is illustrated in the following cases: —

Crocker v. *Crocker* [1921] P. 25.—The wife committed adultery and the husband wrote a letter offering forgiveness on certain conditions. The wife accepted all the conditions and gave up her job in the expectation that her husband would take her back. He changed his mind and it was held that his letters plus the wife's acceptance were not sufficient.

Fearn v. *Fearn* [1948] P. 241.—A husband while on active service abroad received a letter from his wife admitting adultery. He wrote back saying he forgave her, and did not stop her marriage allowance. Later he changed his mind, stopped her allowance and took proceedings for divorce. The petition was dismissed on the ground of condonation but this was reversed on appeal by the Court of Appeal (Tucker, Bucknill and Cohen, L.JJ.). Bucknill, L.J., said at p. 250 (quoting Lord Chelmsford in *Keats* v. *Keats* (1859), 1 Sw. & Tr. 334, at p. 356): —

> " But words, however strong, can at the highest only be regarded as imperfect forgiveness, and, unless followed up by something which amounts to a reconciliation and of a reinstatement of the wife in the condition she was in before she transgressed, it must remain incomplete. . . ."

Hockaday v. *Goodenough* [1945] 2 All E.R. 335.—This was a case of a summons by a married woman claiming maintenance for her bastard child from the putative father. The latter's defence was that as the husband had condoned the adultery she was not a single woman within the meaning of the Bastardy Acts. The husband, who was serving as a soldier in India, had received a letter from his wife telling him that she was pregnant to another man, and he had written to a third party that it was easier to forgive than to forget but as he knew it was best for the children he would try and live it down and go on as if it had not happened. He did not write to his wife. It was held by the Court of Appeal (Mackinnon, L.J., Humphreys and Oliver, JJ.) that as the letter to a third party was only an expression of future intention, in the absence of evidence that he had not only forgiven his wife but reinstated her as his wife, there was no condonation.

2. *A binding legal agreement is sufficient*

This was established by *Rose* v. *Rose* (1883), 8 P.D. 98. A wife, in a deed for which there was monetary consideration, agreed that she would take no proceedings against her husband in respect of any complaint which had arisen before the deed. The husband had been guilty of cruelty. It was held by the Court of Appeal (Jessel, M.R., Baggalay and Lindley, L.JJ.) that subsequent adultery by the husband did not revive the wife's right to complain of cruelty committed before the deed in order to obtain a divorce.

It must be noted that the decision depended on the special words of the deed. The court decided that it was not against public policy to enter into such an agreement. Where, however, the deed provided for the compromise of proceedings by the wife on the ground of her husband's cruelty and it was agreed that on payment by the husband of a certain sum all further proceedings would be stayed, it was decided that as there was nothing in the deed about future proceedings, the husband's subsequent adultery revived the old cruelty (*Norman* v. *Norman* [1908] P. 6). In other words the deed had amounted to condonation but only conditional condonation.

Rose v. *Rose* was followed in *L.* v. *L.* [1931] P. 63, where the parties entered into a separation deed to compromise a suit for judicial separation alleging cruelty by the husband, and it was agreed that neither would sue the other for misconduct which had previously taken place, and such conduct was forgiven and condoned. Subsequently the wife brought proceedings on the ground of the husband's adultery since the deed, and the husband made a countercharge of adultery which had taken place before the deed. Lord Merrivale, P., held that the countercharge must fail, since the provision in the deed was binding and not against public policy.

In *Crocker* v. *Crocker*, *supra*, it was argued that, since the husband had made a conditional offer of condonation which had been accepted unreservedly by the wife, there was a binding agreement. Lord Sterndale, M.R., at [1921] P. 37, dealt with this argument by saying that the parties did not think they were entering into an agreement in the sense of making a binding contract, and that there was no consideration.

3. *Reinstatement*

The cases show that the guilty party must be reinstated as a wife or a husband, as the case may be. Lord Simon pointed this out in *Henderson* v. *Henderson and Crellin* [1944] A.C. 49 in the passage quoted on p. 296, *supra*. If a wife therefore stays on in the house with her guilty husband (or returns) as a housekeeper, that does not amount to reinstatement of the husband.

The Act of 1895 provided in cases of persistent cruelty that the wife had to show that she had been forced to live separate and apart from her husband, but this was repealed by the Act of 1925 and that is the position today under the Act of 1960. Section 7 of the 1960 Act provides that where an order is made while the parties are cohabiting it shall be suspended until cohabitation ceases. This plainly visualises that orders can be made while they are still cohabiting, at any rate in matrimonial offences other than desertion.

Denning, L.J., in *Mackrell* v. *Mackrell* [1948] 2 All E.R. 858 drew attention to the provisions under the old legislation as a reason for showing that the mere fact that the wife stays on in the house is not in itself condonation. It may be a fact from which condonation may be inferred, but in itself it is not conclusive. There must be reinstatement and reconciliation, by mutual consent.

In *Mackrell* v. *Mackrell* the wife had continued to live in the house after her husband had been cruel to her, and Hodson, J., held that this amounted to condonation, but he was reversed by the Court of Appeal.

That reconciliation and reinstatement involve mutuality was emphasised by the Divisional Court (Lord Merriman, P., and Pearce, J.) in *Cook* v. *Cook* [1949] 1 All E.R. 384, where a husband had lived in adultery with his mistress until she left him, and he then asked his wife to come and keep house for him, which she did for about three months, but she did not sleep with him or have intercourse. On an application by the wife for maintenance on the ground of her husband's adultery the magistrates held that her return amounted to condonation.

This was reversed by the Divisional Court.

In a previous case, *Wilmot* v. *Wilmot and Martin* [1948] 2 All E.R. 123, Willmer, J., had held that it was not necessary for the guilty party to consent to the condonation.

Denning, L.J., dissented from this view in *Mackrell* v. *Mackrell*, as also did both judges in *Cook* v. *Cook*. In the words of Pearce, J., at p. 388 :—

> " The words ' resumption of cohabitation' must mean resuming a state of things, that is to say, a setting up of a matrimonial home together, and that involves a bilateral intention on the part of both spouses so to do."

An example of reinstatement without the resumption of sexual intercourse is *Lawrence* v. *Lawrence and Cramner* [1946] W.N. 126. In 1938 the wife told the husband that she was pregnant to another man but if he commenced proceedings she would deny it. The husband did not take proceedings for divorce until 1946. According to the husband for four years before the confession the parties had not had intercourse and since that time they had slept in separate bedrooms and had no intercourse. The wife said they occupied the same bedroom and had intercourse at times. They had continued to live together until 1943. Barnard, J., said that even if the husband's account was true, sexual intercourse was only an element in condonation, and the husband had reinstated his wife to her previous position. They had continued to live on the same terms as before her confession and his forgiveness must be implied from his conduct.

In *Diplock* v. *Diplock* (1966), 109 Sol. J. 50, Sir J. Simon, P., held that the husband had reinstated the wife after her adultery although he had not had sexual intercourse with her after he had forgiven her.

In *Quinn* v. *Quinn* [1969] 3 All E.R. 1212, C.A., the husband had been cruel to his wife and she left him, but returned and had sexual intercourse with him. Later she left again and brought a petition on the ground of cruelty which the trial judge dismissed, holding that the husband's cruelty had been condoned. The Court of Appeal dismissed her appeal, holding that she had not proved she had not forgiven him and that s. 42 of the Act of 1965 did not apply as it had not been jointly agreed that resumption of cohabitation had been for a trial period.

Tynan v. *Tynan and Waldock and Good* [1969] 3 All E.R. 1472 was rather different. The wife separated from her husband and committed adultery, and he issued a petition for divorce on that ground. The wife returned on condition that the petition should be withdrawn, and although the husband took active steps to do this it was not in fact withdrawn. Intercourse was not resumed and after 4½ months they separated again and the husband went on with his petition. Wrangham, J., dismissed the petition on the ground that the wife's adultery had been condoned and s. 42 of the Act of 1965 made it plain that full reconciliation was not an essential constituent of condonation. Wrangham, J., quoted with approval from Rayden on Divorce, 10th ed., at p. 281: —

> " Condonation is the reinstatement in his or her former marital position of a spouse who has committed a matrimonial wrong of which all material facts are known to the other spouse with the intention of forgiving and remitting the wrong. . . ."

Marital intercourse is not essential to reinstatement, though it is good evidence of it. There has to be mutuality. This is illustrated by *Ford* v. *Ford and Stanford* [1970] 3 All E.R. 188 where the husband was an epileptic and had a crippled arm and leg and for the sake of his health had to have less frequent sexual intercourse. This ceased because the wife was offended, and she committed adultery and became pregnant and gave birth to a child. The husband offered to forgive her and accept the child as a child of the family, but the wife completely rejected the offer. When the husband petitioned for divorce the wife alleged condonation since they had lived together in the same house and she had performed domestic duties for her husband but there had been no sexual intercourse although they had slept in the same bed. Lane, J., held there had not been condonation since, although the husband was willing to forgive, the wife had not been willing to be forgiven. There had been no real resumption of cohabitation. He had continued to accept wifely duties and had slept in the same bed because he had been unable to see a way out of his difficulties which another abler man would have been able to find.

4. *Resumption of sexual intercourse*

(a) *Where the husband is the innocent party*

The rule here was clear, and quite arbitrary until 31st July, 1963. If a husband had sexual intercourse with his wife with full knowledge of her offence, then that was conclusive evidence of condonation (*Henderson* v. *Henderson and Crellin* [1944] A.C. 49). In this case the wife, who had committed adultery, promised her husband she would break off all acquaintance with the co-respondent. Intercourse then took place, but the next morning she changed her mind and said she saw no reason why she should not see the co-respondent. The House of Lords held that the adultery was condoned, and that a breach of assurance as to future conduct did not matter, since there was no such thing as contingent condonation. Obviously, the question of forgiveness has no place here.

This decision followed that of McCardie, J., in *Cramp* v. *Cramp and Freeman* [1920] P. 158 and confirmed in effect the words of Sir Cresswell Cresswell in *Keats* v. *Keats and Montezuma* (1859), 1 Sw. & Tr. 334, at p. 347, when he said: —

> " If the husband, knowing that his wife had been guilty of adultery, takes her to his bed again, he clearly being his own master in that particular, and quite able to choose for himself, if he is so regardless of the wrong done to him as to take her back again, it is always held that this is such a proof of condonation, that it cannot be got over."

It is for this reason that McCardie, J., thought that condonation was not forgiveness in the ordinary sense at all, but a conditional waiver of the right of the injured spouse to take matrimonial proceedings.

An example of the strictness of the rule was *Willan* v. *Willan* [1960] 1 W.L.R. 624, which was a case of cruelty by the wife. Part of the cruelty was the wife's insistence on sexual intercourse and if the husband did not comply she kicked and bit him. His health became affected and he decided to leave her. On the last night they slept together, the same acts occurred and in order to appease her he had intercourse with her, and he left the next day. This act of intercourse was held to have condoned her cruelty since it was a voluntary act.

There was one exception to this rule, namely, that if the intercourse was induced by a fraudulent misstatement of fact by the wife, that circumstance will have the effect of preventing the intercourse amounting to condonation. Thus in *Roberts* v. *Roberts and Temple* (1917), 117 L.T. 157, where a wife had admitted adultery, but had denied in answer to her husband's question that she was pregnant in consequence, knowing that her answer was untrue, and she had lied to induce him to blot out the offence, Hill, J., held that as the husband had been induced to have intercourse by fraud, it did not amount to condonation. This case was cited with approval by Lord Simon in *Henderson* v. *Henderson and Crellin* [1944] A.C. 49, at p. 52.

In 1963 the rule in *Henderson's* case was altered by statute, namely s. 1 of the Matrimonial Causes Act, 1963, which has now been repealed and re-enacted by s. 42 (1) of the Matrimonial Causes Act, 1965, which provides:

> " Any presumption of condonation which arises from the continuance or resumption of marital intercourse may be rebutted by evidence sufficient to negative the necessary intent."

In *Blyth* v. *Blyth* [1965] P. 411, C.A., the wife left the husband for a few months and cohabited with the co-respondent. Shortly afterwards the husband and wife met by chance and sexual intercourse took place. The husband petitioned for divorce. His petition was dismissed, and so was his appeal, in spite of s. 1 of the Act of 1963, the Court of Appeal holding that it had not been proved beyond reasonable doubt that the husband had not condoned his wife's adultery.

(b) Where the wife is the innocent party

When the wife is the innocent party, intercourse by her with knowledge of her husband's guilt is not conclusive evidence of condonation. Sir Cresswell Cresswell's words in *Keats* v. *Keats and Montezuma* (1859), 1 Sw. & Tr. 334, at p. 347, have often been approved: —

> " With reference to a wife, to whom a knowledge of her husband's adultery had been brought home, and who has yet continued to share his bed, the rule has not been so strict. The wife is hardly her own mistress; she may not have the option of going away; she may have no place to go to; no person to receive her; no funds to support her; therefore her submission to the embraces of her husband is not considered by any means such strong proof of condonation as the act of a husband in renewing his intercourse with his wife."

Much depends on the individual facts of each case, and it is possible for one act of intercourse by an innocent wife to condone her husband's conduct. Such was the case in *Baguley* v. *Baguley* [1962] P. 59n,* where the husband had been cruel and the wife petitioned for divorce on that ground. Eventually the parties met at a solicitor's office and agreed to become reconciled and a day or two later had intercourse. The husband failed to get a house and the wife resumed the proceedings. The petition was dismissed

---

* This case was heard in October, 1957.

on the ground that the husband's cruelty had been condoned, and
this was upheld by the Court of Appeal. Hodson, L.J., said at
p. 65: —

" The authorities . . . have consistently proceeded on the basis
that the law of condonation is the same for the wife as for the
husband in that sense—namely, that, if she has reinstated him
by submitting voluntarily to his embraces without any
extraneous circumstance weighing against the inference to be
drawn from that submission, she must be held to have
condoned the offence."

Lord Merriman, P., in *Morley* v. *Morley* [1961] 1 W.L.R.
211 said he knew of no authority for this proposition, and indeed
it goes further than any reported case. The Court of Appeal in
Baguley v. *Baguley* recognised that there had to be reconciliation
and reinstatement for condonation, and that the rule was less strict
as regards sexual intercourse where the wife was an innocent
party, but they held there had been a reconciliation at the
solicitor's office and that her voluntary intercourse amounted to
reinstatement. In *Morley's* case the wife had summoned her
husband for persistent cruelty and the hearing before the magistrates was adjourned to see if a reconciliation could be effected.
The parties were in the fairground business and the wife visited her
husband in his caravan to discuss reconciliation and she agreed to
return provided the husband did not hit her again, and that he
travelled in the south of England away from his parents. She
rejoined him and intercourse took place, but on his refusing to
leave the north of England she left him. The magistrates found
there was no condonation, and this was upheld by the Divisional
Court, which held that there was no condonation since the husband
had repudiated the agreement and further that the acts of sexual
intercourse were an attempt towards reconciliation and did not
constitute a reinstatement by her. The Divisional Court found it
hard to reconcile the reasoning in *Baguley* v. *Baguley* with that in
Mackrell v. *Mackrell* [1948] 2 All E.R. 858.

In *Coates* v. *Coates* (1961), *The Times*, 12th October, and see
105 Sol. J. 886 (C.A.), the wife petitioned for a judicial separation
on the ground of her husband's cruelty. The last instance of cruelty
was 5th January, 1958, but she had continued to live with him
for the next four weeks, living a normal married life, sharing a
bed with him, and having sexual intercourse. Then she left without

telling him where she was going. Holroyd Pearce, L.J., said that the question was—Had the wife reinstated the husband? To answer that question her conduct and words must be looked at. The husband had no reason to believe anything other than that he and his wife were reconciled. As far as he was concerned he was fully reinstated. The wife must either show that the question of reinstatement was under discussion, and not decided, or that for some good reason, connected with her status of wife, she had not been able to make the break immediately. Such reasons could be the necessity for making arrangements to leave, that she had nowhere to go, that there were financial reasons for delaying, or that she had to make arrangements for the children, and so on. A wife must be presumed to intend the reasonable consequences of her behaviour towards her husband. If, over a period, she deceived her husband by conduct consistent only with condonation when there were no difficulties in the way of her departure, she could not then claim that in her heart she never forgave her husband and that she was not bound by the natural conclusion to be drawn from her conduct.

(c) *Attempts at reconciliation*

Section 42 (2) of the Matrimonial Causes Act, 1965, provides as follows:

> " For the purposes of the Matrimonial Proceedings (Magistrates' Courts) Act 1960 adultery or cruelty shall not be deemed to have been condoned by reason only of a continuation or resumption of cohabitation between the parties for one period not exceeding three months, or of anything done during such cohabitation, if it is proved that cohabitation was continued or resumed, as the case may be, with a view to effect a reconciliation."

This subsection replaces s. 2 (1) of the Matrimonial Causes Act, 1963. Section 2 (1) of the Act of 1963 was considered in the Court of Appeal in *Herridge* v. *Herridge* [1966] 1 All E.R. 93, and this decision applies of course equally to s. 42 (2), *supra*. The facts were that the wife left her husband on the ground of his cruelty. Three months later she returned with a view to a reconciliation. One month later she left him for good. She petitioned for divorce but this was dismissed. The judge's attention had not been drawn to the Act of 1963. The appeal was allowed. Willmer, L.J., said, at p. 95:—

" The subsection, of course, applies only to a continuation or resumption of cohabitation with a view to effecting a reconciliation. Where a continuation or resumption takes place in fulfilment of a reconciliation which has already been achieved, there the section has no application. That was the subject of actual decision by the learned President himself in *Brown* v. *Brown* [1964] 2 All E.R. 828. . . . Quite clearly the burden of proof lies fairly and squarely on the wife to prove that the cohabitation was resumed with a view to effecting a reconciliation."

5. *Knowledge*

Knowledge of the other spouse's guilt is an essential element in condonation. There must be " full knowledge of all the material facts " (*Tilley* v. *Tilley* [1949] P. 240, at p. 261, per Denning, L.J.; similar expressions may be found in *Henderson* v. *Henderson and Crellin* [1944] A.C. 49, *Bernstein* v. *Bernstein* [1893] P. 292 and *Cramp* v. *Cramp and Freeman* [1920] P. 158). The only exception is that stated by Sir Cresswell Cresswell in *Keats* v. *Keats and Montezuma* (1859), 1 Sw. & Tr. 334, at p. 346, where the spouse says " I care not whether it be true or false; I do not know whether it is true or not; but be it one or be it the other, I would equally take her back to my bed."

It has long been recognised that mere suspicion of guilt is an insufficient basis for condonation (*D'Aguilar* v. *D'Aguilar* (1794), 1 Hagg. Eccl. 773, 786; *Elwes* v. *Elwes* (1794), 1 Hagg. Con. 269, 292, 293).

What amounts to knowledge, as distinguished from belief, was considered by Sachs, J., in *Burch* v. *Burch* [1958] 1 W.L.R. 480. The facts were these. In January, 1945, the husband spent his embarkation leave with his wife and then went abroad. The next month the wife wrote that she was pregnant and a little later mentioned an association with an American soldier. She gave birth to a child in October, 1945, and no question was raised as to its legitimacy. The husband was, however, suspicious. He suppressed his suspicions and resumed normal marital relations with his wife when he returned in February, 1946. This continued to 1952, and until 1956 they lived together but without having sexual intercourse. The wife then discovered that the husband was associating with another woman, and in the discussion which followed, she admitted that she had had one act of intercourse with a Canadian in January, 1945. The husband at once left her and petitioned for divorce.

Sachs, J., said that "knowledge" of the matrimonial offence in condonation cases covers a number of constituent elements. These are (a) the foundation on which the alleged knowledge rests, (b) whether the spouse believes, or must be taken to believe, that which is alleged to be known, and (c) what are the material facts which must be known to be known.

His view was that: —

(a) The foundation must be credible evidence, i.e., such as would prove his case in a court of law;

(b) belief is generally an essential ingredient in the knowledge required for condonation, but belief itself does not constitute such knowledge;

(c) material facts are those which would be so regarded by a reasonable man, and any fact is material which the offending party knows would be so regarded by the innocent spouse.

6. Belief

That belief is essential in addition to knowledge is shown by *Ellis* v. *Ellis and Smith* (1865), 4 Sw. & Tr. 154. In November, 1861, the parties were living separately and the wife was living with her sister, Mrs. Naylor. Mr. Naylor brought an action in the county court against the husband for maintenance, presumably on the ground that he was supplying the wife with necessaries. The husband pleaded that the wife had committed adultery with the co-respondent, but this defence failed. The wife did not give evidence. After the trial there was a meeting between the husband, wife, Mr. and Mrs. Naylor and a Mr. Colvin at which the husband said he did not believe his wife was guilty of adultery, and that the witness against her had given evidence out of spite. The parties became reconciled and lived togther for a few weeks. In December, 1861, the wife left on account of the husband's ill usage, and he was then twice taken before the magistrates on the charge of deserting her.* He again alleged adultery but was ordered to contribute to her support. In 1863 the husband petitioned for divorce on the ground of adultery as previously alleged. The Judge Ordinary, after holding that adultery had been proved, said at p. 157: —

" . . . it is necessary to prove that the husband took the wife back with the intention of forgiving her, believing her to be guilty. [Quoted with approval by McCardie, J., in *Cramp* v. *Cramp* [1920] P. 158, at p. 162.] If the evidence leads the court to the conclusion that the husband did not thoroughly believe that his wife was guilty and therefore did not forgive her when he took her back, condonation is not established. . . . Both Mrs. Naylor and Colvin agree that he said he did not believe that adultery had been committed and he thought that Mrs. Evans had made the charge against her out of spite. The evidence of condonation falls short in this respect."

The husband had indeed good grounds for his belief since a court of competent jurisdiction had dismissed the charge of adultery. See also *Sneyd* v. *Sneyd and Burgess* [1926] P. 27. A man cannot be said not to believe when on the facts an intelligent man must believe.

7. Material facts

The following are examples of facts that may or may not be material: —

(1) It is material if the guilty spouse continues to associate with the other party to the adultery, for it is a fact " which might reasonably be expected to weigh with a reasonable spouse in deciding whether to forgive the other the offence " (per Denning, L.J., in *Tilley* v. *Tilley* [1949] P. 240, at p. 262).

(2) If a wife admits adultery with *A*, and conceals her adultery with *B*, that is a material fact (*Burch* v. *Burch* [1958] 1 W.L.R. 480).

(3) So is the identity of the man (*Burch* v. *Burch, supra*).

(4) But if a wife admits adultery with a certain man but does

---

* At this date courts of summary jurisdiction had no power to hear a complaint by a wife on the ground of her husband's desertion. The report does not state the nature of the proceedings but they were probably taken under the Vagrancy Act, 1824, s. 3 (see *Stopher* v. *National Assistance Board* [1955] 1 Q.B. 486, and particularly the judgment of Goddard, C.J., at p. 494).

not disclose all the occasions when adultery was committed, that is not material (per Lord Goddard, C.J., in *Wells* v. *Wells* [1954] 1 W.L.R. 1390, at p. 1393).

B. Revival

Section 42 (3) of the Matrimonial Causes Act, 1965, provides:

" Adultery which has been condoned shall not be capable of being revived."

Apart from adultery, the offence condoned will be revived if subsequently the guilty party offends again by committing another matrimonial offence. In effect the guilty party is on probation, and is expected to treat the other with " conjugal kindness " (per Sir John Nicholl in *Durant* v. *Durant* (1825), 1 Hagg. Eccl. 733, at p. 762). See *Kemp* v. *Kemp* [1961] 1 W.L.R. 1030, at p. 1032.

The matter has been expressed lucidly by Sir Francis Jeune, P., in *Houghton* v. *Houghton* [1903] P. 150, at p. 152: —

" The principle is as clear as possible. When the law speaks of condonation and revival, it means that the offence is condoned on the condition that there shall be in the future a proper compliance with the matrimonial decencies and duties, and a person who goes back to live with his or her guilty spouse goes back on that implied condition alone."

1. *Matrimonial offence*

What is meant by " matrimonial offence " in this connection? It has been decided that the meaning, for this purpose, has to be considered broadly. A very extensive review of the cases was made by Scott, L.J., in *Beard* v. *Beard* [1946] P. 8 (C.A.), which decided that desertion only for a short period was sufficient to revive condoned adultery. Scott, L.J., said at p. 22: —

" A ' matrimonial ' or ' marital offence within the cognizance of the divorce court ' in my opinion simply means conduct which in the eye of that court is wrong, whether it does or does not reach the duration, or gravity, or completeness which is necessary to permit of a decree, provided always that it be sufficiently serious for the court to regard it as a substantial breach of duty."

The matter was further explored in *Richardson* v. *Richardson* [1950] P. 16, where the husband's adultery had been condoned and subsequently he had been selfish and inconsiderate and had made hurtful remarks to his wife, but the trial judge did not find his conduct had been responsible for the break-up of the marriage. The Court of Appeal refused to hold that the condoned adultery had been revived. Bucknill, L.J., said that if an offence had been condoned for a number of years it would not be revived if the husband had on one occasion slapped his wife's face, or come home drunk. The test was whether his conduct had been such as to make decent married life of the spouses impossible. Denning, L.J., said that conduct short of cruelty will revive condoned adultery, if it consists of harshness or neglect of a real and substantial kind which is such as to be likely to inflict misery on the innocent party and does indeed lead to a breakdown of the marriage.

In *Roe* v. *Roe* [1956] 1 W.L.R. 1380 the wife left the husband on account of his cruelty. He then admitted adultery over five years and begged his wife to return, which she did. The husband thereupon adopted towards her a course of callous indifference and taciturnity, refused sexual intercourse and stayed out late at night without explanation. After three weeks she left. The Divisional Court (Lord Merriman, P., and Collingwood, J.) held that if the adultery had been condoned then his conduct had revived it. Collingwood, J., at p. 1385, said: —

> ". . . the more serious the original offence, the less grave need be the subsequent act to revive it: *Cooper* v. *Cooper* [1950] W.N. 200 and Lord Merriman in *Jamieson* v. *Jamieson* [1952] A.C. 525, at p. 546."

The Court of Appeal considered the question of revival in *Jelley* v. *Jelley* [1964] 1 W.L.R. 1035. This was a case of condoned adultery committed by the husband. Fifteen years later the wife petitioned for divorce on the ground of cruelty but she also alleged that the husband's conduct had revived the old adultery. The commissioner who tried the case rejected the allegation of cruelty, and he also decided that the conduct was not sufficient to revive the adultery, particularly having regard to the lapse of time. The appeal was dismissed. The court held that condonation being conditional, if it was sought to allege revival of a condoned offence by matters amounting to less than a matrimonial offence, they must be such as in fact to break up the marriage and make matrimonial life impossible, and where the lapse of time after condonation was very great it was all the harder to show that conduct less than a matrimonial offence was sufficiently serious to revive the condoned offence.

The Court of Appeal (Willmer, Donovan and Davies, L.JJ.) in *Lewis* v. *Lewis* (1962), 106 Sol. J. 409, upheld the finding of a divorce commissioner that conjugal unkindness revived condoned cruelty. The unkindness referred to was sulking and refusing to speak. The court referred to *Bertram* v. *Bertram* [1944] P. 59, which decided that very little conjugal unkindness was required to revive condoned cruelty.

When an offence is revived, it is revived for all purposes, so that where adultery by a wife which had been condoned had been revived by her subsequent desertion, it mattered not that she had made an offer to return. That could not cancel the desertion, for the purpose of blotting out again the original offence (*Lloyd* v. *Lloyd and Hill* [1947] P. 89).

A Divisional Court in *Dunn* v. *Dunn* [1962] 1 W.L.R. 1480, held that wilful neglect to maintain was a matrimonial wrong sufficient to revive condoned cruelty.

In *H* v. *H* (1964), 108 Sol. J. 544, Wrangham, J., held that condoned cruelty was revived by the husband's conjugal unkindness, which consisted in telling his pregnant younger daughter to leave, as this substantially contributed to the breakdown of the marriage. Similarly the Court of Appeal in *Arthur* v. *Arthur* (1964), 108 Sol. J. 317, held that physical cruelty which had been condoned was revived by subsequent conjugal unkindness.

2. *Absolute condonation*

Up to 31st July, 1963, adultery which had been condoned was capable of revival, but condonation of that offence since that date is absolute (s. 42 (3) of the Matrimonial Causes Act, 1965). This section (originally enacted as s. 3 of the Matrimonial Causes Act, 1963) is not retrospective (*Carson* v. *Carson and Stoyek* [1964] 1 W.L.R. 511).

There are other examples of absolute condonation. For instance, this can be done by agreement of the parties (see *Rose* v. *Rose*, p. 297, *supra*).

It may also occur by the passage of time. In *Beale* v. *Beale* [1951] P. 48 (C.A.), where the cruelty had taken place fifteen years before the incidents which were relied on to revive the offence, and during this time the parties had lived a normal life, it was held that the cruelty was not revived. Denning, L.J., said, at p. 49: —

> " The probationary period does not, however, necessarily last for life, and a point may be reached where the guilty party has, by his good behaviour, proved himself worthy of the trust and confidence of the other. The further that past offences recede into the distance, so much the more does it become difficult to revive them, until the time may come when the proper inference is that the forgiveness is no longer conditional, but has become absolute."

This must now be read in the light of *Jelley* v. *Jelley* [1964] 1 W.L.R. 1035, at p. 1038 (see p. 310).

An example of condonation by the passage of time is *Hearn* v. *Hearn* [1969] 3 All E.R. 417, where the wife had committed adultery and the parties resumed cohabitation but without sexual intercourse and this state of affairs continued for ten years. When the husband left home the wife issued summonses on the grounds of desertion and wilful neglect to maintain. The justices were not satisfied that her adultery had been condoned, but on appeal the Divisional Court held that where cohabitation had continued for ten years the inference of condonation was almost irresistible; that affection was not a necessary element in either forgiveness or reinstatement; that the motive for the resumption of cohabitation (other than reconciliation within s. 42 of the Matrimonial Causes Act, 1965) was irrelevant; and on the facts the only reasonable inference was that the wife's adultery had been condoned.

Just as conduct cannot be considered as cruel if it is not resented at the time, neither can such conduct be sufficient to revive a condoned offence. In *Benton* v. *Benton* [1958] P. 12 a husband had condoned his wife's cruelty by having sexual intercourse with her. He petitioned for divorce on the ground of her cruelty, and in a cross-petition she made unfounded charges of sodomy against him in the pleadings. The Court of Appeal held that the charges were of such a serious nature that they constituted conduct which was capable of reviving antecedent cruelty, even though the charges were made only in the pleadings. However, as the husband had not in that case resented these charges, they did not revive the condoned cruelty.

C. Proof of condonation

Condonation, by evidence of intercourse, sworn to by a respondent wife, does not as a matter of law require corroboration, but the allegation is so easy to make, and so difficult for the husband to refute, that commonsense requires that in the ordinary way the wife's word should be corroborated in a material particular. A judge, however, is entitled to act without corroboration, if he is satisfied on the wife's evidence alone that intercourse has taken place (per Denning, L.J., in *Tilley* v. *Tilley* [1949] P. 240, at p. 261).

He also dealt with the onus of proof. He said that there is a presumption against condonation, but only a provisional one. This may be displaced by evidence which raises a provisional presumption that there has been condonation. Then the petitioner has to take steps to displace it, seeing that the court at the end of the case has to ask itself: Has the legal burden been discharged? Am I satisfied that there has been no condonation?

In divorce petitions the court formerly had to be satisfied that there had been no condonation (s. 5 (3) (*a*) of the Matrimonial Causes Act, 1965), and therefore, if the evidence was so evenly balanced that the court could come to no definite conclusion about it, it could not be said to be satisfied and would have to dismiss the petition (per Bucknill, L.J., in *Tilley* v. *Tilley*, at p. 253). For the present position in the divorce court, see Matrimonial Causes Act, 1973, s. 2.

This reasoning would apply in the magistrates' court, since the court still has to be satisfied that there has been no condonation (s. 2 (3) of the Act of 1960).

III. CONNIVANCE

While connivance has not yet been precisely or comprehensively defined, it may be said to occur when one spouse consents to the adultery of the other spouse, or corruptly and intentionally permits it.

The leading case in modern times is *Churchman* v. *Churchman* [1945] P. 44 (C.A.), where Lord Merriman, P., giving the judgment of the court, said at p. 52: —

" In our opinion, it is of the utmost importance to bear in mind that the issue is whether, on the facts of the particular case, the husband was or was not guilty of the corrupt intention of promoting or encouraging either the initiation or the continuance of the wife's adultery. . . ."

A. Presumption against connivance

In *Churchman* v. *Churchman* the facts were these. The wife, who before her marriage had been mistress both to her husband and the co-respondent, had two months after her marriage gone to live with the co-respondent. The husband sought to make the co-respondent pay a large sum in damages, little or no insistence being laid on the cessation of the adulterous intercourse. The co-respondent refused to pay and the husband petitioned for divorce, but the petition was dismissed by Denning, J., on the ground that the husband had not proved that he had not connived at the adultery. As to this Lord Merriman said, at p. 51: —

"Connivance implies that the husband has been accessory to the very offence on which his petition is founded, or at least has corruptly acquiesced in its commission, and the presumption of law has always been against connivance."

See also *Douglas* v. *Douglas* [1951] P. 85.

B. Should precede the event

Lord Merriman also dealt with this in *Churchman* v. *Churchman*, and at p. 50 he said: —

". . . it is of the essence of connivance that it precedes the event and, generally speaking, the material event is the inception of the adultery and not its repetition, although the facts may be such that connivance at the continuance of an adulterous association shows that the husband must be taken to have connived at it from the first."

This, he said, was illustrated by *Gipps* v. *Gipps* (1864), 11 H.L. Cas. 1, the facts of which bore some resemblance to *Churchman* v. *Churchman*. In *Gipps* v. *Gipps* the husband, having accepted £3,000 in lieu of damages for adultery, sought to make the co-respondent pay a further £4,000 to withdraw divorce proceedings, upon an engagement not to complain of the acts of the wife, when he well knew that his wife was in such a situation that she was bound to continue her adulterous association with the co-respondent. When later the husband brought divorce proceedings he was held to have connived at her adultery.

Lord Chelmsford, at p. 28, said: —

> " It is the first act which constitutes the crime, and though
> the adulterous intercourse between the parties should con-
> tinue for years, there is not a fresh adultery upon every
> repetition of the guilty acts, although all and each of them
> may furnish proof of the adultery itself."

Denning, L.J., after quoting this passage in *Douglas* v. *Douglas*
[1951] P. 85, at p. 96, said that the first act of adultery marks a
turning point in the relationship of the guilty pair. They have,
as it were, crossed the Rubicon, they have passed the point of no
return, and as Denning, L.J., said, repetition then becomes easy
and likely. Therefore, in considering connivance, the conduct of
the spouse complaining of adultery is much more important before
the first act of adultery, rather than after adultery has been
discovered, and is repeated.

C. Volenti non fit injuria

This maxim is frequently referred to in cases on connivance.
" The rule is *volenti non fit injuria*; that is the true principle "
(Lord Stowell in *Moorsom* v. *Moorsom* (1792), 3 Hagg. Eccl.
87, at p. 107). " Did he so behave himself as to give willing
consent to the act? " (Sir Cresswell Cresswell, J.O., in *Marris* v.
Marris (1862), 2 Sw. & Tr. 530, at p. 543, and to the same effect
in *Glennie* v. *Glennie* (1862), 32 L.J.P.M. & A. 17, at p. 20).

In *Douglas* v. *Douglas* [1951] P. 85, at p. 96, Denning, L.J.,
said: —

> " The principle on which connivance is founded is *volenti
> non fit injuria*. . . . *Volenti* is very different from *scienti*. It is
> not the knowledge of what may occur which bars a husband
> from complaining. It is his consent to it. A husband cannot
> complain of his wife's adultery if he has, therefore, by his
> words or conduct, consented to it taking place. But the consent
> to be a bar, must be a consent to the inception of the
> adultery."

A good example of consent is *Gorst* v. *Gorst* [1952] P. 94, where
a husband who was experiencing sexual difficulties with his wife
suggested to her (she being a doctor) that he might be cured if he
had sexual intercourse with a named woman. To this the wife
vehemently objected, but later she agreed that he could commit
adultery but not with the woman mentioned. He did so, and

later told her falsely that the adultery had ceased, and the wife condoned the adultery. Later he admitted that the adultery was with the woman mentioned, and that it had continued. Karminski, J., held that the wife's consent amounted to connivance, even though the adultery was with the woman she had excluded, and even though the motive was to cure him.

D. Clean hands

Another maxim which the judges refer to in this class of case is that the complainant must come into court with clean hands. In other words it would be intolerable for a spouse to complain of the adultery of the other if he himself is implicated and responsible even partly. Lord Stowell in *Lovering* v. *Lovering* (1792), 3 Hagg. Eccl. 85, said at p. 87: —

> "The ecclesiastical court requires two things—that a man shall come with pure hands himself, and shall have exacted a due purity on the part of his wife. . . ."

So that if a man consents to his wife committing adultery with *A* he has also connived at adultery she commits with *B*.

Tucker, L.J., in *Woodbury* v. *Woodbury* [1949] P. 154 (C.A.), at p. 165, said: —

> "The doctrine of connivance is based on the principle that the complaining spouse must come to the court with clean hands and it would be unconscionable to give relief to one who had been willingly blind to, or had encouraged, the adultery of his or her matrimonial partner."

This case also illustrates that the conduct of the parties must be looked at as a whole.

The wife discovered that her husband had been carrying on an adulterous association with the governess of her small child. While still affected by the deep shock she sustained she wrote both to the governess and her husband, in effect that they could continue as friends and lovers but the governess would have no share in the child. The wife began divorce proceedings but these were withdrawn and she became reconciled with her husband. Later the husband resumed his adulterous association with the same woman. The wife again petitioned for divorce and the husband in defence pleaded connivance. The Court of Appeal held that if the letters were taken by themselves they would have amounted to connivance, but in view of the surrounding circumstances, and the conduct of the parties as a whole, connivance had not been proved.

A husband who did not know of the inception of his wife's adultery with their lodger, and did not know it was going on for a long time after, but when he did know was wilfully blind to it, was held by the Court of Appeal to have connived at it (*Rumbelow* v. *Rumbelow* [1965] P. 207).

E. Corrupt intention—to prove or promote adultery?

If the object of the complaining spouse is to cause or permit the other's adultery, this is a corrupt intention on his part, but if the object is merely to prove adultery which is suspected then it is not corrupt and is not connivance. If the object is a mixed one, to promote and to prove adultery, then it will amount to connivance, since the element of promotion taints the whole conduct. "Connivance must have an element of criminality" (Horridge, J., in *Dotzauer* v. *Dotzauer* (1925), 41 T.L.R. 289, at p. 291).

A great many divorce cases based on adultery, and also proceedings in the magistrates' courts, where adultery is alleged, are proved by private detectives, who give evidence of confessions or of observations they have kept on the suspected parties. It was argued in *Mudge* v. *Mudge and Honeysett* [1950] P. 173 that a husband who watched his wife and the co-respondent through a ground floor window, while he was accompanied by detectives, was guilty of connivance. This was rejected by Hodson, J., who said at p. 177: —

> "But if I were to hold that a man was guilty of connivance who acted as the husband did here—who watched his wife to see whether his suspicions were founded or unfounded and, if founded, were well founded, I should be driven into the position of doing what so far has never been done in this country—that is, rejecting the petitions of those who, if not doing the watching themselves, have employed others to do this kind of work for them."

If, however, the agent arranges the adultery, this would be connivance, even if the agent had no instructions to do so, or indeed was given positive instructions to do no such thing (*Gower* v. *Gower* (1872), L.R. 2 P. & D. 428, followed in *Bell* v. *Bell* (1889), 58 L.J.P. 54, where a solicitor's clerk employed by the wife, without instructions to do so, induced the husband to commit adultery).

See also *Picken* v. *Picken and Simmonds* (1864), 34 L.J.P.M. & A. 22, and *Sugg* v. *Sugg and Moore* (1861), 31 L.J.P.M. & A. 41.

Two cases, one on either side of the line, illustrate when conduct promotes, or merely proves adultery.

In *Manning* v. *Manning* [1950] 1 All E.R. 602 (C.A.) Mr. and Mrs. *M*. became friendly with Mr. and Mrs. *F*. Mrs. *M*., realising that she was falling in love with *F*., requested her husband to terminate the association between the two couples but he refused to take any steps in the matter and allowed *F*. to visit his house and left him alone with his wife. *M*. set up a microphone in his sitting room and listened from his garage with Mrs. *F*. On one occasion they heard a conversation suggesting that adultery was likely to take place. They arranged to leave them alone, and then caught them in the act. Up to that time *M*. and Mrs. *F*. lulled their spouses into a sense of security and continued to have sexual intercourse and did not mention their suspicions. Both *M*. and Mrs. *F*. brought petitions for divorce which were dismissed by Willmer, J., on the ground of connivance.

It was argued that the complaining spouses were merely trying to get proof of adultery, but all the judges thought that they had done much more than this, and by their conduct had taken part in promoting and encouraging the adultery, even though they had consulted a solicitor before arranging their trap.

This decision was relied upon by the commissioner who tried *Douglas* v. *Douglas* [1951] P. 85 when he reluctantly dismissed a husband's petition on the ground of his connivance. The Court of Appeal, however, reversed this decision and distinguished *Manning* v. *Manning*.

The husband, a licensee, worked in the bar and his wife in the kitchen. Suspecting his wife of committing adultery with the co-respondent, he adjusted the speaking apparatus between the bar and the kitchen, so that he could overhear what was said in the kitchen. His suspicions having been confirmed by what he saw and heard, he instructed solicitors and through them enquiry agents and at their suggestion absented himself, letting his wife know beforehand. While he was away his agents caught the wife in the act of adultery with the co-respondent. The husband, who was most upset on getting their report, then brought his petition.

It is probable that in *Manning* v. *Manning* no adultery had taken place before the parties were caught out, whereas in *Douglas* v. *Douglas* it was a fair inference that it had been going on some time.

Bucknill, L.J., at p. 93, said: —

> "The application of the law as laid down in *Churchman* v. *Churchman* [1945] P. 44, to particular facts may well raise difficult problems. In the present case, as it seems to me, the husband was not intending to encourage or promote an adulterous association but seeking proof of what, from Christmas, he rightly believed to exist. In every case in which a husband who believes his wife is committing adultery has her watched, it can be said that if he had warned her she was going to be watched, no act of adultery would have taken place on that occasion. It would absurd to suggest that this in itself amounted to connivance: see *Mudge* v. *Mudge* [1950] P.173."

He distinguished *Manning* v. *Manning* because in that case the petitioners were anxious for the adultery to take place, whereas in *Douglas* v. *Douglas* the petitioner regarded it as the end of his world.

Denning, L.J., pointed out at p. 97 that it had never been held to be connivance where the husband's agents had watched a wife, without warning, and the reason it was not, was because for connivance it was essential there should be a corrupt intention. "He is seeking to discover the offence, not to promote or encourage it. Some people may think it discreditable of him to spy on her, but on balance it is more to the good of the community that he should be at liberty to find out her guilt by keeping watch, rather than that she should escape with impunity." He quoted from Sanchez, *de Matrimonio* (1694), lib. 10, disp. 12, No. 52: —

> "Gamekeepers, who absent themselves in order that poachers may come freely and take game are to be punished; but if they do so in order that the poachers may return and be caught, they should be excused. So also a husband cannot complain of adultery which his wife commits with his knowledge and approval; but that is not so when his dissimulation is not by way of consent but in order to gain proof of her adultery."

Where two husbands and wives regularly changed partners, the Court of Appeal held that this amounted to connivance: *Hart Porter* v. *Hart Porter* (1962), *Current Law*, May, para. 363; (1962), *The Guardian*, 3rd May.

In *Bowden* v. *Bowden and Tabner* (1964), 108 Sol. J. 99, the husband petitioned for divorce on the ground of his wife's adultery. He had raised no objection to her becoming the dancing partner of another man, to whom he had said that ballroom dancers should eat, drink and sleep together and think alike. Hewson, J., held that he had connived at the adultery, and refused a decree.

F. Agreements

The words of a separation agreement may amount to connivance. The words must be clear and unambiguous and if they can be construed to have an innocent meaning that meaning will prevail. In *Studdy* v. *Studdy* (1858), 1 Sw. & Tr. 321, the last clause of a separation agreement was to the effect that if the wife did not fulfil her part of the agreement the husband should have the full power of a husband over her whatever his way of living might be. When later the wife petitioned for divorce and alleged adultery the husband pleaded connivance, relying on this clause. The Judge Ordinary said that the clause could be construed innocently. It might refer to the place where he was living, and the mode in which he chose to live, whether in a permanent residence or moving from place to place, and it was unnecessary to resort to the supposition of an immoral contract. He therefore held that there was no connivance.

Nevertheless, if the words of the agreement mean that the wife was consenting to the husband living with another woman that amounts to connivance (*Ross* v. *Ross* (1869), L.R. 1 P. & D. 734; in that case, where the wife suspected but did not know that the husband was living with another woman, the parties entered into a separation agreement, but the court held there was no connivance because there was no provision whatever with regard to the contemplated future life of the husband, and the Judge Ordinary went on to say that the court should not find connivance unless it sees its way very clearly to the conclusion that it was the intention of the parties to connive).

Greenwood v. *Greenwood* [1937] P. 157 was a case where connivance was found. A wife petitioned for divorce on the ground of adultery, but the suit was compromised on payment of an increased allowance. There was a further deed for an increased allowance with mutual condonation of all past offences. The wife knew that her husband was continuing to live with another woman and did not care. Langton, J., relying on *Thomas* v. *Thomas* (1860), 2 Sw. & Tr. 113, where the deed had recited that the husband was living in adultery, held there was connivance.

A separation agreement authorising an adulterous wife to live with whom she liked was held by Lord Merrivale, P., not to amount to connivance as the husband entered into the agreement when terrified (*King* v. *King and Evans* (1929), 142 L.T. 162).

G. Invalid foreign decree of divorce

Parties domiciled in this country sometimes, by arrangement or otherwise, obtain a decree of divorce in a foreign jurisdiction. If the decree is invalid in this country, and one of the parties, relying on the foreign decree, marries again, can the other spouse obtain a divorce in this country on the ground of adultery?

The full court considered this problem in *Palmer* v. *Palmer* (1859), 1 Sw. & Tr. 551. There, the parties though domiciled in England obtained a divorce in the U.S.A. on the petition of the wife based on the adultery of the husband. The husband remarried and, on finding out that the decree was invalid in this country, the wife petitioned for divorce here. The court held that by divorcing him abroad she had connived at his adultery.

This case was followed in *Lankester* v. *Lankester and Cooper* [1925] P. 114. A husband and wife domiciled in England had been advised wrongly that they could obtain a divorce in the U.S.A. and concurred in a scheme for this purpose. The wife had informed her husband that when the divorce was obtained she proposed to marry the co-respondent, which she did. The husband, having been advised that the divorce was invalid, petitioned for a divorce here, on the ground of the wife's adultery with the co-respondent. Lord Merrivale, P., held that this amounted to connivance and conduct conducing to adultery.

Some years later Lord Merrivale distinguished this case in *Clayton* v. *Clayton and Sharman* [1932] P. 45, where the facts were somewhat similar. The parties were married in England but never cohabited. The wife left England and settled in the U.S.A., where she obtained a decree of nullity, which was consented to by the husband. On finding that this decree was invalid in England the husband petitioned for divorce on the ground that the wife had committed adultery by marrying after the decree.

Lord Merrivale said at p. 50: —

> " The elemental fact in the case is that he and the respondent were both advised, and I am satisfied honestly advised, and both believed, that their marriage was effectually annulled by the proceedings in the court of Michigan, and that accordingly they were free . . . In my judgment connivance does involve what in its essence is a guilty act; it does involve what in its essence is a wrongful intention contrary to the law of the land. These people intended to observe the law; they were not aware, and they were honestly and by accident not aware, of the true position. . . ."

In *Preger* v. *Preger* (1926), 42 T.L.R. 281, a wife consented to a Jewish divorce and the husband remarried according to Jewish law. Hill, J., held that on the evidence that was no assent to anything except to a separation and the respondent had failed to prove connivance.

H. Connivance a defence to adultery only

An attempt was made in *Richmond* v. *Richmond* [1952] 1 All E.R. 838 (D.C.) to extend connivance to desertion and wilful neglect to maintain. In August, 1950, Mr. and Mrs. *R* went on a caravan holiday with a Mr. and Mrs. *B* and partners were exchanged, adultery taking place. After returning home the wife gave up her association with *B*. Mrs. *B* gave birth to a child and *R* admitted paternity, and left his wife to live with Mrs. *B* and paid no maintenance to his wife. The wife took out summonses and the magistrates found the husband guilty of adultery, desertion and wilful neglect. It was argued that the wife's connivance at her husband's adultery made it impossible for her to get an order for desertion or wilful neglect. The Divisional Court (Lord Merriman, P., and Karminski, J.) held that the wife had connived at the husband's adultery, and the husband had connived at his wife's adultery. There would therefore be no order on the ground of adultery, but it was not a natural consequence that the husband would desert his wife, or fail to maintain her, and therefore the orders on those grounds held good.

I. Is connivance for ever?

The House of Lords in *Godfrey* v. *Godfrey* [1964] 3 W.L.R.

524, have now answered this question in the negative. There were obiter dicta in *Gipps* v. *Gipps and Hume* (1864), 11 H.L. Cas. 1, to the effect that once connivance always connivance. These dicta have not been followed. Whether connivance has spent itself depends on whether the guilty party—usually the husband—is truly repentant and has done all in his power to repair the damage which he has done, and whether there is a causal connection between the adultery and the connivance. A full and complete reconciliation is not the only means whereby connivance may be terminated.

In *Goodman* v. *Goodman* (1964), *The Times*, 15th February, a wife lived in the same bungalow as her husband and his mistress and his former mistress. Rees, J., held that although she had connived at adultery from June, 1960, to February, 1962, when under great pressure, there had been a short period of genuine reconciliation, followed by further adultery, the connivance had spent itself by February, 1962, and she was entitled to a decree on the grounds both of cruelty and adultery.

IV. CONDUCT CONDUCING

What is the " wilful neglect or the misconduct " which conduces to the adultery of the complainant or the defendant, as the case may be? The Judge Ordinary, in the case of *Dering* v. *Dering and Blakeley* (1868), L.R. 1 P. & D. 531, in directing the jury on what is conduct conducing, said at p. 536: —

" I think that mere carelessness, the mere omission to do something here or there which ought to be done is not sufficient to constitute misconduct. Allowance must be made for men's different dispositions . . . Mere carelessness, therefore, is not sufficient . . . if it were, very few men, probably, would go safely through the ordeal . . . Before you arrive at the conclusion that the petitioner has been guilty of misconduct . . . you ought to be thoroughly satisfied that the intimacy between these parties was of such a character as to be distinctly dangerous, that the husband knew so much of it as to perceive the danger, and that he either purposely or recklessly disregarded it, and forbore to interfere. I have only to add, that in speaking of what the husband knew, I mean what he actually knew, and not what a more suspicious nature or a more active vigilance might have prompted him to discover, unless indeed he should have purposely closed his eyes, which would be wilful misconduct and something more.

It is not necessary that a man should have intended any wrong, but if he saw danger and recklessly allowed his wife to remain exposed to that danger, although without intending wrong, he would be guilty of neglect. But again, you must make allowance for the differences of mind and disposition, for one man may see danger in circumstances from which another would not draw such a conclusion."

A. Absolute bar

In the magistrates' court, misconduct conducing to adultery is an absolute bar to the making of an order, which, if a non-cohabitation clause is included, has the same effect as a decree of judicial separation, and the onus of satisfying the court that his or her misconduct has not conduced to the adultery charged is placed upon the person alleging the adultery. See *Brown* v. *Brown* [1956] P. 438, 448, and *Jenkins* v. *Jenkins* [1956] P. 458, 462.

B. Must cause the adultery

Conduct only conduces to adultery when it is such conduct as is proved to have brought about the adultery (per Denning, L.J., in *Richards* v. *Richards* [1952] P. 307 (C.A.), at p. 310, quoting *Herod* v. *Herod* [1939] P. 11, at p. 21). So where a man was sent to ten years' penal servitude, and his wife committed adultery while he was away, it was held that this did not conduce to her adultery although, no doubt, if he had not gone to prison, she would not have committed adultery. It has to be neglect to the other party, to be conduct conducing.

It is not every neglect or misconduct to the other party which will amount to conduct conducing.

C. Effect of desertion

It has been held that desertion by itself is not conduct conducing (*Richards* v. *Richards*, *supra*, where a husband deserted his wife and later she committed adultery). Mr. Commissioner Rewcastle held that his desertion conduced to her adultery, and this was reversed by the Court of Appeal, Denning, L.J., at p. 310, saying: —

"There must be conduct which is closely and directly connected with the adultery, such as exposing a wife to known
and obvious dangers. Applying this test, I am clearly of the
opinion that desertion by itself is not conduct conducing to
adultery. It would be deplorable if desertion by one party
were thought to be an excuse for the other party to go and
commit adultery."

Butt, J., found conduct conducing where a husband had deserted
his wife because she got him into debt, the husband earning, as
the learned judge said, "good wages" (engine driver, 24s. a
week), but this decision is probably incorrect. The wife went into
domestic service following the desertion, and only later committed
adultery (*Starbuck* v. *Starbuck and Oliver* (1889), 59 L.J.P. 20).

In *Yore* v. *Yore* (1962), *The Times*, 14th November, the husband
admitted adultery, but said it had been conduced to by his wife's
desertion. This raised a question of causation, said Scarman, J.
The question was whether the conduct of the wife caused the
husband to commit adultery. It was incorrect to say that simple
desertion could never amount to conduct conducing, just as it
was incorrect to say that all cases of constructive desertion must
necessarily contain an element of conduct conducing. In the
present case he held that the wife's desertion did not amount to
conduct conducing.

D. Effect of refusal of sexual intercourse

There have been a number of cases where refusal of sexual
intercourse has been held to be conduct conducing to adultery.
In *Plows* v. *Plows* (1928), 44 T.L.R. 263, the wife refused to
consummate the marriage, and eventually left her husband, who
then married bigamously. Lord Merrivale, P., held that there
was conduct conducing to the adultery, but exercised his discretion
in granting her a divorce. The refusal in *Callister* v. *Callister*
[1947] W.N. 221 was for eleven years, and this also was held to
be conduct conducing by the Court of Appeal. On the other
hand, Jeune, P., in *Synge* v. *Synge* [1900] P. 180, at p. 207, held
that refusal of sexual intercourse for a long period was not conduct
conducing, but presumably this is not good law since *Callister* v.
Callister, supra.

Lord Merriman, P., in *Brown* v. *Brown* [1956] P. 438, at p.
452, has pointed out the paradoxical situation that, while refusal

of sexual intercourse can amount to conduct conducing, desertion, which is a graver matrimonial offence and is an offence which necessarily includes the deprivation of sexual intercourse, does not amount to conduct conducing. There is no distinction between simple desertion and constructive desertion for this purpose (*Jenkins* v. *Jenkins* [1956] P. 458), " but if there are facts connected either with the circumstances of simple desertion, or with the circumstances of constructive desertion which are such as to result in causing the deserted spouse to commit adultery, then that is or may be conduct conducing " (Davies, J., in *Jenkins* v. *Jenkins, supra,* at p. 468).

E. Other misconduct

Brown v. *Brown* [1956] P. 438 is important because the Divisional Court reviewed practically all the cases to date on the subject of conduct conducing. The wife had complained to the magistrates of her husband's adultery, and he alleged that she had conduced to it by her loss of interest and affection for him, in consequence of her infatuation for another man. He had not known of this infatuation prior to his adultery, and had attributed her conduct to her fear of childbirth. This, it was argued, was immaterial since her conduct was due to her guilty conscience. The magistrates found that there was conduct conducing due to her improper association with another man, but the Court of Appeal reversed this. The court made the following points: —

(1) The test to be applied is whether the conduct complained of amounted to misconduct and whether it is the cause of the adultery (p. 450).

(2) The cases on this subject are not easy to reconcile.

(3) Adultery itself, or a confession of adultery whether true or false, might amount to conduct conducing (p. 453).

(4) Conduct short of adultery could conduce to adultery. In *Cox* v. *Cox* (1893), 70 L.T. 200, where the husband had paid marked attention to two unmarried ladies over a period of years, said he was infatuated and would have run away with the first if she had consented, and had been familiar with the other by putting his arm around her waist and sitting her on his knee, the Court of Appeal said that when the bare bones of the allegations had been covered with

the flesh and blood of evidence, these allegations might amount to conduct conducing. It was a question of degree whether the husband's misconduct did or did not conduce to his wife's adultery.

F. The first act of adultery, or its repetition

The Judge Ordinary in *St. Paul* v. *St. Paul* (1869), L.R. 1 P. & D. 739, said that the court must be exceedingly careful to hold clear to its way that the husband's conduct amounted to wilful neglect or misconduct, and that such wilful neglect or misconduct really conduced to the fall of the wife. In his view, the husband shall not be deprived of his remedy whenever it can be proved that some conduct on his part has conduced to any particular act of adultery after an adulterous intercourse has once been established, " but it means that his remedy shall be withheld from him if he has so acted as to bring about that intercourse . . . It seems to me that the neglect intended by the legislature is neglect conducing to the woman's fall, and not neglect conducing to any particular act of adultery subsequent to her fall." See Barnes, J., in *Millard* v. *Millard* (1898), 78 L.T. 471, to the same effect (at p. 472).

Perhaps this is too widely stated. There is no doubt that the inception of the adulterous intercourse is the most important time, as in connivance (see p. 314), but it is going too far to say that a husband cannot conduce to subsequent adultery. There may be cases of " voluntary blindness or acquiescence " as in *Robinson* v. *Robinson and Dearden* [1903] P. 155, where the wife carried on with the lodger, the co-respondent, in an obvious way, and even after finding them in a bedroom together, accepting ridiculous excuses, the husband did nothing, and Bucknill, J., found tacit acquiescence amounting to conduct conducing.

G. Failure to pay maintenance order

A wife obtained an order for maintenance on the ground of persistent cruelty. The husband failed to pay, and she committed adultery. The husband sought to have the order revoked, but the magistrates found that his failure to pay had conduced to her adultery. The Divisional Court (Lord Merrivale, P., and Bateson, J.) reversed this decision, Lord Merrivale saying that conduct conducing must be strictly proved, and the conduct must be the direct cause of the adultery (*Norris* v. *Norris* (1930), 94 J.P. 79).

H. Distinction between conduct conducing and connivance

The distinction between the two is not easy to define, and Wrangham, J., in considering this question in *Haynes* v. *Haynes and Sawkill* [1960] 1 W.L.R. 968, said that he had not been referred to any case which assisted him to define it. Of course, in the magistrates' courts the distinction is not of great importance since both connivance and conduct conducing are absolute bars, but in the divorce court, while connivance was an absolute bar, conduct conducing was only a discretionary one.

However, to consider the distinction may help to understand the nature of each. The facts in *Haynes* v. *Haynes and Sawkill*, *supra,* were that the husband petitioned for divorce on the ground of his wife's adultery, and she pleaded condonation, connivance and conduct conducing. The wife left the home in 1957 and began to live in adultery with the co-respondent. Later the husband and wife became reconciled, but shortly afterwards the husband made it clear that his wife must go and his housekeeper must come back. His motive was to get his wife out of the house and not to encourage her adultery, though he foresaw that it would probably continue, which in fact happened. Wrangham, J., said there was no question of the husband conniving at the initiation of the adultery, but it was said that he connived at its continuance. He quoted Lord Merriman in *Churchman* v. *Churchman* [1945] P. 44, at p. 52, to the effect that in connivance there must be a corrupt intention of promoting or encouraging either the initiation or the continuance of the other party's adultery, and said that in *Woodbury* v. *Woodbury* [1949] P. 154, at p. 158, " corrupt intention " appeared to be interpreted as meaning a willing consent; and he went on, at p. 973: —

> " I hope that I have rightly interpreted Lord Merriman if I say that a corrupt intention to encourage the continuance of adultery implies an intention to act with the motive of encouraging the wife's adultery. In other words, a spouse who acts, foreseeing that one of the natural results of his act is adultery on the part of his spouse and in that sense intending it, is conducing to his spouse's adultery; but if the motive for his action is to bring that result about, then he

may . . . be held to be not merely conducing to the adultery, but conniving at it."

In this case the learned judge held that since the husband's motive was to get his wife out and not to encourage her adultery (though he probably foresaw it would happen and did not care whether it did or not), therefore the husband did not connive at the wife's adultery, though he conduced to it.

APPENDIX I

MATRIMONIAL PROCEEDINGS (MAGISTRATES' COURTS) ACT, 1960

Jurisdiction of magistrates' court in matrimonial proceedings

1.—(1) A married woman or a married man may apply by way of complaint to a magistrates' court for an order under this Act against the other party to the marriage on any of the following causes of complaint arising during the subsistence of the marriage, that is to say, that the defendant—

   (*a*) has deserted the complainant; or

   (*b*) has been guilty of persistent cruelty to—

      (i) the complainant; or

      (ii) an infant child of the complainant; or

      (iii) an infant child of the defendant who, at the time of the cruelty, was a child of the family; or

   (*c*) has been found guilty—

      (i) on indictment, of any offence which involved an assault upon the compainant; or

      (ii) by the magistrates' court, of an offence against the complainant under section twenty, forty-two, forty-three or forty-seven of the Offences against the Person Act, 1861, being, in the case of the said section forty-two, an offence for which the defendant has been sentenced to imprisonment or any other form of detention for a term of not less than one month; or

      (iii) of, or of an attempt to commit, an offence under any of sections one to twenty-nine of the Sexual Offences Act, 1956, or under section one of the Indecency with Children Act, 1960, against an infant child of the complainant, or against an infant child of the defendant who, at the time of the commission of or attempt to commit the offence, was a child of the family; or

   (*d*) has committed adultery; or

   (*e*) while knowingly suffering from a venereal disease has insisted on, or has without the complainant being aware of the presence of that disease permitted, sexual intercourse between the complainant and the defendant; or

   (*f*) is for the time being an habitual drunkard or a drug addict; or

   (*g*) being the husband, has compelled the wife to submit herself to prostitution or has been guilty of such conduct as was likely

331

to result and has resulted in the wife's submitting herself to prostitution; or

(*h*) being the husband, has wilfully neglected to provide reasonable maintenance for the wife or for any child of the family who is, or would but for that neglect have been, a dependant; or

(*i*) being the wife, has wilfully neglected to provide, or to make a proper contribution towards, reasonable maintenance for the husband or for any child of the family who is, or would but for that neglect have been, dependant, in a case where, by reason of the impairment of the husband's earning capacity through age, illness, or disability of mind or body, and having regard to any resources of the husband and the wife respectively which are, or should properly be made, available for the purpose, it is reasonable in all the circumstances to expect the wife so to provide or contribute.

* * * *

Order by magistrates' court in matrimonial proceedings

2.—(1) Subject to the proviso to subsection (3) of section one of this Act and to the provisions of this section and of section four of this Act, on hearing a complaint under the said section one by either of the parties to a marriage the court may make an order (in this Act referred to as a " matrimonial order ") containing any one or more of the following provisions, namely—

(*a*) a provision that the complainant be no longer bound to cohabit with the defendant (which provision while in force shall have effect in all respects as a decree of judicial separation);

(*b*) a provision that the husband shall pay to the wife such weekly sum . . . as the court considers reasonable in all the circumstances of the case;

(*c*) where, by reason of the impairment of the husband's earning capacity through age, illness, or disability of mind or body, it appears to the court reasonable in all the circumstances so to order, a provision that the wife shall pay to the husband such weekly sum . . . as the court considers reasonable in all the circumstances of the case;

(*d*) a provision for the legal custody of any child of the family who is under the age of sixteen years;

(*e*) if it appears to the court that there are exceptional circumstances making it impracticable or undesirable for any such child as aforesaid to be entrusted to either of the parties or to any other individual, a provision committing the care of the child to a specified local authority, being the council of the county or county borough in which the child was, in the opinion of the court, resident immediately before being so committed;

(*f*) if, in the case of any child committed by the order to the legal custody of any person, it appears to the court that there are exceptional circumstances making it desirable that the child should be under the supervision of an independent person, a provision that the child be under the supervision—

(i) of a probation officer appointed for or assigned to the petty sessions area in which in the opinion of the court the child is or will be resident; or

(ii) of a specified local authority, being the council of a county or county borough;

(g) a provision for access to any child of the family by either of the parties or by any other person who is a parent of that child, in a case where the child is committed by the order to the legal custody of a person other than that party or parent;

(h) a provision for the making by the defendant or by the complainant or by each of them, for the maintenance of any child of the family, weekly payments, being—

(i) if and for so long as the child is under the age of sixteen years, payments to any person to whom the legal custody of the child is for the time being committed by the order, or by any other order made by a court in England and for the time being in force, or, during any period when the child is in the care of a local authority under the order, to that local authority;

(ii) if it appears to the court that the child is, or will be, or if such payments were made would be, a dependant though over the age of sixteen years, and that it is expedient that such payments should be made in respect of that child while such a dependant, payments to such person (who may be the child or, during any such period as aforesaid, the local authority) as may be specified in the order, for such period during which the child is over that age but under the age of twenty-one years as may be so specified.

(2) Where, on a complaint under section one of this Act, the court makes a matrimonial order on the ground that the defendant is for the time being an habitual drunkard or a drug addict, and the order contains such a provision as is mentioned in paragraph (a) of the foregoing subsection, then, if in all the circumstances, and after giving each party to the proceedings an opportunity of making representations, the court thinks it proper so to do, the court may include in that order—

(a) if the complainant is the husband, a provision such as is mentioned in paragraph (b) of the foregoing subsection; or

(b) if the complainant is the wife, a provision such as is mentioned in paragraph (c) of that subsection;

but save as aforesaid the said paragraph (b) or (c) shall not authorise the court to require any payment such as is therein mentioned to be made by the complainant.

(3) The court hearing a complaint under section one of this Act

shall not make a matrimonial order containing a provision such as is mentioned in paragraph (*a*), (*b*) or (*c*) of subsection (1) of this section—

   (*a*) on the ground that the defendant has committed an act of adultery unless the court is satisfied that the complainant has not condoned or connived at, or by wilful neglect or misconduct conduced to, that act of adultery; or

   (*b*) where the complainant is proved to have committed an act of adultery during the subsistence of the marriage, unless the court is satisfied that the defendant has condoned or connived at, or by wilful neglect or misconduct conduced to, that act of adultery.

  (4) The court shall not make an order containing—

   (*a*) such a provision as is mentioned in paragraph (*d*) or (*e*) of subsection (1) of this section in respect of any child with respect to whose custody an order made by a court in England is for the time being in force;

   (*b*) such a provision as is mentioned in paragraph (*e*), (*f*) or (*g*) of the said subsection (1) in respect of any child who is already for the purposes of Part II of the Children Act, 1948, in the care of a local authority;

   (*c*) such a provision as is mentioned in the said paragraph (*f*) or (*g*) in respect of any child in respect of whom the order contains such a provision as is mentioned in the said paragraph (*e*).

  (5) In considering whether any, and if so what, provision should be included in a matrimonial order by virtue of paragraph (*h*) of subsection (1) of this section for payments by one of the parties in respect of a child who is not a child of that party, the court shall have regard to the extent, if any, to which that party had, on or after the acceptance of the child as one of the family, assumed responsibility for the child's maintenance, and to the liability of any person other than a party to the marriage to maintain the child.

*   *   *   *

APPENDIX II

MATRIMONIAL CAUSES ACT, 1973

Divorce on breakdown of marriage

1.—(1) Subject to section 3 below, a petition for divorce may be presented to the court by either party to a marriage on the ground that the marriage has broken down irretrievably.

(2) The court hearing a petition for divorce shall not hold the marriage to have broken down irretrievably unless the petitioner satisfies the court of one or more of the following facts, that is to say—

    (*a*) that the respondent has committed adultery and the petitioner finds it intolerable to live with the respondent;

    (*b*) that the respondent has behaved in such a way that the petitioner cannot reasonably be expected to live with the respondent;

    (*c*) that the respondent has deserted the petitioner for a continuous period of at least two years immediately preceding the presentation of the petition;

    (*d*) that the parties to the marriage have lived apart for a continuous period of at least two years immediately preceding the presentation of the petition (hereafter in this Act referred to as " two years' separation ") and the respondent consents to a decree being granted;

    (*e*) that the parties to the marriage have lived apart for a continuous period of at least five years immediately preceding the presentation of the petition (hereafter in this Act referred to as " five years' separation ").

(3) On a petition for divorce it shall be the duty of the court to inquire, so far as it reasonably can, into the facts alleged by the petitioner and into any facts alleged by the respondent.

(4) If the court is satisfied on the evidence of any such fact as is mentioned in subsection (2) above, then, unless it is satisfied on all the evidence that the marriage has not broken down irretrievably, it shall, subject to section 3 (3) and 5 below, grant a decree of divorce.

(5) Every decree of divorce shall in the first instance be a decree nisi and shall not be made absolute before the expiration of six months from its grant unless the High Court by general order from time to time fixes a shorter period, or unless in any particular case the court in which the proceedings are for the time being pending from time to time by special order fixes a shorter period than the period otherwise applicable for the time being by virtue of this subsection.

Supplemental provisions as to facts raising presumption of breakdown

2.—(1) One party to a marriage shall not be entitled to rely for the purposes of section 1 (2) (*a*) above on adultery committed by the other if, after it became known to him that the other had committed that adultery, the parties have lived with each other for a period exceeding, or periods together exceeding, six months.

(2) Where the parties to a marriage have lived with each other after it became known to one party that the other had committed adultery, but subsection (1) above does not apply, in any proceedings for divorce in which the petitioner relies on that adultery the fact that the parties have lived with each other after that time shall be disregarded in determining for the purposes of section 1 (2) (*a*) above whether the petitioner finds it intolerable to live with the respondent.

(3) Where in any proceedings for divorce the petitioner alleges that the respondent has behaved in such a way that the petitioner cannot reasonably be expected to live with him, but the parties to the marriage have lived with each other for a period or periods after the date of the occurrence of the final incident relied on by the petitioner and held by the court to support his allegation, that fact shall be disregarded in determining for the purposes of section 1 (2) (*b*) above whether the petitioner cannot reasonably be expected to live with the respondent if the length of that period or of those periods together was six months or less.

(4) For the purposes of section 1 (2) (*c*) above the court may treat a period of desertion as having continued at a time when the deserting party was incapable of continuing the necessary intention if the evidence before the court is such that, had that party not been so incapable, the court would have inferred that his desertion continued at that time.

(5) In considering for the purposes of section 1 (2) above whether the period for which the respondent has deserted the petitioner or the period for which the parties to a marriage have lived apart has been continuous, no account shall be taken of any one period (not exceeding six months) or of any two or more periods (not exceeding six months in all) during which the parties resumed living with each other, but no period during which the parties lived with each other shall count as part of the period of desertion or of the period for which the parties to the marriage lived apart, as the case may be.

(6) For the purposes of section 1 (2) (*d*) and (*e*) above and this section a husband and wife shall be treated as living apart unless they are living with each other in the same household, and references in this section to the parties to a marriage living with each other shall be construed as references to their living with each other in the same household.

(7) Provision shall be made by rules of court for the purpose of ensuring that where in pursuance of section 1 (2) (*d*) above the petitioner alleges that the respondent consents to a decree being granted the respondent has been given such information as will enable him to understand the consequences to him of his consenting to a decree being

granted and the steps which he must take to indicate that he consents to the grant of a decree.

*   *   *   *

Judicial separation

17.—(1) A petition for judicial separation may be presented to the court by either party to a marriage on the ground that any such fact as is mentioned in section 1 (2) above exists, and the provisions of section 2 above shall apply accordingly for the purposes of a petition for judicial separation alleging any such fact, as they apply in relation to a petition for divorce alleging that fact.

(2) On a petition for judicial separation it shall be the duty of the court to inquire, so far as it reasonably can, into the facts alleged by the petitioner and into any facts alleged by the respondent, but the court shall not be concerned to consider whether the marriage has broken down irretrievably, and if it is satisfied on the evidence of any such fact as is mentioned in section 1 (2) above it shall, subject to section 41 below, grant a decree of judicial separation.

(3) Sections 6 and 7 above shall apply for the purpose of encouraging the reconciliation of parties to proceedings for judicial separation and of enabling the parties to a marriage to refer to the court for its opinion an agreement or arrangement relevant to actual or contemplated proceedings for judicial separation, as they apply in relation to proceedings for divorce.

*   *   *   *

APPENDIX III

MATRIMONIAL CAUSES ACT, 1965

* * * *

Condonation

42.—(1) For the purposes of the Matrimonial Proceedings (Magistrates' Courts) Act, 1960, any presumption of condonation which arises from the continuance or resumption of marital intercourse may be rebutted by evidence sufficient to negative the necessary intent.

(2) For the purposes of . . . the Matrimonial Proceedings (Magistrates' Courts) Act, 1960, adultery or cruelty shall not be deemed to have been condoned by reason only of a continuation or resumption of cohabitation between the parties for one period not exceeding three months, or of anything done during such cohabitation, if it is proved that cohabitation was continued or resumed, as the case may be, with a view to effecting a reconciliation.

(3) For the purposes of the Matrimonial Proceedings (Magistrates' Courts) Act, 1960, adultery which has been condoned shall not be capable of being revived.

[This section is printed as amended by the Divorce Reform Act, 1969, and the Matrimonial Causes Act, 1973, Sched. 2, para. 5 (2).]

* * * *

APPENDIX IV

MATRIMONIAL CAUSES ACT, 1973

*   *   *   *

Matters to which court is to have regard in deciding how to exercise its powers under sections 23 and 24

25.—(1) It shall be the duty of the court in deciding whether to exercise its powers under section 23 (1) (*a*), (*b*) or (*c*) or 24 above in relation to a party to the marriage and, if so, in what manner, to have regard to all the circumstances of the case including the following matters, that is to say—

(*a*) the income, earning capacity, property and other financial resources which each of the parties to the marriage has or is likely to have in the foreseeable future;

(*b*) the financial needs, obligations and responsibilities which each of the parties to the marriage has or is likely to have in the foreseeable future;

(*c*) the standard of living enjoyed by the family before the breakdown of the marriage;

(*d*) the age of each party to the marriage and the duration of the marriage;

(*e*) any physical or mental disability of either of the parties to the marriage;

(*f*) the contributions made by each of the parties to the welfare of the family, including any contribution made by looking after the home or caring for the family;

(*g*) in the case of proceedings for divorce or nullity of marriage, the value to either of the parties to the marriage of any benefit (for example, a pension) which, by reason of the dissolution or annulment of the marriage, that party will lose the chance of acquiring;

and so to exercise those powers as to place the parties, so far as it is practicable and, having regard to their conduct, just to do so, in the financial position in which they would have been if the marriage had not broken down and each had properly discharged his or her financial obligations and responsibilities towards the other.

(2) Without prejudice to subsection (3) below, it shall be the duty of the court in deciding whether to exercise its powers under section 23 (1) (*d*), (*e*) or (*f*), (2) or (4) or 24 above in relation to a child of the family and, if so, in what manner, to have regard to all the circumstances of the case including the following matters, that is to say—

339

(*a*) the financial needs of the child;

(*b*) the income, earning capacity (if any), property and other financial resources of the child;

(*c*) any physical or mental disability of the child;

(*d*) the standard of living enjoyed by the family before the breakdown of the marriage;

(*e*) the manner in which he was being and in which the parties to the marriage expected him to be educated or trained;

and so to exercise those powers as to place the child, so far as it is practicable and, having regard to the considerations mentioned in relation to the parties to the marriage in paragraph (*a*) and (*b*) of subsection (1) above, just to do so, in the financial position in which the child would have been if the marriage had not broken down and each of those parties had properly discharged his or her financial obligations and responsibilities towards him.

(3) It shall be the duty of the court in deciding whether to exercise its powers under section 23 (1) (*d*), (*e*) or (*f*), (2) or (4) or 24 above against a party to a marriage in favour of a child of the family who is not the child of that party and, if so, in what manner, to have regard (among the circumstances of the case)—

(*a*) to whether that party had assumed any responsibility for the child's maintenance and, if so, to the extent to which, and the basis upon which, that party assumed such responsibility and to the length of time for which that party discharged such responsibility;

(*b*) to whether in assuming and discharging such responsibility that party did so knowing that the child was not his or her own;

(*c*) to the liability of any other person to maintain the child.

INDEX